Phuoc Tran-Gia and Tobias Hoßfeld

Performance Modeling and Analysis of Communication Networks

Phuoc Tran-Gia and Tobias Hoßfeld

Performance Modeling and Analysis of Communication Networks

A Lecture Note

Würzburg
University Press

Imprint

Julius-Maximilians-Universität Würzburg
Würzburg University Press
University Library Würzburg
Am Hubland
D-97074 Würzburg
www.wup.uni-wuerzburg.de

© 2021 Würzburg University Press
Print on Demand

Cover design: Margarita Paradissi

ISBN 978-3-95826-152-5 (print)
ISBN 978-3-95826-153-2 (online)
DOI 10.25972/WUP-978-3-95826-153-2
URN urn:nbn:de:bvb:20-opus-241920

Preface

Queueing theory is a fundamental methodology which plays an important role in the analysis of communication networks and systems, but also in other domains like manufacturing systems. P. Tran-Gia published a first edition of this text book "Analytical performance evaluation of distributed systems" [108] in German language in 1996 as part of his lecture "Performance Evaluation of Distributed Systems" at the University of Würzburg. A second edition "Introduction to performance evaluation and traffic theory" [110] was published in German language in 2009 taking into account suggestions received from students and employees at the University of Würzburg. Some methods that have been used frequently in research collaborations were added.

The present text book is published in English language in 2021 as open access book by the Würzburg University Press. The book focuses on the fundamental models of queueing theory as well as advanced models for recent communication systems and networks. It gives an introduction in common methods of performance modeling and analysis of communication systems. These methods form the basis of traffic engineering, teletraffic theory, and system analytical dimensioning tools. The fundamentals of probability theory, stochastic processes, Markov processes, and embedded Markov chains are presented. Basic queueing models are described with applications in communication networks. Advanced methods are presented that have been frequently used in practice, especially discrete-time analysis algorithms, or which go beyond classical performance like quality of experience or energy efficiency. Recent examples of modern communication networks include Software Defined Networking or the Internet of Things. Throughout the book, illustrative examples are used to provide practical experience in performance modeling and analysis.

The book is intended for students and scientists in computer science and technical computer science, applied mathematics, operations research, electrical engineering and economics. For the listeners of the lecture "Performance Evaluation of Distributed Systems" at the University of Würzburg, we would like to point out that Chapter 1 up to and including Chapter 5 are used in the course, as well as the analysis algorithm in time domain for the discrete-time GI/GI/1 system in Chapter 6 and selected examples in Chapter 7. The lecture was originally developed by Phuoc Tran-Gia and is given by Tobias Hoßfeld since 2018.

An implementation of the models in the book is available as interactive notebooks online. The scripts will help students to better understand the impact of parameters on performance characteristics, will avoid common pitfalls in the implementation, and provide means for numerical robust and efficient implementations for researchers in the domain. Besides the computational scripts, we provide exercises and solutions.

There are some major changes compared to the second edition [110]. The book was reorganized and includes the following new models and sections per chapter:

- Chapter 1 "Introduction in Performance Modeling": some recent examples on software defined networking, video streaming, resource sharing in cloud computing, internet of things (IoT) and smart city applications, overload control – they will be analyzed throughout the book.

- Chapter 2 "Fundamentals and Prerequisites": more examples on Little's theorem, general results for GI/GI/n delay systems, loss formula for GI/GI/n-S queues, important inequalities (Jensen, Markov, Chebyshev), notion of mixture distribution, concrete substitute distributions.

- Chapter 3 "Elementary Random Processes": strong law of renewal theory, definition of continuous-time Markov chains and their transition behavior, properties of Poisson processes, superposition of renewal processes, Palm-Khintchine theorem.

- Chapter 4 "Analysis of Markovian Systems": arrival theorem introduced in Engset model, processor sharing model M/M/1-PS and its application for data center power consumption as well as virtualized network functions.

- Chapter 5 "Analysis of Non-Markovian Systems": formal definition of discrete-time Markov chains, power method implementation, Kleinrock's result, results for continuous-time GI/GI/1 delay systems, Kingman's approximations of mean waiting times.

- Chapter 6 "Discrete-time Models and Analysis": analysis of idle times, busy times, interdeparture times of discrete-time GI/GI/1 systems, distributional Little's law for queue size derivation of GI/GI/1.

- Chapter 7 "Advanced Models and Applications": video streaming QoS and QoE (M/M/1 with N-policy, GI/M/1 with N-policy), traffic modeling in the IoT (nD/D/1 and M/D/1), order and gap statistics, renewal approximation, random access schemes of IoT sensors (M/D/∞, M/D/1-S), Kleinrock's approach for deriving the operational point, overload control for non-stationary discrete-time models.

This textbook is available as open access document and intended for digital use. Therefore, we took care of including hyperlinks to Chapters, Equations, Figures, etc. as well as clickable literature references which guide the reader to the original documents. The latest computational scripts implementing the models as well as exercises and solutions are available online.

https://modeling.systems

The authors would like to thank especially Stefan Geißler for proofreading and correcting many things, Katharina Dietz, Fabian Poignée, Frank Loh, Florian Wamser for their helpful comments, Claudia Schober, Manuel Beck for their support in the publishing process, and Hermann Gold for his help in implementing the model with batch service and threshold control. We thank you for the many hours and the enormous effort that you have put into improving the book.

Würzburg, August 2021   Phuoc Tran-Gia & Tobias Hoßfeld

Contents

Introduction in Performance Modeling

This chapter opens with discussion of some basic terms for modeling and performance evaluation in the context of analytical methods. Then, Kendall's notation is introduced allowing description of queueing systems in a compact standardized way. Finally, several examples of performance models in computer and communication networks are provided which illustrate the abstraction of a real system into an analytical performance model. The goal of such a model is the analysis of a particular performance measure in a system in light of limiting resources (like processing speed of devices, available memory, or network capacity). Some of the models introduced in this chapter are discussed in detail throughout the book. The models in this book are fundamentals of *queueing theory* providing an analytical framework for describing the operation of systems. Jobs or customers arrive to the queue, possibly may be blocked if the queue's capacity is exceeded or wait some time; then the job is processed which takes some additional processing time, and departs from the queue. This allows to derive performance measures like waiting times, response times, blocking probabilities, but also related measures like energy consumption or user perceived quality.

1.1 Modeling Concept and Levels of Abstraction

When examining complex processes in real systems, performance models are often required during the design but also the operation of the system. This has a long tradition in communication and manufacturing systems with distributed control structures, where performance or teletraffic models based on stochastic theory and queueing theory allow a quantitative and qualitative description of the system operation in real-time coupled with an assessment of the system reaction. In particular, "teletraffic models" – or "traffic models" in short – aim at describing data flows in telecommunication networks, like the Internet or industrial networks. They allow analysis of performance and usage of network resources and to derive engineering practices for those networks like sizing of resources depending on the traffic load in the system and given quality of service (QoS) requirements, e.g. with respect to response times. Literature provides various textbooks on performance modeling and analysis, cf. Kleinrock [61], Daigle [26], Kobayashi [65], Le Boudec [70], Zukerman [125], Van Mieghem [112], Tay [104], Giambene [39].

This text book provides fundamental performance and queueing theory models as well, but focuses on advanced models and recent applications in the area of communication networks, like QoS and QoE for video streaming, traffic modeling for the Internet of Things, energy efficiency in communication networks, or the performance of virtualized network functions, to mention a few examples.

A performance model – or teletraffic model – describes the sequence of events in a (communication) system, taking into account the most relevant temporal and logical relationships between system entities. This is done using a set of abstract model elements that reflect the real system components and the logical interaction between them. As a result, the modeling includes the mapping of the system organization or dynamic system events to corresponding model components and model-related equivalent processes.

Modern communication systems are characterized by ever more extensive functions and increasing complexity. Think of high-speed mobile networks with worldwide Internet connectivity, cyber-physical environments in smart cities, or digital manufacturing systems. The use of various hardware and software components creates ever more powerful and complex systems from a structural and control technology perspective. Often the performance of such systems, due to their functional complexity and their increasingly different performance characteristics, must be examined and proven before the system is deployed. We differentiate between functional and system performance under load.

Functional performance

This includes, among other things, the absence of deadlocks or inconsistencies in the communication protocols implemented in the system, the flawless cooperation of the activated processes and the functional compliance with defined system-specific performance characteristics.

System performance under load conditions

The key aspects are the functionality and compliance with some predefined QoS agreements, e.g. thresholds for the blocking probability, throughput, or waiting times under nominal load conditions, compliance with the specified quality of service under overload, the survivability of the system in the event of extreme load peaks (cf. Heegaard and Trivedi [47]), etc.

Due to the large number of connected entities and system components that work together in real time, as well as the parallel running processes, the sequence of events in a distributed system, e.g. in a communication system or in a manufacturing environment, can be described with the help of random processes. Stochastic methods, especially queueing theory, are used to investigate such processes.

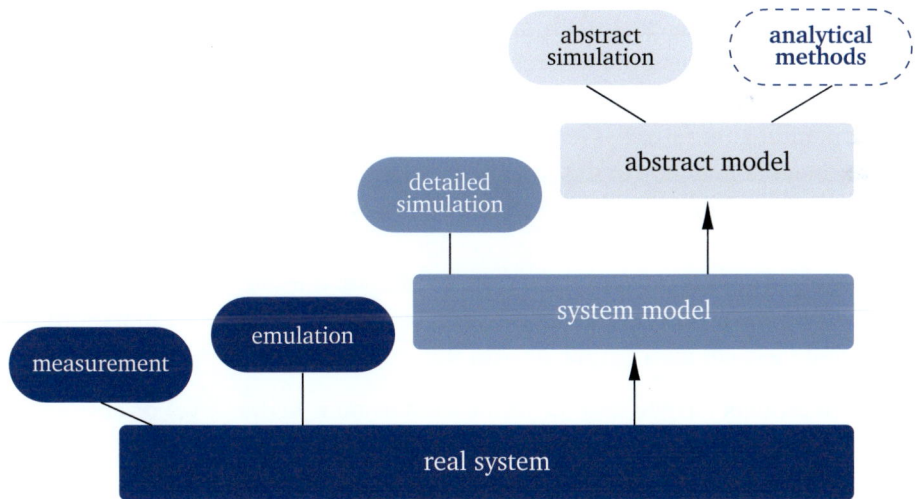

Figure 1.1: Abstraction layering of performance analysis techniques.

Figure 1.1 gives an overview of the methods for the performance evaluation of distributed systems and communication networks.

Measurements If a system is already up and running (i.e. in the operating phase), the functionality can be examined by measurements, with realistic load profiles of connected subscribers, peripheral devices, and other components in the network available for measurement purposes.

Hardware simulation If a prototype of the system to be examined is available, but the users or peripheral devices to be connected are not yet or only partially available, the performance of the system can be examined under real load conditions, e.g. with the help of hardware simulation devices. Users and peripheral processes are simulated by state machines in a timely manner and taking into account real user behavior of the interaction between the users and the system. The system performance can be tested under any load conditions.

Simulation In the design and development phase of a system, performance studies are often carried out using detailed system models or more abstract traffic models. As shown in Figure 1.1, the model can be created on different levels of abstraction. In a detailed system model, model components are still very similar to the system. All structural components and their behavior in real systems are modeled with great attention to detail. This leads to traffic models of high complexity, which can usually only be investigated with the help of system simulations. Because of the inherent complexity, it may be impossible to compute such complex analytical models in practice. Since several system designs and structural alternatives often have to be compared in the development phase, the model simulation at this level of detail leads to a large computational effort. Then, the performance can be examined instead with a system model of higher abstraction, with the essential system features relevant for the examination still having to be contained in the model. Models on this abstraction level, referred to as *traffic* or *performance models,* can be investigated using simulations that require less computing time or with the help of analytical methods.

Analytical models In the case of traffic models on a higher level of abstraction, there are often analytically exact or approximate methods that enable investigations of sufficiently large parameter ranges with considerably less computational effort. Queueing theory offers a framework for analytical models which often provide closed-form solutions. This means that the solution of the traffic models (i.e. equations used to describe changes in a system) can be expressed as a mathematical function depending on relevant input parameters like the load in the system. If there are no closed-form solutions available, approximation methods or numerical methods like time-discrete analysis are provided to quantify the performance of the system depending on the input parameters. Analytical models and their solutions are described in detail later in this textbook.

1.2 Notation for Single-Stage Queueing Models

Single-stage queueing models can be described in a compact way using Kendall's notation, also known as the Kendall notation. Single-stage means that there is a queue where jobs or customers go through before they are served by the server or service unit. Jobs or customers arrive at the queue, get processed, and leave the system. A queueing model requires the definition of the following components.

- *Traffic sources* and associated random *arrival processes* describing the time between arrivals of jobs in the system.

- *Service units* (or servers) and associated random variables for the duration of *service processes*.

- *Queues* and associated waiting room capacity and *operating disciplines*.

Let us consider a simple model for a router in the Internet. The router is responsible for forwarding incoming packets to an appropriate output port by matching incoming packets to an entry in its forwarding table. Forwarding of packets happens on the data plane. This forwarding table is determined by the underlying routing algorithm which is operating on the control plane. For modeling the data plane of the router, we need to describe the arrival process of packets at the router. The router has a certain buffer capacity to store packets. We may assume that at most S packets can be cached in the router. Packets are served in the order of arrival (First-In First-Out, FIFO). The processing time includes a) the lookup time to match the incoming packet with an entry in the forwarding table and b) the transmission time required to transmit the packet on the output port of the router. This processing time may depend on the size of the packet and is described by a random variable. The router can only process a single packet at a time and we therefore have a single service unit for processing the packets. The queueing model is denoted as GI/GI/1-S system in Kendall's notation which will be explained below.

1.2.1 Kendall's Notation

A common notation for single-stage queueing systems was introduced by Kendall in 1954 and is the de facto standard in queueing theory. An often used form of Kendall's notation is shown in Figure 1.2.

If there is a model with special types of arrival and service processes, the shorthand notations of these processes are translated directly into Kendall's notation. The following short notations are often used to identify arrival and service processes – exact definitions of the distributions are given in Chapter 2.4.

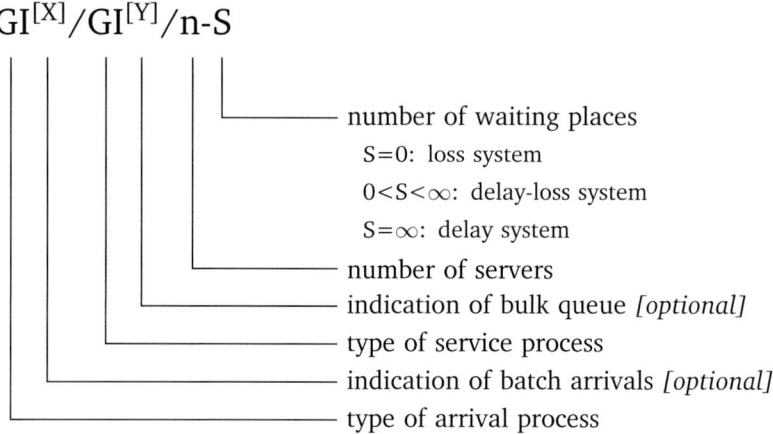

Figure 1.2: Kendall's notation for single-stage queueing models.

GI General Independent. Arrival processes or service process with renewal properties (renewal process, see Chapter 3.2) can be described by means of a random variable. The realizations of these random variables in the arrival or service process are statistically independent of one another.

D Deterministic. The interarrival times or the service times are constant.

M Markov. The corresponding random variable follows a negative exponential distribution (Chapter 2.4.2.2) with a coefficient of variation of 1. A Markovian arrival process is therefore a Poisson process (Chapter 3.3).

E_k Erlang-k. The random variables follow an Erlang-k distribution (Chapter 2.4.2.3) with a coefficient of variation between 0 and 1.

H_k Hyperexponential distribution of order k, i.e. with k phases (Chapter 2.4.2.4) with a coefficient of variation greater than 1.

The parameter S indicates the number of waiting places. For the special cases $S = 0$ (loss system) and $S = \infty$ (waiting or delay system), the parameter is often not indicated to condense the representation even more. Then context information is required to identify a loss or delay system. For example, the GI/GI/n *loss system* corresponds to GI/GI/n-0. The GI/GI/n *delay system* corresponds to GI/GI/n-∞. For $0 < S < \infty$, the queueing system has limited capacity, such that blocking may occur, while non-blocked jobs or customers may also experience some waiting times. Such systems are referred to as *loss and delay systems*. If not stated otherwise, the First-In First-Out (FIFO) operating discipline is assumed. Thus, jobs or customers are served in the order of arrival. An infinite customer population is assumed.

The parameter n indicates the number of servers, e.g. $n = 1$ for a single server system, e.g. $n = \infty$ for infinite number of servers where are all arriving customers are immediately served by another server. It is also differentiated between single arrivals (GI) and batch arrivals (GI$^{[X]}$) with the batch size X being a random variable. Analogously, single service queues (GI) and bulk or batch queues (GI$^{[X]}$) are differentiated. In bulk queues, the arriving customers are served in groups of random size X. If no batch arrival or batch service queue is indicated, a single arrival or single service queue is assumed, respectively. For example, the M/M$^{[2]}$/3 loss system assumes single arrivals and has three batch servers which are serving (deterministically) two customers each. For special systems like a bulk service queue with starting threshold Θ and maximum bulk service size K, literature suggests dedicated notions, for example M/GI$^{[\Theta,K]}$/1, see Chapter 5.5.

1.2.2 Extended Kendall's Notation: A/B/n/S/m/D

Literature also suggests an extended notation which specifies additional elements of the queueing model. The previously introduced compact notation specifies A, B, n, S and assumes $m = \infty$, $D = $ FIFO. Hence, the compact representation is $A/B/n - S$.

A   The time between arrivals to the queue, e.g. M for a Poisson process with exponential interarrival times, e.g. M$^{[X]}$ for a Poisson process with batch arrivals with the random variable X of the batch size, e.g. M(x) for exponential interarrival times with state-dependent arrival rates.

B   The service time distribution, e.g. M for exponential service times, e.g. D for fixed service times, e.g. GI$^{[\Theta,K]}$ for general independent service times with starting threshold Θ and maximum bulk service K (see Chapter 5.5), e.g. C for clocked service (see Chapter 7.4.1).

n   The number of servers or service units, e.g. n=1 for a single server system, e.g. n=∞ for infinite number of servers.

S   The capacity of the waiting queue, e.g. S=0 for a loss system, e.g. S=∞ for a delay system, e.g. 0<S<∞ for a delay-loss system.

m   The size of the (finite or infinite) customer population; if this number is omitted, the population is assumed to be infinite as in a Poisson process.

D   The queueing discipline or service discipline, e.g. FIFO (first if first out), LIFO (last in first out), PS (processor sharing) analyzed in Chapter 4.5.

Please note that some textbooks use the total capacity of the system $S + n$ instead of the capacity S of the waiting queue only. Hence, $A/B/n/n + S/m/D$ is used. Throughout this text book, we refer to the capacity of the waiting queue and use $A/B/n/S/m/D$ or the short notation $A/B/n - S$.

1.2.3   Overview of Queueing Systems Discussed in this Book

The following queueing systems are discussed in this textbook.

- **loss system**: GI/GI/n-0 or in the extended notation GI/GI/n/0/∞/FIFO
  Chapter 4.1: M/M/n-0 and M/GI/n-0 (Erlang-B model, robustness property)

- **delay system**: GI/GI/n-∞ or in the extended notation GI/GI/n/∞/∞/FIFO
  Chapter 4.2: M/M/n
  Chapter 5.3: M/GI/1
  Chapter 7.4.2: M/D/1
  Chapter 5.4: GI/M/1
  Chapter 5.6: GI/GI/1 (continuous-time)
  Chapter 6.4: GI/GI/1 (discrete-time)

- **delay-loss systems**: GI/GI/n-S or in the extended notation GI/GI/n/S/∞/FIFO
  Chapter 3.5.5: Markovian birth-and-death process
  Chapter 7.4.3: M/D/1-S

- **finite population**: GI/GI/n/0/m/FIFO with a finite population of m customers
  Chapter 4.3: M/M/n/0/m/FIFO (Engset model)
  Chapter 4.4: M/M/n/0/m/FIFO with retrial

- **infinite servers**: GI/GI/∞
  Chapter 7.4.1: M/M/∞ and M/GI/∞ (robustness property)

- **processor sharing**: GI/GI/1-PS or in the extended notation GI/GI/1/∞/∞/PS
  Chapter 4.5: M/M/1-PS and M/GI/1-PS (robustness property)

- **N-policy**: delay system GI/GI/1 or GI/GI/1/∞/∞/FIFO with N-policy
  Chapter 7.1: M/M/1 with N-policy

- **state-dependent rates**: the interarrival times and service times follow an exponential distribution with state-dependent arrival and service rates, respectively
  Chapter 3.5.5: M(x)/M(x)/n-S (Markovian birth-and-death process)

- **batch service**: with threshold control: finite system with a single batch server containing a group of K service places; Θ customers are required in the queue before starting the batch service
  Chapter 5.5: M/GI$^{[\Theta,K]}$/1-S

- **discrete-time queues**: GI/GI/1-∞ or GI/GI/1/∞/∞/FIFO
  Chapter 6.3: GEOM(1)/GI/1
  Chapter 6.4: GI/GI/1 (discrete-time)
  Chapter 7.5: GI/D/1 queue with bounded delay (spacer)
  Chapter 7.6: GI/GI/1 with overload control (amount of unfinished work)

1.3 Modeling Examples

To illustrate the concept of a model and the modeling process, this chapter reviews some simple modeling examples. It is important to mention that each model has a certain purpose and is used to answer a particular question. For each example a model summary is provided which summarizes the *limiting resources* in the system, the *performance measure* of interest, and the *goal* of the model.

1.3.1 Handshaking Protocol

A sender sends messages to a receiver in the form of packets (Figure 1.3). According to a handshaking protocol, packets received without errors are acknowledged with a positive message (ACK: positive acknowledgment). If the transmission is incorrect, the recipient sends a negative acknowledgment (NAK: negative acknowledgment), whereupon the sender repeats the transmission of the corresponding packet. The process is repeated until the packet arrives at the receiver without any errors. Then, the next packet can be transmitted from sender to receiver. This simple handshaking protocol only allows a single packet to currently move over the communication channel.

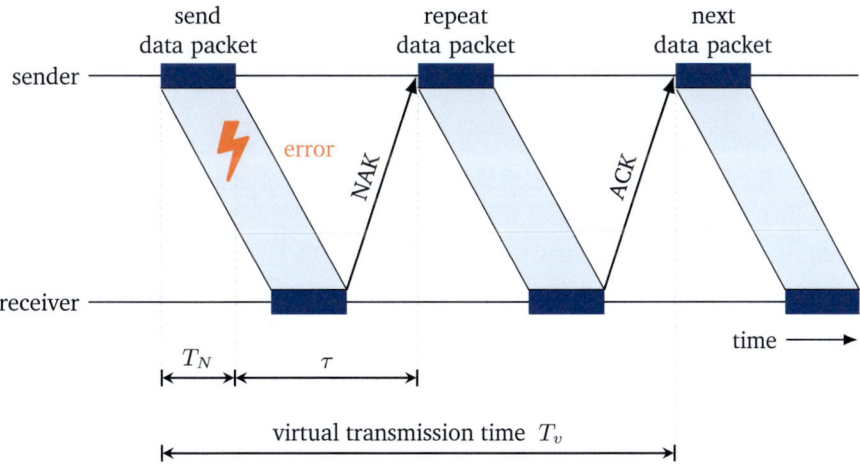

Figure 1.3: Handshaking protocol: illustration how it works.

The packet transmission time is indicated by T_N and the signal propagation delay from sender to receiver and back (round-trip time) is denoted by τ. To model the handshaking protocol, the virtual transmission time T_V of a packet is determined first. The virtual transmission time is defined as the time actually required for the successful transmission of a packet. Let us assume a packet error probability p_B for any packet. If the error events are independent of one another, the virtual transmission time T_V is derived as shown in Figure 1.4. After a single transfer process, the transmission is successful with probability $1 - p_B$ and we obtain $T_V = T_N + \tau$. With probability p_B the transmission is repeated, and T_V is increased by the time for a single (re-)transmission $T_N + \tau$.

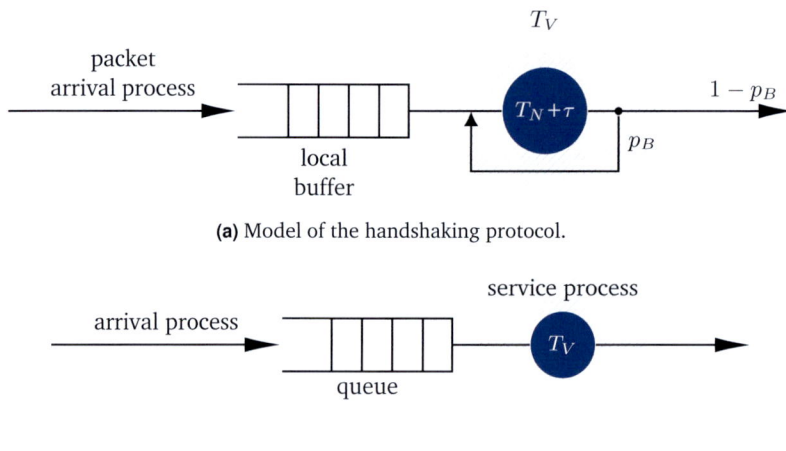

(a) Model of the handshaking protocol.

(b) Queueing model or traffic model.

Figure 1.4: Traffic model of the handshaking protocol.

The traffic model of the handshaking protocol includes an arrival process of the packets as well as waiting room for packets arriving for transmission. The arrival process describes the interarrival time of packets to be transmitted. Since only a single packet can be transmitted over the communication channel, new packets to be transmitted may need to wait until the channel is free for transmission. The communication channel represents the service unit in the system. The service time for processing a single packet corresponds to the virtual transmission time. The service time T_V is a random variable which depends on the number R of required retransmissions. R is also a random variable, since with a certain probability p_B a transmission is repeated. Here R follows a geometric distribution, see Chapter 2.4.1.3. The probability that i retransmissions are required is $p_B^i(1 - p_B)$ which results in the service time $(i + 1)(T_N + \tau)$. Figure 1.4 visualizes the traffic model.

As will be discussed in Chapter 1.2, this is a single-stage queueing system of the type GI/GI/1. The arrival process of the packets is modeled with arbitrarily distributed interarrival times. The transmission duration T_N of packets is also arbitrarily distributed. An analysis of the model provides system characteristics such as waiting time, processing time and throughput depending on the probability of packet errors, etc. The goal of the model is to study the impact of the packet error probability on the response time of the system, which is the waiting time of packets and the virtual transmission time. The response time is also referred to as sojourn time of packets in the system.

Limiting resources
> processing of packets in the system, i.e., sending of packets over the error prone communication channel

Performance measures
> response time of the system (waiting time and virtual transmission time)
> throughput per packet

Goal of model
> impact of packet error probability on performance measures

Queueing model
> GI/GI/1-∞ delay system

1.3.2   Network Dimensioning in Mobile Networks

Consider a cellular radio system in which the geographical area is divided into radio cells for planning purposes. Each cell is served by a base station and mobile subscribers can connect to the base station to get access to the mobile network. The underlying assumption is that each cell offers a limited number of communication channels to the mobile subscribers. A dedicated channel is assigned to each subscriber being connected to the base station in a cell. However, if all communication channels within a cell are already used, a newly requesting subscriber cannot be served and is blocked (admission control).

As a concrete use case for numerical results we examine the cellular radio standard GSM (Global System for Mobile Communication). The model introduced here can also be applied to other mobile networks. The GSM system is the European standard for cellular networks of the 2nd generation. The GSM uses the cellular concept with a base station BTS (Base Transceiver Station) per cell with which the mobile stations connect. A combination of frequency division multiplexing and time division multiplexing is used in GSM to provide communication channels.

The blocking of call requests or call attempts in a GSM cell must not exceed a predetermined blocking probability in order to guarantee the mobile radio subscribers a certain quality of service. For modeling a GSM cell, we have the following two model components: service process and arrival process.

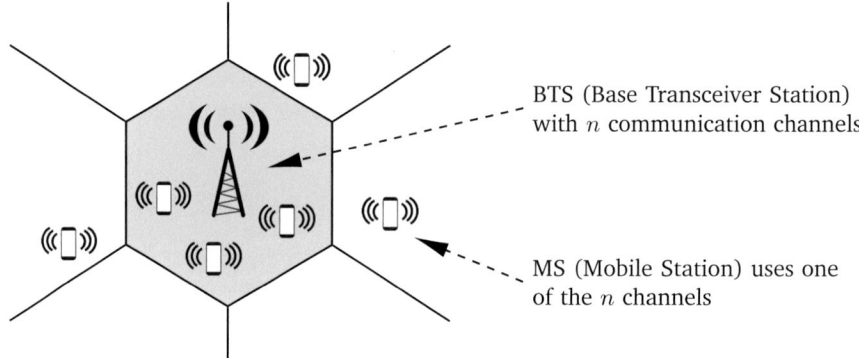

Figure 1.5: GSM cell with n communication channels and several mobile stations.

Service process A GSM cell has n communication channels, i.e. n service units for processing voice traffic. The call duration B is a random variable that can be measured from real-world phone calls in existing systems. An accepted call utilizes one dedicated communication channel for the duration of the voice call. If no communication channel is available at the time of the call attempt, the attempt will be rejected. We refer to this class of models as *loss systems*.

Arrival process In a cell there is a finite number m of mobile subscribers who can be in different states: "idle", "active" (making a phone call) or "wait for retrial". In Chapter 4, three models at different levels of detail are analyzed.

- *Arrival traffic with a finite number of sources*: the number m of participants is finite, the aggregated traffic is the sum of the traffic flows of all participants in the "idle" state. The corresponding traffic model is dealt with in Chapter 4.3 (loss system with finite number of sources).

- *Arrival traffic with an infinite number of sources*: if the number m of participants is sufficiently large, the resulting arrival traffic can be approximately described by an arrival process with an "infinite number of sources". This model approach is usually easier to handle analytically. The corresponding traffic model is described in connection with the well-known Erlang loss formula, which is often used in practice. The analysis can be found in Chapter 4.1 (loss system M/M/n and M/GI/n).

- *Customer retrial model with finite number of sources*: In reality, overload situations may emerge in such systems. The traffic intensity continues to increase and the system performance continues to deteriorate. One reason for this snowball effect is the repetition of calls: the more likely the call attempts of mobile users are blocked, the more impatient rejected callers will become and will try to retry the unsuccessful call attempt at shorter time intervals, thereby overloading the system. The corresponding traffic model is discussed in Chapter 4.4 (customer retrial model with finite number of sources).

In all three cases, the limiting resource is the number of communication channels in a single cell. The performance measure of interest is the blocking probability which depends on the number of sources in a cell as well as the customer retrial behavior.

Limiting resources
> number of communication channels in the mobile cell

Performance measures
> blocking probability of customers' calls

Goal of model
> dimensioning of the number of required communication channels such that the blocking probability is below a QoS threshold for given parameters and user retrial behavior

Queueing model
> M/GI/n-0 loss system

1.3.3   Software Defined Networking and Switch Table Occupancy

Software defined networking (SDN) is a networking paradigm which enables programmable network control with open interfaces. A key principle of SDN is the separation of the control plane and the data plane of switching devices. The switches are responsible for forwarding the traffic, but they are controlled by an external control plane entity referred to as "SDN controller". Hence, control functions are centralized at the controller, e.g. network access control, firewall functionality, load balancing, routing, etc. The controller has the ability to change the forwarding behavior of the network switches directly.

In SDN, each new flow in the network introduces additional signaling traffic between the switch and the controller. Rules are created in the so called *flow table* of the switch, which specify the forwarding or dropping behavior of packets. The controller pushes the SDN rules to the switch based on incoming flows on the data plane. However, the flow table space in terms of TCAM (ternary content-addressable memory) and CAM (content-addressable memory) is the limiting factor of the SDN switches. This kind of memory is expensive and therefore limited. As a consequence, unused flow rules should be removed from the switches. In practice, unused entries in the flow table are removed after a predefined time-out interval τ. A longer time-out interval reduces the signaling traffic between the switch and the controller, but results in increased table occupancy. If the flow table is completely occupied, the rules for newly arriving flows cannot be inserted into the flow table or existing flow rules are overwritten. In both cases, we observe the "blocking" of rules in the flow table. Alternatively, short values of τ quickly release memory at the cost of increased signaling traffic if the flow is still active. The network operator has to define the time-out parameter τ by considering this trade-off.

A basic model for the analysis of the impact of time-out parameter is as follows. The arrival process describes the newly arriving traffic flows in the network which are triggering the establishment of a new rule in the flow table of the switch. The switch has a limited capacity and can only install n flow rules. If there are already n rules in the flow table, new rules cannot be installed and are blocked. The system has n service units corresponding to the capacity in the flow table. The service process is the time B the rule is active and occupies one of the n available memory spaces in the flow table. This time B is a random variable which depends on the type of traffic and the lifetime of the flow, but also on the time-out parameter τ. The parameter τ also influences the arrival process. If an inactivity period of a flow is larger than τ, the flow rule may be deleted; the same flow getting active again (after the inactivity period) will appear as newly arriving flow. In a very simplified way, the system can be described as an M/GI/n loss system – as in the previous example. Hence, we have two completely different use cases (SDN and switch table occupancy; dimensioning of GSM cells) which are described however by the same queueing model.

Limiting resources:
> switch table memory allows the installation of n rules

Performance measures:
> switch table occupancy and blocking probability of flow rules

Goal of model:
> time-out parameter τ triggers arrival rate of new flows and lifetime of flows; parameter sensitivity study on time-out values τ after which flow entries are deleted in the flow table of a switch

Queueing model
> M/GI/n-0 loss system

▣ *Further reading:* Metter et al. (2017) "Analytical model for SDN signaling traffic and flow table occupancy and its application for various types of traffic" [78].

1.3.4 Video Streaming Applications and QoE

Video streaming services currently constitute the majority of Internet traffic. The video service provider platforms offer videos in a variety of quality settings which allow them to adapt the video quality to the available network conditions. The goal is to provide high video quality without any video playout interruptions. This may happen due to insufficient video server capacity, insufficient network data rates as well as varying network conditions when the video contents are not delivered fast enough to the video client, such that the video freezes for some time until the video buffer is filled again and the video playout can be restarted.

For a smooth playout, the video client at the end-user site implements a video buffer. The player fills up the video buffer, e.g. until a certain amount of video data is available in the buffer, before the video playout is started. The video buffer helps to overcome variations in the download throughput (jitter). Once the video buffer empties, the video freezes or stalls until the video buffer is filled again. From an end user's point of view, stalling and video interruptions are the most severe influence factors on the quality of experience (QoE) of video streaming. Service providers therefore aim to avoid stalling, even at the cost of reduced video quality.

In the Internet, HTTP-based adaptive streaming is the de-facto standard for delivering video streaming services. On the server side, the video is split into small segments and each of them is available in different quality levels corresponding to

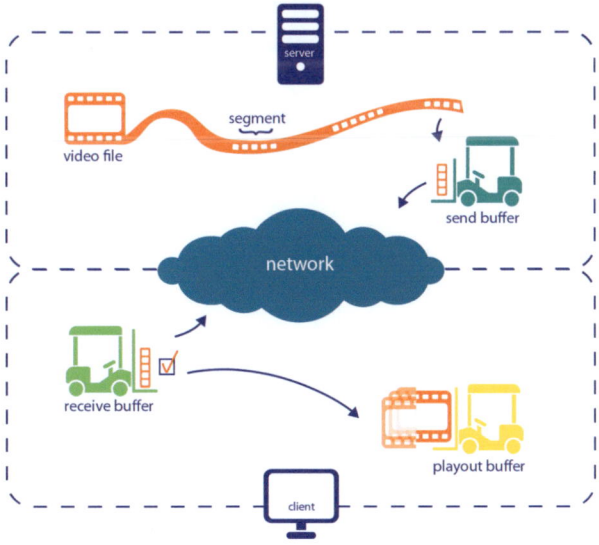

Figure 1.6: Illustration of video streaming buffer (M/M/1 system with N-policy).

different video bit rates, cf. Figure 1.6. Based on network measurements and the current video buffer status, the video client at the user side requests the next part of the video via the HTTP protocol in the appropriate bit rate level which is best suited under current network and video buffer conditions.

It is of particular interest for the service provider to understand the impact of the buffer threshold N which is the number of segments in the video buffer when the video playout starts again after any video interruption. To be more precise, the service provider is interested in the QoE of a user. Thereby, quantifiable QoE models are utilized which model the user perceived quality depending on (network or application-level) Quality of Service (QoS) parameters. For HTTP-based video streaming, the key influence factors (on application layer) on the QoE are the number of video interruptions during the playout, referred to as *stalling*, and the total stall duration. 🖩 *Further reading:* A survey on QoE of HTTP adaptive streaming [96].

Chapter 7.1 provides a queueing model of the video buffer. The arrival process describes the arrival of video segments at the client's video buffer which are transmitted from the video server. The available segments in the video buffer are played out one by one. Hence, the video player is a single service unit which processes a single video segment. The video duration of a segment is a random variable describing the service time of a single segment. The video player however gets only active (i.e. start to play out segments), when the video buffer exceeds N segments. This policy is denoted as *N-policy*.

In particular, Chapter 7.1 analyzes the M/M/1 queue with N-policy. The model provides the probability for the number of segments in the video buffer for a given network data rate and the video bit rate with the buffer threshold N as configuration parameter of the video buffer policy. This allows derivation of various performance parameters: stall ratio, average stall duration, and the stall frequency. These parameters are input for the QoE model, such that we are able to derive the QoE-optimal video buffer parameter N.

Limiting resources:
   downlink network capacity
Performance measures:
   stall ratio, average stall duration, and the stall frequency
Goal of model:
   optimal video buffer threshold N concerning the user perceived quality which is obtained by applying a video streaming QoE model to the performance results
Queueing model
   M/M/1-∞ delay system with N-policy

1.3.5 Resource Sharing in Cloud Computing

Resource sharing mechanisms are implemented in systems with constrained resources. In communication networks this may be the sharing of network resources like network capacity to download data among several users or network devices. In cloud computing environments this limiting resource may be the processing power of data center servers which are shared among several compute jobs. Queueing models with processor sharing are widely used to analyze resource sharing mechanisms where a system capacity is (time-)shared between all users or jobs. Processor sharing models are the ideal, perfect system in which the fraction of the total capacity occupied per user/job is simply the inverse of the number of users/jobs in the system.

A recent application of processor sharing is network function virtualization (NFV). Network functions and network services like firewalls or mobility management and session management were so far hosted on dedicated hardware. With the rise of the cloud computing paradigm and virtualization technologies, such network functions may be implemented within a cloud environment which offers virtual and physical resources of storage, computation, and network. The main idea of NFV is to decouple the network functions from the physical hardware that accommodates them. As a result, virtualized network functions (VNFs) are deployed on virtual resources provided within the NFV infrastructure. The VNF requests share the available resources in the cloud. The cloud computing paradigm allows network operators to scale up their deployments more rapidly and according to the demand of arrival requests.

In Chapter 4.5, the basic egalitarian processor sharing model, which does not differentiate between customers, is analyzed (M/M/1-PS). Due to the insensitivity or robustness property, the results can be generalized for the more general M/GI/1-PS system which means that service time may follow a general random variable. As a concrete example, the power consumption of a data center is considered in Chapter 4.5.6. Initially, the power consumption of a single server is computed. A single server can be described as M/GI/1-PS system. In such a data center, the arrival process characterizes the workload arrival due to new jobs to be processed in the data center. The capacity of the server is shared among the present workload requests which is modeled by the processor sharing discipline. Secondly, the required number n of servers for a certain quality of service requirement is derived. The QoS requirement may consider that the expected sojourn time for 99% of the workload requests are below a threshold $T_{\max}$. Within the data center, n servers are available. To reduce the total energy in the data center, up to m servers may be turned off – which will, however, increase the utilization per server and the response time.

Limiting resources:
> service capacity of a single server within the data center
> total power consumption of data center consisting of n servers

Performance measures:
> response time of jobs and total power consumption

Goal of model:
> minimum number of required servers in the data center such that the expected power consumption in the data center is minimized while the QoS requirements (sojourn time below a pre-defined threshold) are fulfilled

Queueing model
> M/GI/1-PS processor sharing system

1.3.6   Internet of Things and Smart City Applications

The Internet of Things (IoT) is a networking challenge where a potentially huge number of new devices will be interconnected across the digital landscape. On one hand, IoT enables typical smart city applications like environmental sensing of air quality, road traffic conditions, free parking lots, or bike fleet management. Thereby, the IoT data from the sensors is typically transmitted to an IoT cloud which processes the data and offers a platform to access the data or services built on top of the data. On the other hand, the industrial IoT interconnects sensors, actuators, and other devices to realize industrial applications like manufacturing or energy management. As in the case of smart cities, the data may be collected, exchanged, and processed in a data center.

Chapter 7.2 deals with traffic modeling in the Internet of Things for typical smart city applications. Sensors are monitoring the environment and are sending the IoT data for further processing to a central IoT cloud. Hence, the arrival process of data packets sent to the IoT cloud is the superposition of the IoT traffic stemming from a large number of sensors. A typical use case is periodic sensing of the environment. The question arises how such aggregated (periodic) IoT traffic can be modeled. We will see and quantify that for a sufficiently large number of n sensor nodes the aggregated IoT traffic may be approximated by the Poisson process, which has convenient mathematical properties and allows to derive closed-form solutions for many practical questions.

Figure 1.7 illustrates the networking architecture for periodic sensor traffic delivered to a central cloud processing platform over the Internet. The IoT load balancer is the first point of the cloud architecture where the individual traffic flows become aggregated. Due to the large number of IoT devices, the load balancer is required to distribute the workload across back-end servers and may be a potential performance

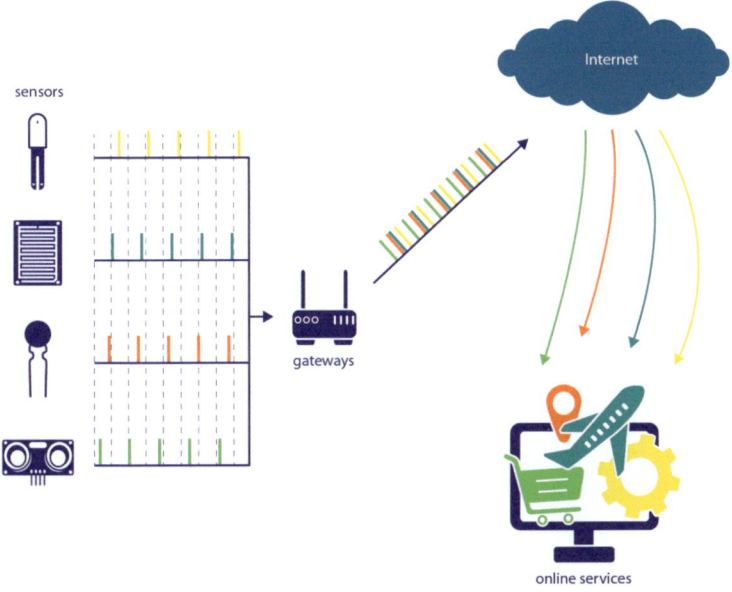

Figure 1.7: Illustration of the IoT cloud for periodic traffic.

bottleneck in the architecture. Data arrives from sensor nodes and is aggregated at the load balancer which forwards the data to the back-end cloud servers. The question arises how to dimension the load balancer in terms of processing power, such that the mean waiting time of IoT data packets is below a certain QoS threshold. We will consider small sensor messages of constant size which are periodically sent from n asynchronous sensors to the IoT cloud. The IoT load balancer therefore has a deterministic processing time to distribute the data across the back-end server. The system is modeled as an (exact) nD/D/1 waiting queue and compared to an (approximating) M/D/1 waiting queue.

Limiting resources:
    IoT cloud load balancer
Performance measures:
    waiting time or response time of IoT data packets at the load balancer
Goal of model:
    dimensioning of the required processing power of the load balancer to keep the mean waiting time below a predefined QoS threshold;
    comparison of exact nD/D/1 model with the approximating M/D/1 queue
Queueing model
    nD/1/1 and M/D/1 delay system

Finally, Chapter 7.2 considers different random access schemes of the IoT sensor nodes with LoRaWAN as smart city infrastructure. The IoT sensor nodes try to send the data over the air interface to an IoT gateway. LoRaWAN (Long Range Wide Area Network) has received public interest through provider-backed installations, but also community-operated or smart city-operated gateway networks. Such LoRaWAN gateways can aggregate the traffic from thousands of devices which is of particular interest in dense urban environments with up to 10,000 households per km^2.

We compare various random access schemes for LoRaWAN sensor nodes which are pure and slotted ALOHA, perfect CSMA/CA as well as energy-aware CSMA/CA with restricted accessibility. The performance measures are the packet loss probability due to potential message collisions on the air interface, the throughput, and the mean response time to send packets to the IoT gateway. The LoRaWAN IoT sensor devices are kept cheap and extremely resource-limited for enabling suggested runtimes of ten years on one reasonably sized battery charge. Thus, energy consumption and energy efficiency is of major interest in that context. This use case nicely demonstrates different fundamental queueing models for those random access mechanisms.

Limiting resources:
   message collision on the air interface between IoT sensor and gateway
Performance measures:
   throughput, packet loss, energy consumption, energy efficiency
Goal of model:
   comparison of different random access mechanisms: pure ALOHA (M/D/∞), slotted ALOHA (M/C/∞), perfect CSMA/CA (M/D/1-∞), energy-aware CSMA/CA with restricted accessibility (M/D/1-S)
Queueing model
   infinite server M/D/∞ and M/C/∞
   M/D/1-∞ delay system
   M/D/1-S delay-loss system

1.3.7   Overload Control in Communication Systems

In communication systems the overload phenomenon and its influence on system performance has become more critical and complex due to the increasing number of new system features, the large number of involved hardware and software components, but also increased service requirements. To guarantee proper system performance and providing appropriate QoS, the sensitivity of communication systems against overload must be taken into account in the design and development phase as well as in the operating phase.

According to [106], we distinguish two classes of modeling approaches for the investigation of the overload phenomenon in communication systems.

- *Overload modeling*: evaluation models for overload indicators and time-dependent requirements for overload detection which include models describing the dynamics of overload situations and those describing behavior of users or network devices.

- *Overload control modeling*: models for performance evaluation of overload control strategies, where aspects like timeliness, influence on other subsystems, etc., are considered.

In communication systems, overload control strategies operate with throttling mechanisms of the input process which we will model with a general queueing system in Chapter 7.6. The main mechanism of these overload control strategies implements workload-driven admission control which uses the actual workload as overload indicator. The actual workload is the amount of unfinished work in the system which still needs to be processed by the system. When this workload exceeds a predefined threshold L, newly arriving jobs are rejected. The basic model of the class of overload control strategy is of type GI/GI/1 with a feedback-controlled input process. Discrete-time analysis methods are used to obtain a generally applicable exact algorithm to obtain numerical results. The key performance measure is the blocking probability of jobs, when the unfinished work exceeds the threshold L. The discrete-time analysis allows to derive results for stationary and non-stationary load conditions, as well as (auto-)correlated arrival and service processes. The input process models the job arrival process, while the service time models the processing time of jobs. In particular, the evaluation of the overload control strategy under short-term overloads is of interest.

Limiting resources:
overload situation results in workload exceeding a threshold L

Performance measures:
blocking probability of jobs

Goal of model:
impact of the threshold L under short-term overloads

Queueing model
discrete-time delay system GI/GI/1 with bounded unfinished work

Fundamentals and Prerequisites

One fundamental relationship in operation research and especially in queueing theory is Little's theorem, which is also known as Little's result or Little's law. Several examples applying Little's theorem as well as the utilization law are discussed. Furthermore, elementary results from probability theory and random variables are introduced. Expected values and functions of random variables are prerequisites in queueing theory. Commonly used transformation methods are introduced which allow to elegantly analyze some queueing systems. Finally, important discrete- and continuous-time functions as well as basic relationships between these are presented.

2.1 Little's Theorem and General Results

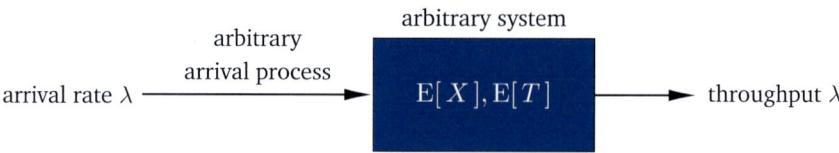

Figure 2.1: On Little's mean value analysis.

We consider a *"system"* which can be understood in a very general context. For the system it is only assumed that the limit values considered below are well-defined constants – and not random variables. The system taken into account can be any selected component of a real system or its model. The following parameters are of interest:

λ mean arrival rate of the arrival process, which can be of generic nature,

$\mathrm{E}[X]$ mean number of customers in system,

$\mathrm{E}[T]$ mean sojourn time of customers in system.

This system assumes it is in statistical equilibrium and the mean number of customers and the mean sojourn time are finite and exist. Therefore, the so-called Little's theorem applies (or Little's formula, Little's law).

$$\lambda \cdot \mathrm{E}[T] = \mathrm{E}[X] \qquad\qquad \textbf{Little's formula} \quad (2.1)$$

Proof of Little's Theorem

The proof of this general relationship is illustrated in Figure 2.2. We observe the system state $X(t)$ over a long time interval t_0. The system state $X(t)$ is the number of all customers in the system at time t. During the interval t_0, a number N of customers arrive to the system, and their respective sojourn times T_i are marked in Figure 2.2.

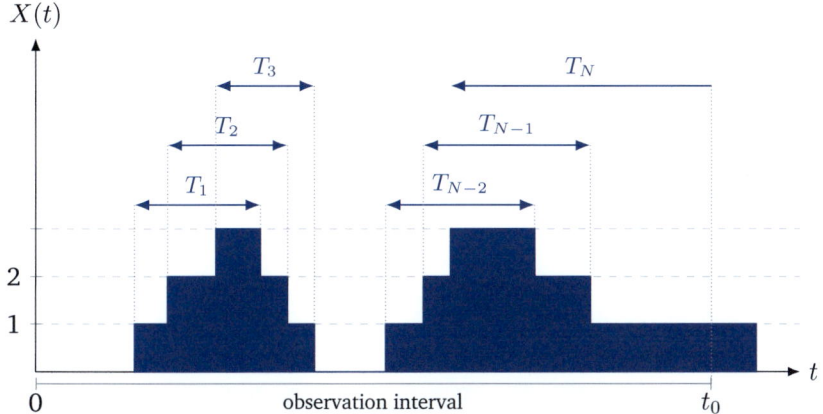

Figure 2.2: On the derivation of Little theorem. During the observation interval of length t_0 there are N arrivals of customers with sojourn times T_i.

The mean sojourn time and the mean number of customers in the system during the finite observation interval t_0:

$$\bar{T} = \frac{1}{N} \sum_{i=1}^{N} T_i \approx \frac{1}{N} \int_0^{t_0} X(t)\, dt \,, \tag{2.2a}$$

$$\bar{X} = \frac{1}{t_0} \int_0^{t_0} X(t)\, dt \,, \qquad \text{i.e.,} \quad \bar{X} \approx \frac{N}{t_0} \bar{T} \,. \tag{2.2b}$$

With

$$\bar{\lambda} = \frac{N}{t_0} \tag{2.2c}$$

we obtain

$$\bar{X} \approx \bar{\lambda} \cdot \bar{T} \,. \tag{2.2d}$$

Since the observation period t_0 is limited, an error can occur, such as the sojourn time of a customer (e.g. of customer N in Figure 2.2) is truncated at the end of the observation period for customers arriving before t_0, but leaving after t_0. Hence, Equation (2.2a) requires '$\approx$'. For the limit $t_0 \to \infty$ this error is negligible.

Considering the limit $t_0 \to \infty$, where

$$\lambda = \lim_{t_0 \to \infty} \bar{\lambda} = \lim_{t_0 \to \infty} \frac{N}{t_0} , \tag{2.3a}$$

$$E[T] = \lim_{t_0 \to \infty} \bar{T} = \lim_{t_0 \to \infty} \frac{1}{N} \sum_{i=1}^{N} T_i , \tag{2.3b}$$

$$E[X] = \lim_{t_0 \to \infty} \bar{X} = \lim_{t_0 \to \infty} \frac{1}{t_0} \int_{0}^{t_0} X(t) \, dt , \tag{2.3c}$$

we obtain Little's result in Equation (2.1).

Extension to Batch Arrivals   It is important to note that Little's law can also be applied to batch arrivals. The arrival rate of batches is λ. The average number of customers in a group is $\overline{N}$. Then, the average arrival rate of customers in the system is $\bar{\lambda} = \overline{N} \cdot \lambda$ and Little's law can be applied.

2.1.1   Little's Law in Finite Systems with Blocking

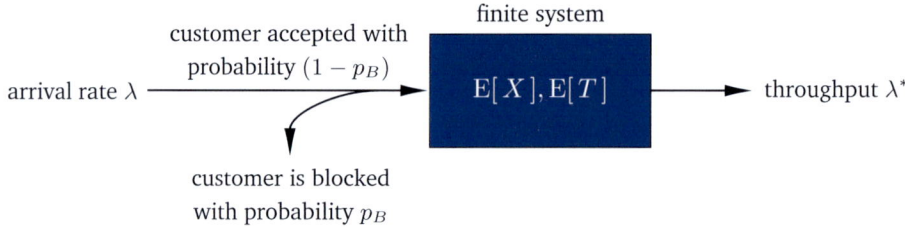

Figure 2.3: Applying Little's theorem to a loss system GI/GI/n-S.

Let's consider a finite system where the number of servers and waiting places is limited. Customers are blocked when all servers and waiting places are occupied. The blocking probability is p_B. An arriving customer is therefore accepted with probability $(1 - p_B)$. The arrival rate is λ which includes the arrival of all customers, i.e. accepted and blocked customers. The arrival rate λ^* of customers who are accepted by the system is

$$\lambda^* = (1 - p_B) \cdot \lambda \tag{2.4a}$$

which represents also the throughput of the system. Little's theorem can now be applied.

$$E[X] = \lambda^* \cdot E[T] = (1 - p_B) \cdot \lambda \cdot E[T] \tag{2.4b}$$

2.1.2 Example: Multiclass Systems

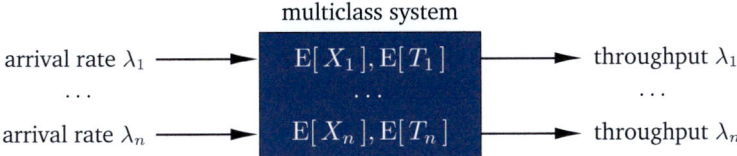

multiclass system

arrival rate λ_1 $\longrightarrow$ $E[X_1], E[T_1]$ $\longrightarrow$ throughput λ_1

$\cdots$ $\cdots$ $\cdots$

arrival rate λ_n $\longrightarrow$ $E[X_n], E[T_n]$ $\longrightarrow$ throughput λ_n

Figure 2.4: Applying Little's theorem to a queueing system with multiple customer classes.

The queueing system consists of n customer classes with arrival rates λ_i for $i = 1, \ldots, n$. We denote the superposition of the customer arrivals within Kendall's notion as $\sum \text{GI}$. Accordingly, if the customer classes have different service times, we may denote the multiclass delay system with n servers as $\sum \text{GI}/\sum \text{GI}/n$. Little's theorem can be applied to every customer class individually.

$$E[X_i] = \lambda_i \cdot E[T_i] \quad \text{for } i = 1, \ldots, n \tag{2.5}$$

The total number of customers in the system is $X = X_1 + \cdots X_n$ and the mean number of customers independent of the customer class is

$$E[X] = E[X_1] + \cdots + E[X_n] \tag{2.6a}$$

while the arrival rate respective throughput is

$$\lambda = \lambda_1 + \cdots + \lambda_n . \tag{2.6b}$$

Hence, the average sojourn time $E[T]$ follows from Little's theorem.

$$E[T] = \frac{E[X]}{\lambda} = \frac{E[X_1] + \cdots + E[X_n]}{\lambda} = \frac{\lambda_1}{\lambda}E[T_1] + \cdots + \frac{\lambda_n}{\lambda}E[T_n] \tag{2.6c}$$

2.1.3 Example: Balking

Consider now a system with user impatience. In particular, consider balking. A customer arrives and sees the system in state i, i.e. there are i other customers in the system. With probability $1 - p_i$ the arriving customer refuses to enter the queue e.g. due to too long waiting time. This means this customer balks from the queueing system. With probability p_i, the arriving customer joins the systems. This behavior can be observed in practice for example when the waiting line is too long in a supermarket, then some customers decided to not go shopping and do not enter the supermarket.

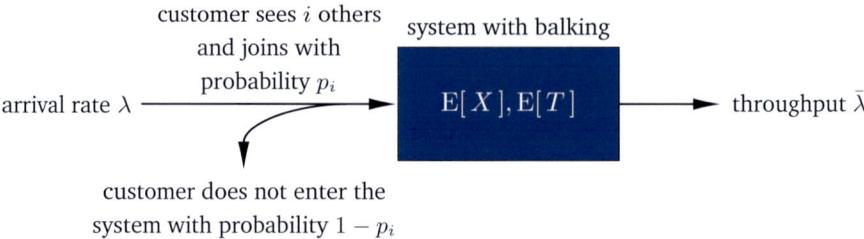

Figure 2.5: Applying Little's theorem to a queueing system with balking.

This creates state-dependent arrival rates. The system is in state i with probability $x(i)$. The effective arrival rate λ_i of customers entering the system when seeing i other customers is

$$\lambda_i = \lambda \cdot p_i . \tag{2.7a}$$

Then, the mean arrival rate to the system is

$$\bar{\lambda} = \sum_{i=0}^{\infty} \lambda_i \cdot x(i) = \sum_{i=0}^{\infty} \lambda \cdot p_i \cdot x(i) , \tag{2.7b}$$

which is equivalent to the throughput of the system. It is

$$E[X] = \sum_{i=0}^{\infty} i \cdot x(i) \tag{2.7c}$$

and therefore

$$E[T] = \frac{E[X]}{\bar{\lambda}} = \frac{\sum_{i=0}^{\infty} i \cdot x(i)}{\sum_{i=0}^{\infty} \lambda \cdot p_i \cdot x(i)} . \tag{2.7d}$$

2.1.4 The Utilization Law

Little's theorem is very powerful, since it makes no assumptions about how arrivals occur or customers are served. The theorem can be applied to *any stable* system and to any *part* of the system. Applying Little's theorem to a server of a queueing system leads to the utilization law. Consider the average number $E[X_B]$ of customers at a *single server* (i.e. not in the waiting queue) which is simply the fraction of the time the server is busy, referred to as *utilization* of the server. Then, Little's law leads to

$$E[X_B] = \lambda_s \cdot E[B] < 1 \tag{2.8}$$

with B being the service time of a customer and λ_s being the arrival rate (of accepted customers) at the server. If the server is overloaded, then $\lambda_s \cdot E[B] > 1$. If there is only a single server in a delay system (GI/GI/1-∞), the utilization law leads to the probability that the system is empty: $x(0) = P(X = 0) = 1 - \lambda_s \cdot E[B]$.

2.1.5 Assumptions and Limits of Little's Law

The proof of Little's theorem did not specify the distribution of the interarrival times or the service times, as well as the scheduling discipline. It is valid for any work-conserving disciplines like FIFO, LIFO, processor sharing (PS), or service in random order (RANDOM) and the order of served customers does not matter. *Work-conserving* means that the system is not idle when there is work and that the system does not introduce overhead, e.g. to wake-up after an idle phase, e.g. preemption in computer system may cause context switches. The capacity of the server is constant and independent of e.g. the length of the queue. In practice, machines may have failures – the server is 'on vacation' when there is work in the system, but the server is not working and serving the customers. Iversen provides a nice example of a queueing discipline which is not work-conserving [56]: "If the server is a human being, the service rate will often increase with the length of the queue, and after some time the server may become exhausted and decrease the service rate."

But Little's law is even more general. Little's law holds for *any* scheduling discipline. Even the interarrival times may be statistically dependent. The only required assumption for Little's law is that two of the quantities $(\mathrm{E}[X], \lambda, \mathrm{E}[T])$, exist and are finite. Then, the third quantity follows, see e.g. Van Mieghem [112]. The steady state assumption is not required for the applicability of Little's law and is stronger than the existence of finite limits. A system in steady state implies the existence of the limit values. Even more, the steady state implies that the entire distributions for T and X reach a limiting distribution, see Equation (3.40). In the steady state, the arrival rate of work for the system is the same as the departure rate of completed work from that system. In other words: throughput, arrival rate, and departure rate are the same, see Figure 2.1. Ramalhoto, Amaral, and Cochito [87] survey literature and discuss the minimal assumptions for Little's law along with corresponding proofs.

In general, Little's law is not valid when the system generates or destroys work. For example, due to a failure in a router, some packets are not forwarded and are not departing from the system or may initiate additional (signaling) traffic within the system. In that case, the sojourn times are unclear. Extensions of Little's law are summarized by Whitt [119] and by Little himself [73].

2.1.6 General Results for GI/GI/n Delay Systems

For a GI/GI/n delay system some general results are available which may be obtained based on Little's law. The average arrival rate λ is the inverse of the average interarrival time, $\lambda = 1/E[A]$. There are n servers with an average service rate μ of a single server, which is the inverse of the average service time for a customer, $\mu = 1/E[B]$. For the delay system, the main interest is the sojourn time, also denoted as response time, the waiting time of a customer, as well as the waiting probability. We use the following notions in this book.

- sojourn time or response time T is the sum of the waiting time W and the service time B: $T = W + B$ (random variables)

- number of customers in the system X is the sum of customers in the queue X_W and in service X_B: $X = X_W + X_B$ (random variables)

The stability of the GI/GI/n system requires the so called *stability condition*.

$$a = \lambda \cdot E[B] < n \qquad \Longleftrightarrow \qquad \rho = \frac{a}{n} = \frac{\lambda}{n\mu} < 1 \qquad \textbf{stability condition} \quad (2.9)$$

This means that the number of arrivals during the mean service time $E[B]$ must be less than the number of available servers. We use the term *offered load* for $a = \lambda E[B]$. In other words, the stability condition demands that the *normalized offered load* $\rho = \frac{\lambda}{n\mu} < 1$ with $\mu = 1/E[B]$. Note that finite buffer systems GI/GI/n-S are always stable due to blocking with a certain blocking probability p_B.

The mean values of the GI/GI/n delay system are as follows:

- mean response time $E[T] = E[W] + E[B]$,
- mean number in system $E[X] = E[X_W] + E[X_B]$,
- mean number of busy servers $E[X_B] = \lambda \cdot E[B] = a$ is identical to the offered load a due to Little's law (note for loss systems, $E[X_B] = (1 - p_B)\lambda \cdot E[B] < a$),
- utilization, i.e. the fraction of time each server is busy, $a/n = \lambda/n \cdot E[B] = \rho$ is identical to the normalized offered load ρ.

If the service time is independent of the actual waiting time (e.g. in a FIFO queue), then $VAR[T] = VAR[W] + VAR[B]$; the sum of two independent random variables, its expectation and variance will be discussed in Chapter 2.2.6.3. Note that some systems may be speeding up and allocate more resources if a certain workload is in the system; or that are shutting down servers in idle periods. This is, for example, done to save energy in data centers. In that scenario, the service time B and the waiting time W are not independent of each other.

2.1.7 Loss Formula for GI/GI/n-S Loss Systems

Consider a single server in a general GI/GI/n-S system with ρ_s being the mean offered load of the server. Customers arrive with rate $\lambda = 1/\mathrm{E}[A]$ to the queue and the mean service time is $\mathrm{E}[B]$. The mean arrival rate at the considered server is $\lambda_s = \lambda/n$.

$$\rho_s = \frac{\lambda \mathrm{E}[B]}{n} = \lambda_s \mathrm{E}[B] \tag{2.10a}$$

Assuming that an arbitrarily chosen server is idle with probability ϕ_s, Hübner [55] provided the following loss formula – in a limited context – which was, however, found to be generally valid by Roberts, Mocci, Virtamo, and Andersen in [89]. The blocking probability that an arbitrary customer is blocked at that server is as follows.

$$p_B = 1 - \frac{1 - \phi_s}{\rho_s} \qquad \textbf{loss formula} \tag{2.10b}$$

This relation follows from considering a large time interval T. The mean number of served customers N_s and of blocked customers N_b during time T is

$$N_s = \frac{(1 - \phi_s)T}{\mathrm{E}[B]} \, , \tag{2.11a}$$

$$N_b = \lambda_s T - N_s \, , \tag{2.11b}$$

with the busy time $(1 - \phi_s)T$ and $\lambda_s T$ total arrivals. This leads to the ratio of blocked customers at that server:

$$\frac{N_b}{\lambda_s T} = 1 - \frac{1 - \phi_s}{\rho_s} \, . \tag{2.11c}$$

Note for a GI/GI/1-∞ delay system, it is $\phi_s = 1 - \rho_s$ (see utilization law in Chapter 2.1.4), and obviously $p_B = 0$.

2.2 Probabilities and Random Variables

Before proceeding, it is important to summarize some basic concepts of probability theory. This discussion is only intended to refresh existing knowledge and is limited to basic relationships that are relevant for the model analysis discussed later. The interested reader is referred to the detailed treatment of probability theory in standard literature (cf. Feller [34], Fisz [37], Ross [91], Kobayashi, Mark, and Turin [66]).

2.2.1 Random Experiments and Probabilities

2.2.1.1 Random Events

Consider the experiment of transmitting a data packet over a computer network. This experiment has two possible outcomes: correct (successful packet transmission) or erroneous (packet error) transmission. For these experiment results, any number can be assigned (e.g. zero {0} erroneous, one {1} for successful transmission). This number can be thought as the result of a mapping and stands for the experiment result.

The samples and sample space are denoted as follows:

ω_i sample or (elementary) experiment result,

Ω sample space, set containing all possible experiment results, $\Omega = \{\omega_1, \omega_2, \ldots\}$ can be an infinite or finite set.

2.2.1.2 Definitions of Probability

Probability as Limit of Relative Frequency   Consider the series of experiments below using the following variables:

n number of experiments,

A_i event (or feature), consisting of a subset of (elementary) experiment results,

n_i number of performed experiments, which delivers experiment results belonging to event A_i.

The relative frequency for the event A_i is defined as follows:

$$h(A_i) = \frac{n_i}{n}. \tag{2.12a}$$

The limit of $h(A_i)$ for an infinite number of experiments is defined as the probability of the event A_i:

$$P(A_i) = \lim_{n \to \infty} \frac{n_i}{n}. \tag{2.12b}$$

There are some basic properties of the probability of an event A_i.

- The value of A_i is bounded in the interval $[0; 1]$.

$$0 \leq h(A_i) \leq 1 \implies 0 \leq P(A_i) \leq 1 \tag{2.13a}$$

- If A_i and A_j are mutually exclusive events, then either event A_i or A_j can occur but never both simultaneously.

$$h(A_i \cup A_j) = h(A_i) + h(A_j) \implies P(A_i \cup A_j) = P(A_i) + P(A_j) \qquad (2.13b)$$

- For a set of $\{A_i\}$ mutually exclusive events with $\bigcup_i A_i = \Omega$, the sum of all probabilities is equal to one.

$$\sum_i h(A_i) = 1 \implies \sum_i P(A_i) = 1 \qquad (2.13c)$$

A-priori Probability   Another approach to define probability is by deductive reasoning. If there are a number of equivalent mutually exclusive alternatives and if they are equally likely, e.g. due to a symmetric property. If

m_i number of alternatives belonging to an event A_i,

m number of all alternatives,

then the so-called "a-priori"-probability – or probability with Laplace assumption – is defined as:

$$P(A_i) = \frac{m_i}{m}. \qquad (2.14)$$

Example   Consider an experiment of tossing a six-sided die where the sample space consists of the elementary events $\{1\}, \{2\}, \{3\}, \{4\}, \{5\}, \{6\}$. If the die is fully symmetric, the elementary events have all the same probability 1/6. Examining an event that the outcome is an odd number ($A_1 = \{$ outcome is odd $\} = \{1, 3, 5\}$), the probability of the event A_1 is

$$\left. \begin{array}{ll} m_1 & = 3 \\ m & = 6 \end{array} \right\} \implies P(A_1) = \frac{1}{2}.$$

2.2.2   Other Terms and Properties

2.2.2.1   Mutually Exclusive Event System

Given a set of events $\{A_i, i = 1, 2, \ldots, N\}$ which belong to a sample space Ω. If the events are pairwise disjoint or mutually exclusive, i.e. $A_i \cap A_j = \emptyset$, $\forall i \neq j$, then yields for the union set $B = A_1 \cup A_2 \cup \cdots \cup A_N$:

$$P(B) = \sum_{i=1}^{N} P(A_i) \,. \tag{2.15}$$

In case that the union set B is the entire sample space ($B = \Omega$), i.e. B contains all (elementary) events in Ω, then $P(B) = 1$ and $\{A_i, \ i = 1, \ldots, N\}$ form a mutually exclusive event system.

2.2.2.2 Joint Probability

Now consider two not necessarily disjoint events A and B. Then:

$$P(A \cap B) = P(A, B) = P(B, A) \,,$$
$$P(A \cup B) = P(A) + P(B) - P(A, B) \,.$$

In the case where $\{A_i, \ \ i = 1, \ldots, N\}$ represents a mutually exclusive event system, the probability of an arbitrary event B can be determined from the probabilities of the joint events (B, A_i) as follows:

$$P(B) = \sum_{i=1}^{N} P(A_i, B) \,. \tag{2.17}$$

2.2.2.3 Conditional Probability

A conditional event $(A|B)$ for the case that an event A occurs under the condition that another event B has occurred ($P(B) > 0$). The probability for this conditional event $(A|B)$ – conditional probability of A given B – is:

$$P(A|B) = \frac{P(A, B)}{P(B)} \,. \tag{2.18}$$

It is obvious that $P(A|B) \geq P(A, B)$.

2.2.2.4 Statistical Independence

Two events A and B are said to be statistically independent, if:

$$P(A|B) = P(A) \quad \text{or} \quad P(A, B) = P(A) \cdot P(B) \,, \tag{2.19}$$

i.e., the occurrence of A happens with the same probability, regardless of whether B already occurs or not.

2.2.2.5 Law of Total Probability

A mutually exclusive event system $\{A_i\}$ and an arbitrary event B are given. If the conditional probabilities $P(B|A_i)$ and the probabilities $P(A_i)$ for the respective condition A_i are known, then the probability for the event B can be calculated as follows:

$$P(B) = \sum_{i=1}^{N} P(A_i, B) = \sum_{i=1}^{N} P(B|A_i) \cdot P(A_i) \,. \tag{2.20}$$

This relationship is referred to as law of total probability. From Equations (2.18) and (2.20) the so-called *Bayes' theorem* can be obtained:

$$P(A_i|B) = \frac{P(B|A_i) \cdot P(A_i)}{P(B)} = \frac{P(B|A_i) \cdot P(A_i)}{\sum\limits_{j=1}^{N} P(B|A_j) \cdot P(A_j)} \,. \tag{2.21}$$

Remark: In the equations in subchapters (2.2.2.1), (2.2.2.2) and (2.2.2.5), the upper limit of the sum N can also be $N = \infty$.

2.2.3 Random Variable, Distribution and Distribution Function

2.2.3.1 Random Variable (R.V.)

A random variable (r.v.) is a function that assigns a real number to each elementary event ω_i in the sample space Ω. Depending on the range of values (codomain of the r.v.), discrete and continuous random variables can be distinguished. This fact is illustrated with the help of the following examples:

- *Discrete random variable:*
  In the random experiment "tossing two dice", the random variable [$X =$ sum of the numbers] is defined. X is a discrete r.v. and can only take integer values. In this example, X has the sample space $\{2, 3, \ldots, 12\}$.

- *Continuous random variable:*
  The round-trip time of an IP packet in a computer network is described with the random variable T. Then, T is a continuous r.v. which may be, for example, in the range of $T_{\min} = 125.21\,\text{ms}$ and $T_{\max} = 525\,\text{ms}$.

In general, a discrete random variable can have any range of values. However, unless otherwise noted, we consider non-negative integer random variables, including zero.

2.2.3.2 Distribution or Probability Mass Function (PMF)

Let X be a discrete random variable. The realization i of this r.v. X occurs with probability

$$x(i) = P(X = i), \quad i = 0, 1, \ldots, X_{\max}, \qquad \text{distribution or PMF} \quad (2.22a)$$

where $X_{\max}$ does not have to be finite. These probabilities form the probability vector $\mathbf{X} = (x(0), x(1), \ldots, x(X_{\max}))$, which represents the distribution of the r.v. X. The following normalization condition holds.

$$\sum_{i=0}^{X_{\max}} x(i) = 1 \qquad \text{normalization condition} \quad (2.22b)$$

The probability distribution for a random variable describes how the probabilities are distributed over the values of the random variable. The distribution $x(i)$ completely characterizes the r.v. X which is denoted as probability mass function (PMF). For a discrete r.v. X the probability distribution is defined by the PMF.

2.2.3.3 Cumulative Distribution Function (CDF)

Let A be an arbitrary (discrete or continuous) random variable. The cumulative distribution function (CDF) of A is defined as

$$A(t) = P(A \leq t), \qquad \text{cumulative distribution function} \quad (2.23)$$

i.e., the probability that the r.v. A is less than or equal to a realization t.

The complementary cumulative distribution function (CCDF), which is also referred to as a tail distribution, is

$$A^c(t) = 1 - A(t) = P(A > t). \qquad (2.24)$$

Fundamental properties of the CDF $A(t)$ are:

$$t_1 < t_2 \implies A(t_1) \leq A(t_2) \qquad \text{monotony} \quad (2.25a)$$
$$t_1 < t_2 \implies P(t_1 < A \leq t_2) = A(t_2) - A(t_1) \qquad (2.25b)$$
$$A(-\infty) = 0, \; A(\infty) = 1 \qquad (2.25c)$$

The CDF $A(t)$ is a complete characterization of a r.v. A. As illustrated in Figure 2.6, a CDF can be a continuous function (Figure 2.6a) or a piece-wise continuous function (Figure 2.6b).

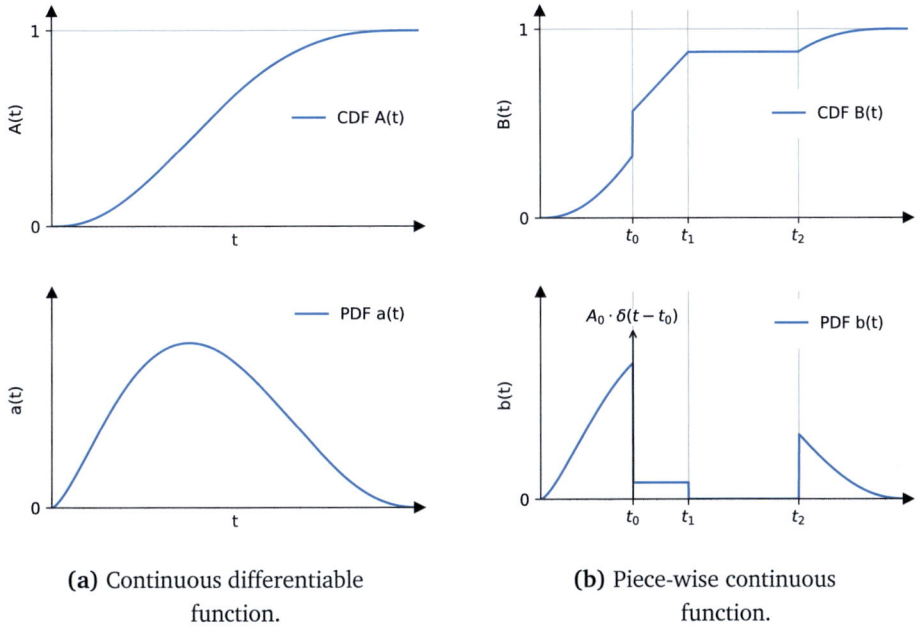

(a) Continuous differentiable function.

(b) Piece-wise continuous function.

Figure 2.6: Cumulative distribution function (CDF) and probability density function (PDF).

2.2.3.4 Probability Density Function (PDF)

The probability density function $a(t)$ (PDF) of a r.v. A – or in brief, density (function) – is defined as the first derivative of the cumulative distribution function $A(t)$:

$$a(t) = \frac{d}{dt}A(t) \,, \qquad \text{probability density function} \quad (2.26a)$$

where the normalization conditions holds:

$$\int_{-\infty}^{+\infty} a(t)\, dt = 1 \,. \qquad \text{normalization condition} \quad (2.26b)$$

When defining the probability density function $a(t)$, it is implicitly assumed that the derivative of the CDF $A(t)$ exists (see example in Figure 2.6a). If $A(t)$ is discontinuous at a certain point, e.g. t_0 with a step of height A_0 (cf. Figure 2.6b), the PDF $a(t)$ can be specified with the help of the Dirac delta function $\delta(t)$, as defined in Equation (2.27). In this example, the corresponding probability density function $a(t)$ has the step height (function value) $A_0 \delta(t - t_0)$ at t_0.

2.2.3.5 Relationship between PMF, CDF, and PDF

According to the above definitions, probability mass functions are used to characterize discrete random variables. Cumulative distribution functions and probability density functions are alternatively used to characterize continuous random variables. The relationship between probability mass function, cumulative distribution function and probability density function is illustrated in Figure 2.7 using an example.

The cumulative distribution function of a discrete r.v. X can be represented by means of the associated probability mass function. A continuous r.v. A can be considered to only take discrete values $t = i \cdot \Delta t$. Here Δt is the so-called discretization constant. The relationship between X and A can be shown in the sequence:

Probability mass function:

$$x(i) = P(X = i) = P(A = i \cdot \Delta t), \quad i = 0, 1, \ldots$$

Cumulative distribution function:

$$A(t) = P(A \leq t) .$$

The cumulative distribution function is step-wise (cf. Figure 2.7b). The step heights correspond to the probabilities.

Probability density function: According to the definition, the corresponding PDF is a weighted sum of Dirac impulses (cf. Papoulis [85]):

$$a(t) = \frac{dA(t)}{dt} = \sum_{i=-\infty}^{+\infty} P(A = t_i) \, \delta(t - t_i) ,$$

where $\delta(t - t_i)$ stands for the Dirac impulse at time $t = t_i$. Formally, the Dirac delta function is

$$\delta(t) = \begin{cases} 0 , & t \neq 0 , \\ \infty , & t = 0 , \end{cases} \qquad \text{Dirac delta function} \quad (2.27a)$$

while satisfying

$$\int_{-\infty}^{+\infty} \delta(t) \, dt = 1 . \qquad (2.27b)$$

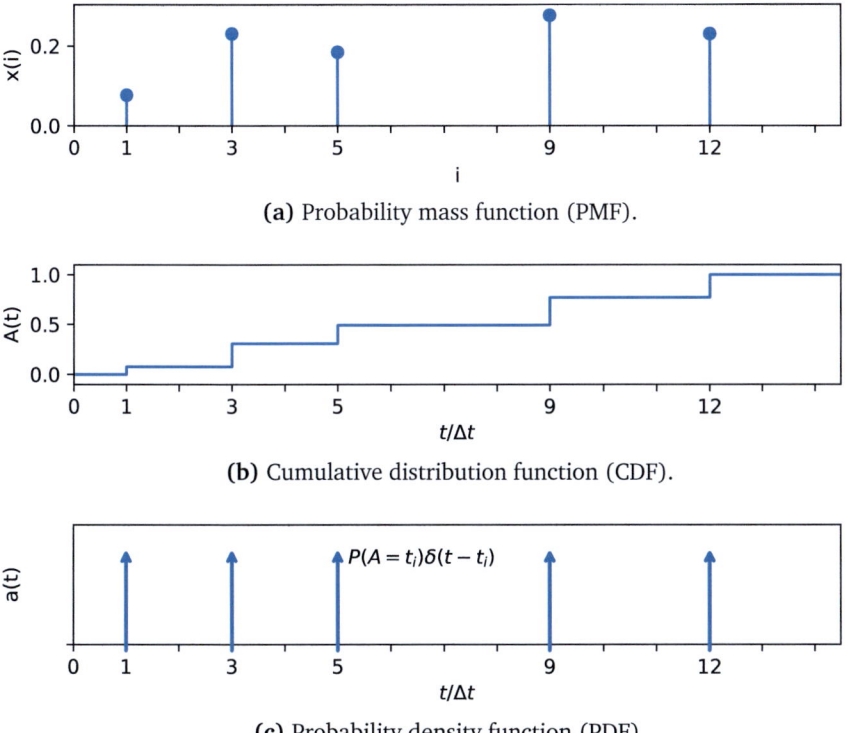

(a) Probability mass function (PMF).

(b) Cumulative distribution function (CDF).

(c) Probability density function (PDF).

Figure 2.7: Characterization of discrete random variables.

2.2.4 Expected Value and Moments

2.2.4.1 Expected Value

Let:

A be a r.v. with probability density function $a(t)$,

$g(A)$ be a function of the r.v. A; then $g(A)$ represents another r.v.

The expected value of $g(A)$ is defined as:

$$\mathrm{E}[\,g(A)\,] = \int_{-\infty}^{+\infty} g(t) \cdot a(t) \, dt \; . \qquad \text{expected value} \quad (2.28)$$

2.2.4.2 Mean of a Random Variable

For the case of $g(A) = A$ we obtain from Equation (2.28) the *mean* or the *expected value* of the random variable A.

$$m_1 = \mathrm{E}[\,A\,] = \int_{-\infty}^{+\infty} t \cdot a(t) \, dt \qquad \text{mean} \quad (2.29)$$

For a *non-negative* random variable A, the mean can also be computed by integrating the complementary cumulative distribution function (CCDF):

$$\mathrm{E}[\,A\,] = \int_{t=0}^{+\infty} P(A > t) \, dt = \int_{t=0}^{+\infty} \int_{\tau=t}^{+\infty} a(\tau) \, d\tau \, dt = \int_{\tau=0}^{+\infty} \int_{t=0}^{\tau} a(\tau) \, dt \, d\tau$$

$$= \int_{\tau=0}^{+\infty} \left[t \cdot a(\tau) \right]_0^{\tau} d\tau = \int_{\tau=0}^{+\infty} \tau \cdot a(\tau) \, d\tau = \mathrm{E}[\,A\,]. \qquad (2.30)$$

2.2.4.3 Moments of a Random Variable

By inserting $g(A) = A^k$ into Equation (2.28) we obtain the definition of the k-th (ordinary) moment of a random variable A:

$$m_k = \mathrm{E}[\,A^k\,] = \int_{-\infty}^{+\infty} t^k \cdot a(t) \, dt, \qquad k = 0, 1, \dots \; . \qquad (2.31)$$

$$k\text{-th (ordinary) moment}$$

2.2.4.4 Central Moments of a Random Variable

Central moments describe the fluctuation of a random variable around its mean m_1. These can be found by inserting $g(A) = (A - m_1)^k$ into Equation (2.28):

$$\mu_k = \mathrm{E}[\,(A - m_1)^k\,] = \int_{-\infty}^{+\infty} (t - m_1)^k \cdot a(t)\, dt, \qquad k = 0, 1, \dots\,. \tag{2.32}$$

k-th central moment

Especially for $k = 2$ we obtain the variance of the random variable A:

$$\mu_2 = \mathrm{E}[\,(A - m_1)^2\,] = \mathrm{VAR}[\,A\,] \qquad\qquad \text{variance (2.33a)}$$

or

$$\mathrm{VAR}[\,A\,] = \mathrm{E}[\,(A - m_1)^2\,] = \mathrm{E}[\,A^2 - 2m_1 A + m_1^2\,]$$
$$= \mathrm{E}[\,A^2\,] - 2m_1 \mathrm{E}[\,A\,] + m_1^2 = m_2 - m_1^2 = \mathrm{E}[\,A^2\,] - \mathrm{E}[\,A\,]^2\,. \tag{2.33b}$$

In addition, the following measures are commonly used:

$$\sigma_A = \mathrm{STD}[\,A\,] = \sqrt{\mathrm{VAR}[\,A\,]}\,, \qquad\qquad \text{standard deviation (2.34)}$$

$$c_A = \frac{\sigma_A}{m_1} = \frac{\mathrm{STD}[\,A\,]}{\mathrm{E}[\,A\,]} \quad (m_1 > 0)\,. \qquad\qquad \text{coefficient of variation (2.35)}$$

2.2.5 Functions of Random Variables and Inequalities

2.2.5.1 Function of a Single Random Variable

In the evaluation of systems, the performance like download times are often mapped to key quality indicators (KQIs) or costs, e.g. server utilization and energy consumption of those servers. KQIs are often indicators for the perceived quality and they are typically based on performance measures. Quality of experience models may directly allow the mapping of performance measures to the user perceived quality when using a particular service. In the simplest case, a mapping function $f(x)$ exists which maps the performance parameter x to a QoE value, e.g. in the range from 0 ('poor quality') to 1 ('excellent quality'). A random variable X with CDF $X(t)$ describing the performance of a system may then be mapped to a random variable Y of QoE values and we obtain the following properties. If the inverse function f^{-1} exists, the cumulative distribution function $Y(\nu)$ and the probability density function $y(\nu)$ can be derived.

$$Y = f(X) \text{ with } f : x \mapsto \mathbb{R}^+ \qquad\qquad \text{function of a random variable}$$

$$Y(\nu) = P(Y \le \nu) = P(f(X) \le \nu) = P(X \le f^{-1}(\nu)) = X(f^{-1}(\nu)) \quad \text{(2.36a)}$$

$$y(\nu) = \frac{d}{d\nu} Y(\nu) = x(f^{-1}(\nu)) \cdot \frac{d}{d\nu} f^{-1}(\nu) \qquad\qquad\qquad\qquad \text{(2.36b)}$$

$$\text{In general: } E[Y] = E[f(X)] \ne f(E[X]) \qquad\qquad\qquad\qquad \text{(2.36c)}$$

2.2.5.2 Jensen's Inequality

Consider the real-valued function f. Jensen's inequality for random variables states the following for a random variable X.

$$f(E[X]) \le E[f(X)], \quad \text{if } f \text{ is convex} \qquad\qquad\qquad \text{(2.37)}$$

$$f(E[X]) \ge E[f(X)], \quad \text{if } f \text{ is concave} \qquad\qquad \textbf{Jensen's inequality}$$

A function f is concave if the first derivative is monotonically decreasing or the second derivative is non-positive on its entire domain.

$$\frac{d}{dx} f(x) = f'(x) \text{ is monotonically decreasing} \qquad \Longleftrightarrow \quad f \text{ is concave} \quad \text{(2.38a)}$$

$$\frac{d^2}{dx^2} f(x) = f''(x) \le 0 \qquad\qquad\qquad\qquad\qquad \Longleftrightarrow \quad f \text{ is concave} \quad \text{(2.38b)}$$

In a similar way, a function f is convex if the first derivative is monotonically increasing or the second derivative is non-negative on its entire domain.

$$\frac{d}{dx} f(x) = f'(x) \text{ is monotonically increasing} \qquad \Longleftrightarrow \quad f \text{ is convex} \quad \text{(2.39a)}$$

$$\frac{d^2}{dx^2} f(x) = f''(x) \ge 0 \qquad\qquad\qquad\qquad\qquad \Longleftrightarrow \quad f \text{ is convex} \quad \text{(2.39b)}$$

Only in the case of a linear function $f(x) = ax + b$, it is

$$E[f(X)] = E[aX + b] = aE[X] + b = f(E[X]) . \qquad\qquad\qquad \text{(2.40)}$$

Example: Network Throughput The download time X of a certain web page on a web server is measured and is randomly distributed in the interval $[1\,s; 9\,s]$. To be more precise, X follows a uniform distribution with PDF $x(t) = 1/8$ for $1\,s \le t \le 9\,s$ and $x(t) = 0$ otherwise. The average download time is $E[X] = 5\,s$ and the (constant) size of the page is $c = 2\,MB$ reflecting the median size of web pages in the Internet in 2021. It is tempting to compute the average throughput as $c/E[X] = 0.4\,MBps$.

However, Jensen's inequality shows that the average throughput $E[f(X)]$ with $f(x) = c/x$ is indeed larger due to the convexity of f. It is

$$E[f(X)] = E[c/X] = \int_{t=0}^{\infty} \frac{c}{t} x(t) \, dt \approx 0.55 \, \text{MBps} \quad > \quad \frac{c}{E[T]} = 0.5 \, \text{MBps} \, .$$

Example: QoE Consider an exponential mapping function between the performance x and the QoE which is often observed in practice according to the IQX hypothesis by Fiedler, Hoßfeld, and Tran-Gia [35] who postulate that the Interdependency between QoS and QoE is eXponential. In its simplest form, $f(x) = e^{-x}$. The exponential function is convex, since $f''(x) = e^{-x} > 0$. The mean QoE $E[f(X)]$ is therefore larger or equal to the mean QoS parameter $E[X]$ mapped to QoE, $f(E[X]) \leq E[f(X)]$.

2.2.5.3 Markov's Inequality

Markov's inequality gives a relation between the probability that a non-negative random variable is larger than a certain value $a > 0$ and its mean value.

$$P(X \geq a) \leq \frac{E[X]}{a} \tag{2.41}$$

It is worth mentioning that there are no assumptions on the shape of the distribution function. However, for some values of a, the inequality provides meaningless results, e.g. for $a = E[X]$ we observe $P(X \geq E[X]) \leq 1$. In practice, Markov's inequality may be used to consider the probability that the random variable is larger than the c-fold of the mean value, $P(X \geq c \cdot E[X]) \leq 1/c$.

2.2.5.4 Chebyshev's Inequality

The relationship between the standard deviation and the distance to the mean is provided by Chebyshev's inequality. In particular, no more than a ratio of $1/c^2$ of the distribution's values can be more than c standard deviations away from the mean. The only assumptions required by this inequality are that the mean and the standard deviation are finite and $c > 0$. However, Chebyshev's inequality is only meaningful for $c > 1$.

$$P(|X - E[X]| \geq c \cdot \text{STD}[X]) \leq \frac{1}{c^2} \tag{2.42}$$

2.2.6 Functions of Two Random Variables

2.2.6.1 Two-dimensional Random Variables

Consider first the general case of multi-dimensional random variables and their associated distribution functions. If $A_1, A_2, \ldots, A_i$ are arbitrary, non-negative random variables, the joint event can be defined

$$\{A_1 \leq t_1, A_2 \leq t_2, \ldots, A_i \leq t_i\} \tag{2.43a}$$

with the joint cumulative distribution function

$$A(t_1, t_2, \ldots, t_i) = P(A_1 \leq t_1, A_2 \leq t_2, \ldots, A_i \leq t_i) . \tag{2.43b}$$

In later chapters the case of two-dimensional random variables (A_1, A_2) is often encountered. The definition of the *joint cumulative distribution function* is

$$A(t_1, t_2) = P(A_1 \leq t_1, A_2 \leq t_2) . \tag{2.43c}$$

For the limits $t_1 \to \infty$ or $t_2 \to \infty$ we obtain the *marginal cumulative distribution function* and the corresponding *marginal probability density function* as follows:

$$A_1(t_1) = \lim_{t_2 \to \infty} A(t_1, t_2) , \quad a_1(t_1) = \frac{d}{dt_1} A_1(t_1) , \tag{2.44a}$$

$$A_2(t_2) = \lim_{t_1 \to \infty} A(t_1, t_2) , \quad a_2(t_2) = \frac{d}{dt_2} A_2(t_2) . \tag{2.44b}$$

The probability of an event R defined as

$$R = \{t_{11} < A_1 \leq t_{12}, t_{21} < A_2 \leq t_{22}\} \tag{2.45a}$$

can be determined with the joint cumulative distribution function as:

$$P(R) = A(t_{12}, t_{22}) - A(t_{12}, t_{21}) - A(t_{11}, t_{22}) + A(t_{11}, t_{21}) . \tag{2.45b}$$

Analogous to one-dimensional random variables, the joint density function of two-dimensional random variables can be specified:

$$a(t_1, t_2) = \lim_{\Delta t_1 \to 0} \lim_{\Delta t_2 \to 0} \frac{P(t_1 < A_1 \leq t_1 + \Delta t_1, t_2 < A_2 \leq t_2 + \Delta t_2)}{\Delta t_1 \cdot \Delta t_2}$$

$$= \lim_{\Delta t_1 \to 0} \lim_{\Delta t_2 \to 0} \left(\frac{A(t_1 + \Delta t_1, t_2 + \Delta t_2) - A(t_1 + \Delta t_1, t_2)}{\Delta t_1 \cdot \Delta t_2} - \frac{A(t_1, t_2 + \Delta t_2) - A(t_1, t_2)}{\Delta t_1 \cdot \Delta t_2} \right)$$

$$= \frac{\partial^2 A(t_1, t_2)}{\partial t_1 \, \partial t_2} , \tag{2.46}$$

where the following properties are obvious:

$$\int_0^\infty \int_0^\infty a(\xi_1, \xi_2) \, d\xi_1 \, d\xi_2 = 1 , \tag{2.47a}$$

$$\int_0^{t_2} \left(\int_0^{t_1} a(\xi_1, \xi_2) \, d\xi_1 \right) d\xi_2 = A(t_1, t_2) , \tag{2.47b}$$

$$\int_{a_2}^{b_2} \left(\int_{a_1}^{b_1} a(\xi_1, \xi_2) \, d\xi_1 \right) d\xi_2 = P(a_1 < A_1 \leq b_1, a_2 < A_2 \leq b_2) . \tag{2.47c}$$

2.2.6.2 Moments and Correlation Coefficient

Analogous to the definition in Equation (2.28), the expected value for a two-dimensional random variable can be defined:

$$E[\, A_1^{k_1} A_2^{k_2} \,] = \int_0^\infty \int_0^\infty t_1^{k_1} t_2^{k_2} a(t_1, t_2) \, dt_1 \, dt_2 , \tag{2.48a}$$

$$\text{moment of } (k_1, \, k_2)\text{-th order}$$

$$\mu_{k_1 k_2} = E[\, (A_1 - m_1)^{k_1} (A_2 - m_2)^{k_2} \,] \tag{2.48b}$$

$$\text{central moment of } (k_1, \, k_2)\text{-th order}$$

and especially for $k_1 = k_2 = 1$:

$$\text{COV}[A_1, A_2] = \mu_{11} = E[\, (A_1 - m_1)(A_2 - m_2) \,] \tag{2.49}$$

$$= E[\, A_1 \cdot A_2 \,] - E[\, A_1 \,]E[\, A_2 \,] . \qquad \text{covariance}$$

The correlation coefficient r of two r.v. A_1 and A_2 is a measure how strong the statistical dependency between them looks like, and is given as:

$$r = \text{COR}[A_1, A_2] = \frac{\mu_{11}}{\sigma_{A_1}\sigma_{A_2}} = \frac{\text{E}[(A_1 - m_1)(A_2 - m_2)]}{\sqrt{\text{E}[(A_1 - m_1)^2]}\sqrt{\text{E}[(A_2 - m_2)^2]}}$$

$$= \frac{\text{E}[A_1 \cdot A_2] - \text{E}[A_1]\text{E}[A_2]}{\sqrt{\text{E}[(A_1 - m_1)^2]}\sqrt{\text{E}[(A_2 - m_2)^2]}} \ . \tag{2.50}$$

correlation coefficient

It is $-1 \leq r \leq 1$, while $|r| = 1$ implies a linear relationship between A_1 and A_2.

For two statistically independent r.v.s A_1, A_2 (cf. Equation (2.58a) in next section):

$$\text{E}[A_1 \cdot A_2] = \text{E}[A_1] \cdot \text{E}[A_2] \quad \text{and} \quad r = 0 \ . \tag{2.51}$$

According to Equations (2.49) and (2.50) the covariance and the correlation coefficient of two random variables vanish if these random variables are statistically independent of each other. This means that statistical independence includes the uncorrelated property. It should be noted that, conversely, the uncorrelated nature of two stochastic processes does not always result in statistical independence.

2.2.6.3 Sum of Two Continuous Random Variables

Given A is the sum of two non-negative random variables A_1 and A_2,

$$A = A_1 + A_2 \ , \qquad A_1, A_2 \geq 0 \ , \tag{2.52a}$$

with the joint density function $a(t_1, t_2)$ and the marginal density functions $a_1(t)$ and $a_2(t)$. The r.v. A_1 and A_2 themselves can be statistically dependent on each other. The cumulative distribution function

$$A(t) = P(A \leq t) = P(A_1 + A_2 \leq t) \tag{2.52b}$$

and its properties will be investigated in the sequence.

In the realization (ξ_1, ξ_2) of the tuple (A_1, A_2), the points for $A = A_1 + A_2$ lie on a straight line (see Figure 2.8). This figure shows also that the cumulative distribution function of A can be directly determined by the integral within the marked triangle:

$$A(t) = \int_{\xi_1 + \xi_2 \leq t} a(\xi_1, \xi_2) \, d\xi_1 \, d\xi_2 = \int_{\xi_1 = 0}^{t} \left(\int_{\xi_2 = 0}^{t - \xi_1} a(\xi_1, \xi_2) \, d\xi_2 \right) d\xi_1$$

$$= \int_{u=0}^{t} \int_{v=u}^{t} a(u, v - u) \, dv \, du \ . \tag{2.53}$$

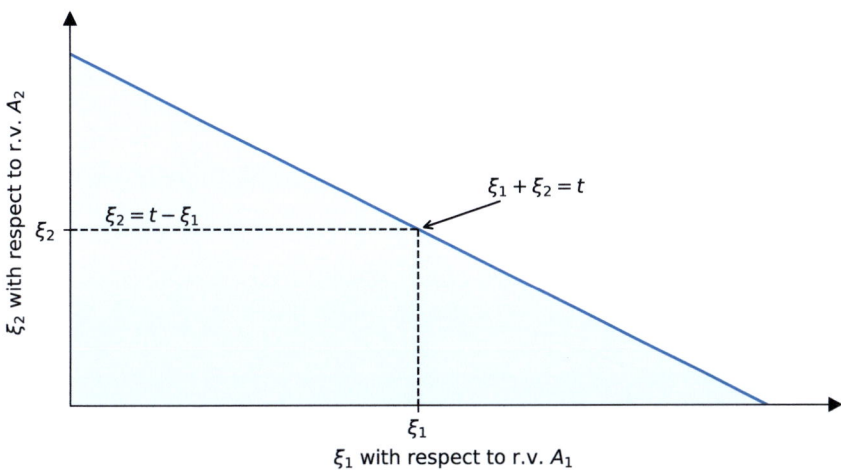

Figure 2.8: Computation of the sum of two random variables in Equation (2.53).

The first two moments and the variance of the sum A can be determined as:

$$E[A] = E[A_1 + A_2]$$

$$= \int_0^\infty \int_0^\infty (t_1 + t_2) a(t_1, t_2) \, dt_1 dt_2$$

$$= \int_0^\infty t_1 \left[\int_0^\infty a(t_1, t_2) \, dt_2 \right] dt_1 + \int_0^\infty t_2 \left[\int_0^\infty a(t_1, t_2) \, dt_1 \right] dt_2$$

$$= \underbrace{\int_0^\infty t_1 a_1(t_1) \, dt_1}_{E[A_1]} + \underbrace{\int_0^\infty t_2 a_2(t_2) \, dt_2}_{E[A_2]} = E[A_1] + E[A_2], \quad (2.54a)$$

$$E[A^2] = E[(A_1 + A_2)^2] = E[A_1^2 + 2A_1 A_2 + A_2^2]$$

$$= E[A_1^2] + 2E[A_1 A_2] + E[A_2^2], \quad (2.54b)$$

$$VAR[A] = E[A^2] - E[A]^2$$

$$= VAR[A_1] + VAR[A_2] + 2 \underbrace{(E[A_1 A_2] - E[A_1] \cdot E[A_2])}_{COV[A_1, A_2]}. \quad (2.54c)$$

Special Case: Statistically Independent R.V. A_1 and A_2 If the two random variables A_1 and A_2 are statistically independent of each other, their joint density function consists of the product of the marginal density functions:

$$a(t_1, t_2) = a_1(t_1) \cdot a_2(t_2). \quad (2.55)$$

The probability density function $a(t)$ is the convolution of the PDFs $a_1(t)$ and $a_2(t)$. This property can be derived from Equation (2.53) as follows. With

$$A(t) = \int_{u=0}^{t} \int_{v=u}^{t} a(u, v - u) \, dv \, du$$

$$= \int_{u=0}^{t} \int_{v=u}^{t} a_1(u)a_2(v - u) \, dv \, du = \int_{u=0}^{t} a_1(u)A_2(t - u) \, du \tag{2.56}$$

we obtain:

$$a(t) = \frac{dA(t)}{dt} = \int_{u=0}^{t} a_1(u)a_2(t - u) \, du$$

$$\overset{\text{def}}{=} a_1(t) * a_2(t) \overset{\text{def}}{=} (a_1 * a_2)(t) \,, \qquad \textbf{convolution} \tag{2.57}$$

where the symbol "$*$" represents the notation for the (continuous) convolution operation. Both notations $a_1(t) * a_2(t)$ and $(a_1 * a_2)(t)$ are common in literature. Note that the convolution is an operation between two functions a_1 and a_2, not between the two numbers $a_1(t)$ and $a_2(t)$ – which is expressed by $(a_1 * a_2)(t)$. Due to the statistical independence of A_1 and A_2:

$$E[A_1 \cdot A_2] = \int_0^\infty \int_0^\infty t_1 t_2 a(t_1, t_2) \, dt_1 \, dt_2 = \int_0^\infty \int_0^\infty t_1 t_2 a_1(t_1)a_2(t_2) \, dt_1 \, dt_2$$

$$= \int_0^\infty t_1 a_1(t_1) \int_0^\infty t_2 a_2(t_2) \, dt_2 \, dt_1$$

$$= E[A_1] \cdot E[A_2] \,. \tag{2.58a}$$

The variance of the sum follows from Equation (2.54c):

$$\text{VAR}[A] = \text{VAR}[A_1 + A_2] = \text{VAR}[A_1] + \text{VAR}[A_2] \,. \tag{2.58b}$$

In general, the sum A is obtained for several statistically independent r.v.s

$$A = \sum_{i=1}^{k} A_i$$

with the mean and the variance

$$E[A] = \sum_{i=1}^{k} E[A_i] \,, \tag{2.59a}$$

$$\text{VAR}[A] = \sum_{i=1}^{k} \text{VAR}[A_i] \,. \tag{2.59b}$$

Note that Equation (2.59a) also applies to arbitrary, not necessary independent random variables.

2.2.6.4 Sum of Discrete Random Variables

Let X be the sum of two *non-negative* discrete random variables X_1 and X_2 with the distributions $x_1(i)$ and $x_2(i)$:

$$X = X_1 + X_2 \, .$$

Furthermore, the r.v.s X_1 and X_2 are statistically independent of each other. We apply the law of total probability to determine the distribution of X:

$$
\begin{aligned}
x(i) = P(X = i) &= P(X_1 + X_2 = i) \\
&= \sum_{j=0}^{i} P(X_1 = i - j | X_2 = j) P(X_2 = j) \\
&= \sum_{j=0}^{i} x_1(i - j) \cdot x_2(j) \\
&\overset{\text{def}}{=} x_1(i) * x_2(i) \overset{\text{def}}{=} (x_1 * x_2)(i) \, .
\end{aligned}
\qquad \textbf{discrete convolution} \quad (2.60)
$$

The distribution of the sum is accordingly the discrete convolution (with the symbol "$*$") of the distributions of X_1 and X_2.

2.2.6.5 Difference of Discrete Random Variables

The difference X of two *non-negative* discrete random variables X_1 and X_2 with the respective distributions $x_1(i)$ and $x_2(i)$ (i.e., $x_1(i) = 0$ and $x_2(i) = 0$ for negative values of i):

$$X = X_1 - X_2 \, .$$

The r.v.s X_1 and X_2 are statistically independent. The distribution of the difference X can be determined as follows:

$$
\begin{aligned}
x(i) = P(X = i) &= P(X_1 - X_2 = i) \\
&= \sum_{j=0}^{+\infty} P(X_1 = i + j | X_2 = j) \cdot P(X_2 = j) \\
&= \sum_{j=0}^{+\infty} x_1(i + j) x_2(j) \\
&\overset{\text{def}}{=} x_1(i) * x_2(-i) \overset{\text{def}}{=} (x_1 * -x_2)(i) \, ,
\end{aligned}
\qquad (2.61)
$$

where $x(i)$ can exist for negative values of i. In this book, the notation $x_1(i) * x_2(-i)$ is used, which is common in engineering.

2.2.6.6 Maximum of Random Variables

Let A be the maximum of two statistically independent random variables:

$$A = \max(A_1, A_2) ,$$

we obtain

$$\{A \le t\} \ \text{ for } \ \{A_1 \le t \ \text{ and } \ A_2 \le t\}$$

or

$$P(A \le t) = P(A_1 \le t) \cdot P(A_2 \le t) ,$$

i.e.

$$A(t) = A_1(t) \cdot A_2(t) \tag{2.62a}$$

$$a(t) = \frac{d}{dt} A(t) = a_1(t) A_2(t) + a_2(t) A_1(t) . \tag{2.62b}$$

In general, the following relationship can be obtained for the maximum of multiple statistically independent random variables $\{A_i\}$ with the respective cumulative distribution functions $\{A_i(t)\}$:

$$A = \max(A_1, A_2, \ldots, A_k) , \tag{2.63a}$$

$$A(t) = \prod_{i=1}^{k} A_i(t) . \tag{2.63b}$$

2.2.6.7 Minimum of Random Variables

We consider the minimum of two statistically independent random variables:

$$A = \min(A_1, A_2) .$$

The minimum can also be formulated as:

$$\{A > t\} \ \text{ for } \ \{A_1 > t \ \text{ and } \ A_2 > t\}$$

or

$$P(A > t) = P(A_1 > t) \cdot P(A_2 > t) ,$$

i.e.,

$$(1 - A(t)) = (1 - A_1(t)) \cdot (1 - A_2(t))$$

or

$$A(t) = A_1(t) + A_2(t) - A_1(t) \cdot A_2(t) , \qquad (2.64a)$$

$$a(t) = \frac{d}{dt}A(t) = a_1(t)(1 - A_2(t)) + a_2(t)(1 - A_1(t)) . \qquad (2.64b)$$

In general, the same applies to the minimum of multiple statistically independent random variables $\{A_i\}$ with the cumulative distribution functions $\{A_i(t)\}$:

$$A = \min(A_1, A_2, \ldots, A_k) , \qquad (2.65a)$$

$$A(t) = 1 - \prod_{i=1}^{k}(1 - A_i(t)) . \qquad (2.65b)$$

2.3 Transform Methods

Transform methods are often employed in analytical treatment of performance models and are briefly discussed in this chapter. The definition equations formulated below normally apply to general random variables. However, unless otherwise noted, they are given for non-negative random variables.

We use the following notation:

Time Domain	**Transform Domain**
Function ∘——●	Transform (or transformed function)

2.3.1 Generating Function

2.3.1.1 Definition

Given a discrete random variable X with the distribution

$$x(i) = P(X = i) , \quad i = 0, 1, \ldots .$$

The *probability generating function* (or, for short, generating function GF) for the random variable X is defined as

$$X_{GF}(z) = GF\{x(i)\} = \sum_{i=0}^{\infty} x(i)z^i = E[z^X] , \qquad \text{generating function} \quad (2.66)$$

where z is a complex(-valued) Variable. Since the sum $\sum_{i=0}^{\infty} x(i) = 1$ is bounded, $X_{GF}(z)$ converges within and on the unit circle ($|z| \leq 1$). The generating function contains a complete characterization of the distribution $x(i)$.

2 Fundamentals and Prerequisites

2.3.1.2 Properties of the Generating Function

Moments   The moments of the random variable X can directly be determined in transform domain:

$$X_{GF}(1) = \sum_{i=0}^{\infty} x(i) = 1 \tag{2.67a}$$

$$X'_{GF}(1) = \left.\frac{dX_{GF}(z)}{dz}\right|_{z=1} = \left.\sum_{i=0}^{\infty} x(i)\, i\, z^{i-1}\right|_{z=1} = \mathrm{E}[\,X\,] \tag{2.67b}$$

$$X''_{GF}(1) = \left.\frac{d^2 X_{GF}(z)}{dz^2}\right|_{z=1} = \mathrm{E}[\,X^2\,] - \mathrm{E}[\,X\,] \tag{2.67c}$$

$$\mathrm{VAR}[\,X\,] = \mathrm{E}[\,X^2\,] - \mathrm{E}[\,X\,]^2 = X''_{GF}(1) + X'_{GF}(1) - X'_{GF}(1)^2 \tag{2.67d}$$

Inverse Transform of GF   As the name "probability generating function" already suggests, the distribution $x(i)$ can be obtained from the generating function.

$$x(i) = GF^{-1}\{X_{GF}(z)\} = \left.\frac{1}{i!}\, \frac{d^i X_{GF}(z)}{dz^i}\right|_{z=0} \tag{2.68}$$

According to Equation (2.68) the distribution $x(i)$ can in principle be derived from the *(probability)* generating function. The inverse transformation can numerically be carried out more efficiently with the Discrete Fourier Transform (DFT) or the Fast Fourier Transform (FFT), see e.g. Cavers [18], Cooley and Tukey [22], Henrici [48].

Convolution Theorem for Discrete Random Variables   Let X be the sum of two statistically independent discrete random variables X_1 and X_2 with corresponding distributions $x_1(i)$ and $x_2(i)$. The sum

$$X = X_1 + X_2$$

has the distribution (derivation in Chapter 2.2.6)

$$x(i) = x_1(i) * x_2(i)$$

$$= \sum_{j=-\infty}^{\infty} x_1(j)\, x_2(i-j) = \sum_{j=-\infty}^{\infty} x_1(i-j)\, x_2(j). \qquad \text{convolution} \tag{2.69a}$$

The symbol "$*$" stands here for the discrete convolution operation. The transform using the generating function turns the convolution of the distributions into a multiplication of the transforms.

$$x(i) \quad = \quad x_1(i) \quad * \quad x_2(i)$$

$$\Big\downarrow \text{GF} \qquad \Big\downarrow \text{GF} \qquad \Big\downarrow \text{GF} \qquad \qquad \textbf{discrete convolution} \qquad \text{(2.69b)}$$
$$\textbf{theorem}$$

$$X_{GF}(z) \quad = \quad X_{1,GF}(z) \quad \cdot \quad X_{2,GF}(z)$$

2.3.1.3 Z-Transform

A closely related form to the generating function (GF) is the Z-transform (ZT), which is widely used in discrete-time signal processing. The Z-transform of the distribution $x(i)$ of a non-negative discrete random variable X is defined as

$$X_{ZT}(z) = ZT\{x(i)\} = \sum_{i=0}^{\infty} x(i) z^{-i} = \mathrm{E}[z^{-X}]\,. \qquad \textbf{Z-transform} \quad \text{(2.70)}$$

Here, the difference to the definition of the generating function in Equation (2.66) is just the use of z^{-1} instead of z. The corresponding properties can be derived in the same way as for the generating function (cf. Oppenheim and Schafer [82]).

2.3.2 Laplace and Laplace-Stieltjes Transforms

2.3.2.1 Definition

The Laplace transform (LT) or respectively the Laplace-Stieltjes transform (LST) play a central role in analysis methods of continuous-time system theory.

Let $A(t)$ be the cumulative distribution function and $a(t)$ the density function of a non-negative continuous random variable A. The Laplace-Stieltjes transform of $A(t)$ and the Laplace transform of $a(t)$ are defined as follows:

$$\Phi_A(s) = \text{LST}\{A(t)\} = \int_0^{\infty} e^{-st}\, dA(t) \qquad \qquad \text{(2.71a)}$$

$$= \text{LT}\{a(t)\} = \int_0^{\infty} e^{-st} a(t)\, dt \qquad \qquad \text{(2.71b)}$$

$$= \mathrm{E}[e^{-sA}]\,, \quad Re(s) \geq 0\,, \qquad \textbf{Laplace transform} \quad \text{(2.71c)}$$

for a complex variable s with non-negative real part $Re(s) \geq 0$. The integral in Equation (2.71a) is formulated in Lebesgue-Stieltjes sense. The relationship between LT and LST is illustrated in Figure 2.9.

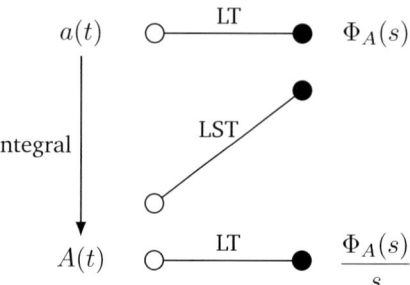

Figure 2.9: Laplace and Laplace-Stieltjes transforms.

A detailed discussion of the Laplace transform can e.g. be found in Doetsch [28] or Spiegel [98].

2.3.2.2 Properties of Laplace Transform

In the following, important properties of the Laplace transform are listed which contribute to the understanding of later chapters. We use hereby the notation $\Phi_A(s) = LT\{a(t)\}$.

Computation of Moments using Laplace Transform

$$E[A^k] = \int_0^\infty t^k a(t)\, dt = (-1)^k \left. \frac{d^k \Phi_A(s)}{ds^k} \right|_{s=0} \qquad (2.72)$$

Laplace Transforms of Integral and Derivative

$$A(t) \quad \overset{LT}{\circ\!\!-\!\!\bullet} \quad \frac{1}{s}\Phi_A(s) \qquad (2.73a)$$

$$\frac{d}{dt}a(t) \quad \overset{LT}{\circ\!\!-\!\!\bullet} \quad s\Phi_A(s) - a(0) \qquad (2.73b)$$

Laplace Transform Limit Theorems

$$\lim_{t\to 0} a(t) = \lim_{s\to\infty} s\cdot\Phi_A(s) \qquad (2.74a)$$

$$\lim_{t\to\infty} a(t) = \lim_{s\to 0} s\cdot\Phi_A(s) \qquad (2.74b)$$

Laplace Transform and Convolution Operation Given are two *non-negative*, statistically independent random variables A_1 and A_2 with the probability density functions $a_1(t)$ and $a_2(t)$, and the Laplace transforms $\Phi_{A_1}(s)$ and $\Phi_{A_2}(s)$. The sum

$$A = A_1 + A_2$$

has the probability density function

$$a(t) = a_1(t) * a_2(t) = \int_{\tau=0}^{t} a_1(\tau) \cdot a_2(t - \tau)\, d\tau\,, \tag{2.75a}$$

where the symbol "$*$" represents the continuous convolution operation. Thus, the Laplace transform converts the convolution operation into a multiplication:

$$
\begin{array}{ccccc}
a(t) & = & a_1(t) & * & a_2(t) \\
\Big\updownarrow \text{LT} & & \Big\updownarrow \text{LT} & & \Big\updownarrow \text{LT} \\
\Phi_A(s) & = & \Phi_{A_1}(s) & \cdot & \Phi_{A_2}(s)\,.
\end{array}
\qquad
\begin{array}{l}
\text{continuous convolution} \\
\text{theorem}
\end{array}
\tag{2.75b}
$$

2.4 Some Important Distributions

2.4.1 Discrete Distributions

Commonly used discrete distributions and their transforms are introduced.

2.4.1.1 Bernoulli Experiment and Distribution (BER)

Given a so-called Bernoulli experiment X with two possible outcomes: *"success"* with the probability p, and *"failure"* with the complementary probability $q = (1 - p)$. The random variable X follows a Bernoulli distribution with success probability p:

$$X \sim \mathrm{BER}(p) \quad \text{with}\ \ 0 \le p \le 1 \qquad\qquad \text{Bernoulli distribution}$$

$$x(i) = P(X = i) = \begin{cases} 1 - p & ,\ i = 0 \quad \text{(failure)} \\ p & ,\ i = 1 \quad \text{(success)} \end{cases} \tag{2.76a}$$

$$\mathrm{E}[\,X\,] = p\,, \qquad c_X = \sqrt{\frac{1-p}{p}} \tag{2.76b}$$

$$X_{GF}(z) = (1 - p) + pz\,. \tag{2.76c}$$

2.4.1.2 Binomial Distribution (BINOM)

Carrying out a number N of statistically independent Bernoulli experiments with success probability p, while letting X be the random variable for the number of successes in this series of experiments we achieve the following results. If we look at the case $X = i$, there are in total $\binom{N}{i}$ patterns of i successes and each pattern occurs with probability $p^i (1-p)^{N-i}$. The random variable X follows a Binomial distribution with N experiments and success probability p:

$$X \sim \text{BINOM}(N,p) \quad \text{with} \ \ 0 \le p \le 1 \ , \ N \in \mathbb{N}^+ \qquad \text{binomial distribution}$$

$$x(i) = \binom{N}{i} p^i \, (1-p)^{N-i} \ , \quad i = 0,1,\ldots,N \tag{2.77a}$$

$$\text{E}[\,X\,] = Np \, , \qquad c_X = \sqrt{\frac{1-p}{Np}} \tag{2.77b}$$

$$X_{GF}(z) = \Big((1-p) + pz \Big)^N \tag{2.77c}$$

The term $\binom{a}{k}$ denotes a binomial coefficient. From Equation (2.77c) it can be seen that the binomial distribution represents the N-fold convolution of the Bernoulli distribution with itself. Figure 2.10 shows the typical course of the binomial distribution for different means $\text{E}[\,X\,]$. To show how the probabilities belong together, the discrete values of the probability mass function are interconnected.

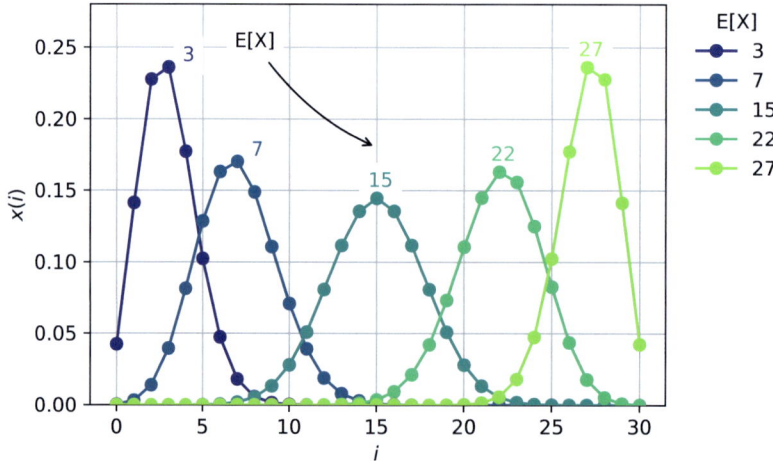

Figure 2.10: Binomial distribution $X \sim \text{BINOM}(N,p)$ with parameters $N = 30$ and $p = \text{E}[\,X\,]/N$.

2.4.1.3 Geometric Distribution (GEOM)

We perform a series of Bernoulli experiments until we get the first "success"-outcome. The Random variable X stands for the number of failures before the first success. For a realization of $X = i$, the probability for i unsuccessful experiments is $(1 - p)^i$ and for the successful experiment p which ends the test series. The random variable X follows a geometric distribution with success probability p:

$$X \sim \text{GEOM}(p) \quad \text{with} \quad 0 \le p \le 1 \qquad \text{geometric distribution}$$

$$x(i) = (1 - p)^i \cdot p \,, \quad i = 0, 1, \ldots \qquad (2.78a)$$

$$\text{E}[X] = \frac{1 - p}{p} \,, \quad c_X = \frac{1}{\sqrt{1 - p}} \qquad (2.78b)$$

$$X_{GF}(z) = \frac{p}{1 - z + pz} \qquad (2.78c)$$

In Figure 2.11 the characteristics of the geometric distribution for different mean values $\text{E}[X]$ are shown, whereby the discrete values belonging to the same distribution are interconnected. The linear decrease, typical for geometric distributions, is visible in Figure 2.11b, where the y-axis is logarithmically scaled. This property is also referred to as the *geometric tail*, and also for other distributions, if a straight characteristic of the tail distribution can be observed on a semi-logarithmic scale.

Shifted Geometric Distribution (GEOM$_m$) A common generalization of the geometric distribution is the shifted geometric distribution. The distribution arises when the geometric distribution is shifted by m positions:

$$X \sim \text{GEOM}_m(p) \quad \text{with} \quad 0 \le p \le 1 \,, \, m \in \mathbb{N}_0 \qquad \text{shifted geometric distribution}$$

$$x(i) = (1 - p)^{i-m} \cdot p \,, \quad i = m, m+1, \ldots \qquad (2.79a)$$

$$\text{E}[X] = \frac{1 - p}{p} + m \,, \quad c_X = \frac{\sqrt{1 - p}}{1 - p + m \cdot p} \qquad (2.79b)$$

$$X_{GF}(z) = \frac{pz^m}{1 - z + pz} \qquad (2.79c)$$

For $m = 0$, we simply write GEOM instead of GEOM$_0$, which is the regular unshifted geometric distribution. If $X = X_0 + m$ with $X_0 \sim \text{GEOM}_0(p)$, then $Y \sim \text{GEOM}_m(p)$.

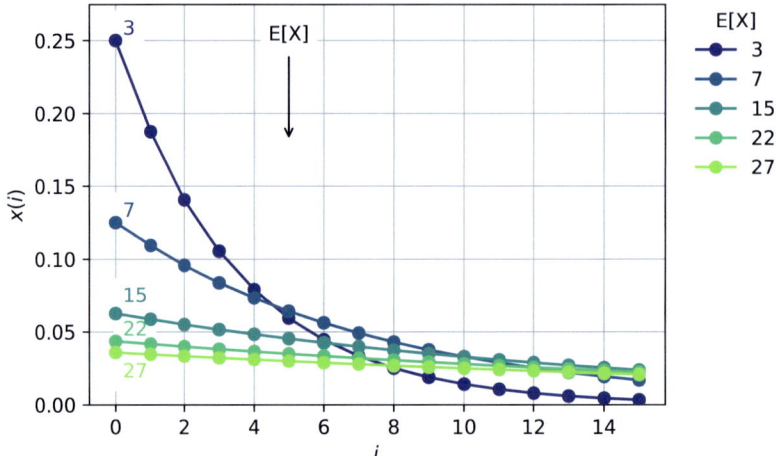

(a) Linear scale of x-axis and y-axis.

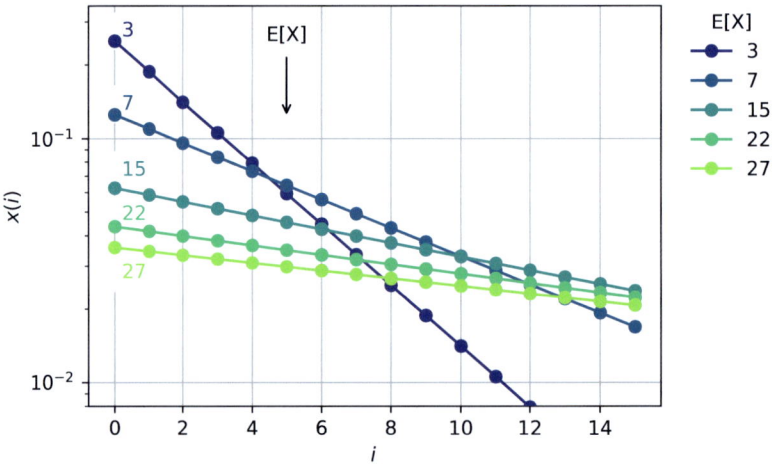

(b) Logarithmic scale of y-axis and linear scale of x-axis.

Figure 2.11: Geometric distribution $X \sim \mathrm{GEOM}(p)$ with $p = \dfrac{1}{\mathrm{E}[X]+1}$.

2.4.1.4 Negative Binomial Distribution (NEGBIN)

The negative binomial distribution X models the number of failures in a sequence of independent and identically distributed Bernoulli trials with success probability p, before a specified (real valued) number of successes y occurs. A discrete random variable X follows a negative binomial distribution with parameters y and p:

$$X \sim \text{NEGBIN}(y, p) \quad \text{with} \quad 0 \leq p \leq 1 \,, \ y > 0 \qquad \text{negative binomial distribution}$$

$$x(i) = \binom{y + i - 1}{i} p^y (1 - p)^i \,, \quad i = 0, 1, \ldots \tag{2.80a}$$

$$\mathrm{E}[\,X\,] = \frac{y(1 - p)}{p} \,, \qquad c_X = \frac{1}{\sqrt{y(1 - p)}} \tag{2.80b}$$

$$X_{GF}(z) = \left(\frac{p}{1 - z + pz} \right)^y \tag{2.80c}$$

Equation (2.80c) implies that the negative binomial distribution results from a (not necessarily integer valued) y-fold convolution of the geometric distribution with itself. The parameters y and p of the negative binomial distribution can be determined from a given mean value $\mathrm{E}[\,X\,]$ and a coefficient of variation c_X as follows:

$$p = \frac{1}{\mathrm{E}[\,X\,] \cdot c_X^2} \,, \qquad y = \frac{\mathrm{E}[\,X\,]}{\mathrm{E}[\,X\,] \cdot c_X^2 - 1} \,, \tag{2.81}$$

where the condition $\mathrm{E}[\,X\,] \cdot c_X^2 > 1$ holds.

This implies that by means of negative binomial distributions, two-parametric distributions with any given mean value $\mathrm{E}[\,X\,]$ and coefficient of variation c_X according to Equation (2.81) and the condition $\mathrm{E}[\,X\,] \cdot c_X^2 > 1$ can be generated. This property is very beneficial when a systematic parameter study is to be carried out. Figure 2.12 visualizes the possible parameter combinations $(\mathrm{E}[\,X\,], c_X)$ in the marked area.

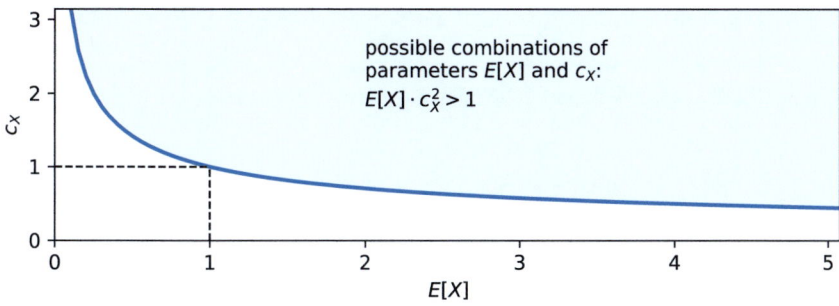

Figure 2.12: Possible parameter combinations for a negative binomial distribution X such that the condition $\mathrm{E}[\,X\,] \cdot c_X^2 > 1$ holds.

2.4.1.5 Poisson Distribution (POIS)

The Poisson distribution plays an important role in queueing theory. The distribution provides the probability of a given number $X = i$ of events occurring in a fixed interval of time Δt if these events randomly occur with a mean rate λ. In particular, we may consider arrivals to a queueing system with arrival rate λ. The mean number of arrivals within the interval is $y = \lambda \cdot \Delta t$. The random variable X models the number of arrivals within the interval.

The Poisson distribution is defined as follows with a parameter $y > 0$:

$$X \sim \text{POIS}(y) \ \text{ with } \ y > 0 \qquad\qquad \text{Poisson distribution}$$

$$x(i) = \frac{y^i}{i!}\, e^{-y}\,, \quad i = 0, 1, \dots \tag{2.82a}$$

$$\text{E}[\,X\,] = y\,, \qquad c_X = \frac{1}{\sqrt{y}} \tag{2.82b}$$

$$X_{GF}(z) = e^{-y(1 - z)} \tag{2.82c}$$

Figure 2.13 illustrates the Poisson distribution for different mean values $\text{E}[\,X\,]$. The discrete values of the same distribution are interconnected by a line.

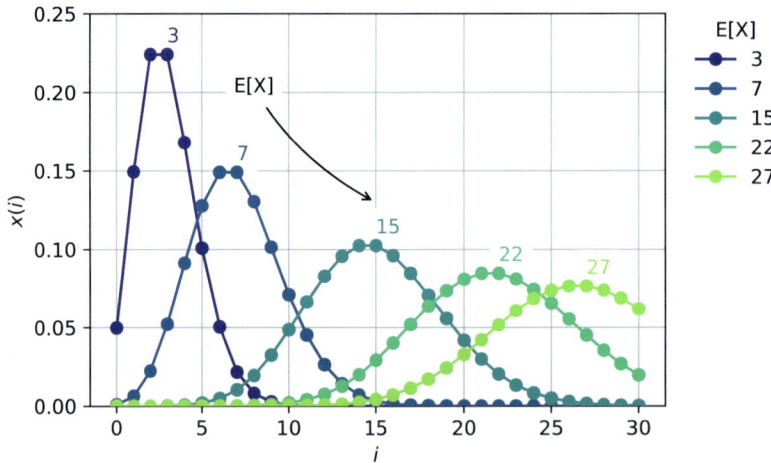

Figure 2.13: Poisson distribution $X \sim \text{POIS}(y)$ with parameter $y = \text{E}[\,X\,]$.

2.4.2 Continuous Distributions

This section introduces commonly used continuous distributions. The associated random variables are represented with symbolic phase representations, if appropriate.

2.4.2.1 Deterministic Distribution (D)

In principle, a deterministic variable is not a random variable. For systematic reasons, e.g. to have a distribution function with coefficient of variation *zero*, the deterministic distribution is introduced.

The r.v. A takes a constant value t_0, whereby the randomness does not apply. The cumulative distribution function is a shifted step function.

$A \sim D(t_0)$ with $t_0 \in \mathbb{R}$ deterministic distribution

$$A(t) = \begin{cases} 0, & t < t_0 \\ 1, & t \geq t_0 \end{cases} \tag{2.83a}$$

$$a(t) = \delta(t - t_0) \tag{2.83b}$$

$$\mathrm{E}[A] = t_0, \qquad c_A = 0 \tag{2.83c}$$

$$\Phi_A(s) = \mathrm{LST}\{A(t)\} = e^{-st_0} \tag{2.83d}$$

The correspondent phase representation is indicated in Figure 2.16a.

2.4.2.2 Negative Exponential Distribution (EXP)

Due to its memoryless property (or Markov property) the negative exponential distribution or, in short, exponential distribution plays a central role in performance modeling and analysis (see elementary processes in Chapter 3.1.3 and in particular the Poisson process in Chapter 3.3).

$A \sim \mathrm{EXP}(\lambda)$ with $\lambda > 0$ exponential distribution

$$A(t) = 1 - e^{-\lambda t}, \quad t \geq 0 \tag{2.84a}$$

$$a(t) = \lambda e^{-\lambda t} \tag{2.84b}$$

$$\mathrm{E}[A] = \frac{1}{\lambda}, \qquad c_A = 1 \tag{2.84c}$$

$$\Phi_A(s) = \frac{\lambda}{\lambda + s} \tag{2.84d}$$

The abbreviation "M" (Markov) is used in Kendall's notation and in the phase representation (Figure 2.16b) for the negative exponential distribution.

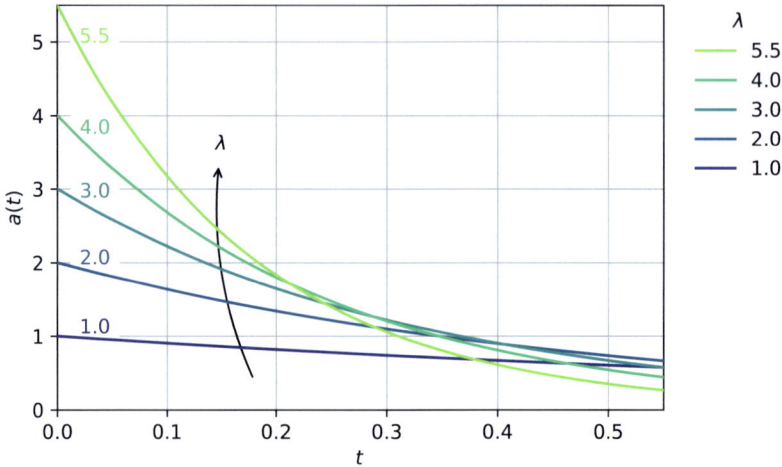

(a) Probability density function (PDF).

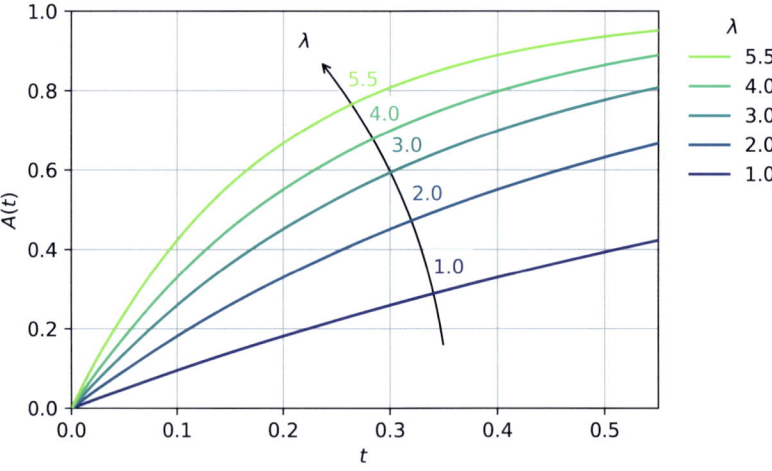

(b) Cumulative distribution function (CDF).

Figure 2.14: Negative exponential distribution $A \sim \mathrm{EXP}(\lambda)$ with mean $\mathrm{E}[A] = \frac{1}{\lambda}$.

Figure 2.14 visualizes the probability density function $a(t)$ and the cumulative distribution function $A(t)$ for different parameters λ in the range $[1.0, 5.5]$. Please note that we will often consider Poisson arrival processes where the interarrival times A follow an exponential distribution with parameter λ, see Chapter 3.3. The values of the r.v. A are then provided in an appropriate time unit, e.g. t in seconds $[\mathrm{s}]$. The unit of λ is then s^{-1}, corresponding to the mean arrival rate. It is $\lambda = 1/\mathrm{E}[A]$.

Remark: Relation between exponential and geometric distribution   Considering the exponential distribution $A \sim \text{EXP}(\lambda)$ with parameter λ. The continuous random variable A is now discretized with a constant Δt which leads to a discrete random variable X denoted by

$$X = \left[\frac{A}{\Delta t} \right]$$

with the probability mass function

$$\begin{aligned}
x(i) &= A\big((i+1)\Delta t\big) - A\big(i\Delta t\big) \\
&= e^{-\lambda i \Delta t} - e^{-\lambda(i+1)\Delta t} = e^{-\lambda i \Delta t}\big(1 - e^{-\lambda \Delta t}\big) \\
&= (1-p)^i \cdot p \quad \text{with } p = 1 - e^{-\lambda \Delta t}, \quad i = 0, 1, \dots .
\end{aligned}$$

Thus, X follows a geometric distribution with parameter p: $X \sim \text{GEOM}(1 - e^{-\lambda \Delta t})$.

2.4.2.3 Erlang-k Distribution (E_k)

Let A be the sum of k exponentially distributed phases, each with parameter λ:

$$\begin{aligned}
A &= A_1 + A_2 + \dots + A_k , \\
A_i(t) &= 1 - e^{-\lambda t}, \quad i = 1, 2, \dots, k .
\end{aligned}$$

The r.v. A follows an Erlang-k distribution (or Erlang-distribution of k-th order).

$$A \sim \text{E}_k(\lambda) \text{ with } \lambda > 0, \ k \in \mathbb{N}^+ \qquad\qquad \text{Erlang-}k \text{ distribution}$$

$$A(t) = 1 - \sum_{i=0}^{k-1} \frac{(\lambda t)^i}{i!} e^{-\lambda t}, \quad t \geq 0 \tag{2.85a}$$

$$a(t) = \frac{\lambda(\lambda t)^{k-1}}{(k-1)!} e^{-\lambda t} \tag{2.85b}$$

$$\text{E}[A] = \frac{k}{\lambda}, \qquad c_A = \frac{1}{\sqrt{k}} \tag{2.85c}$$

$$\Phi_A(s) = \left(\frac{\lambda}{\lambda + s} \right)^k \tag{2.85d}$$

According to the construction of A as the summation of k exponentially distributed phases (cf. Figure 2.16c) and as shown in Equation (2.85d) it can be seen that the Erlang-k distribution is the k-fold convolution of the negative exponential distribution (Equation (2.84d)) with itself. For the limit $k \to \infty$, $\lambda \to \infty$ ($\frac{k}{\lambda}$ remains constant) the Erlang-k distribution function approaches the deterministic distribution.

2.4.2.4 Hyperexponential Distribution (H$_k$)

A hyperexponentially distributed random variable A results from a selection between k different exponentially distributed phases A_i with parameters λ_i , $i = 1, 2, \ldots, k$, where the respective phase A_i is chosen with probability p_i (cf. Figure 2.16d).

$$A = A_i \quad \text{with probability } p_i , \quad i = 1, 2, \ldots, k ,$$

$$A_i \sim \text{EXP}(\lambda_i) , \quad A_i(t) = 1 - e^{-\lambda_i t} .$$

We obtain with $\boldsymbol{\Lambda} = (\lambda_1, \ldots, \lambda_k)$ and $\mathbf{p} = (p_1, \ldots, p_k)$

$$A \sim \text{H}_k(\boldsymbol{\Lambda}, \mathbf{p}) , \quad \sum_{i=1}^{k} p_i = 1 \qquad\qquad \text{hyperexponential distribution}$$

$$A(t) = \sum_{i=1}^{k} p_i (1 - e^{-\lambda_i t}) = 1 - \sum_{i=1}^{k} p_i e^{-\lambda_i t} , \quad t \geq 0 , \tag{2.86a}$$

$$a(t) = \sum_{i=1}^{k} p_i \lambda_i e^{-\lambda_i t} , \tag{2.86b}$$

$$\text{E}[A] = \sum_{i=1}^{k} \frac{p_i}{\lambda_i} , \quad c_A = \sqrt{ 2 \left(\sum_{i=1}^{k} \frac{p_i}{\lambda_i^2} \right) \Big/ \left(\sum_{i=1}^{k} \frac{p_i}{\lambda_i} \right)^2 - 1 } , \tag{2.86c}$$

$$\Phi_A(s) = \sum_{i=1}^{k} p_i \frac{\lambda_i}{\lambda_i + s} . \tag{2.86d}$$

Special Case: Hyperexponential Distribution of Second Order (H$_2$) The H$_2$-distribution (or hyperexponential distribution of second order) is used quite often to represent two-parametric distributions in system modeling. Originally, it has four parameters $(p_1, p_2, \lambda_1, \lambda_2)$. Since $p_1 + p_2 = 1$ and another parameter is eliminated by an arbitrarily chosen symmetry assumption ($\frac{p_1}{\lambda_1} = \frac{p_2}{\lambda_2}$), two parameters remain:

$$A(t) = 1 - p_1 e^{-\lambda_1 t} - p_2 e^{-\lambda_2 t} , \tag{2.87a}$$

$$p_1 + p_2 = 1 , \tag{2.87b}$$

$$\frac{p_1}{\lambda_1} = \frac{p_2}{\lambda_2} . \qquad\qquad \text{symmetry assumption} \tag{2.87c}$$

2.4.2.5 Uniform Distribution (U)

A continuous random variable A is said to follow a uniform distribution on the interval $[a, b]$ if:

$$A \sim U(a, b) \quad \text{with } a < b \qquad\qquad \text{uniform distribution}$$

$$A(t) = \begin{cases} \frac{t-a}{b-a} , & a \leq t \leq b \\ 1 , & t > b \end{cases} \tag{2.88a}$$

$$a(t) = \frac{1}{b-a} , \quad a \leq t \leq b \tag{2.88b}$$

$$\mathrm{E}[A] = \frac{a+b}{2} , \qquad c_A = \frac{1}{\sqrt{3}} \cdot \frac{b-a}{a+b} \tag{2.88c}$$

$$\Phi_A(s) = \frac{e^{-sa} - e^{-sb}}{s(b-a)} \tag{2.88d}$$

The density has a rectangular characteristic and is constant in the interval $[a, b]$.

2.4.2.6 Mixture Distribution (MIX)

Consider a set of independent random variables $A_1, \ldots, A_k$. A random variable A is now constructed in such a way that with the probability p_i the random variable A_i is selected.

$$A = \begin{cases} A_1 \text{ with } p_1 \\ \quad \ldots \\ A_k \text{ with } p_k \end{cases}$$

The resulting random variable A has a so-called *mixture distribution* with the following formal definition:

A mixture distribution A is derived from a collection of k other independent random variables $A_1, \ldots, A_k$. With probability p_i, the random variable A_i is chosen, for $i = 1, \ldots, k$. Then, the value of the selected random variable A_i is realized. Thus, the random variable A follows A_i with probability p_i. We obtain the following relations.

$$A \sim \text{MIX}\big((A_1, \ldots, A_k), (p_1, \ldots, p_k)\big) \qquad \text{mixture distribution}$$

$$a(t) = \sum_{i=1}^{k} p_i \cdot a_i(t) \,, \qquad A(t) = \sum_{i=1}^{k} p_i \cdot A_i(t) \tag{2.89a}$$

$$\text{E}[\,A\,] = \sum_{i=1}^{k} p_i \cdot \text{E}[\,A_i\,] \,, \qquad \text{E}[\,A^n\,] = \sum_{i=1}^{k} p_i \cdot \text{E}[\,A_i^n\,] \tag{2.89b}$$

$$\Phi_A(s) = \int_0^\infty e^{-st} a(t)\, dt = \int_0^\infty e^{-st} \sum_{i=1}^{k} p_i \cdot a_i(t)\, dt = \sum_{i=1}^{k} p_i \cdot \Phi_{A_i}(s) \tag{2.89c}$$

It should be noted that the hyperexponential distribution is a special mixture distribution, where each of the r.v. $A_1, \ldots, A_k$ is exponentially distributed.

Figure 2.15 illustrates an example of a mixture distribution A. With probability $p = 1/2$, the distribution A follows an exponential distribution $X \sim \text{EXP}(\lambda)$ with $\lambda = 1$. With probability $p = 1/2$, the distribution A follows a deterministic distribution $Y \sim \text{D}(t_0)$ with $t_0 = 1$. Please note that the sum $Z_0 = X + Y$ follows a shifted exponential distribution with PDF $z_0(t) = e^{-(t-0.5)}$ for $t \geq t_0$ and $z_0(t) = 0$ for any other t. Hence, the weighted sum of distributions ($Z = \frac{1}{2}X + \frac{1}{2}Y$) differs from the mixture distribution $A = \text{MIX}((X, Y), (\frac{1}{2}, \frac{1}{2}))$, see Figure 2.15.

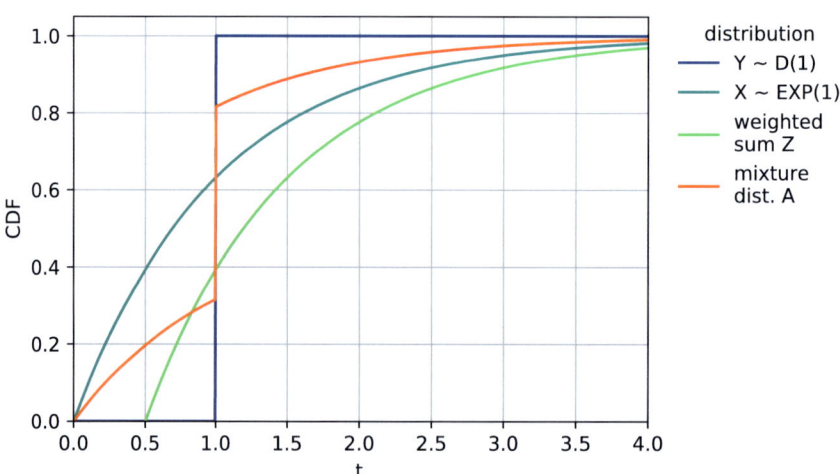

Figure 2.15: Mixture distribution $A = \text{MIX}((X, Y), (\frac{1}{2}, \frac{1}{2}))$ vs. weighted sum of distributions $Z = \frac{1}{2}X + \frac{1}{2}Y$.

2.4.2.7 Representations of Distributions

Phase Representations of Random Variables and Distribution Random variables which are composed of other known distributions are often described in the form of *phase representations*. As shown in Figure 2.16, an Erlang-k distributed random variable (E_k) can be visualized as a series of exponentially distributed phases (M or Markov phases). The phase representation of a hyperexponentially distributed random variable (H_k) e.g. is a parallel connection of exponentially distributed phases reflecting the mixture distribution.

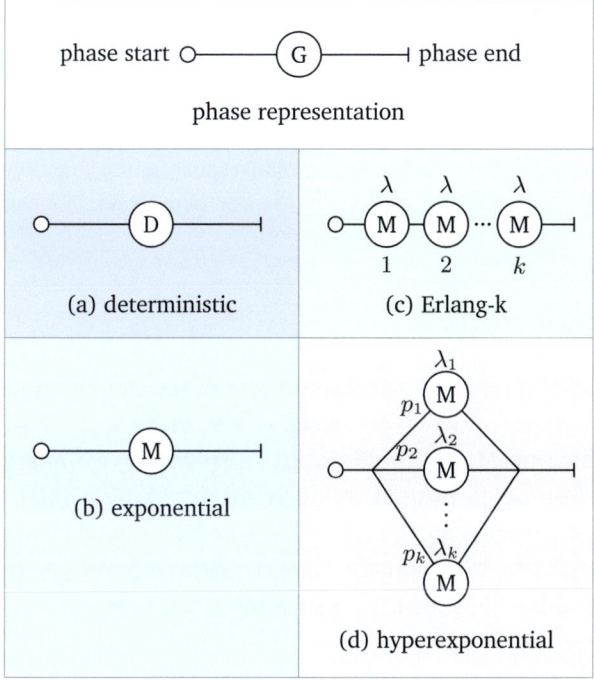

Figure 2.16: Phase representation of common distribution functions.

Graphs of Common Distributions Figure 2.17 shows some common cumulative distribution functions with the same mean E[A]: D, M, E_k and H_k as discussed above. It can be seen that D can be interpreted as the limit of the Erlang distribution E_k for $k \to \infty$. It can also be observed that for r.v.s with higher coefficients of variation the curve is flatter and the limit value $\lim_{t\to\infty} A(t) = 1$ is approached more slowly.

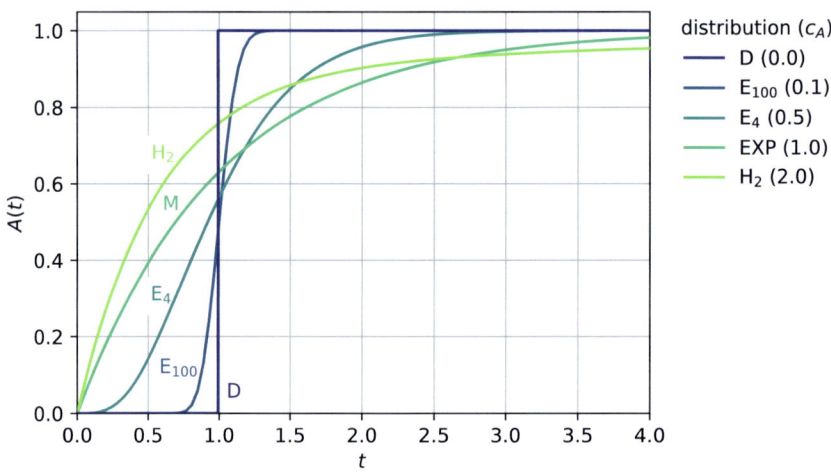

Figure 2.17: Comparison of relevant cumulative distribution functions ($\mathrm{E}[\,A\,] = 1$).
The coefficient of variation c_A is given in the legend for each distribution.

2.4.2.8 Substitute Distributions

In the performance modeling practice we often face the challenge to describe a random variable, where only two parameters – e.g. mean and variance – are roughly obtained from measurements. In literature, a so-called two-moment substitution distribution is often taken instead of a general distribution [40]. This substitute distribution A has the same mean and variance as the original distribution A^*, but is analytically more tractable. To obtain a desired expectation $\mathrm{E}[\,A\,]$ and coefficient of variation c_A, the following substitute distributions are used:

Case: $c_A > 1$

2nd order hyperexponential distribution with symmetry assumption, $A \sim \mathrm{H}_2$

$$A(t) = 1 - p \cdot e^{-t/t_1} - (1 - p) \cdot e^{-t/t_2} \ ,$$

where $\ t_1 = \mathrm{E}[\,A\,] \left(1 + \sqrt{\dfrac{c_A^2 - 1}{c_A^2 + 1}} \right)^{-1}$, $\quad t_2 = \mathrm{E}[\,A\,] \left(1 - \sqrt{\dfrac{c_A^2 - 1}{c_A^2 + 1}} \right)^{-1}$,

and $\ p = \dfrac{\mathrm{E}[\,A\,]}{2t_1}$.

It is $pt_1 = (1 - p)t_2$ (symmetry assumption).

Case: $0 < c_A \leq 1$

Shifted exponential distribution, $A \sim \text{Exp}\left(\dfrac{1}{t_2}\right) + t_1$

$$A(t) = \begin{cases} 0 & 0 \leq t < t_1 \\ 1 - e^{-(t-t_1)/t_2} & t \geq t_1 \end{cases}$$

where $t_1 = \text{E}[A](1 - c_A)$ and $t_2 = \text{E}[A]c_A$.

Figure 2.18 illustrates the substitute distribution for the case $c_A \leq 1$. In the example, the mean is $\text{E}[A] = 5$ and the different curves correspond to various coefficients of variation. It can be seen that all cumulative distribution functions go through the same point at $t = \text{E}[A] = t_1 + t_2$. Computing the cumulative distribution function at that point yields $A(t_1 + t_2) = 1 - e^{-1}$, which is independent of t_1 and t_2 and, thus, the input parameters $\text{E}[A]$ and c_A.

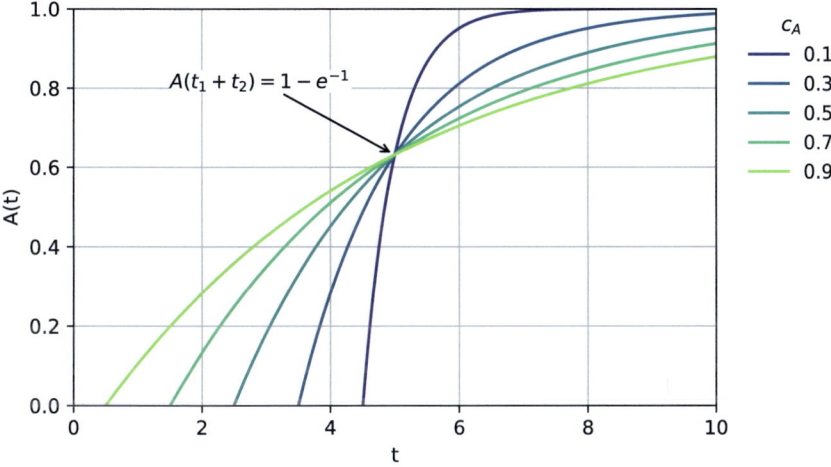

Figure 2.18: Substitute distribution with $\text{E}[A] = 5$ and $c_A < 1$ is a shifted exponential distribution: $A \sim \text{Exp}\left(\frac{1}{t_2}\right) + t_1$ with $t_1 = \text{E}[A](1 - c_A)$ and $t_2 = \text{E}[A]c_A$.

2.4.3 Relationship between Continuous and Discrete Distribution

Consider a continuous r.v. A whose realizations only have (discrete) values at the points $t_i = i\Delta t, i = 0, 1, \ldots$. This continuous r.v. A can be represented by a non-negative discrete r.v. X. The corresponding functions and their transforms are as follows.

Discrete r.v.

X

Distribution

$$x(i) = P(X = i) , \quad i = 0, 1, \ldots$$

Equivalent continuous r.v.

$$A = X \cdot \Delta t$$

Cumulative distribution function

$$A(t) = P(A \le t) = P(X \le \frac{t}{\Delta t}) = \sum_{k=0}^{i} x(k) , i = \left\lfloor \frac{t}{\Delta t} \right\rfloor$$

Probability density function

$$a(t) = \sum_{i=0}^{\infty} x(i) \, \delta(t - i\Delta t)$$

Generating function

$$X_{GF}(z) = \sum_{i=0}^{\infty} x(i) z^i$$

Laplace transform

$$\Phi_A(s) = \int_0^{\infty} e^{-st} a(t) \, dt = \int_0^{\infty} e^{-st} \sum_{i=0}^{\infty} x(i)\delta(t - i\Delta t) \, dt$$

$$= \sum_{i=0}^{\infty} x(i) \cdot \underbrace{\int_0^{\infty} e^{-st}\delta(t - i\Delta t) \, dt}_{e^{-si\Delta t}}$$

(sampling property
(or stifting property)
of Dirac function)

$$= X_{GF}\left(e^{-s\Delta t}\right)$$

3

Elementary Random Processes

.

Chapter 3 is also introductory focusing first on definitions of elementary stochastic processes. Basic properties of the class of renewal processes are then derived. The important Poisson process and the properties of the Poisson process are highlighted. A closer look is taken at the superposition of general arrival processes and the Palm-Khintchine theorem. Finally, continuous-time Markov chains are introduced, and the transition behavior of such Markovian state processes are derived. As a result, a system of state equations is formulated which is solved to obtain the steady state probabilities. Concrete examples of transition probability densities are discussed, before the birth-and-death processes as special form of Markov processes – often found in practice – are analyzed.

3.1 Stochastic Processes

3.1.1 Definition

To evaluate the performance of technical systems, it is often necessary to model the random time sequences of signals and data exchanged between system components and software processes. These sequences can be described and analyzed using characterization with stochastic processes. In the following, stochastic processes, in particular stochastic state processes, are introduced, defined and classified.

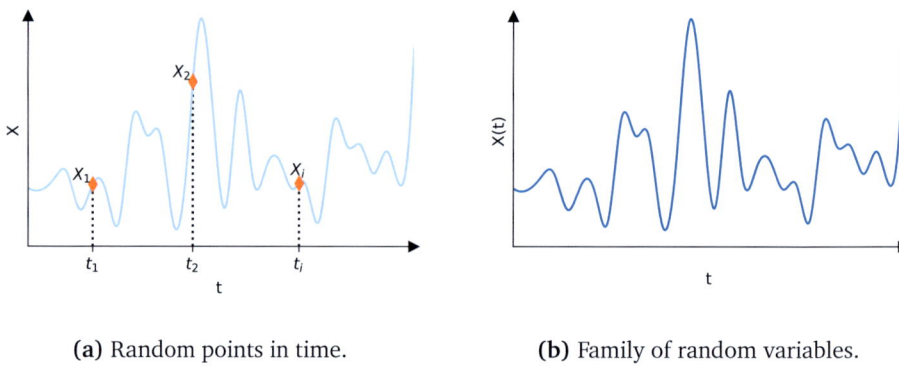

(a) Random points in time.   **(b)** Family of random variables.

Figure 3.1: Stochastic process.

Start by examining the random events in a system at different points on the time axis $t_i, i = 1, 2, ...$, where a specific variable X is pursued. Principally, the random development of the quantity X can be described with the tuples $\{X(t_i), t_i\}$, for $i = 1, 2, ...,$, where $X(t_i)$ represents a random variable (cf. Figure 3.1).

Another possibility to characterize the system development is to generalize the tuples $\{X(t_i), t_i\}$, $i = 1, 2, ...$, in a family of random variables $\{X(t), t\}$, for $t \in \Gamma$, as illustrated in Figure 3.1. The set Ξ denotes the *state space* of the variable $X(t)$, while Γ denoted the *index set* or *parameter set*. The values assumed by the r.v. $X(t)$ are called states and the collection of all possible values forms the state space Ξ. Such a family of random variables is called a *stochastic process*.

In the performance models discussed in this context, the variable X often characterizes the state of the system to be analyzed. A typical example for X is the number of data packets waiting in a device of a computer network. In most process considerations, the continuous or discretized time axis usually represents the index set. Instead of the "index set" we will refer to as "time" for simplicity.

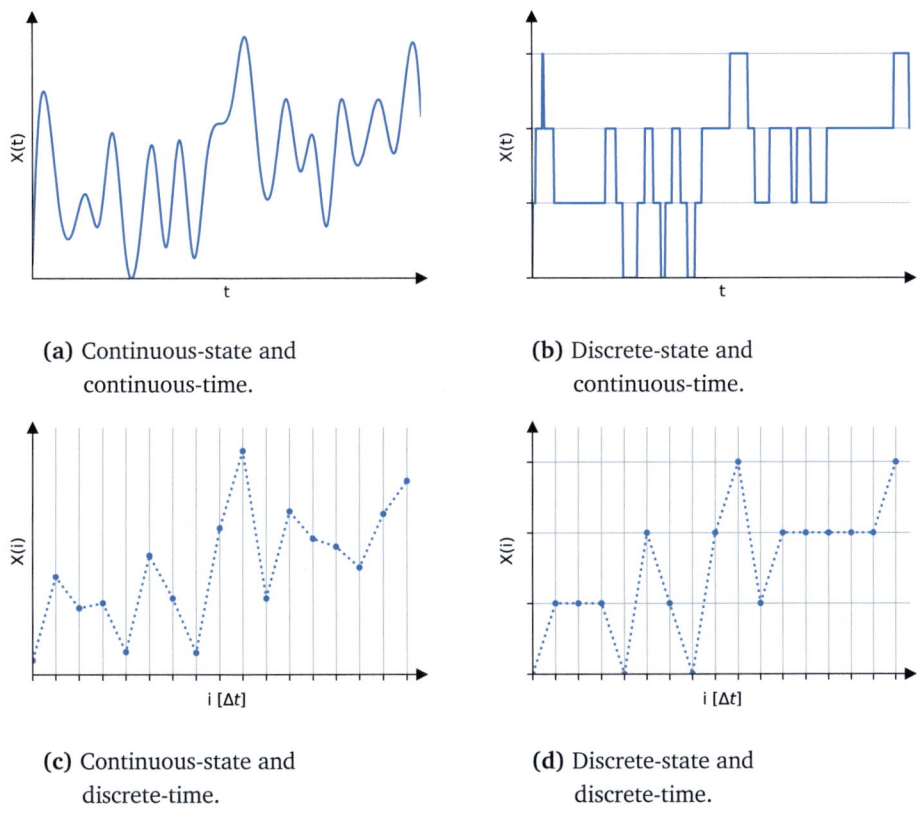

(a) Continuous-state and continuous-time.

(b) Discrete-state and continuous-time.

(c) Continuous-state and discrete-time.

(d) Discrete-state and discrete-time.

Figure 3.2: Classification of stochastic state processes.

The time-dependent variable $X(t)$ indicates the state of a stochastic process at time t. Accordingly, the terms "time" or "state" are used below for the classification of stochastic processes.

With regard to the state space (cf. Figure 3.2), we distinguish between two classes of stochastic processes:

- *Continuous-state stochastic processes*:
  The state space Ξ here is composed of intervals on the axis of real numbers. Examples are processes to characterize unfinished work in a queueing system, the remaining waiting time for customers, etc.

- *Discrete-state stochastic processes*:
  The state space Ξ is here finite or countable; $X(t)$ can e.g. only be an integer, and the range of values are finite. Discrete-state processes are e.g. used to describe the number of data packets in a router or the number of workpieces in

the processing phase in a manufacturing system. Discrete-state processes are also often referred to as *chains* (see Figure 3.2).

Stochastic processes can also be classified according to the index set "time":

- *Continuous-time stochastic processes*:
  The index set Γ consists of intervals of the real time axis. If the process is also state-discrete, then $X(t)$ is a step function (cf. Figure 3.2b).

- *Discrete-time stochastic processes*:
  The index set Γ is finite or countably infinite. The time axis is viewed as discretized in this case. The state $X(t)$ of the process is observed *only* at the instances $t_i = i\Delta t, i = 0, 1, ...$ As shown in Figure 3.2, the state process consists only of a sequence of discrete realizations of the process. The class of discrete-time processes plays an important role in evaluating the performance of modern computer networks and communication systems. Analysis methods for discrete-time processes are discussed in more detail in Chapter 6.

3.1.2 Markov Processes

Markov processes form a special class of stochastic processes. They play an essential role in the performance analysis and teletraffic theory, as analysis methods for Markov processes are well-developed.

A stochastic process $\{X(t), t\}$ is called a Markov process, if its future development only depends on the current process state. If x_n is the state of the process at an observation instance t_n, the Markov property can be formulated as follows for $t_0 < t_1 < \ldots < t_n < t_{n+1}$ using the random variables $X(t)$:

$$P(X(t_{n+1}) = x_{n+1} | X(t_n) = x_n, \ldots, X(t_0) = x_0) \qquad \textbf{Markov property}$$
$$= P(X(t_{n+1}) = x_{n+1} | X(t_n) = x_n) \qquad (3.1)$$

From a process point in time t_n, the future development of the process depends only on the state $[X(t_n) = x_n]$. The development path of the process in the past $(t < t_n)$ until it reaches the state $[X(t_n) = x_n]$ is not decisive for the further development of the process, but only the state x_n at the observation time t_n (cf. Figure 3.3). This is also called the *memoryless property* of Markov processes.

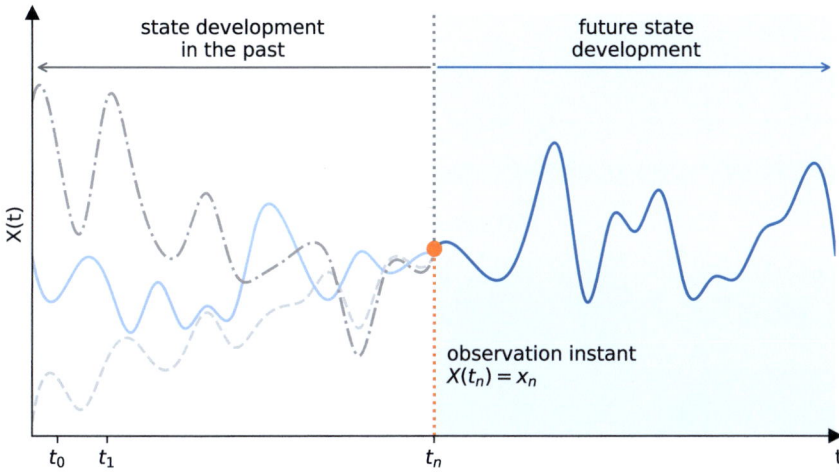

Figure 3.3: The future development of the Markov process only depends on the state $x_n = X(t_n)$ at time t_n, but not on the state development in the past.

As explained in the next subchapter, the Markov property can apply to several types of processes, like arrival, service and state processes.

3.1.3 Elementary Processes in Performance Models

3.1.3.1 Arrival Processes

In the context of performance models, arrival processes are often stochastic processes with which the chronological sequences of arrival events in a system are described. As shown in Figure 3.4, an arrival process describes a sequence of occurrences or events, e.g. arrivals of customers, signals, data packets, work items. In case one single customer arrives at an event time, it is a *single arrival process*. If several customers arrive at the same time, the arrival process is a *batch arrival process*. The group size can statistically be described e.g. with a probability distribution.

An often used description method for a random arrival process is the application of a *renewal process* (cf. Chapter 3.2). In Figure 3.4a, a single arrival process is depicted, where the arrival process is characterized with a random variable A. Assuming that there is a renewal process, the interarrival intervals are independently and identically distributed and can be described with a cumulative distribution function $A(t)$.

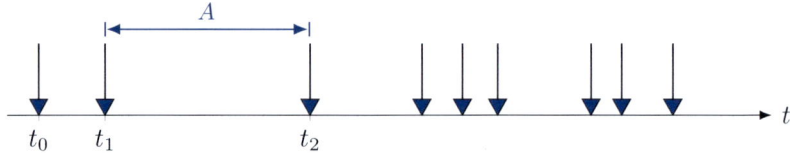

(a) Arrival proccess.

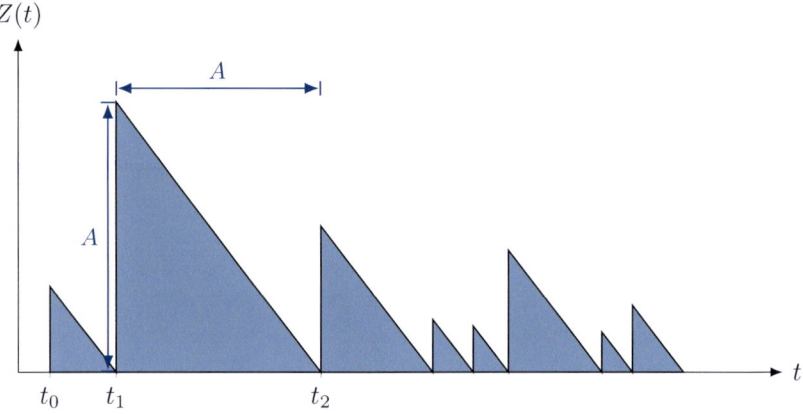

(b) Arrival process as a state process.

Figure 3.4: Characterization forms of an arrival process.

An arrival process can also be interpreted as a state process (cf. Figure 3.4b) by viewing the remaining time $Z(t)$ until the next arrival occurs. Here, the resulting stochastic process $\{Z(t), t\}$ is continuous-time and continuous-state. Immediately after an arriving event, the remaining time $Z(t)$ increases by the corresponding interarrival time A.

Arrival Process with Markov Property   According to the definition of the Markov property, an arrival process is memoryless at any point in time if the distribution function of the remaining time $Z(t)$ (Figure 3.4b) is independent of the past of the process, up to the point of observation. This means that the distribution function of the remaining time does not depend on the age of the last arrival. In Chapter 3.2 this is formulated as follows: "The forward recurrence time of the interarrival time has the same cumulative distribution function as that of the interarrival time itself".

It can be shown that in the case of continuous-time arrival processes, the Poisson process is the only single arrival process with Markov property.

3.1.3.2 Service Process

In a performance model, the service process characterizes the mode of operation of a server or a group of servers where the chronological sequence of operating phases is described. Figure 3.5 shows the service process of a server which is either free or busy (occupied). The service time (e.g. the transmission time of a data packet, the processing time of a switch for an IP packet) is characterized by means of a random variable B for the service time, which is described with a cumulative distribution function $B(t)$.

Several consecutive service times constitute a busy period (cf. Figure 3.5). Between busy periods there is an idle period during which there are no customers in service or waiting in the system.

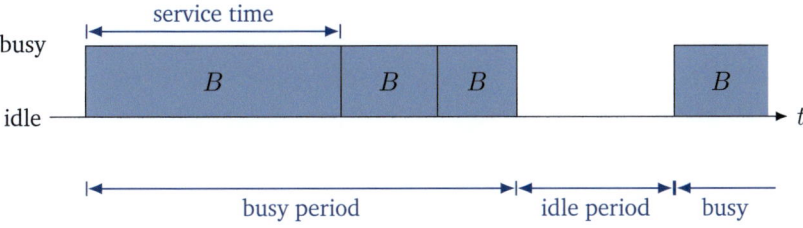

Figure 3.5: Server with service process.

Service Process with Markov Property   Consider a server in active state. The associated service process is called memoryless – or has the Markov property – if the remaining time until the end of the current service process has the same cumulative distribution function at every point of observation. The distribution of the remaining service time does not depend on the age of the ongoing service. When dealing with renewal processes in Chapter 3.2, this property is formulated as follows: "The forward recurrence time of the service time has the same cumulative distribution function like the service time itself".

In case of continuous service time distributions, the exponential distribution function is the only distribution which has the Markov property.

3.1.3.3 State Process

State processes are often considered in performance model analysis. Depending on the traffic model and the appropriate analysis method, different forms of the state process description are considered, as shown in Figure 3.6: *number of customers* or *unfinished work* in the observed system.

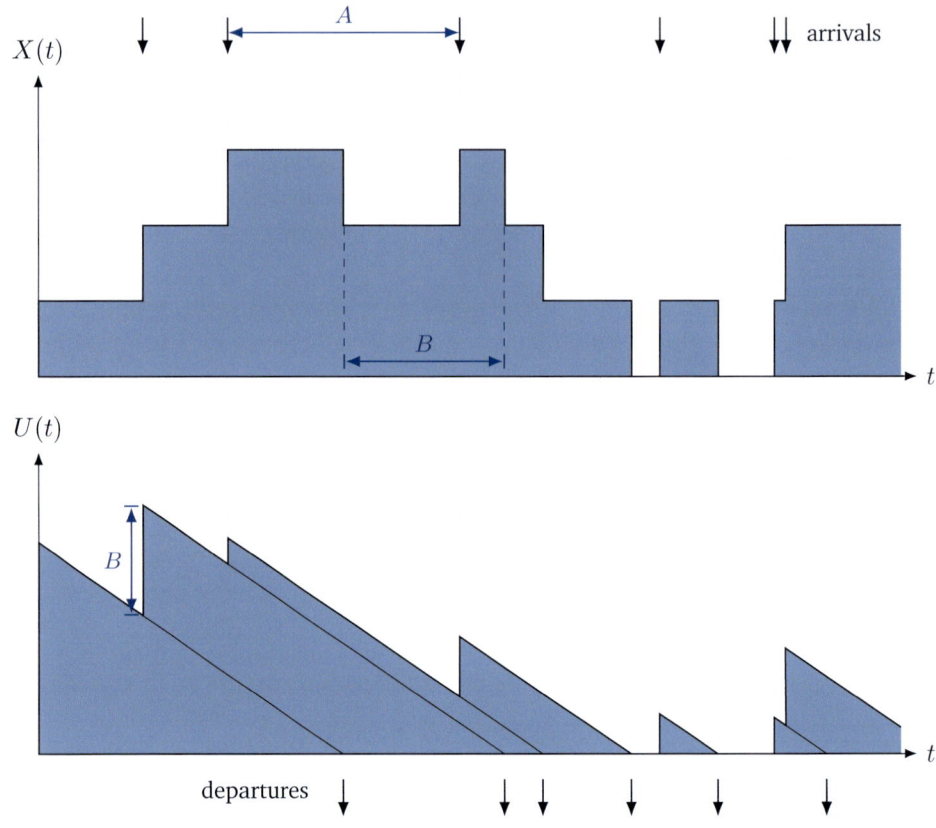

Figure 3.6: Representations of state processes.

- $X(t)$: *Number of customers in system*
  Each arriving and accepted customer increases $X(t)$ by one, each service termination decrements $X(t)$. Since the state space is integer valued, the process is a discrete-state stochastic process $\{X(t), t\}$, which can be depicted by a step-function. This form of state process description is used later e.g. in the analysis of elementary Markov models and of models of type GI/M/1 and M/GI/1.

- $U(t)$: *Unfinished work in system (total amount of remaining work)*
  An incoming and accepted customer increases the state $U(t)$ by a random quantum B of unfinished work. The amount B is here identical to the service duration of the customer. As the unfinished work $U(t)$ is continuously reduced over time t, the shape of a continuous-state stochastic process as shown in Figure 3.6 is obtained. This form of state process is e.g. used in the analysis of GI/GI/1.

3.2 Renewal Processes

In model-driven performance investigations, traffic streams are often characterized by arrival processes that statistically describe the stochastic input and output traffic flows in these systems. In this analytical context, renewal processes play an important role in the representation of arrival processes.

Renewal processes and their properties are presented below. Further literature can be found e.g. in Cox and Miller [25] or Cox [24].

3.2.1 Definition

Point Process   A point process is a finite or infinite sequence of random points in time or occurrences (arrival times of customers) on the real time axis (cf. Figure 3.7). In the general case of a point process, the interarrival distances A_i between customer arrivals t_{i-1} and t_i can have different cumulative distribution functions $A_i(t)$.

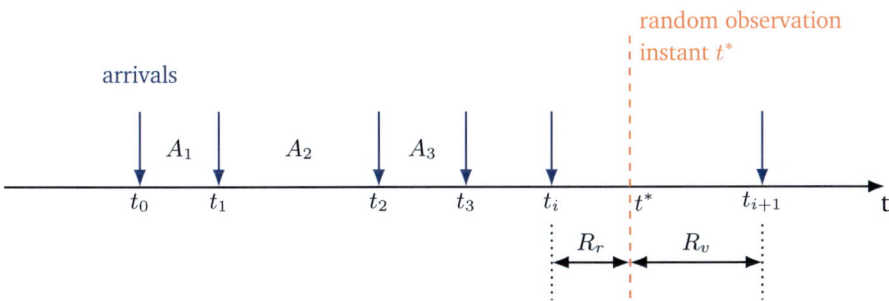

Figure 3.7: Definition of random variables.

Renewal Process   A renewal process is a point process, in which the interarrival intervals A_i between successive points in time are independently and identically distributed (*iid*):

$$A_i(t) = A(t) \qquad \text{for all } i \,. \tag{3.2}$$

If the distribution function $A_1(t)$ of the first interval A_1 deviates from the other distribution functions $A_i(t)$, $i \neq 1$, the process is referred to as a *modified* renewal process.

Law of Large Numbers for Renewal Processes   A fundamental result of renewal theory is the law of large numbers for renewal processes. The total number $N(t)$ of arrival events in the interval $[0; t]$ is counted for a renewal process with interarrival time A. We obtain a stochastic process $\{N(t), t\}$ which is referred to as *counting process*. For any $t \geq 0$, the r.v. $N(t)$ can be defined as

$$N(t) = \sum_{n=1}^{\infty} \mathbb{1}_{\{t_i \leq t\}} \qquad \text{with } \mathbb{1}_C = \begin{cases} 1 & \text{if condition } C \text{ is true} \\ 0 & \text{if condition } C \text{ is false} \end{cases} \qquad (3.3a)$$

where $\mathbb{1}$ is the indicator function counting the arrivals before time t: $\mathbb{1}_{\{t_i \leq t\}}$.

The law of large numbers for renewal processes considers a renewal process with mean interarrival time $E[A]$. With probability 1, observe the following relation between the arrival rate $\frac{N(t)}{t}$ and the mean interarrival time.

$$\lim_{t \to \infty} \frac{N(t)}{t} = \frac{1}{E[A]} \qquad \qquad \textbf{strong law for renewal processes} \quad (3.3b)$$

The relationship follows directly from the strong law of large numbers in statistics which says that the sample average converges to the expected value with probability 1.

$$\lim_{n \to \infty} \frac{t_n}{n} = \lim_{n \to \infty} \frac{1}{n} \sum_{i=1}^{n} A = E[A] \qquad (3.4a)$$

Per definition, it is

$$t_{N(t)} \leq t \leq t_{N(t)+1} \qquad (3.4b)$$

and hence

$$\frac{t_{N(t)}}{N(t)} \leq \frac{t}{N(t)} \leq \frac{t_{N(t)+1}}{N(t)} = \frac{t_{N(t)+1}}{N(t)+1} \cdot \frac{N(t)+1}{N(t)} \qquad (3.4c)$$

which is converging for $t \to \infty$ using Equation (3.4a):

$$\frac{1}{E[A]} \leq \frac{N(t)}{t} \leq \frac{1}{E[A]} . \qquad (3.4d)$$

Hence, Equation (3.3b) follows.

Recurrence Time   Figure 3.7 shows a renewal process (i.e. all A_i are identically distributed) with the arrival times t_i, in which

A random variable of the interarrival time,

$A(t)$ cumulative distribution function of A,

$a(t)$ probability density function of A.

The process is observed by an independent outside observer at time t^*. The following intervals are marked in Figure 3.7:

R_v forward recurrence time; interval from the observation time to the next arrival;

R_r backward recurrence time; interval from the last arrival to the observation time.

The random observation time t^* can be "equally likely" at any time on the time axis. Thus, the time axis, in terms of observing a renewal process, is reversible, i.e. the forward and backward recurrence times have the same statistical properties. For this reason, only the recurrence time R is examined below instead of both R_v and R_r.

3.2.2   Analysis of Recurrence Time

Cumulative Distribution Function of Recurrence Time   The probability density function $r(t)$ of the recurrence time R of a renewal process can be derived from the cumulative distribution function $A(t)$ of the interarrival time A according to:

$$r(t) = \frac{1}{\mathrm{E}[A]} \cdot (1 - A(t)) = \lambda \, A^c(t) = \lambda \int_{\tau=t}^{\infty} a(\tau) \, d\tau \qquad \textbf{recurrence time} \quad (3.5)$$

where $\lambda = \dfrac{1}{\mathrm{E}[A]}$ is the arrival rate.

The proof of this relationship is detailed below and takes into account that the observation time t^* is in an interarrival of length $A = \tau$. Thus:

$a(\tau)$ probability density of the *occurrence* of an interval of exact length τ.

q_τ probability density for an outside observer to *randomly encounter* an interarrival interval of length τ. It is obvious that this density is proportional to the length τ itself, since a longer interval is more likely to be encountered by a random observer then a shorter one. Hence, $q_\tau = a(\tau) \, \tau \, c_0$.

c_0 is just a standardization constant, where

$$\int_{\tau=0}^{\infty} q_\tau \, d\tau = \int_{\tau=0}^{\infty} a(\tau) \cdot \tau \cdot c_0 \, d\tau = c_0 \cdot \mathrm{E}[A] = 1 \,,$$

yielding:

$$c_0 = \frac{1}{\mathrm{E}[A]} = \lambda \quad \text{or} \quad q_\tau = \lambda \cdot \tau \cdot a(\tau) \,.$$

During the encountered interval of length $A = \tau$, the observation instant is also equally likely for each position. The conditional probability density function of the recurrence time is therefore

$$r(t|A = \tau) = \begin{cases} \dfrac{1}{\tau} & \text{für } t \in (0, \tau) , \\ 0 & \text{otherwise.} \end{cases}$$

Applying the law of total probability we arrive at:

$$r(t) = \int_{\tau=0}^{\infty} r(t|A = \tau)\, q_\tau \, d\tau = \int_{\tau=t}^{\infty} \frac{1}{\tau} \lambda\, \tau a(\tau) \, d\tau$$

$$= \lambda\, A(\tau) \Big|_t^{\infty} = \lambda\, A^c(t) , \qquad \text{q.e.d.}$$

The Laplace transform of the recurrence time is thus

$$\Phi_R(s) = \frac{\lambda}{s} \cdot (1 - \Phi_A(s)) \qquad \textbf{Laplace transform of recurrence time} \quad (3.6)$$

with $\Phi_R(s) = \mathrm{LT}\{\, r(t)\,\}$ and $\Phi_A(s) = \mathrm{LT}\{\, a(t)\,\}$. From Equation (3.5) it is obvious that

- $r(t)$ can be unambiguously be determined from $a(t)$, whereas
- the probability density function $a(t)$ of the interarrival time cannot be unambiguously calculated from the density function $r(t)$. For a computation of $a(t)$ from $r(t)$ we additionally need the mean value $\mathrm{E}[\,A\,]$ of the interarrival time.

Moments of Recurrence Time The relationship between the moments of the interarrival time and the recurrence time can be determined as follows:

$$\mathrm{E}[\,R^k\,] = \int_{u=0}^{\infty} u^k r(u) \, du = \int_{u=0}^{\infty} u^k \lambda(1 - A(u)) \, du = \lambda \int_{u=0}^{\infty} u^k \int_{t=u}^{\infty} a(t) \, dt \, du$$

$$= \lambda \int_{t=0}^{\infty} a(t) \underbrace{\int_{u=0}^{t} u^k \, du}_{\frac{t^{k+1}}{k+1}} dt = \frac{1}{(k+1)\mathrm{E}[\,A\,]} \underbrace{\int_{t=0}^{\infty} t^{k+1} a(t) \, dt}_{\mathrm{E}[\,A^{k+1}\,]}$$

or

$$\mathrm{E}[\,R^k\,] = \frac{\mathrm{E}[\,A^{k+1}\,]}{(k+1)\mathrm{E}[\,A\,]} . \qquad\qquad (3.7)$$

Especially for the mean, it holds

$$\mathrm{E}[R] = \frac{\mathrm{E}[A^2]}{2\mathrm{E}[A]} = \frac{c_A^2 + 1}{2} \cdot \mathrm{E}[A] , \tag{3.8}$$

i.e. for

$$c_A < 1 : \quad \mathrm{E}[R] < \mathrm{E}[A] , \tag{3.9a}$$
$$c_A = 1 : \quad \mathrm{E}[R] = \mathrm{E}[A] , \tag{3.9b}$$
$$c_A > 1 : \quad \mathrm{E}[R] > \mathrm{E}[A] . \tag{3.9c}$$

For processes with higher coefficients of variation ($c_A > 1$) the mean recurrence time is greater than the mean interarrival time. This is at first difficult to understand intuitively, since R "lies within" A (cf. Figure 3.7). To explain this property, we consider all realizations of A, where longer intervals are more frequently encountered by the outside observer and thus, larger intervals contribute more often to the recurrence time (cf. Equation (3.9c)).

3.3 Poisson Process

The Poisson process plays an essential role in queueing theory. Poisson processes are often observed in practice when a large number of independent sources are generating requests in a system. A prominent example is the modeling of incoming telephone calls which was introduced and validated by Erlang in 1909 [32]. Recent measurement studies revealed that the Poisson process may be used e.g. to model the users' video view requests in popular Internet platforms for the vast majority of videos [36]. Another example are block completions of mining nodes in Blockchain systems [84] or the aggregation of IoT traffic at different points like IoT gateways or at a cloud instance for further processing. The association of Poisson Processes with the superposition of periodic IoT messages will be discussed in detail in Chapter 7.2. The fundamental principle why Poisson process approximations are often observed in practice is the Palm-Khintchine theorem, cf. Chapter 3.4.

3.3.1 Definition of a Poisson Process

There are different ways of defining a Poisson process. The Poisson process is a counting process which counts the number $N(t)$ of (arrival) events that have occurred by time t. A counting process is a stochastic process in which $N(t)$ takes on non-negative integer values ($N(t) \geq 0$) and is non-decreasing in time. Thus, $N(t_2) \geq N(t_1)$ for $t_2 > t_1$. In queueing systems, the counting process reflects the number of customer arrivals to the queue over time.

Definition of a Poisson process as counting process

Let $\lambda > 0$. The counting process $\{N(t), t \geq 0\}$ is called a Poisson process with rate λ if the following assumptions are fulfilled:

1. $N(0) = 0$.

2. $N(t)$ has independent increments. The number of arrivals during non-overlapping time intervals are independent random variables.

3. $N(t)$ has stationary increments. The distribution of the number of arrivals between t and $t + \tau$ depends only on the length of the interval τ, not on the starting point t.

Independent increments of the process $N(t)$ mean that for a series of time instants $0 \leq t_0 < t_1 < \cdots < t_n$, the random variables $N(t_0)$, $N(t_1) - N(t_0)$, $N(t_2) - N(t_1), \ldots$, $N(t_n) - N(t_{n-1})$ are independent. It can be shown that the number $N(t)$ of arrivals by time t follows a Poisson distribution with parameter λt: $N(t) \sim \text{POIS}(\lambda t)$ with the probability $P(N(t) = k) = e^{-\lambda t} \frac{(\lambda t)^k}{k!}$, $k \geq 0$.

Alternatively, the Poisson process can be defined through interarrival times of events. For the Poisson process, the interarrival times are independent exponentially distributed random variables. The Poisson process is a special point process. We are speaking of a *homogeneous Poisson process* if the interarrival times between consecutive events in time are independently and identically distributed (iid) with rate λ: $A \sim \text{EXP}(\lambda)$.

Definition of a Poisson process as a renewal process of interarrival times

A Poisson process with rate $\lambda > 0$ is a renewal process in which the interarrival time distribution follows a negative exponential distribution with rate λ. The interarrival times $\{A_i : i \geq 1\}$ are iid for all i: $A_i \sim \text{EXP}(\lambda)$ with cumulative distribution function $A_i(t) = 1 - e^{-\lambda t}$ for $t \geq 0$.

Please note that a non-homogeneous Poisson process allows a time-varying arrival rate $\lambda(t)$, e.g. M(t)/GI/1. In this textbook, the focus is on the homogeneous Poisson process with constant rate λ which is simply denoted as Poisson process.

3.3.2 Properties of the Poisson Process

The Poisson process has several relevant properties which are essential for the analysis of queueing systems with a Poisson arrival process. The two definitions for a Poisson process from above are equivalent and the properties can be derived from any of the two definitions.

Memoryless Property for Poisson Process   The special role of the Poisson process is its memoryless property. We define the memoryless property of a positive r.v. A, if for every $t \geq 0$ and $s \geq 0$ the following condition holds.

$$P(A > s + t | A > s) = P(A > t) \qquad \text{memoryless property of r.v.} \quad (3.10)$$

The meaning of the memoryless property is as follows. If an observer has already waited a time s without seeing an event $(A > s)$, the probability that an event won't occur in the next t minutes, $P(A > t + s | A > s)$, is the same as if the observer hadn't already waited the time s, $P(A > t)$. Hence, the system is memoryless from the previous waiting time.

It is the exponential distribution, which is the only continuous distribution that has the memoryless property. Consider $A \sim \text{EXP}(\lambda)$ with $A(t) = 1 - e^{-\lambda t}$.

$$\begin{aligned} P(A > s + t | A > s) &= \frac{P(A > s + t, A > s)}{P(A > s)} = \frac{P(A > s + t)}{P(A > s)} \\ &= \frac{e^{-\lambda(s+t)}}{e^{-\lambda s}} = e^{-\lambda t} = P(A > t) \end{aligned} \qquad (3.11a)$$

The memoryless property of the Poisson process manifests when considering the recurrence times.

Poisson Process as Renewal Process   For the case of a Poisson arrival process, the interarrival time A is (negative) exponentially distributed:

$$A(t) = 1 - e^{-\lambda t}, \qquad a(t) = \lambda e^{-\lambda t}. \qquad (3.11b)$$

The recurrence time R of the interarrival time A for a Poisson process with rate λ follows directly from Equation (3.5):

$$r(t) = \frac{1}{\mathrm{E}[A]}(1 - A(t)) = \lambda e^{-\lambda t} = a(t) \qquad (3.11c)$$

or for the cumulative distribution function

$$R(t) = A(t). \qquad (3.11d)$$

The recurrence time and the interarrival time follow both an exponential distribution with rate λ. This means that the remaining interval R until the next arrival, as seen by an independent observer, has the same distribution as if the observation time was exactly at the last arrival. From the observation time t^* on, the process develops completely independently of its past. Accordingly, we can state that the Poisson process has the memoryless property (or the Markov property).

Formally: For a Poisson process with rate λ, the memoryless property of the exponential distribution can be utilized to show that for any $t^* > 0$, the length R of the interval from t^* until the first arrival after t^* follows an exponential distribution with rate λ. The r.v. R is independent of all arrivals before the time t^*. This is denoted as *memoryless property for the Poisson process*. An intuitive interpretation of the Poisson process is that the distribution of time until the next event is always the same – no matter what point in time is considered.

PASTA Property   A consequence of the memoryless property of the Poisson process is the PASTA property: Poisson Arrivals See Time Averages (cf. Wolff [121]). Let us consider a system in the long run which is described by a discrete random variable X^*, e.g. the number of customers in the system. An independent observer considers the system at a random time t^*. The probability that the random observer finds the system in state $[X^* = i]$ is denoted as $x^*(i) = P(X^* = i)$. Now, the system is considered by an arriving customer, and the system state observed by an arriving customer is X_A. Hence, the probability that the arriving customer finds the system in state $[X_A = i]$ is denoted as $x_A(i) = P(X_A = i)$.

The PASTA property states that the probability $x^*(i)$ of the state as seen by a random observer is the same as the probability $x_A(i)$ of the state seen by an arriving customer.

$$x^*(i) = x_A(i) , \quad i = 0, 1, \ldots \qquad \text{PASTA property} \quad (3.12)$$

The PASTA property is often utilized in the analysis of queueing systems, for example the derivation of the blocking probability of arriving customers in the M/M/n loss system (Equation (4.4)), for example the derivation of system state probabilities $x^*(i)$ for the M/GI/1 delay system (Equation (5.45)).

A simple counter-example that PASTA is not valid for any arrival process is a deterministic D/D/1 queue with $\mathrm{E}[A] = 1$ and $\mathrm{E}[B] = 1/2$. Then, the random observer sees $x^*(0) = x^*(1) = 1/2$. However, the arriving customer finds an empty system: $x_A(0) = 1$ and $x_A(1) = 0$.

Number of Poisson Arrivals in Fixed Interval   Consider a fixed interval of length t. Then, consider the r.v. $N_t = N(t)$ counting the number of events occurring in this time interval $[0; t]$. The time instants t_i denote the i-th arrival event. It is $t_k = A_1 + \cdots + A_k$, cf. Figure 3.8. Then, t_k follows an Erlang-k distribution (Chapter 2.4.2.3) with parameter λ, i.e. $t_k \sim E_k(\lambda)$. The cumulative distribution function is

$$P(t_k \le t) = 1 - \sum_{i=0}^{k-1} \frac{(\lambda t)^i}{i!} e^{-\lambda t} , \; t \ge 0. \qquad (3.13)$$

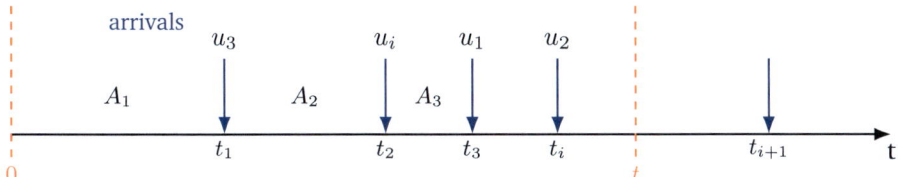

Figure 3.8: Number of Poisson arrivals in a fixed interval of length t.

If there are at least k arrival events in the interval t, then the arrival time t_k must be less than or equal to t.

$$P(N(t) \geq k) = P(t_k \leq t) = 1 - \sum_{i=0}^{k-1} \frac{(\lambda t)^i}{i!} e^{-\lambda t} = \sum_{i=k}^{\infty} \frac{(\lambda t)^i}{i!} e^{-\lambda t} \qquad (3.14a)$$

$$P(N(t) \leq k) = \sum_{i=0}^{k} \frac{(\lambda t)^i}{i!} e^{-\lambda t} \qquad (3.14b)$$

$$P(N(t) = k) = \frac{(\lambda t)^k}{k!} e^{-\lambda t} \qquad (3.14c)$$

Hence, N_t follows a Poisson distribution with mean λt: $N_t = N(t) \sim \text{POIS}(\lambda t)$.

Stationary and Independent Increment Property   As already stated in the first definition of a Poisson process, a counting process $\{N(t); t > 0\}$ has the *stationary increment property* if for every $t + \tau > t > 0$, the distribution function $N(t+\tau) - N(t)$ has the same distribution function as $N(\tau)$. Thus, the distribution of the number of arrival events only depends on the length of the interval τ, but not on the starting point.

The *independent increment property* means that the r.v.s counting the events in non-overlapping intervals are statistically independent. Let us define arbitrary times $0 \leq t_0 < t_1 < t_2 < \cdots < t_k$. Note that these times are arbitrary and do not correspond to arrival times of events. Indeed, there are now non-overlapping time intervals $(0; t_0]$, $(t_0; t_1]$, $(t_1; t_2]$, etc. The number of arrival events in these time intervals is a random variable denoted by $\Delta_0, \Delta_1, \Delta_2$, etc., respectively. These r.v.s are statistically independent.

Poisson processes have both the stationary increment and independent increment properties. The r.v.s $\Delta_0 \sim \text{POIS}(\lambda t_0)$, $\Delta_1 \sim \text{POIS}(\lambda(t_1 - t_0))$, $\Delta_2 \sim \text{POIS}(\lambda(t_2 - t_1))$ follow a Poisson distribution, are all statistically independent, and only dependent on the length of the respective interval.

Uniform Distribution of Poisson Arrivals Consider a Poisson process with rate λ. There are n arrivals within an fixed interval of duration t. Then these arrivals are uniformly distributed within this interval. Figure 3.8 illustrates the arrivals within the interval $[0; t]$. The n arrivals are uniformly distributed and occur at times $u_1, u_2, u_3, \ldots, u_n$. Note that the times u_i are not ordered. The r.v.s $u_1, u_2, \ldots, u_n$ follow all the same uniform distribution.

$$u_i \sim U(0, t) \quad \text{for} \quad i = 1, 2, \ldots, n \tag{3.15}$$

The ordered random variables $(t_1, t_2, \ldots, t_n)$ reflect the series of arrival events. This is denoted as *order statistics* and will be discussed for aggregated IoT traffic in Chapter 7.2.

Merging of Poisson Processes The superposition of Poisson processes remains a Poisson process. Consider n independent Poisson processes with arrival rates $\lambda_1, \ldots, \lambda_n$. Figure 3.9 shows the merging of two Poisson processes into one total process. The two processes are independently generating arrival events at rates λ_1 and λ_2, respectively.

Consider an arbitrary point in time t^*. Due to the memoryless property of the exponential distribution, the forward recurrence time of the process 1 and process 2 is $A_1 \sim \text{EXP}(\lambda_1)$ and $A_2 \sim \text{EXP}(\lambda_2)$, respectively.

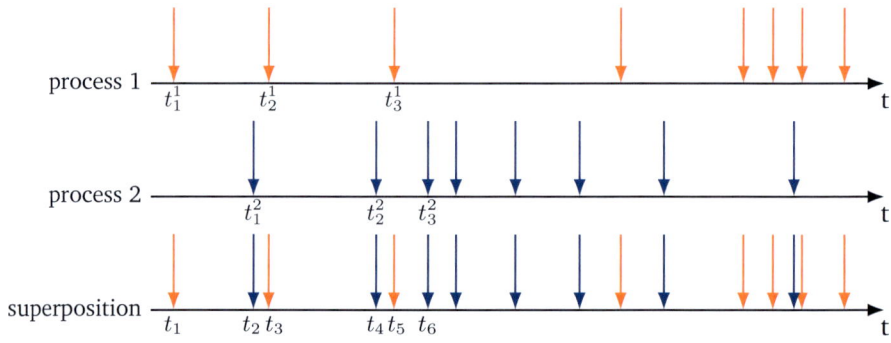

Figure 3.9: Merging of Poisson processes.

The next arrival after time t^* is the minimum of the forward recurrence times of both processes. Hence, the minimum of two r.v.s is obtained, see Section 2.2.6.7.

$$A = \min(A_1, A_2) \quad \text{with } A_1 \sim \text{EXP}(\lambda_1), \; A_2 \sim \text{EXP}(\lambda_2) \tag{3.16a}$$

$$A(t) = 1 - (1 - A_1(t)) \cdot (1 - A_2(t)) = 1 - e^{-(\lambda_1 + \lambda_2)t} \tag{3.16b}$$

The recurrence time to the next arrival follows an exponential distribution with rate $\lambda_1 + \lambda_2$. Hence, the superposition of the two processes is again a Poisson process with the total rate $\lambda_1 + \lambda_2$.

Following the same argument, the superposition of n independent Poisson process with arrival rates $\lambda_1, \ldots, \lambda_n$ follows a Poisson process with the total rate $\sum_{i=1}^{n} \lambda_i$.

$$A = \min(A_1, \ldots, A_n) \quad \text{with } A_1 \sim \text{EXP}(\lambda_1), \ \ldots, \ A_n \sim \text{EXP}(\lambda_n) \tag{3.17a}$$

$$A(t) = 1 - \prod_{i=1}^{n}(1 - A_i(t)) = 1 - e^{-(\sum_{i=1}^{n} \lambda_i)t} \tag{3.17b}$$

Random Thinning of Poisson Processes An original Poisson process is considered which has an arrival rate λ. With a certain probability p, the arrival event is considered in the thinned process. Since this is done in a random way, the resulting thinned process stays a Poisson process with rate $p \cdot \lambda$. Figure 3.10 illustrates the arrival events of the original process and the resulting arrival process after random thinning. The gray arrows indicate that the original event is not considered in that sub-process. We can also say that the original process is split into two sub-processes. The first sub-process is indicated by the blue arrows (rate $p\lambda$); the second sub-process is composed of the gray arrows (rate $(1 - p)\lambda$).

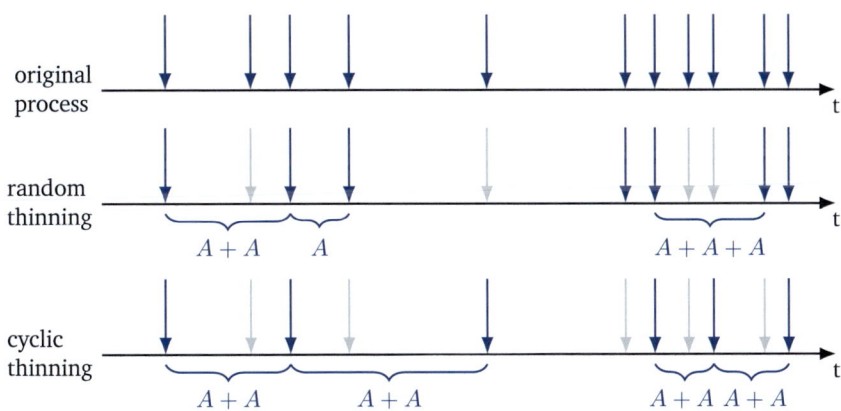

Figure 3.10: Random and deterministic (cyclic) thinning of a Poisson process.

Now consider the first sub-process in Figure 3.10 after random thinning. The interarrival times of the original process are described by A. In the thinned process, with probability p the next arrival is taken and the interarrival time is also A. However, with probability $p \cdot (1 - p)$, the next event is not taken, but the event after. Hence, the interarrival time is $A + A$. The probability that k consecutive events are not taken and the $k + 1$-st event is taken is $p(1 - p)^k$; the resulting interarrival time is then a sum of exponentially distributed r.v.s which is an Erlang-$k + 1$ distribution:

$$\sum_{i=1}^{k+1} A \sim E_{k+1}(\lambda) \quad \text{with probability } p(1 - p)^k \tag{3.18a}$$

The interarrival time A^* of the thinned Poisson process is a mixture distribution.

$$A^* = \begin{cases} A & \text{with probability } p \\ A + A & \text{with probability } p(1 - p) \\ A + A + A & \text{with probability } p(1 - p)^2 \\ \cdots \\ \sum_{i=1}^{k+1} A & \text{with probability } p(1 - p)^k \\ \cdots \end{cases} \tag{3.18b}$$

The probability distribution follows using the Erlang distribution in Equation (2.89).

$$a^*(t) = \sum_{k=0}^{\infty} (1 - p)^k \cdot p \cdot \lambda e^{-\lambda t} \frac{(\lambda t)^k}{k!}$$

$$= p\lambda e^{-\lambda t} \underbrace{\sum_{k=0}^{\infty} \frac{((1 - p)\lambda t)^k}{k!}}_{e^{(1-p)\lambda t}} = p\lambda e^{-p\lambda t} \tag{3.18c}$$

Thus, $a^*(t)$ is the probability density function of an exponential distribution with parameter $p\lambda$. Random thinning of a Poisson process results in a Poisson process with smaller rate.

Remark: In contrast to random thinning, the deterministic or cyclic thinning of a Poisson process leads to a different process. Figure 3.10 also shows cyclic thinning of the original Poisson process. In the example, every second arrival event is skipped. Hence, the interarrival time is the sum of two exponential phases which follows an Erlang distribution: $A + A \sim E_2(\lambda)$.

3.3.3 Poisson Arrivals during an Arbitrarily Distributed Interval

An arrival process is called a Poisson process if its interarrival times are independent and (negative) exponentially distributed (cf. Equation (2.84)). The number Γ of observed arrivals during a constant interval τ follows a Poisson distribution (cf. Equation (2.82a)).

In case the observation interval B is no longer constant, but is now arbitrarily distributed with probability density function $b(t)$, the distribution of the number Γ of arrivals during B will be derived in the following. Here the Poisson process has the rate λ, the observation window of length B (cf. Figure 3.11) is seen from an independent outside observer.

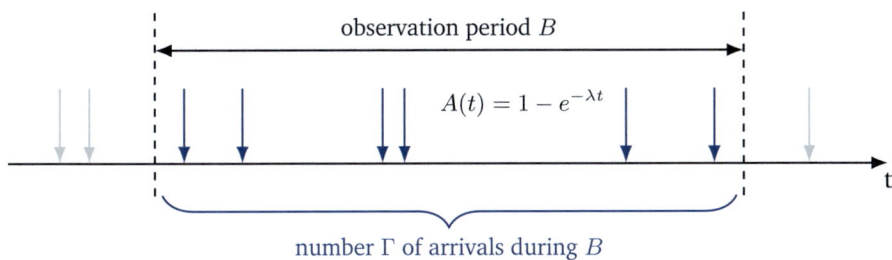

Figure 3.11: Poisson arrivals during an arbitrarily distributed interval B.

The number Γ of arrivals during B and its corresponding generating function are:

$$\gamma(i) = P(\Gamma = i) \quad \overset{\text{GF}}{\circ\!\!-\!\!\bullet} \quad \Gamma_{GF}(z) = \sum_{i=0}^{\infty} \gamma(i) z^i \ . \tag{3.19a}$$

Starting with the condition that the window is of exact length $B = \tau$, then Γ is Poisson distributed according to:

$$P(\Gamma = i \,|\, B = \tau) = \frac{(\lambda\tau)^i}{i!} e^{-\lambda\tau} \ . \tag{3.19b}$$

Applying the law of total probability, we obtain:

$$\gamma(i) = \int_0^{\infty} P(\Gamma = i \,|\, B = \tau) \underbrace{b(\tau)\, d\tau}_{P(B=\tau)} = \int_0^{\infty} \frac{(\lambda\tau)^i}{i!} e^{-\lambda\tau} b(\tau)\, d\tau \tag{3.19c}$$

with the generating function

$$\Gamma_{GF}(z) = \sum_{i=0}^{\infty} \gamma(i) z^i = \sum_{i=0}^{\infty} \int_0^{\infty} \frac{(\lambda\tau)^i}{i!} e^{-\lambda\tau} b(\tau) \, d\tau \; z^i$$

$$= \int_0^{\infty} e^{-\lambda\tau} b(\tau) \underbrace{\sum_{i=0}^{\infty} \frac{(\lambda\tau z)^i}{i!}}_{e^{\lambda\tau z}} \, d\tau = \int_0^{\infty} b(\tau) e^{-\lambda(1-z)\tau} \, d\tau \qquad (3.19d)$$

or finally

$$\Gamma_{GF}(z) = \Phi_B\Big(\lambda(1-z)\Big). \qquad (3.20)$$

This relationship is used in later chapters, e.g. in the analysis of the M/GI/1 system in Chapter 5.3.4.

Example: Poisson Arrivals During an Exponentially Distributed Interval The observation interval B follows a negative exponential distribution with parameter μ: $B \sim \mathrm{EXP}(\mu)$. The Laplace transform of the exponential distribution is $\Phi_B(s) = \frac{\mu}{\mu+s}$, see Equation (2.84d). Then, the generating function of the number Γ of arrivals during B is

$$\Gamma_{GF}(z) = \Phi_B\Big(\lambda(1-z)\Big) = \frac{\mu}{\mu + \lambda(1-z)} = \frac{\mu}{\mu + \lambda - z\lambda - z\mu + z\mu}$$

$$= \frac{\mu}{(\lambda + \mu) - z(\lambda + \mu) + z\mu} = \frac{\frac{\mu}{\lambda+\mu}}{1 - z + z\frac{\mu}{\lambda+\mu}}$$

$$= \frac{p}{1 - z + z \cdot p} \quad \text{with} \quad p = \frac{\mu}{\lambda + \mu}.$$

This is the probability generating function $\Gamma_{GF}(z)$ of a geometric distribution with parameter $p = \frac{\mu}{\lambda+\mu}$, see Equation (2.78c): $\Gamma_{GF}(z) = \frac{p}{1-z+pz}$.

This can be interpreted in the following way. There is a series of events following a Poisson process with rate $\lambda + \mu$. With probability p, the event terminates the observation interval. With probability $q = 1 - p = \frac{\lambda}{\lambda+mu}$, the event is an arrival event. The number of arrival events during the exponentially distributed interval follows therefore a geometric distribution.

3.4 Superposition of Independent Renewal Processes

Here it is appropriate to take a generalized look at the superposition of renewal processes. In the context of a queueing system, the arrival stream of all customers into a system is the superposition of the customers which are coming from n distinct sources. If the individual processes emerging from the sources are Poisson processes, the superposition will also be a Poisson process (see Figure 3.9). Even if the n single processes are not Poisson processes and if n is large enough, it is possible to approximate the superposition by a Poisson process which is formulated as the Palm-Khintchine theorem.

It is important to take notice that, in general, the superposition of independent renewal processes is not necessarily a renewal process. A simple example are deterministic sources which are generating periodic arrivals. However, even in that case, we may approximate the superposition as a Poisson process, which will be discussed in detail in Chapter 7.2.1 on advanced traffic models in the Internet of Things.

3.4.1 Superposition of Poisson Processes

The superposition of n independent Poisson processes with arrival rates $\lambda_1, \ldots, \lambda_n$ follows a Poisson process with the total rate $\sum_{i=1}^{n} \lambda_i$, which has been derived already in Equation (3.17).

$$A_i \sim \text{EXP}(\lambda_i) \tag{3.21a}$$

$$A \sim \text{EXP}(\sum_i \lambda_i) \qquad \text{superposition of Poisson processes} \tag{3.21b}$$

3.4.2 Palm-Khintchine Theorem

In practice, a large number of independent sources which are generating requests in a system is often observed. The superposition of the arrival requests is then the total arrival process A^* in such a system. Assuming that the arrival processes $i = 1, \ldots, n$ are independent, and renewal processes with distribution A_i, the arrival rate of the individual renewal processes is then $\lambda_i = \frac{1}{\text{E}[A_i]}$ according to the strong law for renewal processes (cf. Chapter 3.2.1).

Palm-Khintchine Theorem

The superposition of a large number of independent renewal processes, each with a finite intensity, behaves asymptotically like a Poisson process for $n \to \infty$:

$$A^* \sim \mathrm{EXP}(\sum_i \lambda_i) \tag{3.22}$$

if the following two conditions are fulfilled:

1. the overall load is finite, $\sum_i \lambda_i < \infty$,

2. no single process dominates the superposition, $\lambda_k \ll \sum_i \lambda_i$ for any k.

Example: Superposition of Uniformly Distributed Interarrival Times   As an example consider the superposition of n processes with uniformly distributed interarrival times in the interval $[0; 2]$: $A_i \sim U(0, 2 \cdot n)$. The mean interarrival time is $\mathrm{E}[A_i] = n$ with rate $\lambda_i = 1/n$. Then, the superposition process has an overall rate λ^* which is the sum of the individual rates: $\lambda^* = \sum_{i=1}^{n} \lambda_i = \frac{n}{n} = 1$. Hence the overall load λ^* is finite, and no single process dominates the superposition.

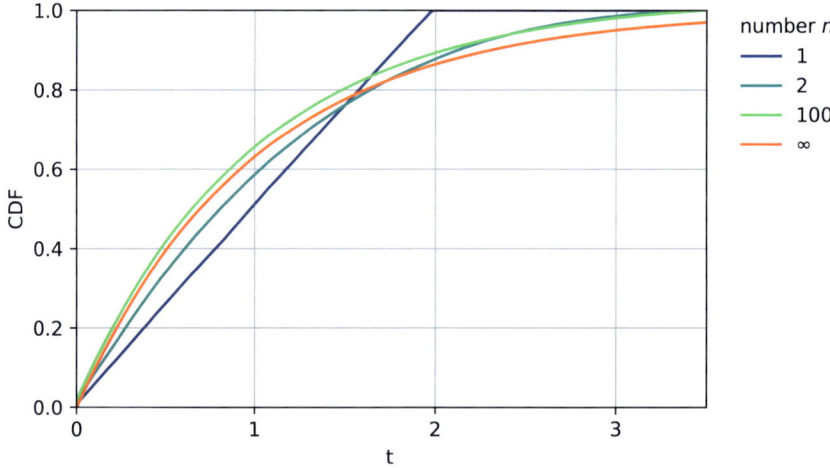

Figure 3.12: Superposition of n processes with uniformly distributed interarrival times converges towards a Poisson process with the corresponding rate; $\lambda^* = 1$ in this example.

Figure 3.12 shows the cumulative distribution function of the interarrival times A^* of the superposition process for different number of n independent sources for this example. If there is only a single source ($n = 1$), a uniform distribution is observed. With increasing n, the distribution A^* converges towards an exponential distribution with rate λ^*. If there are only 100 independent sources, the difference to the Poisson process may be negligible. In Chapter 7.2.1, we derive guidelines and quantify when is n large enough, such that the bias between the approximating Poisson process and the superposition process is below a threshold.

Remark: In Kendall's notation the superposition of the arrival process is often denoted in the following way: $\sum_i GI_i/\bullet/\bullet$. Please note that the sum sign in Kendall's notation must not be confused with the sum of r.v.s. If the individual arrival processes follow the same distribution, this is also denoted as $n \cdot GI/\bullet/\bullet$. In particular, this may be used for aggregated periodic arrival streams, e.g. $nD/M/1$.

3.5 Markov State Process

This section discusses the analysis of the class of discrete-state, continuous-time state processes which have the Markov property (or memoryless property) as characterized in Equation (3.1). The index set of this class of stochastic processes is normally the real values on the time axis, and the state space are non-negative integers. A formal definition of the continuous-time Markov chain is given in the following.

3.5.1 Definition of Continuous-Time Markov Chain

A *continuous-time Markov process* is a stochastic process $\{X(t), t \geq 0\}$ which has the Markov property. The future evolution of the process only depends on the current system state $X(t)$ at time t. If the state space S is discrete (which is the case here), we obtain a special type of Markov process, referred to as *continuous-time Markov chain (CTMC)*. This definition includes

- finite or countable state space S, e.g. $S = \{0, 1, 2, \ldots\}$ is the number of customers in a system,

- transition rates $q_{ij} \geq 0$ for $i \neq j$ and $i, j \in S$,

- initial state $X(0)$, i.e. a probability distribution for initial state.

The probability $P(X(t) = i) = x(i, t)$ for $i \in S$ describes the system at time t which is the probability that the system is in state $[X = i]$ at time t. The vector $\mathbf{X}(t) = \big(x(t, 0), x(t, 1), x(t, 2), \ldots\big)$ is a compact representation.

For $i \neq j$, the rates q_{ij} are non-negative and describe the rate of the process transitions from state i to state j. The rates are aggregated in the rate matrix Q with $q_{ii} = -\sum_{i \neq j} q_{ij}$. This allows a compact notation of the evolution of the Markov chain (Kolmogorov equations in Chapter 3.5.3) in the matrix representation. Note that the row-wise sums of Q are 0.

For a continuous-time Markov chain, the system remains in the state i for a period of time T_i that is exponentially distributed with rate $q_i = -q_{ii} > 0$, whenever the process enters state i. The reason is that the time T_{ij} which is required to change from state i to j is assumed to follow an exponential distribution, $T_{ij} \sim \text{EXP}(q_{ij})$. The minimum of T_{ij} for any $j \neq i$ follows also an exponential distribution, as shown in Chapter 2.2.6.7.

$$T_i = \min_{i \neq j}\{T_{ij}\} \sim \text{EXP}(q_i) \text{ with } q_i = \sum_{i \neq j} q_{ij} = -q_{ii} \tag{3.23}$$

When the process leaves state i, the state $j \neq i$ is reached with probability p_{ij}.

$$p_{ij} = \frac{q_{ij}}{q_i} = \frac{q_{ij}}{\sum_{i \neq j} q_{ij}} \tag{3.24}$$

In the following, the system is analyzed and the transition behavior of the Markovian state process is derived leading to the Kolmogorov equations.

3.5.2 Transition Behavior of Markovian State Processes

If the state of the process is known at a certain time t_n, then, according to the Markov property, the future development of the process only depends on the state $[X(t_n) = x_n]$. The state $[X(t_n) = x_n]$ is thought of to contain all information relevant to estimate the process development in the future.

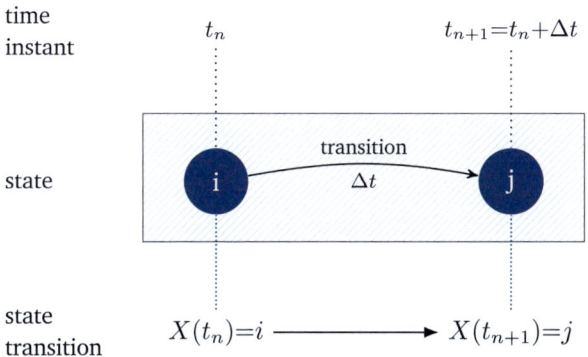

Figure 3.13: State transition from state i at time t_n to state j at time t_{n+1}.

Transition Probability   Consider the development of the process during the interval between two successive process times t_n and t_{n+1} with the respective states $[X(t_n) = i]$ and $[X(t_{n+1}) = j]$ (cf. Figure 3.13).

The state transition $i \rightarrow j$ during this interval occurs with the transition probability

$$p_{ij}(t_n, t_{n+1}) = P(X(t_{n+1}) = j | X(t_n) = i) . \tag{3.25}$$

If the state process is time-homogeneous, i.e. the transition behavior is identical for each process point in time, the transition probability is independent of the observation instant, i.e.

$$p_{ij}(t_n, t_{n+1}) = p_{ij}(t_{n+1} - t_n) = p_{ij}(\Delta t) , \tag{3.26a}$$

with the standardization condition

$$\sum_j p_{ij}(\Delta t) = 1 , \quad \Delta t \geq 0 , \tag{3.26b}$$

which holds for all i. The transition probability $p_{ij}(\Delta t)$ in this equation describes the transition behavior of the state process during an interval of length Δt.

The transition probabilities $\{p_{ij}(\Delta t)\,,\ i,j=0,1,\dots\}$ form the transition matrix:

$$
\mathcal{P}(\Delta t) =
\begin{pmatrix}
p_{00}(\Delta t) & p_{01}(\Delta t) & \cdots & p_{0j}(\Delta t) & \cdots \\
p_{10}(\Delta t) & p_{11}(\Delta t) & \cdots & p_{1j}(\Delta t) & \cdots \\
\vdots & \vdots & & \vdots & \\
p_{i0}(\Delta t) & p_{i1}(\Delta t) & \cdots & p_{ij}(\Delta t) & \cdots \\
\vdots & \vdots & & \vdots &
\end{pmatrix}.
\tag{3.27}
$$

3.5.3 State Equations and State Probabilities

Kolmogorov Forward Equation   At the starting point $t_0 = 0$ the process is in a starting state $[X(0) = i]$ (cf. Figure 3.14). As the development proceeds, the system passes various possible intermediate states k to reach the target state $[X(t+\Delta t) = j]$.

The matrices of the transition probabilities for the intervals t and Δt are $\mathcal{P}(t)$ and $\mathcal{P}(\Delta t)$. The resulting transition matrix is the product of these sub-matrices:

$$
\mathcal{P}(t + \Delta t) = \mathcal{P}(t) \cdot \mathcal{P}(\Delta t)
\qquad
\textbf{Chapman-Kolmogorov equation}
\tag{3.28a}
$$

or

$$
p_{ij}(t + \Delta t) = \sum_{k} p_{ik}(t) \cdot p_{kj}(\Delta t) .
\tag{3.28b}
$$

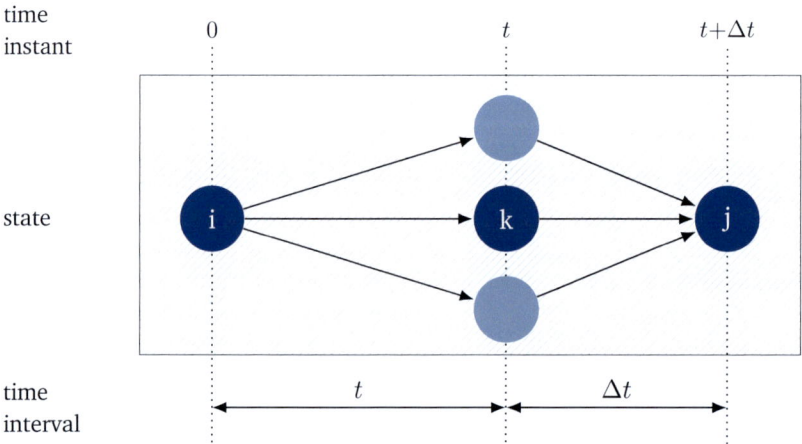

Figure 3.14: On the derivation of the Kolmogorov forward equation.

State Equations   Equation (3.28b) can be formulated as

$$\frac{p_{ij}(t + \Delta t) - p_{ij}(t)}{\Delta t} = \sum_{k \neq j} p_{ik}(t) \frac{p_{kj}(\Delta t)}{\Delta t} - p_{ij}(t) \frac{1 - p_{jj}(\Delta t)}{\Delta t} \tag{3.29a}$$

where at the limit $\Delta t \to 0$ the interpretations of the terms of this equation are:

- $$\lim_{\Delta t \to 0} \frac{p_{ij}(t + \Delta t) - p_{ij}(t)}{\Delta t} = \frac{d}{dt} p_{ij}(t) \tag{3.29b}$$
  first derivative of the transition probabilities $p_{ij}(t)$ at time t

- $$\lim_{\Delta t \to 0} \frac{p_{kj}(\Delta t)}{\Delta t} = q_{kj} , \quad k \neq j \tag{3.29c}$$
  transition probability density for the transition $k \to j$

- $$\lim_{\Delta t \to 0} \frac{1 - p_{jj}(\Delta t)}{\Delta t} = q_j = \sum_{k \neq j} q_{jk} \tag{3.29d}$$
  transition probability density for leaving of the state j

With the limit $\Delta t \to 0$ in this equation, we are dealing with a new probabilistic measure: the *transition probability density* which is often also referred to as *rate*. This has the unit $[\frac{1}{s}]$ and describes the "tendency to change" of a probability in an infinitesimally small interval. The Kolmogorov forward equation for transition probabilities is obtained from Equation (3.29a) and with the limits in Equations (3.29b)–(3.29d):

$$\frac{d}{dt} p_{ij}(t) = \sum_{k \neq j} q_{kj} p_{ik}(t) - q_j p_{ij}(t) . \tag{3.30}$$

Kolmogorov Forward Equation in Matrix Notation   Similar to the matrix notation of the transition probabilities $\mathcal{P}(t)$ in Equation (3.27) the matrix for transition probability densities is defined

$$\mathcal{Q} = \begin{pmatrix} q_{00} & q_{01} & \cdots & q_{0j} & \cdots \\ q_{10} & q_{11} & \cdots & q_{1j} & \cdots \\ \vdots & \vdots & \ddots & \vdots & \\ q_{j0} & q_{j1} & \cdots & q_{jj} & \cdots \\ \vdots & \vdots & & \vdots & \ddots \end{pmatrix} . \qquad \text{rate matrix} \tag{3.31a}$$

This matrix $\mathcal{Q}$, also called the *rate matrix* and is the infinitesimal generator matrix of the continuous-time Markov process.

The row-wise sum is

$$\sum_{k} q_{jk} = 0 \, , \tag{3.31b}$$

and the probability density for remaining in the state j:

$$q_{jj} = -\sum_{k \neq j} q_{jk} = -q_j \, . \tag{3.31c}$$

It should be noted here that the notation "$-q_j$" does not imply that there is a negative rate or negative probability density; it is solely the notation for the "rate" to stay in state j. In doing so it complies with the Kolmogorov equation notation that the sum of all elements in a row of the matrix is zero.

Finally, from Equation (3.30) the matrix notation of the Kolmogorov forward equation is obtained.

$$\frac{d\mathcal{P}(t)}{dt} = \mathcal{P}(t) \cdot \mathcal{Q} \qquad \text{**Kolmogorov forward equation**} \tag{3.32}$$

The solution of Equation (3.32) requires the computation of the matrix exponential of the matrix $t\mathcal{Q}$ for which efficient implementations exist [93, 33]:

$$\mathcal{P}(t) = e^{t\mathcal{Q}} = \sum_{k=0}^{\infty} \frac{(t\mathcal{Q})^k}{k!} \, . \tag{3.33}$$

Kolmogorov Backward Equation In the derivation of the Kolmogorov forward equation, the future development of the state process from the current process state is considered. With this equation the future development of the process can be investigated.

Alternatively, if the goal is to investigate the development path of the process until the state at the time of observation is reached, the so-called *Kolmogorov backward equation* can be derived with similar steps. As shown in Figure 3.15, the process is in state $[X(0) = j]$ at the observation time $t = 0$. The initial state at time $-t - \Delta t$ is $[X(-t - \Delta t) = i]$. The development path of the state process passes through various intermediate states k before reaching the target state.

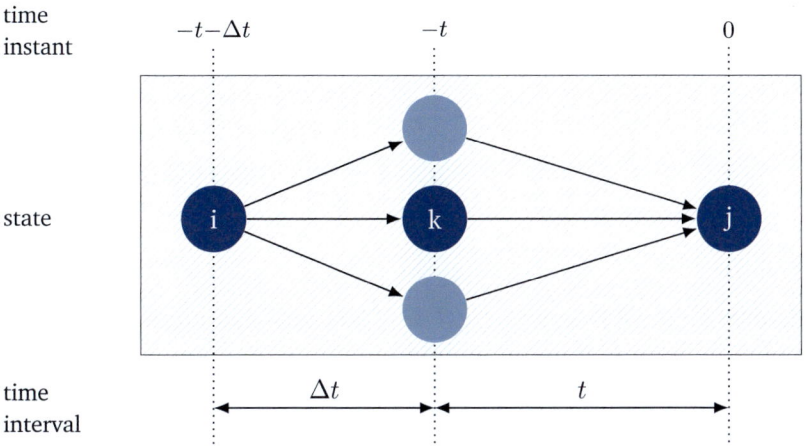

Figure 3.15: On the derivation of the Kolmogorov backward equation.

The transition matrices for the intervals Δt and t are $\mathcal{P}(\Delta t)$ and $\mathcal{P}(t)$. Analogous to the Chapman-Kolmogorov equation, the resulting transition matrix is the product of these transition matrices:

$$\mathcal{P}(t + \Delta t) = \mathcal{P}(\Delta t) \cdot \mathcal{P}(t) \tag{3.34}$$

or

$$p_{ij}(t + \Delta t) = \sum_k p_{ik}(\Delta t) \cdot p_{kj}(t)$$

or

$$\frac{p_{ij}(t + \Delta t) - p_{ij}(t)}{\Delta t} = \sum_{k \neq i} \frac{p_{ik}(\Delta t)}{\Delta t} \cdot p_{kj}(t) - p_{ij}(t) \cdot \frac{1 - p_{ii}(\Delta t)}{\Delta t} \ .$$

With the limit $\Delta t \to 0$ we obtain

$$\frac{d}{dt} p_{ij}(t) = \sum_{k \neq i} q_{ik} \cdot p_{kj}(t) - p_{ij}(t) \cdot \underbrace{q_i}_{-q_{ii}}$$

$$= \sum_k q_{ik} \cdot p_{kj}(t) \ .$$

In matrix notation we arrive at the Kolmogorov backward equation:

$$\frac{d\mathcal{P}(t)}{dt} = \mathcal{Q} \cdot \mathcal{P}(t) \, . \qquad \textbf{\textcolor{blue}{Kolmogorov backward equation}} \quad (3.35)$$

While the Kolmogorov forward equation is suitable for analyzing state probabilities, the Kolmogorov backward equation is often used to investigate sojourn time distribution functions in performance models.

Kolmogorov Forward Equation for State Probabilities   Beginning with

$$x(j, t) = P(X(t) = j) \, , \quad j = 0, 1, \dots \, ,$$

then the probability exists for the system to be in state j at time t. From the initial state $x(i, 0)$, the state $x(j, t)$ can be determined applying the law of total probability:

$$x(j, t) = \sum_i P(X(t) = j | X(0) = i) \cdot P(X(0) = i) = \sum_i x(i, 0) \cdot p_{ij}(t). \quad (3.36)$$

After multiplying the terms of the Kolmogorov forward equation (3.30) with $x(i, 0)$ and summing for all i, the result is

$$\underbrace{\sum_i \frac{d}{dt} p_{ij}(t) \, x(i, 0)}_{\frac{\partial}{\partial t} x(j, t)} = \sum_{k \neq j} q_{kj} \underbrace{\sum_i \left(p_{ik}(t) \, x(i, 0) \right)}_{x(k, t)} - \underbrace{\sum_i \left(q_j \, p_{ij}(t) \, x(i, 0) \right)}_{q_j \cdot x(j, t)} \, .$$

$$(3.37)$$

From Equation (3.37) we can derive the system of differential equations

$$\frac{\partial}{\partial t} x(j, t) = \sum_{k \neq j} q_{kj} \, x(k, t) \; - \; q_j \, x(j, t) \, , \quad j = 0, 1, \dots \, , \qquad (3.38a)$$

Kolmogorov forward equation for state probabilities

$$\sum_j x(j, t) = 1 \, . \qquad (3.38b)$$

The Kolmogorov forward equation for state probabilities describes the development of state process $X(t)$ which are in state j at time t. An infinitesimally small time window dt is considered immediately after the observation time t.

Using the system of differential equations (3.38a) transient state probabilities can be calculated for the general case of non-stationary Markov state processes. The result are the non-stationary state probabilities $\{x(j, t), \; j = 0, 1, \dots\}$. A transient state process analysis is e.g. necessary in performance evaluation of overload behavior in communication systems.

A compact representation of the Kolmogorov forward equation for state probabilities uses again the matrix notation. The vector $\mathbf{X}(t)$ contains the state probabilities $x(j, t)$ at time t for $j = 0, 1, \ldots$:

$$\mathbf{X}(t) = \big(x(0, t), x(1, t), \ldots, x(j, t), \ldots \big), \tag{3.39a}$$

and with the initial system state $\mathbf{X}(0)$ and the transition probability matrix $\mathcal{P}$:

$$\mathbf{X}(t) = X(0) \cdot \mathcal{P}(t). \tag{3.39b}$$

Finally, the matrix notation of the Kolmogorov forward equation for state probabilities is obtained:

$$\frac{d}{dt}\mathbf{X}(t) = \mathbf{X}(t) \cdot \mathcal{Q}. \qquad \textbf{Kolmogorov forward equation} \atop \textbf{for state probabilities} \tag{3.39c}$$

A detailed derivation of the stationary and transient state equations presented here can be found e.g. in Cooper [23] and Syski [100].

Stationary State Equation System If the system state stops changing, it reaches a steady state condition, where the state probability no longer depends on time t, i.e.

$$\frac{d}{dt}P(X(t) = j) = \frac{\partial}{\partial t}x(j, t) = 0, \tag{3.40}$$

the state process is said to reach a *statistical equilibrium* or is *stationary*. The stationary state probabilities are accordingly:

$$x(j) = \lim_{t \to \infty} P(X(t) = j), \quad j = 0, 1, \ldots. \tag{3.41}$$

Equations (3.38a) and (3.40) form an equation system for the analysis of stationary state probabilities of Markovian state processes:

$$q_j\, x(j) = \sum_{k \neq j} q_{kj} \cdot x(k), \quad j = 0, 1, \ldots, \qquad \text{stationary state equations} \tag{3.42a}$$

$$\sum_j x(j) = 1. \tag{3.42b}$$

The individual terms of the steady state equations (3.42a) can be interpreted as follows, whereby the state $[X = j]$ is balanced with the associated transitions with regard to the probability densities. We observe hereby the state $[X = j]$.

- $q_j \cdot x(j)$ - - - - - - - ►   (leaving state j in Figure 3.16)
  probability densities (rates) for leaving state j. Each rate is weighted with the state probability $x(j)$ itself.

- $\displaystyle\sum_{k \neq j} q_{kj} \cdot x(k)$ ──────►   (reaching state j in Figure 3.16)
  probability densities (rates) for reaching state j from other states $k \neq j$. Each rate is weighted with the probability $x(k)$ of state k, from which the respective transition starts.

- If the system is in stationary condition, the flows of weighted probability densities for reaching and leaving a state must be in equilibrium, i.e. they are the same, so that the state probability no longer changes in time. This fact is also called the *principle of maintaining statistical equilibrium* (cf. Bolch [12]) and leads to Equation (3.42). This is illustrated in Figure 3.16.

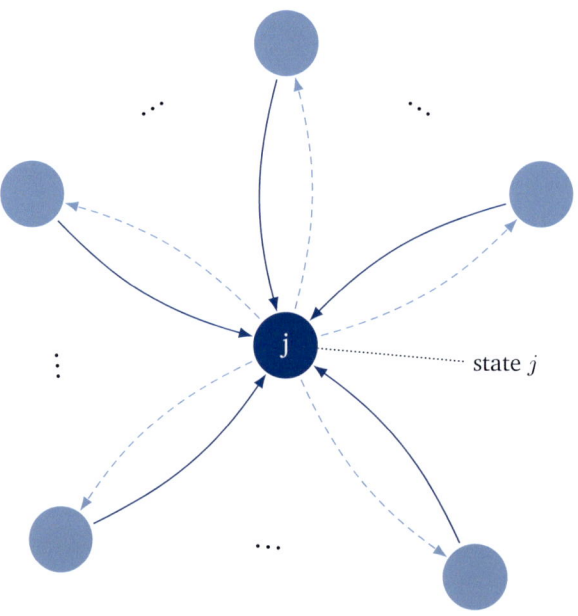

Figure 3.16: State $[X = j]$ in statistical equilibrium. Dashed arrows and solid arrows indicate leaving and reaching state j, respectively.

The state equation system in (3.42) is an important and frequently used relationship in the analysis of Markov state processes.

Matrix Notation for State Equations With the probabilities combined into a stationary state probability vector

$$\mathbf{X} = \big(x(0), x(1), \ldots, x(j), \ldots\big) , \tag{3.43}$$

the state equation system (3.42) can be written in matrix notation as:

$$\mathbf{X} \cdot Q = \mathbf{0} , \qquad\qquad \text{state equation system} \tag{3.44a}$$

where the normalization condition holds

$$\sum_j x(j) = 1 \quad \text{or} \quad \mathbf{X}\,\mathbf{e} = 1 . \tag{3.44b}$$

Here, e is a column vector which contains only ones.

For the solution of this equation system, a linear dependency between the state equations must be taken into account. This is discussed in the next section.

Linear Dependency of State Equations The equation system (3.42) to determine the state probabilities should now be examined in more detail. To accomplish this consider a finite state space $\{0, 1, \ldots, N\}$ with the state vector

$$\mathbf{X} = \big(x(0), x(1), \ldots, x(j), \ldots, x(N)\big) . \tag{3.45}$$

The stationary system of equations according to (3.42) then reads:

$$q_j\, x(j) = \sum_{k \neq j} q_{kj}\, x(k) , \quad j = 0, 1, \ldots, N , \tag{3.46a}$$

$$\sum_j x(j) = 1 \tag{3.46b}$$

and consists of $(N + 2)$ equations for $(N + 1)$ unknowns (state probabilities) $\{x(0), x(1), \ldots, x(N)\}$. The initially over-determined system of equations (3.46a) can easily be modified to a non-overdetermined system, since any arbitrarily chosen equation out of (3.46a) can be omitted due to linear dependency. The reason being that each equation in (3.46a) results from the summation of the remaining equations.

Macro State and Global Equilibrium Equation The construction of each equation of type (3.42a) or (3.46a) is based on the balance of the probability densities with regard to leaving and reaching a state $[X = j]$. A single state that cannot be further decomposed is also called a micro state. The equation system (3.42) or (3.46) is therefore called the stationary equation system for micro states.

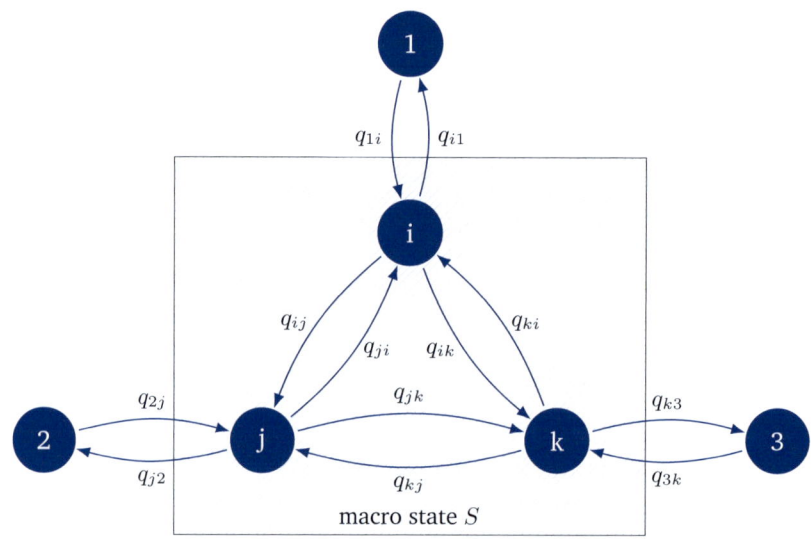

Figure 3.17: Macro state and related transitions.

The combination of any set of micro states leads to a macro state. Figure 3.17 shows an example of a macro state S which is composed of the states i, j and k. We sum up equations of all micro states contained in the macro state S:

$$+\begin{cases} (q_{i1} + q_{ij} + q_{ik})x(i) = q_{1i}x(1) + q_{ji}x(j) + q_{ki}x(k) \\ (q_{j2} + q_{jk} + q_{ji})x(j) = q_{2j}x(2) + q_{kj}x(k) + q_{ij}x(i) \\ (q_{k3} + q_{ki} + q_{kj})x(k) = q_{3k}x(3) + q_{ik}x(i) + q_{jk}x(j) \end{cases}$$

$$q_{i1}x(i) + q_{j2}x(j) + q_{k3}x(k) = q_{1i}x(1) + q_{2j}x(2) + q_{3k}x(3) \tag{3.47}$$

The result is the stationary state equation of the macro state S. The left side of Equation (3.47) contains the weighted rates (weighted transition probability densities) for leaving the macro state S, while the right side describes the rates for reaching S.

In general, the state equation for an *arbitrary* macro state can be given as follows:

$$\underbrace{\sum_{j \,\in\, S,\, u \,\notin\, S} q_{ju} x(j)}_{\substack{\text{weighted rates for leaving} \\ \text{the macro state } S}} \quad = \quad \underbrace{\sum_{u \,\notin\, S,\, j \,\in\, S} q_{uj} x(u)}_{\substack{\text{weighted rates for reaching} \\ \text{the macro state } S}} \qquad (3.48)$$

This equation puts in relation the transition probability densities between a macro state and the rest in the state space. It is a generalized form of the equilibrium equation, now applied on a set of micro states. The global equilibrium equations are also referred to as full or global balance equations.

It should be noted here that the purpose of Equation (3.48) is not to calculate the state probability of the entire macro state S. The terms for reaching or leaving the macro state contain state probabilities of the micro states inside and outside the macro state. As will be shown in later analysis examples, the clever selection of a macro state can often provide a simpler – and more structured – equation system to calculate the micro state probabilities.

3.5.4 Examples of Transition Probability Densities

Analytic performance models with Markov property, as discussed in the next chapter, often contain components such as Poisson arrival processes and servers with negative exponentially distributed service times. The corresponding rates (or transition probability densities) are derived below.

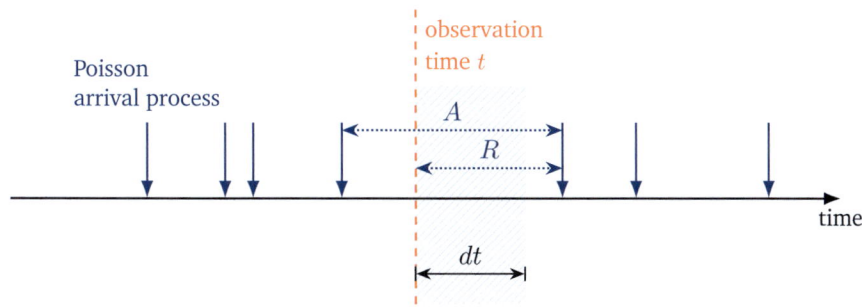

Figure 3.18: Transition probability density of Poisson arrival process during time dt.

Transition Probability Density of Poisson Arrival Process   Figure 3.18 depicts a state process with Poisson input traffic. The interarrival time A and its recurrence time have the same distribution function:

$$A(t) = R(t) = 1 - e^{-\lambda t} . \tag{3.49a}$$

The state process $X(t)$ at time t, assuming the state $[X(t) = i]$ can be observed. Analyzing the process development during the following *infinitesimal* short interval dt (cf. marked area in Figure 3.18), the probability density for a state transition $i \rightarrow i+1$, i.e. for a customer arrival during the period dt, is

$$\begin{aligned} q_{i,i+1} &= \lim_{dt \to 0} \frac{p_{i,i+1}(dt)}{dt} \\ &= \lim_{dt \to 0} \frac{P(R \leq dt)}{dt} = \lim_{dt \to 0} \frac{1 - e^{-\lambda dt}}{dt} \underset{\text{L'Hospital}}{=} \lambda \end{aligned} \tag{3.49b}$$

using L'Hospital's rule to derive the limit $\frac{0}{0}$.

Transition Probability Density for Exponential Service Time   Consider a state process $X(t)$. At time t there are k ongoing services in the system, i.e. k servers are active. The service times of the servers are independent and exponentially distributed.

Since the service process is memoryless, the recurrence time R of the service time B has the same distribution function as the service time itself:

$$R(t) = B(t) = 1 - e^{-\mu t} . \tag{3.50a}$$

As shown in Figure 3.19, the interval R^* until the next service termination is the minimum of k independent recurrence times:

$$R^* = \min\{\underbrace{R, \ \ldots, \ R}_{k\text{-times}}\}, \tag{3.50b}$$

i.e. according to Equation (2.65)

$$R^*(t) = 1 - \prod_{i=1}^{k}(1 - R(t)) = 1 - e^{-k\mu t} . \tag{3.50c}$$

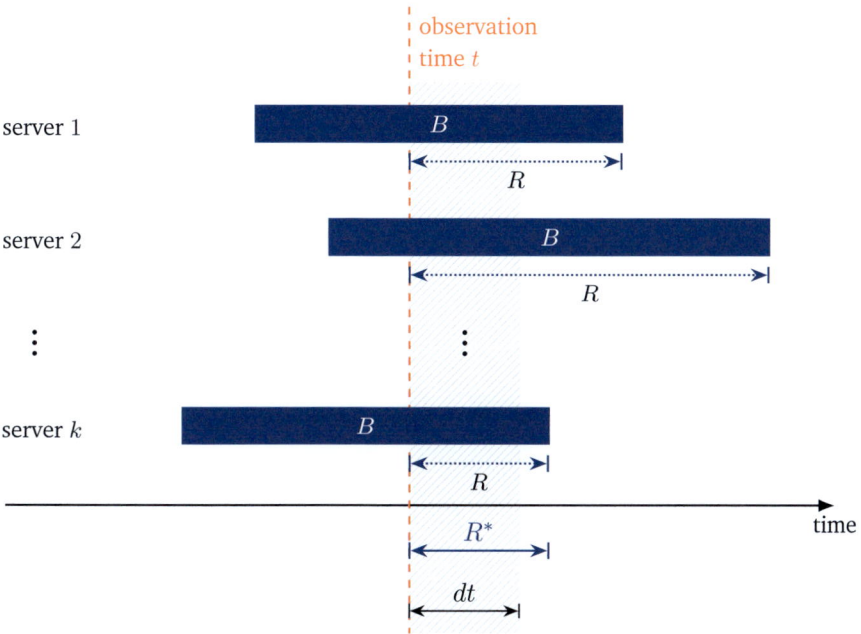

Figure 3.19: Transition rate for k exponential service times at time t.

Take an infinitesimally short interval dt. During this interval, the probability that several service times terminate is negligible. The probability density for a service termination, i.e. for a transition $k \to k - 1$, during this infinitesimally short interval $(t, t + dt)$ is analogous to Equation (3.49b):

$$
\begin{aligned}
q_{k,k-1} &= \lim_{dt \to 0} \frac{p_{k,k-1}(dt)}{dt} \\
&= \lim_{dt \to 0} \frac{P(R^* \leq dt)}{dt} = \lim_{dt \to 0} \frac{1 - e^{-k\mu dt}}{dt} \underset{\text{L'Hospital}}{=} k\mu \,.
\end{aligned}
\tag{3.50d}
$$

3.5.5 Birth-and-Death Processes

3.5.5.1 Definition and State Process Description

Birth-and-Death processes (BD processes) are Markov processes in which only transitions between neighboring states occur. We often have BD processes having state processes with one-dimensional state space, in which the neighborhood of a state (cf. Figure 3.20) is unambiguously defined. In some Markov models with multi-dimensional state spaces, however, the term BD process is used when there are only transitions between neighboring states in each direction of the state space.

Consider a finite-state, one-dimensional Birth-and-Death process, as depicted in Figure 3.20.

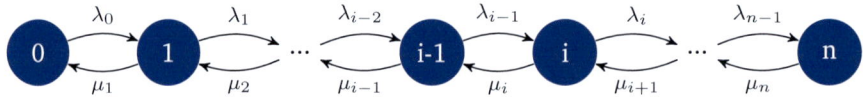

Figure 3.20: Finite-state, one-dimensional birth-and-death process.

The transition probability densities (rates) are:

$$q_{ij} = \begin{cases} \lambda_i & i = 0, 1, \ldots, n-1, \quad j = i+1 \quad \text{birth rate} \\ \mu_i & i = 1, 2, \ldots, n, \qquad j = i-1 \quad \text{death rate} \\ 0 & \text{otherwise} \end{cases} \tag{3.51}$$

with the special cases:

- all $\mu_i = 0$: pure birth process; in statistical equilibrium the state process approaches
  $x(n) = P(X = n) = 1$, $x(i) = 0$ otherwise;

- all $\lambda_i = 0$: pure death-process; in statistical equilibrium the state process approaches
  $x(0) = P(X = 0) = 1$, $x(i) = 0$ otherwise.

3.5.5.2 Non-stationary Birth-and-Death Processes

In the general non-stationary case, the state equations to determine transient (time-dependent) state probabilities of the Birth-and-Death process, with the state space depicted in Figure 3.20, can be derived from Equation (3.38a) as follows:

$$\frac{\partial}{\partial t}x(0,t) = -\lambda_0 x(0,t) + \mu_1 x(1,t) , \qquad\qquad i = 0 , \qquad\qquad (3.52\text{a})$$

$$\frac{\partial}{\partial t}x(i,t) = -(\lambda_i + \mu_i)x(i,t) + \lambda_{i-1}x(i-1,t) + \mu_{i+1}x(i+1,t) , \qquad (3.52\text{b})$$

$$i = 1,\ldots,n-1 ,$$

$$\frac{\partial}{\partial t}x(n,t) = -\mu_n x(n,t) + \lambda_{n-1}x(n-1,t) , \qquad\qquad i = n . \qquad\qquad (3.52\text{c})$$

The solution of this differential equation system with the initial conditions

$$\{x(i,0) , i = 0,\ldots,n\} \qquad\qquad (3.53\text{a})$$

leads to the state probability vector

$$\mathbf{X}(t) = \big(x(0,t), x(1,t), \ldots, x(n,t)\big) \qquad\qquad (3.53\text{b})$$

at observation time t.

Example: Poisson Process as Pure Birth Process The Poisson process and its properties have been discussed in Chapter 3.3. Consider now the Poisson process as pure birth process. The customer arrival process of a system is modeled with a Poisson process with rate λ. We observe the number $X(t)$ of customers in the system at time t

$$P(X(t) = i) = x(i,t) . \qquad\qquad (3.54\text{a})$$

Starting the observation at time $t_0 = 0$, we want to know how many customers are in the system at time t. At start, there are no customers in the system

$$x(0,0) = 1 ; \quad x(i,0) = 0 , \quad i = 1,2,\ldots . \qquad\qquad (3.54\text{b})$$

The resulting state process with infinite state space ($n \to \infty$) is a pure birth process with the birth rate λ:

$$q_{ij} = \begin{cases} \lambda & \text{for } j = i+1, \quad i = 0,1,\ldots \\ 0 & \text{otherwise} . \end{cases} \qquad\qquad (3.55)$$

From Equation (3.52a) for non-stationary state analysis, the state equation system is obtained

$$\frac{\partial}{\partial t}x(0,t) = -\lambda x(0,t) \qquad\qquad (3.56\text{a})$$

$$\frac{\partial}{\partial t}x(i,t) = -\lambda x(i,t) + \lambda x(i-1,t) , \quad i = 1,2,\ldots . \qquad\qquad (3.56\text{b})$$

Applying Laplace transform

$$x(i, t) \overset{LT}{\circ\!\!-\!\!\bullet} \Phi_X(i, s)$$

$$\frac{\partial}{\partial t} x(i, t) \overset{LT}{\circ\!\!-\!\!\bullet} s\Phi_X(i, s) - x(i, 0)$$

the differential equation system (3.56) is converted to a linear equation system as follows:

$$s\Phi_X(0, s) - 1 = -\lambda\Phi_X(0, s) \tag{3.58a}$$

$$s\Phi_X(i, s) - 0 = -\lambda\Phi_X(i, s) + \lambda\Phi_X(i - 1, s), \quad i = 1, 2, \dots. \tag{3.58b}$$

With successive insertion, it results in:

$$\Phi_X(i, s) = \frac{\lambda^i}{(s + \lambda)^{i+1}}, \quad i = 0, 1\dots \tag{3.59a}$$

$$\updownarrow LT$$

$$x(i, t) = P(X(t) = i) = \frac{(\lambda t)^i}{i!} e^{-\lambda t}, \quad i = 0, 1, \dots, \quad t \geq 0. \tag{3.59b}$$

$X(t)$ follows the Poisson distribution, which was derived here using a pure birth process model in accordance to non-stationary Birth-and-Death processes.

3.5.5.3 Stationary Birth-and-Death Processes

In statistical equilibrium, the equation system (3.42) for the micro states of the state space in Figure 3.20 results in:

$$\lambda_0 x(0) = \mu_1 x(1), \tag{3.60a}$$

$$(\lambda_i + \mu_i)x(i) = \lambda_{i-1}x(i-1) + \mu_{i+1}x(i+1), \quad i = 1, 2, \dots, n-1, \tag{3.60b}$$

$$\lambda_{n-1}x(n-1) = \mu_n x(n), \tag{3.60c}$$

$$\sum_{i=0}^{n} x(i) = 1, \tag{3.60d}$$

where again, any equation from (3.60a), (3.60b), (3.60c) is the result of summing all the other equations. By eliminating an equation from (3.60a), (3.60b), (3.60c) we obtain together with Equation (3.60d) an equation system of $n + 1$ equations to determine the $n + 1$ state probabilities.

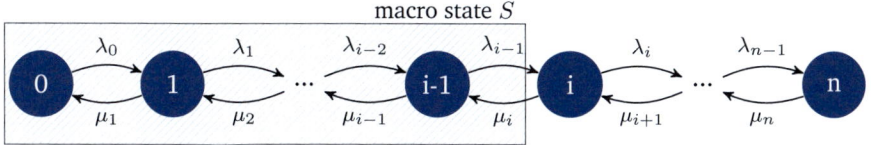

Figure 3.21: Macro state consideration for macro state equation system.

With the choice of the macro state S which consists of the micro states $\{X = 0, 1, \ldots, i - 1\}$ (cf. Figure 3.21) a simpler equation system can be derived using the macro state observation:

$$\lambda_{i-1}\, x(i - 1) = \mu_i\, x(i)\,, \quad i = 1, 2, \ldots, n \tag{3.61a}$$

$$\sum_{i=0}^{n} x(i) = 1\,. \tag{3.61b}$$

The solution of this equation system can be obtained by successively inserting Equation (3.61a) in itself:

$$x(i) = x(0) \cdot \frac{\displaystyle\prod_{k=0}^{i-1} \lambda_k}{\displaystyle\prod_{k=1}^{i} \mu_k}\,, \quad i = 1, 2, \ldots, n\,. \tag{3.62a}$$

The still unknown probability $x(0)$ can be calculated using the normalization condition from Equation (3.61b):

$$1 = \sum_{i=0}^{n} x(i) = x(0) + x(0) \sum_{i=1}^{n} \frac{\displaystyle\prod_{k=0}^{i-1} \lambda_k}{\displaystyle\prod_{k=1}^{i} \mu_k} \tag{3.62b}$$

yielding

$$x(0)^{-1} = 1 + \sum_{i=1}^{n} \frac{\displaystyle\prod_{k=0}^{i-1} \lambda_k}{\displaystyle\prod_{k=1}^{i} \mu_k}\,. \tag{3.62c}$$

Example: Delay-Loss System with State-dependent Rates   A delay-loss system is now investigated which consists of two servers, each working with service rate μ. The service time B follows an exponential distribution with parameter μ: $B \sim \text{EXP}(\mu)$. The system has one single waiting place if an arriving customer finds both servers occupied. The system can be in state $[X = i]$ for $i = 0, 1, 2, 3$. Figure 3.22 visualizes the state transition diagram for the system.

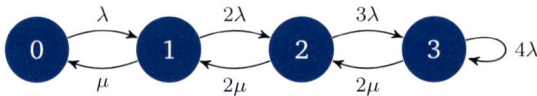

Figure 3.22: Delay-loss system M(x)/M/2-1 as an example for birth-and-death process with state-dependent arrival rates.

Customers arrive to the system with state-dependent arrival rates:

$$\lambda_i = (i + 1)\lambda , \quad i = 0, 1, 2, 3 .$$

Hence, the interarrival times A_i depend on the actual system state $[X = i]$ and follow an exponential distribution:

$$A_i \sim \text{EXP}(\lambda_i) , \quad i = 0, 1, 2, 3 .$$

Kendall's notation for the system is M(x)/M/2-1 whereby M(x) indicates state-dependent arrival rates. Therefore, the arrival process is *not* a Poisson process, and the PASTA property must not be used: $x_A(i) \neq x^*(i)$.

The arbitrary-time state probabilities $x^*(i) = x(i)$ are provided in Equation (3.62) for a birth-and-death process. However, we are interested in the blocking probability p_B and the waiting probability p_W which requires $x_A(i)$ for *arriving customers*.

The expected number of arrivals when the system is in state $[X = i]$ is

$$n_A(i, T) = \lambda_i \cdot x(i) \cdot T \tag{3.63a}$$

in an interval of length T. Hence, the time in state $[X = i]$ is $x(i) \cdot T$. The expected total number $n_A(T)$ of arrivals in an interval of length T is

$$n_A(T) = \sum_i n_A(i, T) = \sum_i \lambda_i \cdot x(i) \cdot T = \bar{\lambda} \cdot T \text{ with } \bar{\lambda} = \sum_i \lambda_i x(i) . \tag{3.63b}$$

Then, the steady state probability than an arriving customers finds the system in state $[X = i]$ for $i = 0, 1, \ldots$ is

$$x_A(i) = \lim_{T \to \infty} \frac{n_A(i, T)}{n_A(T)} = \frac{\lambda_i \cdot x(i)}{\sum_k \lambda_k \cdot x(k)}, \qquad \text{strong law of large numbers for} \quad (3.63c)$$

strong law of large numbers for Markov chains (3.63c)

which is known as the strong law of large numbers for Markov chains (cf. Fisz [37]).

Coming back to the previous example in Figure 3.22, the following arbitrary-time probabilities are obtained with Equation (3.62) and $\lambda = \mu = 1$:

$$x(0) = \left(1 + \frac{\lambda_0}{\mu_1} + \frac{\lambda_0 \lambda_1}{\mu_1 \mu_2} + \frac{\lambda_0 \lambda_1 \lambda_2}{\mu_1 \mu_2 \mu_3} \right)^{-1} = \frac{4}{18}$$

$$x(1) = x(0) \cdot \frac{\lambda_0}{\mu_1} = \frac{4}{18}$$

$$x(2) = x(0) \cdot \frac{\lambda_0 \lambda_1}{\mu_1 \mu_2} = \frac{4}{18}$$

$$x(3) = x(0) \cdot \frac{\lambda_0 \lambda_1 \lambda_2}{\mu_1 \mu_2 \mu_3} = \frac{6}{18}$$

The steady state probabilities for arriving customers are provided in Equation (3.63c) with the mean arrival rate $\bar{\lambda}$:

$$\bar{\lambda} = \sum_{i=0}^{3} \lambda_i x(i) = \frac{8}{3}$$

$$x_A(0) = \lambda_0 x(0) / \bar{\lambda} = \frac{1}{12}$$

$$x_A(1) = \lambda_1 x(1) / \bar{\lambda} = \frac{2}{12}$$

$$x_A(2) = \lambda_2 x(2) / \bar{\lambda} = \frac{3}{12}$$

$$x_A(3) = \lambda_3 x(3) / \bar{\lambda} = \frac{6}{12}$$

Finally, an arriving customer is blocked, when there are $[X_A = 3]$ other customers in the system (two customers are served, one customer is waiting). The blocking probability is $p_B = x_A(3)$. Analogously, the waiting probability is $p_W = x_A(2)$ if both servers are occupied, but the waiting place is empty, and the system is in state $[X_A = 2]$.

Analysis of Markovian Systems

Queueing systems with Markov property (or memoryless property) form the majority of models employed in performance modeling in general and of communication systems in particular. They belong to the basic repertoire of classic traffic models, which are dealt with in most textbooks in great detail (Cooper [23], Gross and Harris [41, 97], Kleinrock [61, 62], Tijms [105], Daigle [26]). In this chapter a number of key queueing models with Markov property are described and analyzed. Here, we consider models which consist mainly of Poisson arrival processes and negative exponentially distributed service times.

4.1 Loss System M/M/n

4.1.1 Model Structure and Parameters

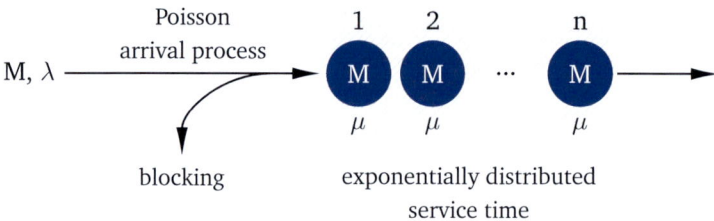

Figure 4.1: Loss system M/M/n.

The structure of the M/M/n loss system (or M/M/n-0 system) is depicted in Figure 4.1. According to the Kendall notation, the arrival process is a Poisson process, i.e. the interarrival time A is (negative) exponentially distributed. The service time B also follows a (negative) exponential distribution:

$$A(t) = P(A \leq t) = 1 - e^{-\lambda t} , \qquad E[A] = \frac{1}{\lambda} ,$$

$$B(t) = P(B \leq t) = 1 - e^{-\mu t} , \qquad E[B] = \frac{1}{\mu} .$$

The parameter λ is the arrival rate, which stands for the mean number of customer arrivals per time unit. Analogously μ is called the service rate, which can be thought of as a measure for the speed of the server.

Here, we consider the pure loss or blocking operation mode, i.e. an arriving customer finding all servers occupied upon arrival will be blocked. Those customers leave the system and will have no further impact on the system state process.

4.1.2 State Process and State Probabilities

The number $X(t)$ of busy servers in the system at time t is used to characterize the state process. This state process is a discrete-state and continuous-time stochastic process. A sample path of the state process is depicted in Figure 4.2. When an arriving customer is accepted, the system state $X(t)$ is incremented. The state is decremented when a service is terminated. Due to the Markov property of the arrival and service processes, the state process $X(t)$ has also the memoryless property. This Markov property applies for every arbitrary instance of the process development.

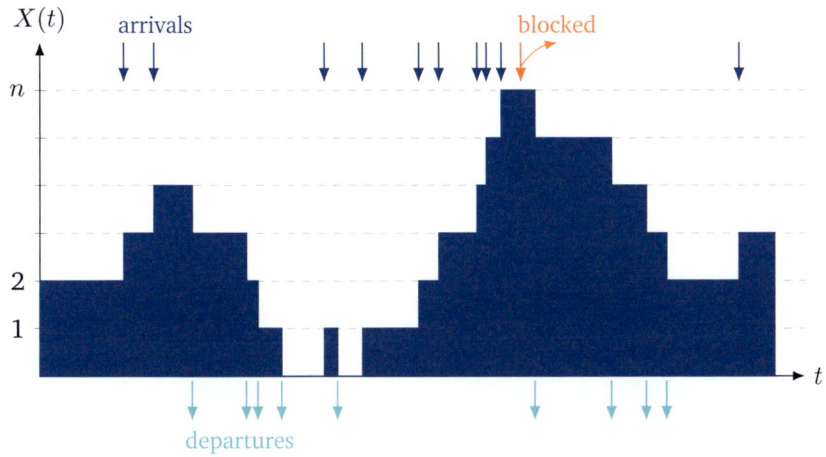

Figure 4.2: Sample state process of an M/M/n loss system.

Beginning with a start state $X(0)$, the state process generally evolves first through a non-stationary phase before it reaches the stationary condition or steady state. In this statistical equilibrium the state of the system varies in time in a stochastic sense but the probability of the system to be in a certain state doesn't change any more. The state of the system in statistical equilibrium is described by the random variable X. The state probabilities

$$x(i) = P(X(t) = i) = P(X = i) , \quad i = 0, 1, \ldots, n \tag{4.1}$$

form a state probability vector $\mathbf{X} = \big(x(0), x(1), \ldots, x(n) \big)$ which characterizes the statistical properties of the state process at an arbitrary instant. According to the derivation of the arrival and service rates in Chapter 3.5.4 we obtain the following transition probability density (or rate) q_{ij} (cf. Figure 4.3):

- *Customer arrival:* For the Poisson arrival process, the transition $[X = i] \rightarrow [X = i + 1]$ occurs with rate λ (cf. Equation (3.49b)), when an arriving customer is accepted ($i = 0, \ldots, n - 1$). In case that an arriving customer finds the system fully occupied $[X = n]$, it is blocked, and the system remains in this state.

- *Service termination:* In the system state $[X = i]$ there are i customers in the service phase. From Equation (3.50d) we have the transition $[X = i] \rightarrow [X = i - 1]$ with the rate $i\mu$ ($i = 1, \ldots, n$); this transition occurs when the service time of one of the i customers in the service phase is ended.

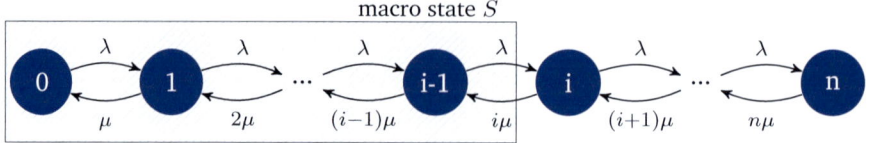

Figure 4.3: State transition diagram of an M/M/n loss system.

The state transition diagram of an M/M/n loss system has the form of a one-dimensional, finite-state Birth-and-Death process. Figure 4.3 shows the state space together with the respective rates q_{ij} for the transition $i \to j$.

In choosing the macro state S consisting of the micro states $\{X = 0, 1, \ldots, i - 1\}$, we arrive at the equation system

$$\lambda\, x(i - 1) = i\, \mu\, x(i)\,, \quad i = 1, 2, \ldots, n \tag{4.2a}$$

$$\sum_{i=0}^{n} x(i) = 1\,. \tag{4.2b}$$

By successive insertion of Equation (4.2a) in itself we obtain the state probabilities of the M/M/n loss system:

$$x(i) = \frac{\dfrac{a^i}{i!}}{\displaystyle\sum_{k=0}^{n} \dfrac{a^k}{k!}} \qquad \textbf{Erlang formula for loss systems} \tag{4.3a}$$

with

$$a = \frac{\lambda}{\mu}\,. \qquad\qquad \text{offered traffic} \tag{4.3b}$$

The offered traffic a and the mean offered traffic per server ρ are usually given in the pseudo-unit "Erlang" [Erl].

$$\rho = \frac{a}{n}\,. \qquad\qquad \text{normalized offered traffic} \tag{4.3c}$$

The Erlang-B formula for loss systems is used in a large number of dimensioning problems in technical systems in general, and in communication systems and networks in particular. It is still one of the most "powerful" formulas in classical performance analysis. As we have derived it for Markovian service time (M), according to its so-called *"insensitivity property"* or *"robustness property"*, it is also valid for generally distributed service time (GI), see Chapter 4.1.4.

As discussed above the state probabilities $\{x(i),\ i = 0, 1, \ldots, n\}$ derived here are valid at arbitrary instants of the stationary state process of the M/GI/n loss system.

Figure 4.4 depicts the state distribution of the of the M/M/n loss system (for $n = 30$). The normalized offered traffic $\rho = \frac{a}{n}$ appears here as a parameter. It can be seen in this diagram that with increasing values of ρ, i.e. the load in the system is increasing, more servers are occupied and the mass of state probabilities is shifted to the right side at higher value of i. At the special value of $i = n = 30$ where all servers are occupied, we have the blocking case and the blocking probability is marked accordingly in Figure 4.4. Note that the normalized offered traffic ρ may be $\rho > 1$, while the utilization per server is $\frac{\mathrm{E}[X]}{n} = (1 - p_B)\rho < 1$ which follows from Little's law, see also Equation (4.6b).

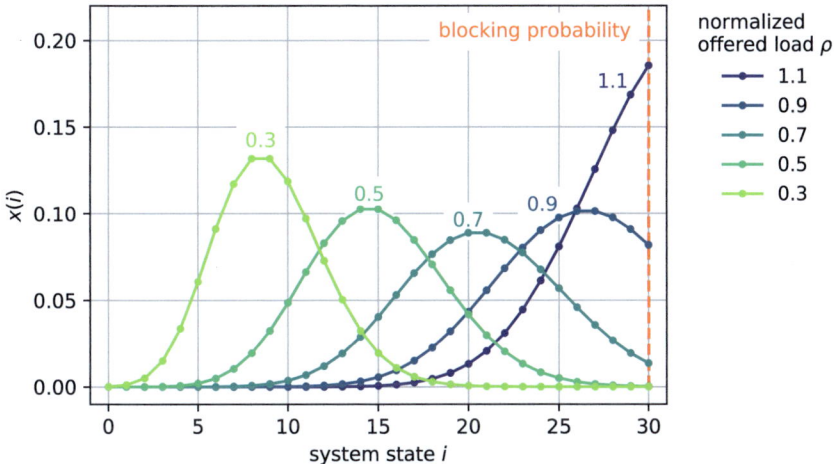

Figure 4.4: Steady state distribution of an M/M/n loss system (n=30) depending on the normalized offered load ρ.

We briefly discuss the validity of the state probabilities given in Equation (4.3a). Originally these state probabilities are derived for arbitrary instants. They are observed by an arbitrary independent observer at random time. Due to the memoryless property of the Poisson process, these arbitrary-time state probabilities in Equation (4.3a) are also valid at arrival instants of arriving customers. This means that the arrival-time state probabilities $\{x_A(i), \quad i = 0, 1, \ldots, n\}$ are identical with the arbitrary-time state probabilities $\{x(i)\}$ in Equation (4.3a):

$$x_A(i) = x(i), \quad i = 0, 1, \ldots, n. \qquad \textbf{PASTA property} \quad (4.4)$$

This is called the PASTA property, see Equation (3.12) in Chapter 3.3.2, and represents an important property of systems with Poisson arrival processes.

4.1.3 Other System Characteristics

4.1.3.1 Blocking Probability

A blocking event occurs when an arriving customer (test customer) is rejected. The blocking probability p_B is thus the probability that the test customer finds all servers busy upon arrival:

$$p_B = x_A(n) = x(n) = \frac{\dfrac{a^n}{n!}}{\displaystyle\sum_{k=0}^{n} \frac{a^k}{k!}} \ . \qquad\qquad \textbf{Erlang-B formula} \ \ (4.5)$$

4.1.3.2 Carried Traffic

The mean number of occupied servers in the system is called carried traffic Y:

$$Y = \mathrm{E}[X] = \sum_{i=0}^{n} i \cdot x(i) \ . \qquad\qquad\qquad (4.6a)$$

The carried traffic Y is given in pseudo-unit "Erlang" [Erl]. We derive Y by employing Little's theorem, considering the following system (as depicted in Figure 2.1):

System: the entire set of servers with

- *arrival rate:* rate of accepted customers $\lambda(1 - p_B)$,

- *mean sojourn time in the system:* mean service time $\mathrm{E}[B] = \dfrac{1}{\mu}$,

- *mean number of customers in the system:* carried traffic $Y = \mathrm{E}[X]$.

By applying Little's law according to Equation (2.1) on this *system*, we obtain the carried traffic in dependence of the offered traffic and the blocking probability as:

$$Y = \lambda\,(1 - p_B)\,\frac{1}{\mu} \ = \ a\,(1 - p_B) \ . \qquad\qquad \text{carried traffic} \ \ (4.6b)$$

The carried traffic represents the utilization of the entire system (mean number of occupied servers). With $\rho = a/n$, the utilization of a single server is

$$\frac{Y}{n} = \rho\,(1 - p_B) \ . \qquad\qquad \text{utilization per server} \ \ (4.6c)$$

The balance of traffic flows in an M/M/n loss system is illustrated in Figure 4.5. The stream of arriving customers is considered to be divided into two sub-flows: accepted traffic and rejected traffic. Only the stream of accepted customers contributes to the carried traffic of the system.

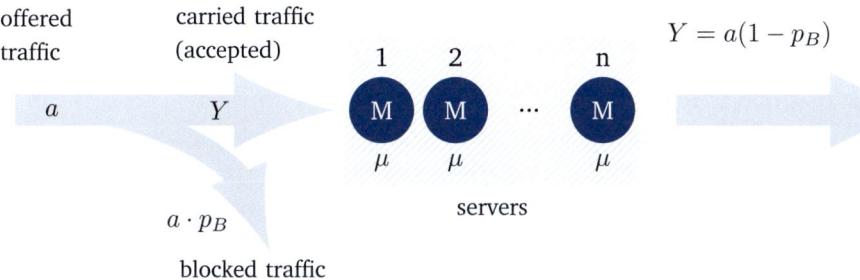

Figure 4.5: Traffic flows in M/M/n loss system.

4.1.4 Generalization to Loss System M/GI/n

The state probabilities in Equation (4.3a) are first derived under the assumption that the service time B is Markovian, i.e., B is (negative) exponentially distributed. This is valid originally for loss systems of type M/M/n.

However, it can be shown that these state probabilities in Equation (4.3a) are also valid for general service times. This insensitivity or robustness property of the Erlang loss formula implies that the state probabilities – and thus, also the blocking probability (cf. Equation (4.5)) – hold also for loss systems of type M/GI/n (or M/GI/n-0). A proof of this generalization property can be found e.g. in Syski [100]. This property extends the applicability of the Erlang loss formula in practical models considerably.

Example: M/GI/1-0 The M/GI/1 loss system with a single server leads to a blocking probability of

$$p_B = \frac{a}{1 + a} \tag{4.7a}$$

and the carried traffic, which is identical to the server's utilization here,

$$Y = \frac{a}{1 + a} . \tag{4.7b}$$

4.1.5   Modeling Examples and Applications

Dimensioning of Trunk Size in Telephone Networks   The best-known and earliest application of the M/M/n or M/GI/n loss system – in connection with the Erlang loss formula – is the dimensioning of trunk groups in telephone networks. The modeling steps and model components are:

- *Arrival process:* process of call attempts to use the trunk group. If a sufficiently large group of telephone subscribers is considered, the arrival process can be modeled with a Poisson process. This initially simplifying assumption, which leads to a simpler analysis due to the Markov property of the Poisson process, has been repeatedly confirmed with measurements in conventional telephone networks.

- *Service process:* An accepted call attempt occupies one line of the trunk group for the duration of the call. One line corresponds to one server in the service stage; the call duration corresponds to the service time B. In pure loss mode, an incoming call attempt is rejected if all n lines are busy at the time of arrival. Since the Erlang loss formula applies to general loss systems M/GI/n, the call duration can also be arbitrarily distributed.

We consider a group of n servers. The number of servers should be dimensioned in such a way that the blocking probability for customers – the guaranteed quality of service – is kept below a certain predefined value according to a Service Level Agreement (SLA).

This dimensioning exercise can be applied in several systems like in i) finding the number of IP addresses a DHCP server should have in an ISP environment, ii) the number of channel pairs (uplink and downlink) in mobile communication systems or more classical, the number of lines of a trunk group to carry an amount of traffic with a certain QoS or SLA.

The example of dimensioning a trunk group in telephone networks is discussed in more detail in the following. We consider a trunk group consisting of n lines. The blocking probability p_B for customers should be kept below a certain value. With the given customer traffic intensity λ and the mean call duration $E[B]$, the offered traffic is $a = \lambda \cdot E[B]$.

With the Erlang formula, it is clear that n cannot explicitly be given as a function of p_B and a. For dimensioning purposes the trunk group size n was traditionally listed in tables for different values of a and p_B (cf. Kühn [69], Seelen et al [95]). We can nowadays easily numerically derive the required trunk group size n.

In Figure 4.6 the number of servers is depicted as a function of the offered traffic, where the curves are illustrated for constant blocking probabilities. For a given value of the offered traffic a and the blocking probability p_B, the required number n can be obtained.

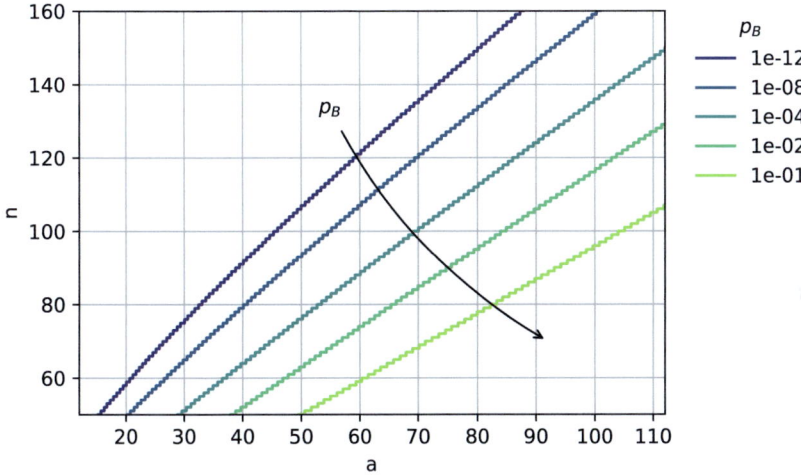

Figure 4.6: Dimensioning of trunk groups in an M/M/n loss system for given service level agreement in terms of guaranteed blocking probability p_B.

We take the example of a trunk group with a guaranteed blocking probability $p_B = 10^{-2}$, an arrival traffic rate of $\lambda = 30$[call attempts per minute] and a mean call duration $E[B] = 90$ s. The offered traffic results in $a = \lambda \cdot E[B] = 45$[Erl]. We can read out of Figure 4.6 that a minimum of $n = 58$ lines is needed. In case we want to offer a better quality of service, with say $p_B = 10^{-12}$, the required number of lines increases to about $n = 100$.

Economy of Scale The economy of scale describes the phenomenon that if many server groups are merged together into a larger server group the resulting QoS – in terms of blocking probability – is increasing. A larger server group thus operates more economically. With the Erlang formula we can show this effect quantitatively.

In Figure 4.7 the normalized carried traffic Y/n, i.e. the utilization of a single server, is depicted as a function of the number of servers n, where the curves are drawn for constant blocking probabilities p_B. We can observe the following from Figure 4.7:

- The server utilization Y/n increases with the number of servers, when we keep the required QoS, i.e. the blocking probability p_B, constant. This indicates that a larger trunk size is more economical.

- The increase of the factor Y/n corresponds to the *economy of scale*. However, this gain cannot be visibly optimized with ever larger bundles. This is reflected in the flatter shape of the curves in Figure 4.7 with larger values of n.

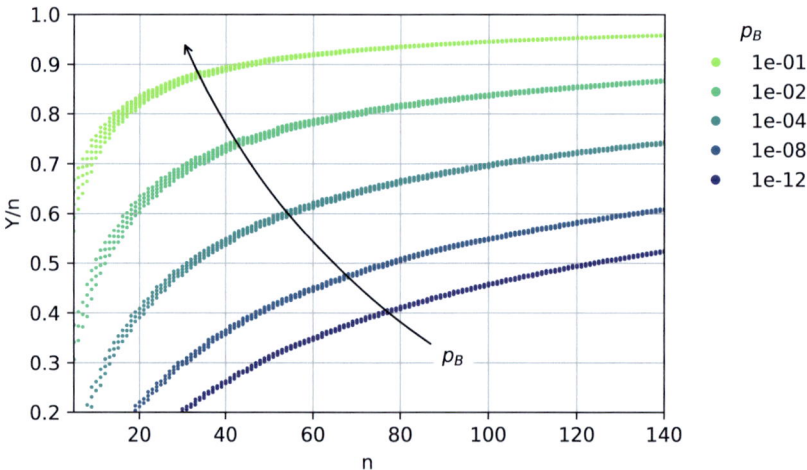

Figure 4.7: Economy of scale for the M/M/n loss system. The server utilization is plotted depending on the number n of servers and the ensured blocking probability p_B.

4.2 Delay System M/M/n

4.2.1 Model Structure and Parameters

The structure of the M/M/n delay system (or M/M/n-∞ system) is depicted in Figure 4.8. According to the Kendall notation the arrival process is a Poisson process, i.e., the interarrival time A is (negative) exponentially distributed. The service time B also follows a (negative) exponential distribution:

$$A(t) = P(A \le t) = 1 - e^{-\lambda t}, \qquad E[A] = \frac{1}{\lambda},$$

$$B(t) = P(B \le t) = 1 - e^{-\mu t}, \qquad E[B] = \frac{1}{\mu}.$$

The arrival rate λ corresponds to the mean number of incoming customers per time unit. Analogously, μ is the service rate.

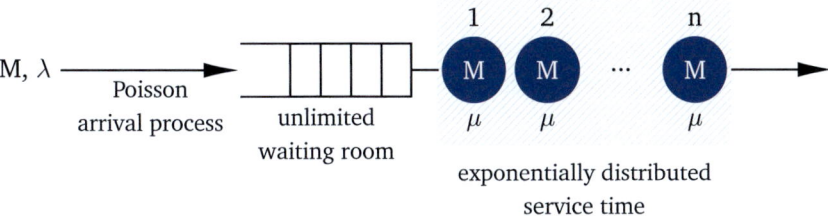

Figure 4.8: Delay system M/M/n.

The queue – i.e. the number of waiting places – is assumed to be unlimited; we consider here the pure delay operating mode. An arriving customer finding upon arrival all servers occupied will join the queue until a server becomes available. A customer is transferred from the queue to the server stage according to a queueing discipline (or service discipline). Examples of queueing disciplines are: FIFO (first-in, first-out) or FCFS (first-come, first-served), LIFO (last-in first-out), RANDOM (cf. Kleinrock [61], Takagi [103]), etc.

For pure delay systems the mean number of occupied servers $E[X]$ is identical to the offered traffic

$$a = \frac{\lambda}{\mu} = \lambda \cdot E[B], \qquad\qquad \text{offered traffic (4.8)}$$

which is given in the pseudo-unit Erlang [Erl]. Correspondingly the utilization or occupancy of *one* server is identical to the mean offered traffic per server ρ

$$\frac{E[X]}{n} = \frac{a}{n} = \rho. \qquad\qquad \text{server utilization (4.9)}$$

Since $\lambda \cdot \mathrm{E}[B]$ in Equation (4.8) is the mean number of arrivals during a service time, the system can become unstable. The waiting time of customers approaches infinity, if on average more customers arrive than can be served. As $a = \lambda \cdot \mathrm{E}[B]$ customers arrive on average in a service duration, during which at most n customers can be served, the stability condition of a pure delay system is

$$a < n \quad \text{or} \quad \rho < 1 . \hspace{4cm} \text{stability condition} \quad (4.10)$$

4.2.2 State Process and State Probabilities

Let $X(t)$ denote the state process at time t, where $X_B(t)$ customers are in the server stage and $X_W(t)$ customers are waiting in the queue. With the two random variables $X_B(t)$ and $X_W(t)$ the state process at time t can completely be characterized.

However, if not all servers are busy ($X_B(t) < n$), the queue must be empty ($X_W(t) = 0$). Thus, to characterize the system state at time t we just need the number $X(t)$ of all customers in the system instead of $\{X_B(t), X_W(t)\}$.

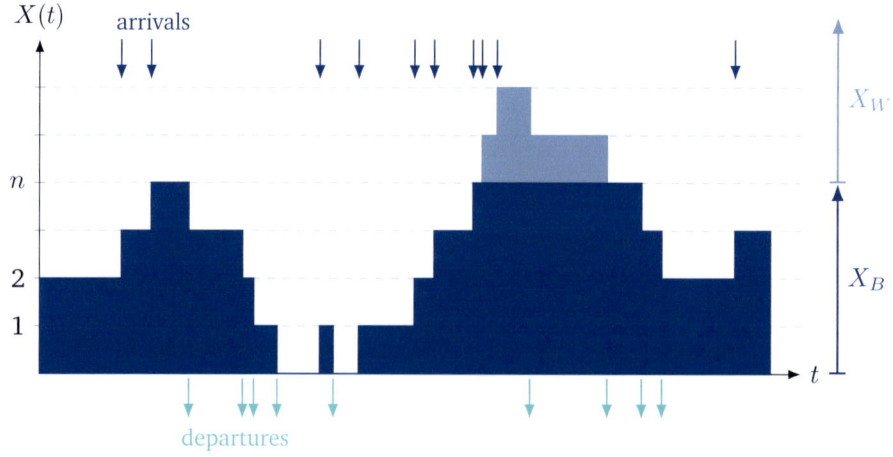

Figure 4.9: Sample state process of an M/M/n delay system.

The state process is a discrete-state and continuous-time stochastic process. A sample path of the state process is depicted in Figure 4.9. Upon the arrival of a customer, $X(t)$ is incremented. The state $X(t)$ is decremented when a service time is terminated. Since the Markov property applies for both arrival and service processes, the state process $X(t)$ also has the memoryless property. Note that this Markov property applies for every arbitrary instance of the process development.

In case the state process $X(t)$ has reached the steady state (or is in statistical equilibrium), its statistical properties no longer depend on the observed time t. In this stationary case, the dependency on time can be omitted and the system state is then described by means of the random variables $\{X_B, X_W\}$ or just X. The state probabilities

$$x(i) = P(X(t) = i) = P(X = i), \quad i = 0, 1, \dots ,$$

hold then for arbitrary observation instants.

According to the derivation of the arrival and service rates in Chapter 3.5.4 we obtain the following rate (or transition probability density) q_{ij} (cf. Figure 4.10):

- *Customer arrival*: Due to the Poisson arrival process, the transition $[X = i] \rightarrow [X = i + 1]$ occurs with the rate λ for $i = 0, \dots, \infty$ (see Equation (3.49b)).

- *Service termination*: Transition $[X = i] \rightarrow [X = i - 1]$

    ◇ $X \leq n$:
    There are $X = i$ servers active. As discussed in Chapter 3.5.4, the time to the next service termination is the minimum of i negative exponentially distributed intervals. Thus, the transition $[X = i] \rightarrow [X = i - 1]$ for $i = 1, \dots, n$ occurs with the rate $i\mu$ (cf. Equation (3.50d)); this transition corresponds to the termination of a service.

    ◇ $X > n$:
    In this case, where all n servers are occupied and $(X - n)$ customers are in the queue, the transition $[X = i] \rightarrow [X = i - 1]$ takes place with the rate $n\mu$ $(i = n + 1, \dots, \infty)$.

As depicted in Figure 4.10, the state transition diagram of the M/M/n delay system has the form of a one-dimensional birth-and-death process with infinite state space.

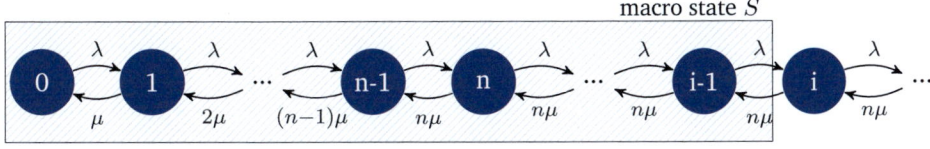

Figure 4.10: State transition diagram of an M/M/n delay system.

With the choice of the macro state S as shown in Figure 4.10, where S consists of the set of micro states $\{X = 0, 1, \ldots, i-1\}$, we arrive at the following state transition equation system:

$$\lambda x(i-1) = i\mu x(i) , \quad i = 1, 2, \ldots, n , \tag{4.11a}$$

$$\lambda x(i-1) = n\mu x(i) , \quad i = n+1, \ldots , \tag{4.11b}$$

$$\sum_{i=0}^{\infty} x(i) = 1 . \tag{4.11c}$$

By successive insertion of Equation (4.11a) and Equation (4.11b) in itself we obtain the state probabilities of the M/M/n delay system:

$$x(i) = \begin{cases} x(0)\dfrac{a^i}{i!} , & i = 0, 1, \ldots, n \\[3mm] x(0)\dfrac{a^n}{n!}\left(\dfrac{a}{n}\right)^{i-n} = x(n)\rho^{i-n} , & i > n \end{cases} \tag{4.12a}$$

and

$$\left(x(0)\right)^{-1} = \sum_{k=0}^{n-1}\frac{a^k}{k!} + \frac{a^n}{n!}\sum_{k=0}^{\infty}\rho^k \tag{4.12b}$$

or for $a < n$

$$\left(x(0)\right)^{-1} = \sum_{k=0}^{n-1}\frac{a^k}{k!} + \frac{a^n}{n!}\frac{1}{1-\rho} . \tag{4.12c}$$

It can be seen in Equation (4.12a) that, starting with $i \geq n$, the development of the state probabilities follows the form of a geometric distribution. This property is called the *geometric tail behavior*.

In Figure 4.11 an example of the state distribution of the M/M/n delay system is displayed for $n = 10$. The location of the mass of the probabilities is visible in this diagram, particularly in dependence of the system load ρ. From the semi-logarithmic scale in Figure 4.11b the geometric tail is obvious as the curves become linear for values of $i > n$.

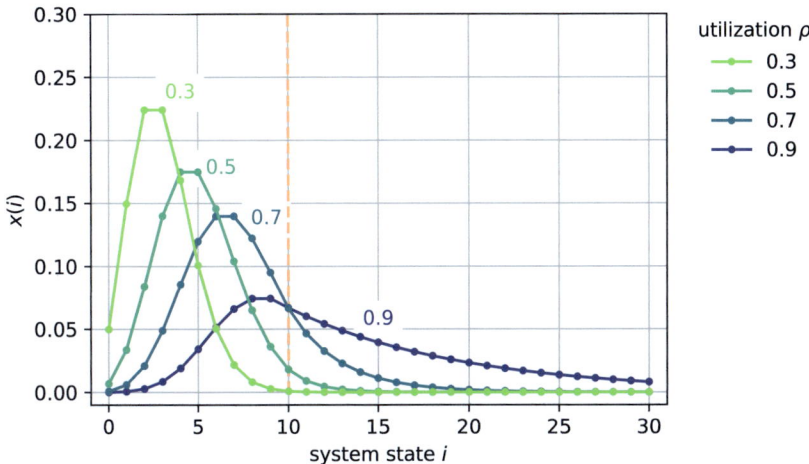

(a) Linear scale of x-axis and y-axis.

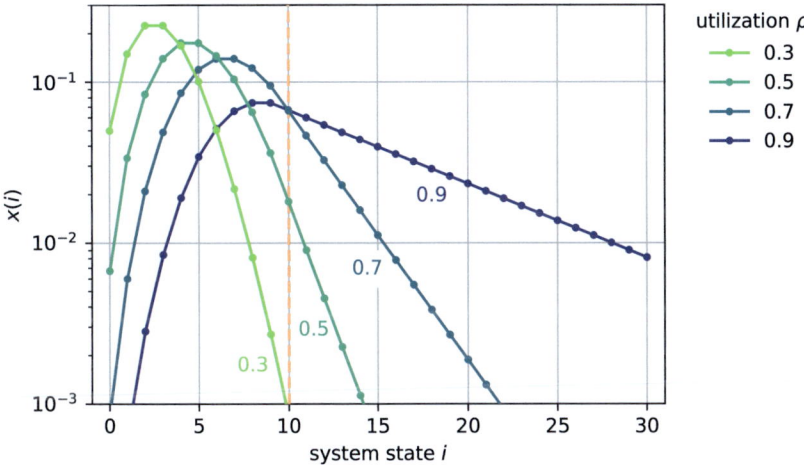

(b) Logarithmic scale of y-axis and linear scale of x-axis.

Figure 4.11: Steady state distribution of the delay system M/M/n-∞ for $n = 10$.

4.2.3 Other System Characteristics

From the state probabilities which are obtained for arbitrary observation instants different system characteristics of the M/M/n delay system will be derived next.

Waiting Probability   An arriving customer has to enter the queue when all servers are occupied at the time of arrival. The corresponding waiting probability p_W is thus

$$p_W = \sum_{i=n}^{\infty} x(i) = x(n) \sum_{i=0}^{\infty} \rho^i = x(n)\,\frac{1}{1-\rho} \tag{4.13a}$$

or after inserting of $x(n)$ (Equation (4.12))

$$p_W = \frac{\dfrac{a^n}{n!}\dfrac{1}{1-\rho}}{\displaystyle\sum_{i=0}^{n-1}\frac{a^i}{i!} + \frac{a^n}{n!}\frac{1}{1-\rho}}\,. \qquad\qquad \textbf{\textcolor{teal}{Erlang-C formula}} \tag{4.13b}$$

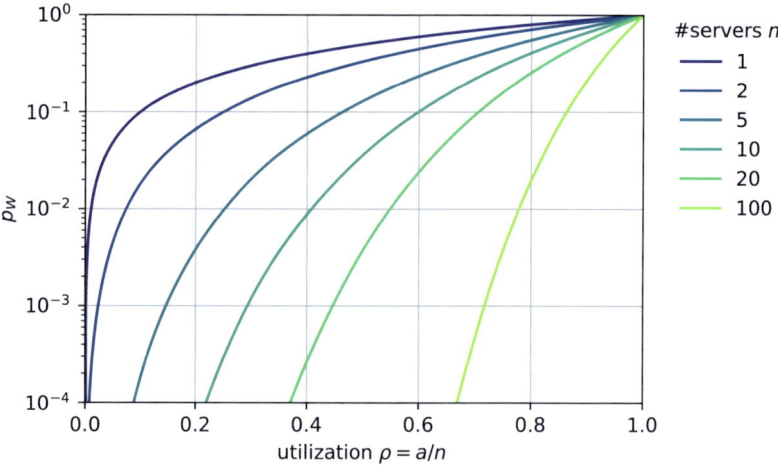

Figure 4.12: Waiting probability for an M/M/n-∞ delay system for various n.

This formula is often called *Erlang-C* formula. Figure 4.12 illustrates the waiting probability for various numbers of servers n. It can be seen that if the utilization per server ρ is kept constant, the waiting probability decreases with the increasing number of servers. This means that grouping of servers leads to a more efficient system operation, as customers experience lower waiting probability. This effect can also be interpreted as the *economy of scale in delay systems*.

For the M/M/1 delay system, the waiting probability follows from Equation (4.13b): $p_W = \rho$. This result can also be derived by means of the utilization law in Chapter 2.1.4. For single server systems, it is $x(0) = 1 - \rho$ and $p_W = 1 - x(0)$ due to the PASTA property.

Carried Traffic It is defined as the mean number of occupied servers:

$$Y = \mathrm{E}[X_B] = \sum_{i=0}^{n-1} i \cdot x(i) + n \sum_{i=n}^{\infty} x(i) = a \ . \qquad\qquad \text{carried traffic} \quad (4.14)$$

The carried traffic Y is given in pseudo-unit "Erlang" [Erl]. The relationship in the equation above can simply be verified using Little's theorem. Therefore, we take into account the following system:

System: all servers in the server stage (cf. Figure 2.1) with

- *mean arrival rate in the system:* identical with the arrival rate λ,

- *mean sojourn time in the system:* mean service time $\mathrm{E}[B] = \dfrac{1}{\mu}$,

- *mean number of customers in system:* carried traffic Y.

Applying the Little formula, the carried traffic is simply:

$$Y = \frac{\lambda}{\mu} = a \ .$$

Mean Queue Length The mean queue length, i.e. the mean number of customers in the waiting space is

$$\Omega = \mathrm{E}[X_W]$$

$$= \sum_{i=n}^{\infty} (i - n)\, x(i) = \sum_{i=n}^{\infty} (i - n)\, x(n)\, \rho^{i-n}$$

$$= x(n) \sum_{i=0}^{\infty} i\, \rho^i = x(n)\frac{\rho}{(1-\rho)^2} = x(0)\frac{a^n}{n!}\frac{\rho}{(1-\rho)^2} \qquad (4.15a)$$

or with Equation (4.13a)

$$\Omega = p_W \cdot \frac{\rho}{1-\rho} \ . \qquad\qquad\qquad (4.15b)$$

Mean Waiting Time In the following, we distinguish between two mean waiting times: the mean waiting time $\mathrm{E}[W]$ of all arriving customers and the mean waiting time $\mathrm{E}[W_1]$ of those customers who have to wait, i.e. whose waiting time is non-zero and positive. As depicted in Figure 4.13 all incoming traffic is divided into two traffic flows: customers who are served directly, and customers who have to wait in the queue first. To apply the Little formula, we consider accordingly two different systems.

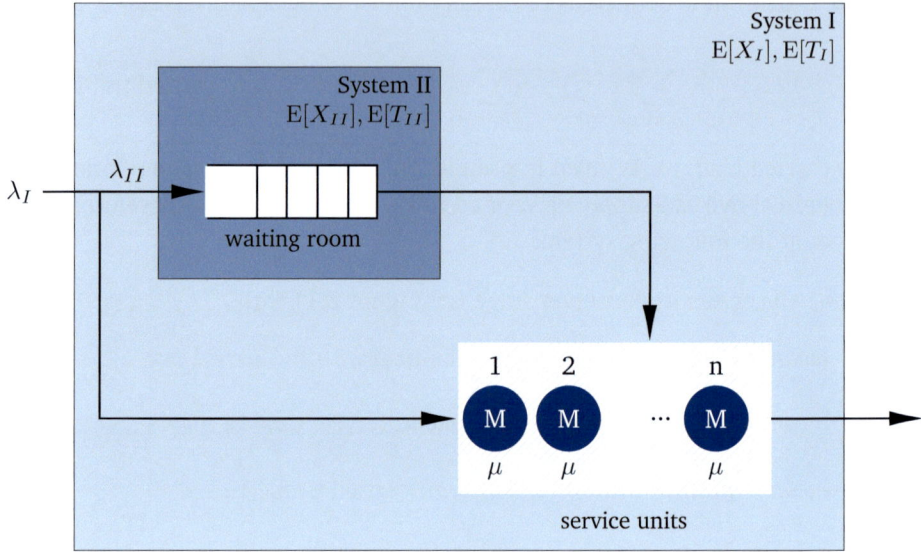

Figure 4.13: On the derivation of mean waiting times of all customers (system I) and of waiting customers (system II), respectively.

Mean waiting time considering all customers (System I) The mean waiting time for all customers considers the entire M/M/n system.

System I (all customers): entire M/M/n system

- *mean arrival rate λ_I:* is the total arrival rate
  $$\lambda_I = \lambda$$

- *mean number of customers in system $E[X_I]$:* sum of all customers in the queue and in service:
  $$E[X_I] = E[X_W] + E[X_B] = \Omega + Y,$$

- *mean sojourn time in system $E[T_I]$:* sum of customer sojourn time in the queue and in the server stage:
  $$E[T_I] = E[W] + E[B].$$

Following Little's formula $\lambda_I \cdot E[T_I] = E[X_I]$ or

$$E[W] = \frac{\Omega}{\lambda}. \tag{4.16}$$

Mean waiting time considering waiting customers (System II)   To compute the mean waiting time for customers who have to wait we consider only the waiting stage (the queue):

System II (only waiting customers): waiting queue of the M/M/n system

- *mean arrival rate λ_{II}:* arrival rate of waiting customers
  $$\lambda_{II} = \lambda \cdot p_W,$$

- *mean number of customers in system $\mathrm{E}[X_{II}]$:* is the mean queue length
  $$\mathrm{E}[X_{II}] = \Omega,$$

- *mean sojourn time in system $\mathrm{E}[T_{II}]$:* is the mean waiting time of waiting customers $\mathrm{E}[W_1]$.

With the Little formula $\lambda_{II} \cdot \mathrm{E}[T_{II}] = \mathrm{E}[X_{II}]$ we finally obtain the mean waiting time of waiting customers:

$$\mathrm{E}[W_1] = \frac{\Omega}{\lambda \cdot p_W} = \frac{1}{\lambda} \cdot \frac{\rho}{1-\rho} = \frac{\mathrm{E}[W]}{p_W}. \tag{4.17}$$

Note W is a mixture distribution (Chapter 2.4.2.6) from which Equation (4.17) directly follows: $W \sim \mathrm{MIX}\big((0, W_1), (1 - p_W, p_W)\big)$ and thus $\mathrm{E}[W] = p_W \mathrm{E}[W_1]$.

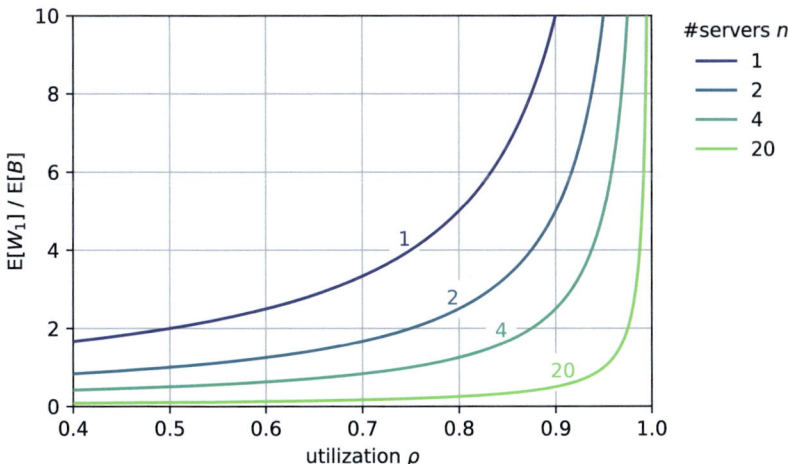

Figure 4.14: Mean waiting time of waiting customers in the M/M/n delay system.

In Figure 4.14 the mean waiting time of waiting customers is shown as a function of the system load ρ. Near the stability boundary $\rho = 1$ the mean waiting time increases sharply. This shows that a delay system should not be dimensioned according to or operate in this area ($\rho \geq 0.7$), since a transient load fluctuation can make the system unstable and the waiting time could multiply to make the quality of service or quality of experience undesirable. This effect can seriously endanger a system, e.g. under overload conditions in computer systems or buffer overflow in transit nodes of a data network. Dimensioning the operation point in the range of $\rho = 0.5$ would lead to a much more resilient and stable system operation.

4.2.4 Delay Distribution

To derive the delay distribution function we look at the probability that a customer experiences a positive waiting time W_1 being a conditional r.v. $W_1 = W|W>0$:

$$P(W_1 > t) = P(W > t \mid W > 0) = \frac{P(W > t,\, W > 0)}{P(W > 0)} = \frac{P(W > t)}{P(W > 0)} \quad (4.18a)$$

with

$$P(W > 0) = p_W = x(n)\,\frac{1}{1-\rho}\,. \quad (4.18b)$$

Further, we consider a randomly selected test customer, who finds a system with Θ customers upon arrival. A positive waiting time exists only for $\Theta \geq n$, or

$$P(W > t) = \sum_{i=0}^{\infty} P(W > t \mid \Theta = i+n) \cdot P(\Theta = i+n)\,, \quad (4.19a)$$

where

$$P(\Theta = i+n) = x(i+n) = x(n)\,\rho^i\,. \quad (4.19b)$$

With Equations (4.18b), (4.19a), and (4.19b) we obtain

$$P(W > t | W > 0) = \sum_{i=0}^{\infty} P(W > t \mid \Theta = i+n)\,(1-\rho)\rho^i\,. \quad (4.20)$$

Assuming the queueing discipline FIFO (first-in, first-out), the probability $P(W > t|\Theta = i+n)$ can be derived as follows (cf. Akimaru [2]). The test customer meets $\Theta = i+n$ customers in the system upon arrival, i.e., all servers are occupied and i customers are waiting in the queue. These $\Theta = i+n$ customers are in front of the test customer and have to be served prior to the test customer. Since all n servers are occupied, the interval $\widehat{B}$ between two successive service terminations is negative exponentially distributed (cf. Chapter 3.5.4):

$$\widehat{B}(t) = P(\widehat{B} \leq t) = 1 - e^{-n\mu t}\,.$$

The waiting time of the test customer consists of two parts:

- Interval from the arrival of the test customer until the first service termination. This interval is the forward recurrence time of $\widehat{B}$. Since $\widehat{B}$ is (negative) exponentially distributed, its forward recurrence time has the same distribution.

- Interval from the first service termination until all $i = \Theta - n$ customers in the server stage have been finished. This interval consists of i periods of type $\widehat{B}$.

Taking these two parts together, the test customer waiting time consists of $i + 1$ intervals of type $\widehat{B}$. It is therefore given by an Erlang-(i+1) distribution with rate $n\mu$:

$$P(W > t|\Theta = i + n) = e^{-n\mu t} \sum_{k=0}^{i} \frac{(n\mu t)^k}{k!} \tag{4.21a}$$

or from Equation (4.20)

$$P(W > t|W > 0) = e^{-n\mu t}(1 - \rho) \sum_{i=0}^{\infty} \sum_{k=0}^{i} \rho^i \frac{(n\mu t)^k}{k!}$$

$$= e^{-n\mu t}(1 - \rho) \sum_{k=0}^{\infty} \frac{(n\mu t)^k}{k!} \sum_{i=k}^{\infty} \rho^i = e^{-(1-\rho)n\mu t}, \tag{4.21b}$$

resulting in the cumulative distribution function

$$W_1(t) = P(W_1 \le t) = 1 - P(W > t|W > 0) = 1 - e^{-(1-\rho)n\mu t}. \tag{4.21c}$$

Hence, the waiting time distribution of waiting customers follows an exponential distribution: $W_1 \sim \text{EXP}((1 - \rho)n\mu)$.

From Equation (4.21b) and Equation (4.18b) the waiting time distribution of all customers follows:

$$P(W > t) = P(W > t|W > 0) \cdot P(W > 0)$$

$$= e^{-(1-\rho)n\mu t} p_W = 1 - W(t). \tag{4.22a}$$

Finally the waiting time distribution function $W(t)$ of an M/M/n delay system is

$$W(t) = 1 - p_W \cdot e^{-(1-\rho)n\mu t}. \tag{4.22b}$$

Note that W is *not* following an exponential distribution.

Figure 4.15 depicts the complementary distribution function of the waiting time in delay systems of type M/M/n for different load ρ and number of servers n. Due to the exponential characteristic of the waiting time distribution function, the complementary distribution function has the form of a straight line on a semi-logarithmic scale. The probability to wait longer increases with increasing load ρ and decreases with increasing number of servers n.

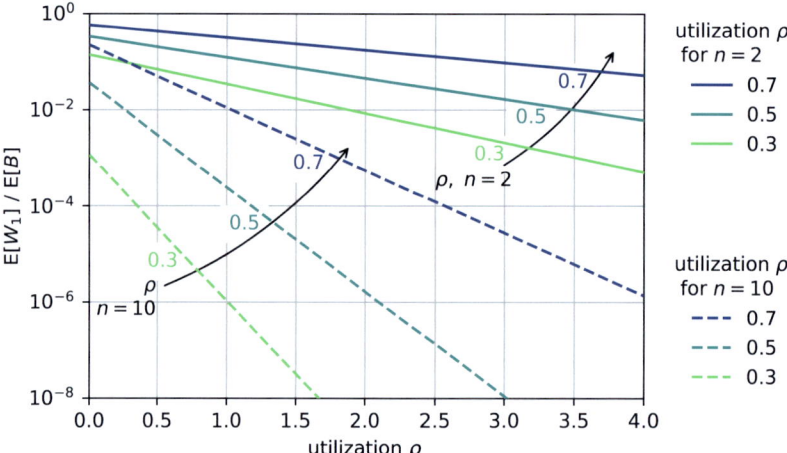

Figure 4.15: Complementary distribution function (CCDF) of the waiting time of waiting customers in an M/M/n delay system.

4.2.5 Example: Single Server Delay System

For the M/M/1-∞ delay system, the server utilization is ρ which leads to the steady state probabilities according to Equation (4.12a):

$$x(0) = 1 - \rho , \tag{4.23}$$

$$x(i) = x(0) \cdot \rho^{i-1} = (1 - \rho) \cdot \rho^{i-1} . \tag{4.24}$$

Hence, $X \sim \text{GEOM}(1-\rho)$ and $x(1) = (1-\rho)\rho$. The waiting probability follows from the Erlang-C formula or Equation (4.13a):

$$p_W = x(1) \cdot \frac{1}{1-\rho} = \rho . \tag{4.25}$$

Then, the waiting time W of all customers (Equation (4.22b)) has the following CDF:

$$W(t) = 1 - \rho \cdot e^{-(1-\rho)n\mu t} . \tag{4.26}$$

4.3 Loss System with Finite Number of Sources

4.3.1 Model Structure and Parameters

The structure of a loss system with finite number of sources is shown in Figure 4.16. The service stage consists of n servers with (negative) exponentially distributed service time B:

$$B(t) = P(B \leq t) = 1 - e^{-\mu t}, \qquad \mathrm{E}[B] = \frac{1}{\mu}.$$

In contrast to models with Poisson arrival processes, where arriving traffic flows are thought of to be generated by an infinite number of customers, we consider here – more realistically – a finite number m of customers that generate the arrival traffic $(m > n)$. Note for $m < n$, a customer is always served and no blocking occurs.

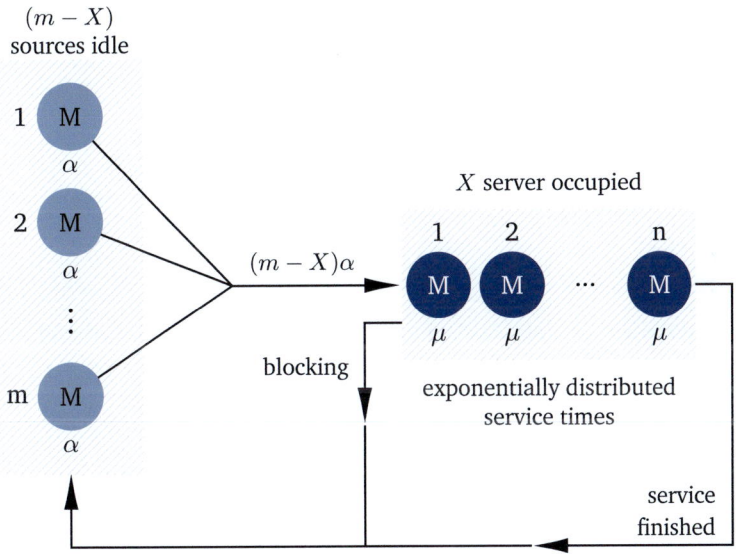

Figure 4.16: Engset model: loss system with finite number of sources.

The behavior of a customer is modeled as follows, where two states are identified:

- *active:* the customer is being served and occupies a server. The length of the active time is the service time B.

- *idle:* customers stay in this state until the next attempt. After a service period or after an unsuccessful attempt where the customer is blocked, the customer returns to the state *idle* (cf. Figure 4.16). The duration of the idle state is assumed to follow a (negative) exponential distribution with rate α:

$$I(t) = P(I \leq t) = 1 - e^{-\alpha t}, \qquad \mathrm{E}[I] = \frac{1}{\alpha}.$$

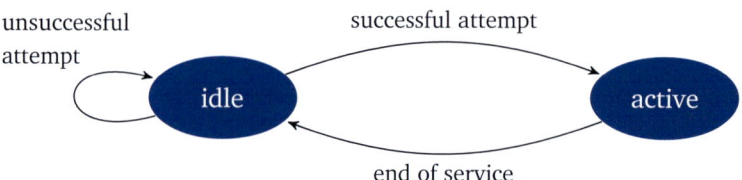

Figure 4.17: Model of customer behavior.

From the customer perspective the behavior of a traffic source (cf. Figure 4.17) is modeled as follows. After a service termination the customer enters an *idle* period with length I. At the end of the *idle* phase the customer starts an attempt to activate a service phase. If a server is available, the customer enters the state *active*, otherwise the customer will be blocked and returns to the state *idle* and starts an idling duration I again. The model is referred to as M/M/n/0/m or *Engset model*.

4.3.2 State Process and State Probabilities

Since the population of all m customers in the system remains constant, the system state can be characterized by the r.v. X of active customers in the server stage, as the $(m - X)$ remaining customers must be in the idle state.

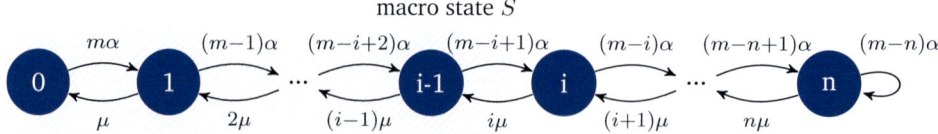

Figure 4.18: State transition diagram of loss system with finite number of sources.

The state process is a one-dimensional Birth-and-Death process with a finite number of states. The state X is incremented in case an activation attempt is accepted and decremented when a service is terminated. In view of the Markov property of the idle and active phases the state process X is also memoryless. This is valid at every arbitrary instant.

The state transition diagram of a loss system with finite number of sources, as shown in Figure 4.18, has the following transitions:

- *Successful activation attempt:*
  In state $[X = i]$ there are $(m - i)$ *idle* customers, each of them can initiate an attempt for a service with rate α. Following the derivation of state transition rates in Chapter 3.5.4 (Equation (3.50d)) the transition $[X = i] \to [X = i + 1]$ $(i = 0, 1, \ldots, n - 1)$ occurs with the rate $(m - i)\,\alpha$, in case the service attempt is accepted. If the attempt finds the system in state $[X = n]$, the attempt is blocked and the system remains in this state.

- *Service termination:*
  In state $[X = i]$ there are i customers in the service stage. With Equation (3.50d) the rate for the state transition $[X = i] \to [X = i - 1]$ $(i = 1, \ldots, n)$ is $i\mu$. This state transition takes place if one of the i ongoing services terminates.

With the choice of a macro state S consisting of the micro states $\{X = 0, 1, \ldots, i - 1\}$ as shown in Figure 4.18 we obtain the following equation system

$$(m - i + 1)\,\alpha\,x(i - 1) = i\,\mu\,x(i), \quad i = 1, 2, \ldots, n, \tag{4.27a}$$

$$\sum_{i=0}^{n} x(i) = 1. \tag{4.27b}$$

By successive insertion of Equation (4.27a) in itself we obtain the steady state probabilities $x(i) = P(X = i)$ for $i = 0, 1, \ldots, n$ in statistical equilibrium:

$$x(i) = \frac{\binom{m}{i} a^{*i}}{\sum_{k=0}^{n} \binom{m}{k} a^{*k}}, \tag{4.28a}$$

with

$$a^* = \frac{\alpha}{\mu} \tag{4.28b}$$

representing the offered traffic *of an idle customer.*

Blocking Probability The state probabilities in Equation (4.28a) give the percentage of time the process is in state $[X = i]$. They are referred to as the outside-observer state probabilities. To derive the blocking probability an arbitrary customer experiences when initiating an activation attempt, we need the state probabilities at arrival instances, i.e., the arrival-time state probabilities.

To derive the arrival-time state probabilities, we consider a test customer S which is part of the system. We virtually take the test customer to be "outside the system" and let him observe the remaining system with the remaining population of $m - 1$ customers. The observed "virtual remaining system" with $m - 1$ customers constitutes in turn a state process of a loss system with a finite number of $m - 1$ sources with known state probabilities. The outside-observer state probabilities of this reduced-source system is identical with the arrival-time state probabilities $x_A(i)$ seen by the test customer. We obtain from Equation (4.28a) the following distribution for X_A:

$$x_A(i) = \frac{\binom{m-1}{i} a^{*i}}{\sum\limits_{k=0}^{n} \binom{m-1}{k} a^{*k}}. \qquad (4.29)$$

A blocking event occurs in case the test customer finds the system state $[X_A = n]$. We finally obtain the following relationship called the Engset formula:

$$p_B = x_A(n) = \frac{\binom{m-1}{n} a^{*n}}{\sum\limits_{k=0}^{n} \binom{m-1}{k} a^{*k}}. \qquad \textcolor{blue}{\textbf{Engset formula}} \quad (4.30)$$

In Figure 4.19 the blocking probability following the Engset formula is depicted for different values of population m. As expected, for the limiting case $m \to \infty$ the loss system with finite sources approaches the M/M/n loss system. The Erlang-B loss formula is thus the limiting case of the Engset formula for $m \to \infty$. As m grows, we can observe that the curves of the Engset formula approximate the curve of the Erlang-B loss formula for M/M/n loss systems.

Generalization of Engset formula   According to the above derivation, the state probabilities given in Equation (4.28a) and Equation (4.30) apply initially only for a negative exponentially distributed service time B. However, it can be shown (cf. Syski [100]) that these state probabilities also hold for general service times. This is referred to as robustness property of the Engset formula which can be applied for finite population M/GI/n-0 loss systems, i.e. an M/GI/n/0/m queue.

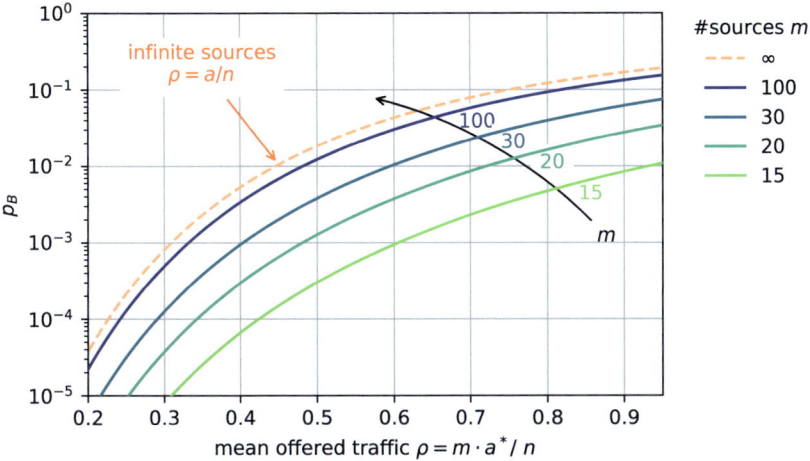

Figure 4.19: Blocking probability according to Engset formula for $n = 10$ servers depending on the mean offered traffic ρ per server.

Arrival Theorem: Random Observer Property In general, the system state i as seen by an incoming customer has a different distribution than the state seen by a random observer. The approach to derive the Engset formula is generalized and known as the *arrival theorem*. In queueing theory, the arrival theorem (also referred to as the random observer property) states that upon arrival at a server, a customer observes the system as if in steady state at an arbitrary instant for the system without that customer.

For closed networks, i.e. with a finite number of m customers, the state probabilities $x_A^m(i)$ seen by a customer entering a state i are the same as the arbitrary-time probabilities $x^{m-1}(i)$ in a system with $m - 1$ customers.

$$x_A^m(i) = x^{m-1}(i) , \quad i = 0, 1, \ldots \qquad \textbf{arrival theorem} \ (4.31)$$

For Poisson processes, there are $m = \infty$ sources. In that case, the probability of the state as seen by an outside random observer is the same as the probability of the state seen by an arriving customer. The property is often referred to as the PASTA property (Poisson Arrivals See Time Averages), see Chapter 3.3.2.

📘 *Further reading:* General investigation when arrivals see time averages (ASTA) by Melamed and Whitt (1990) "On arrivals that see time averages" [76].

4.3.3 Example: Mobile Cell with Finite Number of Sources

We consider now a cell in a mobile communication network, like in systems based on the cellular radio standard GSM (Global System for Mobile Communication). The model is a loss system with a finite number of sources. The Engset formula in Equation (4.30) is used to dimension the number of required channels in a cell. The parameters of the model in the numerical example below are as follows.

- *Service process:* The mobile cell has n user channel pairs (uplink and downlink). The length of channel occupation is B, $E[B] = 1/\mu$. As the results of the M/M/n loss system with a finite number of sources are also valid for M/GI/n loss systems with a finite number of sources due to the insensitivity property, the duration B can be arbitrarily distributed.

- *Arrival process:* There are a population of m customers in the cell. The offered traffic of an idle customer is $a^* = \alpha E[B] = \alpha/\mu$[Erl]. The total offered traffic if all customers are idle is then $a = m \cdot a^* = m \cdot \alpha \cdot E[B]$[Erl]. In the limit $m \to \infty$, the arrival process is a Poisson process with rate $\lambda = \alpha \cdot m$ and the system is the M/M/n-0 loss system.

An accepted call attempt requires a user channel pair for the duration B of the connection. If no channel pair is available upon arrival, the attempt is rejected. The number n of channel pairs should be dimensioned in such a way that for a given total offered traffic a, the blocking probability does not exceed a certain value.

Figure 4.20 shows the blocking probability depending on the available channel pairs. It is assumed that the total offered load of the customer population in the cell is $a = m \cdot a^* = 8$[Erl]. The blocking probability decreases very quickly with increasing number of available channel pairs. It can also be seen that the simplifying assumption of an infinite number of sources represents the upper limit with regard to the blocking behavior. This means that for dimensioning purposes, the modeling approach with infinite number of sources, i.e. with the loss system M/GI/n leading to the Erlang loss formula corresponds to a rather pessimistic and conservative dimensioning.

Figure 4.21 shows the blocking probability depending on the total traffic intensity $\alpha \cdot m$ given in [connection requests per minute]. The mean service time is assumed to be $E[B] = 2\,\text{min}$, The number of channel pairs available is $n = 30$. If the number m of participants increases while the overall traffic intensity remains the same, the blocking probability increases. This effect can also be formulated that the blocking probability increases with the granularity of the traffic. If the same total traffic is generated by a larger number of customers, the blocking probability increases. The limit of the blocking probability approaches the modeling case with the assumption of infinite number of sources ($m \to \infty$).

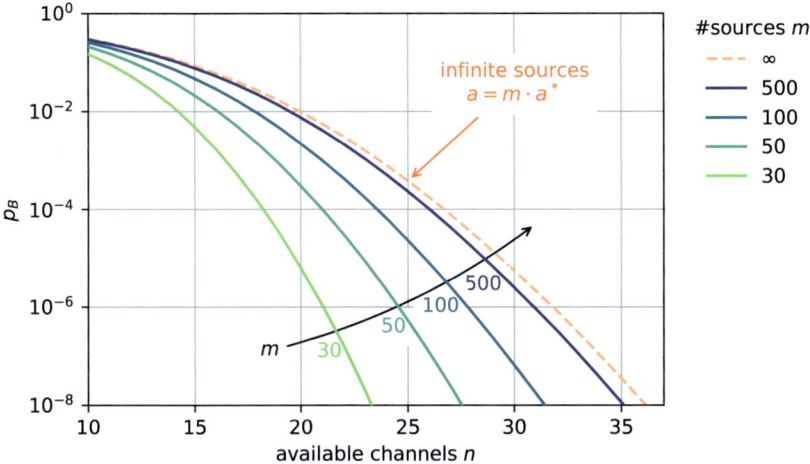

Figure 4.20: Blocking probability depending on the number of channels ($a = 12\,[\mathrm{Erl}]$).

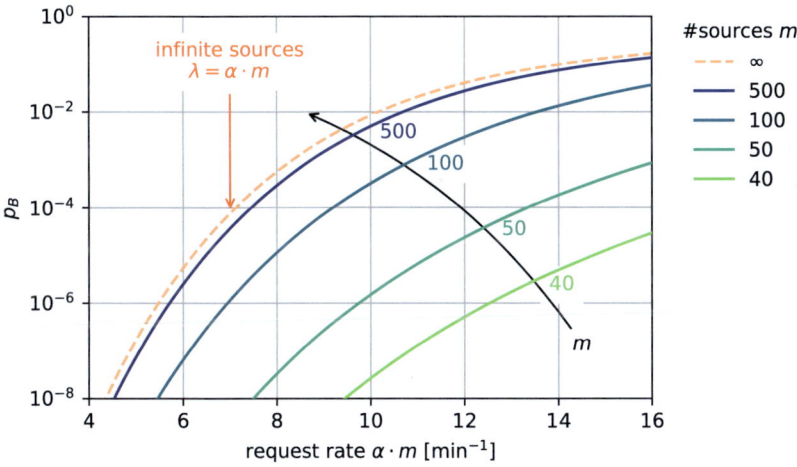

Figure 4.21: Blocking probability for increasing load ($n = 30, \mathrm{E}[\,B\,] = 2\,\mathrm{min}$).

4.4 Customer Retrial Model with Finite Number of Sources

In communication networks, especially for systems operating in loss mode, rejected customer requests sooner or later lead to new attempts – this happens rather sooner. This effect which changes the system dynamic has not been taken into account in the previous Chapter 4.3. Especially when looking at systems with a finite number of sources, this effect has a significant impact on the overall range of traffic and on the performance of the system. In this chapter we are looking at an extension of the loss system with finite number of sources, to a more realistic model considering this retrial or repeated-attempt modeling approach.

The customer model now includes the retrial behavior: if a customer is blocked, a new attempt starts, after a wait-for-retrial time. The wait-for-retrial time is normally shorter than the time to a new "fresh" attempt if the customer would have neglected and "forgotten" the unsuccessful attempt. First, an analysis is presented in which a two-dimensional Markov state process is analyzed using a recursive algorithm. The model is then used to investigate a mobile radio cell with a finite number of subscribers and retrial effect, see Tran-Gia and Mandjes [111].

The retrial phenomenon also occurs in other areas than the modeling of cellular networks, e.g. in optical networks, cognitive radio networks, local area networks operating with random access protocols [86]. On the application layer, customer retrial behavior will also occur for a variety of services, e.g. in call centers, for cloud services, etc.

4.4.1 Model Structure and Parameters

The main extension in the model of customer behavior is illustrated in Figure 4.22, while the overall system model is depicted in Figure 4.23. Model components are explained in more detail in the following.

Customer Behavior Model with Retrial   In the description of the model to follow, based on applications in circuit-switching telephony, we use the terms "connection request", "call attempt" or "attempt" equivalently to describe the attempt to occupy a server or a telephone line. If the subscriber tries to activate a call after a long regular break without a previous blocking event, we call this a "fresh attempt". If it is a retry after blocking, we refer to it as a "retrial" or "reattempt".

Each customer follows the behavior model consisting of three states:

- *Idle state with duration I and mean $1/\alpha$.* After finishing a service phase, a customer will stay in this state until generating the next fresh attempt. In case of request rejection, the customer will enter the *Wait-for-retrial* state with the retrial probability Θ or abandon the call attempt and remain in *Idle state* with the complementary probability $(1 - \Theta)$.

- *Active state with duration B and mean $1/\mu$.* The customer is being served and occupying a server. This state represents e.g. the use of a channel, while its duration B is the connection duration. At the end of a service phase the customer will enter the *Idle state* and stay there until the next attempt.

- *Wait-for-retrial state with duration R and mean $1/\alpha_0$.* The customer will stay in this state until generating the next attempt. When this attempt is rejected, the customer will reenter the *Wait-for-retrial state* with the retrial probability Θ or abandon the call and transfer to the *Idle state* with probability $(1 - \Theta)$.

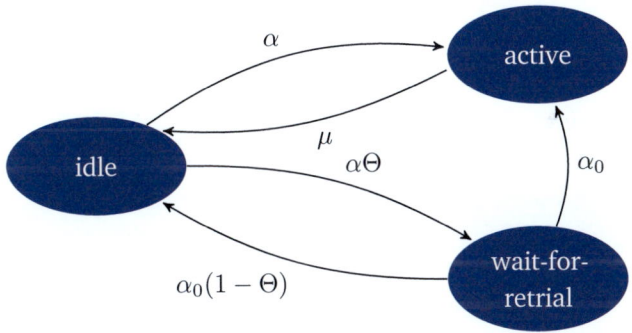

Figure 4.22: Model of customer behavior with retrial.

For the sake of mathematical tractability, all of the three random variables I, B and R are assumed to be (negative) exponentially distributed and are thus Markovian. In reality, the average wait-for-retrial interval is considerably smaller than the average idle time, i.e. $E[R] \ll E[I]$. This reflects customer impatience, which is important when analyzing overload control phenomena. The transitions between the three basic states of a customer shown in Figure 4.22 depend on whether the call attempt (fresh or retrial) is accepted or not. The parameter Θ is the retrial probability and models the customer's persistence. This probability characterizing the patience is generally decreasing with the number of repetitions. For the model discussed here, Θ is assumed to be constant.

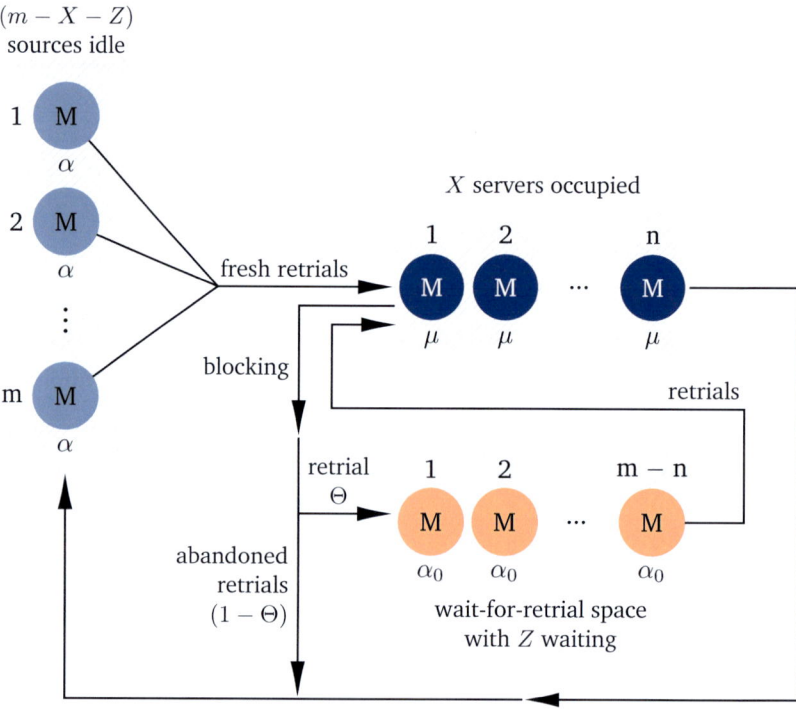

Figure 4.23: Retrial model with finite number m of sources, n servers, retrial probability Θ.

System Model The overall structure of the extended model with retrial is depicted in Figure 4.23. There are m customers sharing n servers in the service stage. Realistically, $m \geqslant n$. The stages and traffic flows in the model are

- *Traffic sources:* There are a finite number of m customers in the system. Each customer is either in the idle state or is in the server stage (occupying a server) or in the wait-for-retrial state. The idle duration I is assumed to follow the exponential distribution:

$$I(t) = P(I \leq t) = 1 - e^{-\alpha t}, \qquad \mathrm{E}[\,I\,] = \frac{1}{\alpha} \,.$$

If there are i customers in the idle stage, the rate to leave the idle stage and initiate a fresh call is $i\alpha$.

- *Server stage:* There are a number of n servers which represent in the context of telephony the number of available lines or channels. The service time B is assumed here to be (negative) exponentially distributed, the associated service rate is μ:

$$B(t) = P(B \leq t) = 1 - e^{-\mu t} , \qquad E[B] = \frac{1}{\mu} .$$

The system is operating as a loss system, i.e. if all servers are occupied, call attempts are rejected. A rejected call – fresh call or retrial – will be repeated with the probability Θ or abandoned with the complementary probability $(1 - \Theta)$. If there are j customers in the server stage, the rate to leave the server stage is $j\mu$.

- *Wait-for-retrial stage:* Customers stay here until the next retrial. Since the number of sources is m and the number of servers n, a maximum of $(m - n)$ customers can wait in parallel for a retrial. The interval R to the next retrial is also assumed to be exponentially distributed:

$$R(t) = P(R \leq t) = 1 - e^{-\alpha_0 t} , \qquad E[R] = \frac{1}{\alpha_0} .$$

If there are k customers waiting for the next retrial, the rate to leave the wait-for-retrial stage is thus $k\alpha_0$.

Since the total number of customers in the system is limited by m it holds $(i + j + k) = m$. In summary, we use the following notation for the analysis below:

α	call rate of a customer in the idle state
m	number of sources,
μ	service rate of a server in the server stage
n	number of servers
α_0	retrial rate of a customer in the wait-for-retrial state
Θ	retrial probability of customers
X	r.v. for the number of occupied servers
Z	r.v. for the number of customers waiting for retrial
$x(i,j)$	$P(X = i, Z = j) = x(i,j), \quad i = 0, 1, \ldots, n, \quad j = 0, 1, \ldots, m - n$
	probability that i customers are in server stage and j customers are in the wait-for-retrial stage.

State Transition Diagram   The state process of the system can be completely described with the r.v.s X and Z. Since all model components are memoryless, in the stationary case the state process can be described with a two-dimensional Markov process, of which the state transition diagram is shown in Figure 4.24.

We observe now the state $[X = i, Z = j]$ (for $i < n$ and $j = 0, 1, \ldots, m - n$), where the following transitions can occur:

- *Fresh call attempt:*
  There are $(m - i - j)$ *idle* customers, each of them can initiate a fresh call with rate α. Following the derivation of state transition rates in Chapter 3.5.4 (Equation (3.50d)) the transition $[X = i, Z = j] \rightarrow [X = i + 1, Z = j]$ $(i = 0, 1, \ldots, n - 1, \ j = 0, 1, \ldots, n)$ occurs with the rate $(m - i - j)\alpha$ to the target state $[X = i + 1, Z = j]$.

- *Retrial:*
  There are j customers in the wait-for-retrial state $(Z = j)$, the target state $[X = i + 1, Z = j - 1]$ is reached with the rate $j\,\alpha_0$.

- *Service termination:*
  There are i active customers, the target state $[X = i - 1, Z = j]$ is reached with the rate $i\,\mu$.

The blocking states are located in the last row $[X = n, Z = j]$ and have the following transitions:

- *Fresh call attempt:*
  Since all servers are occupied, the attempt is blocked. The rejected customer enters the wait-for-retrial stage with retrial probability Θ, the corresponding transition occurs with rate $(m - n - j) \cdot \Theta \cdot \alpha$.

- *Retrial:*
  With the probability $(1 - \Theta)$ the customer will abandon the call. The total rate of the transition is $j \cdot (1 - \Theta) \cdot \alpha_0$.

4.4.2 Recursive Analysis Algorithm

In principle, the state transition diagram in Figure 4.24 is a two-dimensional Markov process with a finite number of $(n + 1) \cdot (m - n + 1)$ states. A system of equations of micro states can be set up and numerically solved.

Alternatively – and in this case, more efficiently – the concept of macro state can be applied to simplify the system of equations. Together with suitable choices of macro states (cf. Tran-Gia and Mandjes [111]) and corresponding macro state equations, a recursive algorithm can be derived to obtain the state probabilities which deliver system characteristics of interest. The macro states S_1 and S_2 used in the algorithm are marked in Figure 4.24.

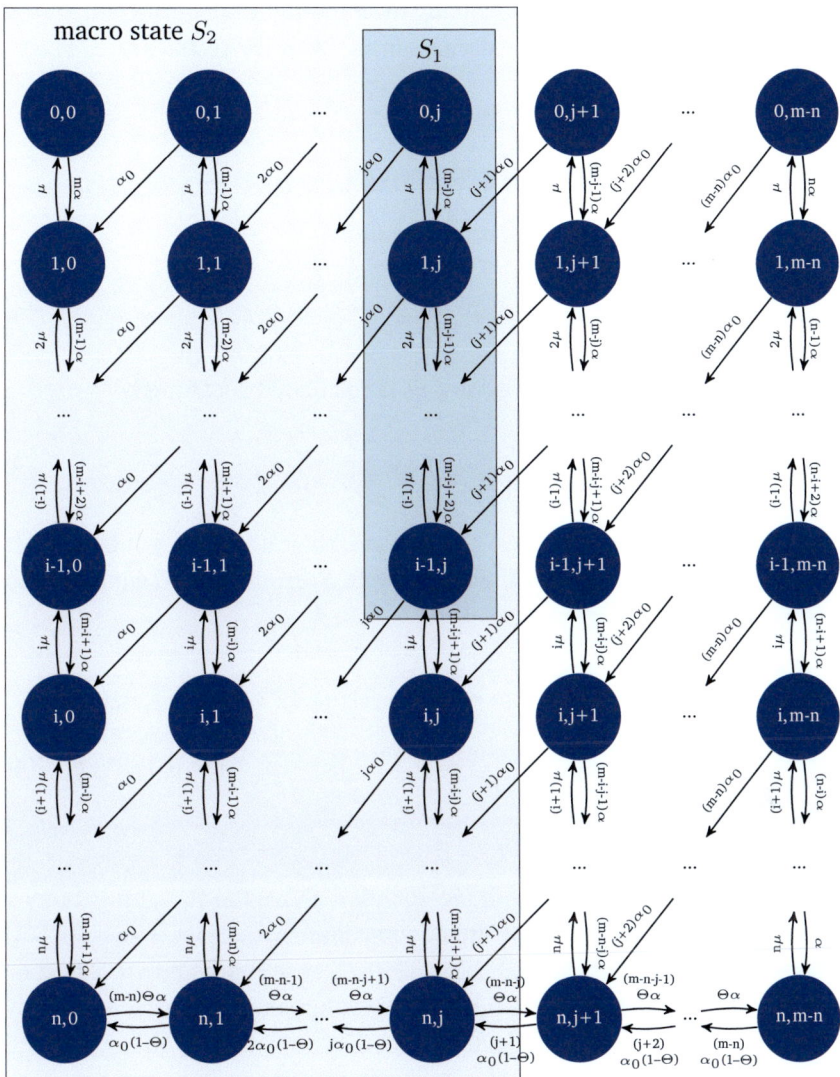

Figure 4.24: State transition diagram of the customer retrial model with finite sources.

Choice of Macro State S_1 and State Transition Equation The macro state S_1 is chosen to include the states with exactly j customers in the wait-for-retrial stage and $0, \ldots, i-1$ occupied servers, as depicted in Figure 4.24. This macro state can be reached from neighboring states, e.g. from the states in the adjacent right column which correspond to $j+1$ customers waiting for retrial and less than $i-1$ occupied servers. These state transitions, diagonally from top right to bottom left, correspond to retrials from one of the $j + 1$ customers in the wait-for-retrial stage. The sum of all of those rates is

$$\sum_{k=0}^{i-2}(j+1) \cdot \alpha_0 \cdot x(k, j+1). \tag{4.32a}$$

The rates for reaching macro state S_1 result in

$$(j + 1) \cdot \alpha_0 \sum_{k=0}^{i-2} x(k, j+1) + i \cdot \mu \cdot x(i, j). \tag{4.32b}$$

The transition probability for leaving S_1 is calculated accordingly

$$j \cdot \alpha_0 \sum_{k=0}^{i-1} x(k, j) + (m - (i - 1) - j) \cdot \alpha \cdot x(i - 1, j). \tag{4.32c}$$

If the macro state S_1 is in statistical equilibrium, the rates for reaching and leaving the state are equal, so we get for the macro state S_1 from the two equations above

$$i\mu x(i, j) = j\alpha_0 \sum_{k=0}^{i-1} x(k, j) + (m - i - j + 1)\,\alpha{\cdot}x(i-1, j) - (j+1)\alpha_0{\cdot}\sum_{k=0}^{i-2} x(k, j+1),$$

$$j = 0, 1, \ldots, m - n, \quad i = 0, 1, \ldots, n, \quad (4.32d)$$

where $x(i, j) = 0$ for $j > m - n$.

It should be noted here that with the equation above the state probability $x(i, j)$ can be computed if all states of the upper sub-column $(x(k, j), k = 0, \ldots, i - 1)$ and the sub-column on the right $(x(k, j + 1), k = 0, \ldots, i - 2)$ are known. Based on this property, the state probabilities are calculated in columns from right to left and within a column from top to bottom in the algorithm described later in this subchapter.

Choice of Macro State S_2 and State Transition Equation   The macro state S_2, as shown in Figure 4.24, is chosen to consist of all states with any number of servers and $0, \ldots, j$ customers waiting for retrial. With regard to transitions, the macro state S_2 can only be left if a fresh call changes from the wait-for-retrial stage to join the server stage. We obtain for S_2:

$$(m - n - j) \cdot \Theta \cdot \alpha \cdot x(n, j) = (j + 1) \cdot \alpha_0 \sum_{k=0}^{n-1} x(k, j+1) + (j + 1) \cdot (1 - \Theta) \cdot x(n, j+1),$$

$$j = 0, 1, \ldots, m - n - 1. \quad (4.33)$$

Recursive Algorithm The Equations (4.32d) and (4.33) are used together with the normalization equation

$$\sum_{i=0}^{n} \sum_{j=0}^{m-n} x(i,j) = 1 \tag{4.34}$$

to formulate the recursion algorithm.

For efficient numerical calculation even for larger systems, an algorithm was developed (cf. Tran-Gia and Mandjes [111]). The number of required operations is essentially proportional to the number of states of the underlying Markov process. The idea here is to first initialize the state probability $x(0, m - n)$ with a constant K_0 and then to use the macro state S_1 to calculate the probabilities for the right most column in Figure 4.24 as a function of K_0. This works particularly because this column cannot be reached by other columns.

Applied successively to the other columns from right to left in Figure 4.24, their probabilities can first be expressed as a function of K_0 and another constant K_1, e.g. by setting $x(0, m - n - 1) = K_1$ for the second column from the right. The second constant K_1 can then be eliminated again with the use of the macro state S_2. This works in particular since S_2 can only be reached by states whose probabilities have already been calculated as a function of K_0 and can only be left by one transition. This procedure once again illustrates the usefulness of macro states when solving the linear equation system for the state probabilities numerically.

The algorithm consists of the following steps.

1. Set $x(0, m - n) = K_0$.

2. Define $x(i, m - n) = c(i, m - n) \cdot K_0$. The coefficients $c(i, m - n)$, $i = 1, 2, \ldots, n$ can be recursively calculated using Equation (4.32d). The probabilities $x(i, m - n)$, $i = 0, 1, \ldots, n$ then depend only on $x(0, m - n) = K_0$.

3. Set $j = m - n - 1$ and $x(0, j) = K_1$.

4. Define $x(i, j) = u(i, j) \cdot K_0 + v(i, j) \cdot K_1$. The coefficient $u(i, j)$ and $v(i, j)$, $i = 1, 2, \ldots, n$ can be recursively computed using Equation (4.32d). We arrive at the following expression.

$$x(n, j) = u(n, j) \cdot K_0 + v(n, j) \cdot K_1 \tag{4.35a}$$

Alternatively, according to Equation (4.33) we can calculate $x(n, j)$ such that

$$x(n, j) = w(j) \cdot K_0 . \tag{4.35b}$$

With Equations (4.35a) and (4.35b), we can relate K_1 and K_0.

$$K_1 = \frac{w(j) - u(n, j)}{v(n, j)} \cdot K_0 = r(j) \cdot K_0 \qquad (4.35c)$$

5. Using Equations (4.35a) and (4.35c), the probabilities $x(i, j)$, $i = 0, 1, \ldots, n$ can be given as

$$x(i, j) = (u(i, j) + r(j) \cdot v(i, j)) \cdot K_0 = c(i, j) \cdot K_0, i = 0, 1, \ldots, n. \quad (4.35d)$$

The probabilities $x(i, k)$, $i = 0, 1, \ldots, n$, $k = j, j + 1, \ldots, m - n$ are then only given in terms of K_0.

6. Recursive calculation according to steps 3), 4) and 5) for $j = m - n - 2, \ldots, 1, 0$. The state probabilities of the entire state space are now given only in terms of K_0.

7. Normalization of state probabilities according to Equation (4.34).

$$\sum_{i=0}^{n} \sum_{j=0}^{m-n} x(i, j) = \sum_{i=0}^{n} \sum_{j=0}^{m-n} c(i, j) \cdot K_0 = 1 \text{ or } K_0 = \left(\sum_{i=0}^{n} \sum_{j=0}^{m-n} c(i, j) \right) \quad (4.36)$$

4.4.3 Calculation of Traffic Flows

To calculate system characteristics, we first determine the rates of traffic processes in the model. The traffic flows are illustrated in Figure 4.25.

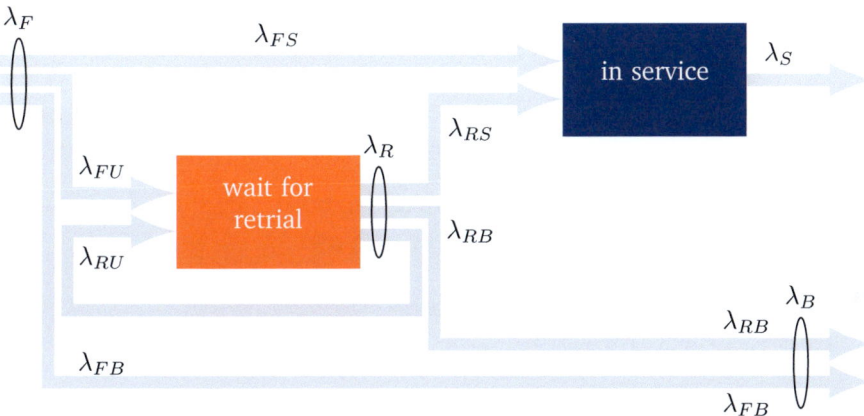

Figure 4.25: Traffic flows in the customer retrial model.

The indices of the traffic flows are defined as follows.

F fresh call, first attempt
R retrial, repeated call
S successful call, completed call
U unsuccessful call or blocked call which will be repeated
B unsuccessful call or blocked call which is abandoned

According to this indexing scheme, λ_{FS} is e.g. the rate (in [calls per unit of time]) of fresh calls that are accepted and immediately served.

The traffic rates of fresh calls shown in Figure 4.25 can be determined from the state probabilities as follows.

$$\lambda_{FS} = \alpha \sum_{i=0}^{n-1} \sum_{j=0}^{m-n} (m - i - j) \cdot x(i,j) \tag{4.37a}$$

$$\lambda_{FU} = \Theta \cdot \alpha \sum_{j=0}^{(m-n)-1} (m - n - j) \cdot x(n,j) \tag{4.37b}$$

$$\lambda_{FB} = (1 - \Theta) \cdot \alpha \sum_{j=0}^{(m-n)-1} (m - n - j) \cdot x(n,j) \tag{4.37c}$$

We obtain analogously for the retrial traffic flows.

$$\lambda_{RS} = \alpha_0 \sum_{i=0}^{n-1} \sum_{j=0}^{m-n} j \cdot x(i,j) \tag{4.38a}$$

$$\lambda_{RU} = \Theta \cdot \alpha_0 \sum_{j=0}^{m-n} j \cdot x(n,j) \tag{4.38b}$$

$$\lambda_{RB} = (1 - \Theta) \cdot \alpha_0 \sum_{j=0}^{m-n} j \cdot x(n,j) \tag{4.38c}$$

The total load of the system is made up of two traffic flows: the fresh call traffic with the mean rate λ_F and the retrial traffic with rate λ_R.

$$\lambda_F = \lambda_{FS} + \lambda_{FU} + \lambda_{FB} \tag{4.39a}$$

$$\lambda_R = \lambda_{RS} + \lambda_{RU} + \lambda_{RB} \tag{4.39b}$$

The blocking probability experienced by a user initiating a fresh call is given as

$$p_{B_F} = \frac{\lambda_{FU} + \lambda_{FB}}{\lambda_F} . \tag{4.40}$$

A characteristic performance measure for the retrial effect is the average number of calls – including the initiating fresh calls – that a call has to make

$$\eta = \frac{\lambda_R + \lambda_F}{\lambda_F} = 1 + \frac{\lambda_R}{\lambda_F} . \tag{4.41}$$

Regarding only successful calls, we obtain the mean number of attempts which have been made by a successful call.

$$\eta_F = \frac{\lambda_{FU} + \lambda_{FS} + \lambda_{RU} + \lambda_{RS}}{\lambda_{FS} + \lambda_{RS}} = \frac{\lambda_F + \lambda_R - \lambda_B}{\lambda_F - \lambda_B} = 1 + \frac{\lambda_R}{\lambda_F - \lambda_B} \tag{4.42}$$

4.4.4 Example: Mobile Cell with Customer Retrials

Now the application example GSM from Chapter 1.3.2 and Chapter 4.3.3 is modified by taking the retrial phenomenon into account. The number of subscribers in the cells and especially in the microcells of modern mobile radio networks is rather small and therefore necessitates the model approach with finite number of sources and retrial. We consider a mobile radio cell with m subscribers and a number n of available channel pairs (servers). In the idle state, a mobile radio subscriber generates calls with rate α. The connection duration is a negative exponentially distributed random variable B with service rate μ. The retrial interval R between the fresh call and the subsequent call or between two subsequent calls is also negative exponentially distributed with rate α_0. The retrial probability is Θ. The system load is specified by the standardized traffic intensity, which stands for the offered load per server:

$$\rho_0 = \frac{\alpha \cdot m}{\mu \cdot n} \, .$$

Figure 4.26 shows the average number of call attempts that a subscriber has to make per call with different system loads ρ_0 for different values of the retrial probability Θ. The mobile radio cell has $n = 15$ channels, $m = 100$ subscribers are in the cell. The mean service time is $E[B] = 120\,\text{s}$, the mean retrial interval is $E[R] = 6\,\text{s}$. In this way, the guaranteed QoS in term of the number of call attempts can be monitored and the cell parameters can be adjusted accordingly. For decreasing retrial probability Θ, the expected number of retrials converges towards 1. For increasing Θ, the system load and the blocking probability increases leading to a significant increase in the expected number of retrials. It can be seen that as the load increases, a subscriber has to make more calls to obtain a successful call. This is the cause of the positive feedback from overload phenomena in communication systems (the often observed "snowball effect"): increasing load leads to an increased blocking probability; this causes retrials, which in turn incur a higher system load.

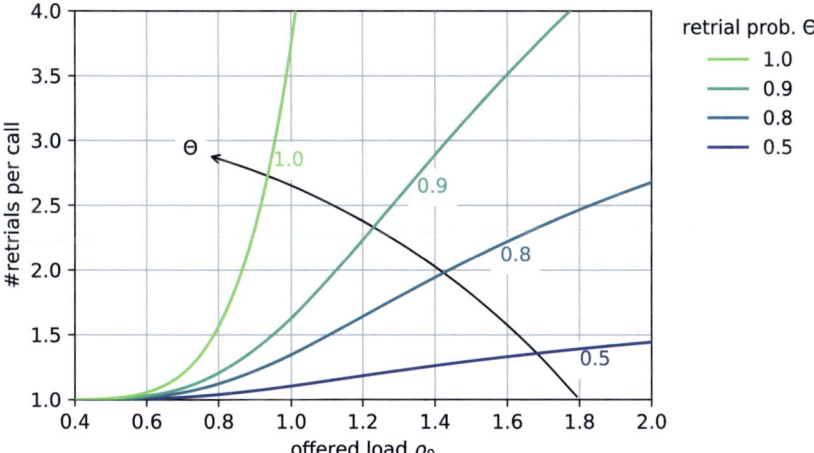

Figure 4.26: QoS degradation caused by retrial phenomenon in terms of increased number of retrials in a mobile cell ($m = 100, n = 15, \alpha_0/\mu = 20$).

The dependence of the blocking probability for fresh calls p_{B_F} on the number of subscribers in the system as a result of retrial effect is shown in Figure 4.27. Here the granularity of the source number, i.e. the need to use models with finite number of sources in performance assessments of such systems, is obvious. For different values of the number of sources, the blocking probability for fresh calls is plotted in Figure 4.27 as a function of the traffic intensity. An infinite number of sources corresponds to the "worst case" with regard to blocking. This finding justifies the modeling assumption with an infinite number of sources for the investigation of mobile communication networks in the literature.

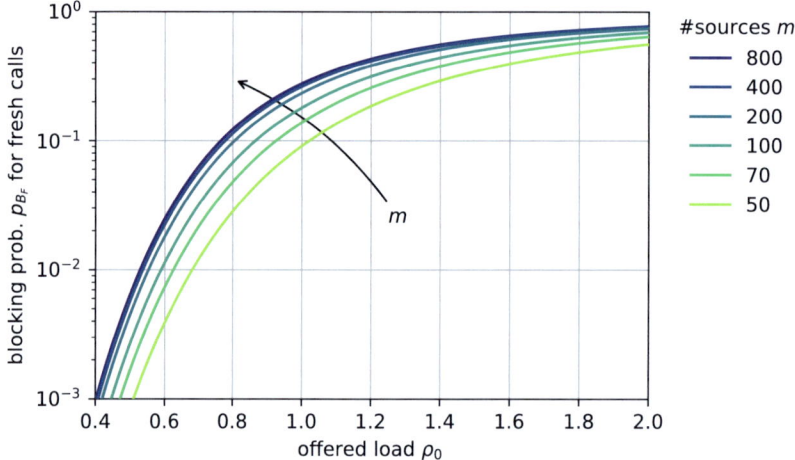

Figure 4.27: Influence of the granularity of number of sources on the blocking probability for fresh calls ($\Theta = 0.8, n = 15, \alpha_0/\mu = 20$).

📖 *Further reading:* An approximation for the blocking probability of the M/M/n-0 retrial queue has been discussed by Shortle, Thompson, Gross, and Harris (2018) *Fundamentals of Queueing Theory* [97]. Artalejo and Falin (2002) "Standard and retrial queueing systems: A comparative analysis" [5].

4.5 Processor Sharing Model M/M/1-PS

In communication networks, models with processor sharing are widely used to analyze resource sharing mechanisms where a system capacity is (time-)shared between all users. Kleinrock [63] introduced the processor sharing model for time-shared computer or processing facilities, where the entire processing capacity is equally shared among all users or jobs. Inspired from a round-robin scheduling behavior, where the users get the entire capacity for a fixed time, the processor sharing models the ideal, perfect system in which assigned time slots are infinitesimal small and the fraction of the total capacity occupied per user is simply the inverse of the number of users, i.e. a perfect share as idealization of round-robin scheduling.

Applications of the processor sharing model range from resource constrained environments like wireless cellular networks, data centers and clouds, web servers [123], etc. Thereby, processor sharing allows to model the flow-level performance of bandwidth–sharing protocols in packet-switched communication networks [38], e.g. TCP behavior in a network of routers with active queue management [17]. Recent applications include cellular network offloading [31] or content distribution systems with impatient customers [49]. An excellent survey on advances of the analysis of processor sharing queues is provided by Yashkov and Yashkova [123], while Altman, Avrachenkov, and Ayesta [123] focus on the multi-class generalization of the egalitarian processor sharing model, also known as discriminatory processor sharing, where the capacity is shared according to positive weight factors for the different classes.

We consider the basic egalitarian processor sharing model without differentiating between customers. First, we describe the system model and the state transition diagram, before relevant system characteristics in terms of expected sojourn times are derived. Especially important is the insensitivity or robustness property which allows analysis of M/GI/1-PS, similar to the robustness property of the M/GI/n-0 loss system. Of particular interest is the consideration of fairness in processor sharing queues in comparison to FIFO queues.

4.5.1 Model Structure and Parameters

The structure of the M/M/1 processor sharing system (or M/M/1-PS system) is depicted in Figure 4.28. Customers arrive in the system according to a Poisson process, i.e. the interarrival time A is (negative) exponentially distributed. All customers in the system simultaneously obtain service and the entire service capacity C is equally shared among all customers. The service capacity indicates how many operations per time or how much data per time can be processed by the system. For example, consider a server from which customers are downloading contents. In that case, the bottleneck is the upload capacity of the server reflecting the entire service capacity in the processor sharing model. Customers want to download files with file sizes B following an exponentially distributed random variable with mean $E[B]$ (in Mbit) and the server capacity is C (in Mbps).

$$A(t) = P(A \leq t) = 1 - e^{-\lambda t}, \qquad E[A] = \frac{1}{\lambda},$$

$$B(x) = P(B \leq x) = 1 - e^{-\mu x}, \qquad E[B] = \frac{1}{\mu}.$$

The arrival rate λ corresponds to the mean number of incoming download requests per time unit (s^{-1}). The service rate of the system is $C/E[B] = C\mu$ and corresponds to the mean number of completed downloads per time unit (s^{-1}). It can also be interpreted as the download rate if a customer is alone in the system and utilizes the entire capacity. Due to egalitarian processor sharing, all customers receive an equal fraction of the service capacity available. If there are n customers currently downloading, the service capacity per customer is C/n.

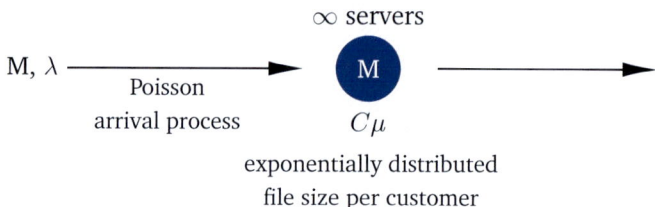

M, λ —— Poisson arrival process —— M —— $C\mu$

∞ servers

exponentially distributed file size per customer

Figure 4.28: Processor sharing M/M/1-PS with server capacity C and service rate $C\mu$.

The system is assumed to be unlimited. As soon as a customer arrives, its service starts. Hence, a customer experiences no waiting time. If a new test customer arrives in the system and sees $n - 1$ other customers, all customers will obtain the same share C/n immediately after arrival of the test customer. Due to the memoryless property of the exponential distribution, the remaining file size per customer to be downloaded is $B^* = B$ which requires an exponentially distributed download time with rate $C\mu/n$. Accordingly, a customer departing from the system results in an increase of the capacity per customer. The sojourn times of customers corresponds to the download time for the file contents, i.e. the actual service time for that customer. In contrast to the FIFO discipline, the download rate of a customer changes over time and depends on the number of other customers at its arrivals, as well as on subsequent arrivals and departures.

For the egalitarian processor sharing systems the offered load or offered traffic is

$$\rho = \frac{\lambda}{C\mu} = \lambda \cdot \frac{\mathrm{E}[B]}{C} \ , \qquad\qquad \text{offered traffic} \quad (4.43)$$

which is given in the pseudo-unit Erlang [Erl].

The system can become unstable, if on average more customers arrive than the mean service time of a customer being alone in the system. Hence, the stability condition is $\mathrm{E}[B] < \mathrm{E}[A]$ (or $\mu > \lambda$) or

$$\rho < 1 \ . \qquad\qquad \text{stability condition} \quad (4.44)$$

4.5.2 State Process and State Probabilities

Let $X(t)$ denote the state of the process at time t which is the number of customers being served simultaneously. The state process is a discrete-state and continuous-time stochastic process. In the stationary case, the dependency on time can be omitted and the system state is then described with the random variable X. The state probabilities

$$x(i) = P(X(t) = i) \ = \ P(X = i) \ , \quad i = 0, 1, \ldots$$

hold then for arbitrary time instants. In the following, we consider the transition rates for the number of customers in the M/M/1-PS system.

- *Customer arrival*: The transition $[X = i] \to [X = i+1]$ occurs with the rate λ $(i = 0, \ldots, \infty)$ according to the Poisson arrival process (cf. Equation (3.49b)).

- *Service completion*: There are $[X = i]$ customers currently being served. For each customer, the time to the next service completion, i.e. finishing the download, is exponentially distributed with rate $C\mu/i$. As discussed in Chapter 3.5.4, the time to the next service completion is the minimum of i negative exponentially distributed intervals. Thus, the transition $[X = i] \to [X = i-1]$ occurs with the rate $iC\mu/i = C\mu$ for $i = 1, \ldots$ (cf. Equation (3.50d)). This transition corresponds to the end of a service.

As depicted in Figure 4.29, the state transition diagram of the M/M/1-PS system has the form of a one-dimensional Birth-and-Death process with infinite state space. All other rates are equal to zero, since the probability of having more than one arrival or departure event at the same time is equal to zero.

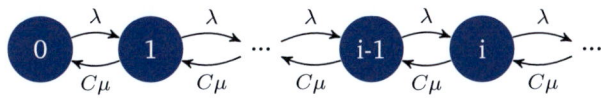

Figure 4.29: State transition diagram of an M/M/1-PS system.

We observe that the state transition diagram is identical to the M/M/1-∞ delay system with arrival rate λ and service rate $C\mu$. According to Equation (4.12), we obtain the steady state probabilities for the M/M/1-PS system.

$$x(i) = \rho^i(1 - \rho) \quad \text{for} \quad i = 0, 1, \ldots \tag{4.45}$$

Thus, X follows a geometric distribution with parameter $\rho = \frac{\lambda}{C\mu}$, which we denote with $X \sim \text{GEOM}(\rho)$ or $X \sim \text{GEOM}_0(\rho)$. From a statistical point of view, the process of number of customers in an M/M/1-PS system is the same as in the M/M/1-FIFO queue.

4.5.3 Other System Characteristics

The mean number of customers in the system, reflecting the mean number of parallel downloads, is simply the mean of the geometric distribution (cf. Chapter 2.4.1.3)

$$\text{E}[X] = \sum_{i=0}^{\infty} i \cdot x(i) = \frac{\rho}{1 - \rho} = \frac{\lambda}{C\mu - \lambda}. \tag{4.46}$$

Again, the stability condition can be observed, such that $C\mu = C/\text{E}[B] > \lambda$. We can derive the mean sojourn time, i.e. mean download time, by employing Little's theorem.

$$\text{E}[T] = \frac{\text{E}[X]}{\lambda} = \frac{1}{C\mu - \lambda}. \tag{4.47}$$

It should be noted that the derivation of the sojourn time distribution in this case is more challenging, since the sojourn time of a customer also depends on the subsequent arrivals and departures after the arrival of the test customer. Instead, we focus here on the mean sojourn time of customers downloading a file of size s. Thus, we are analyzing the *conditional sojourn time* $T|s$ which is a conditional random variable depending on the file size s. Zukerman [125] inspired the derivation by starting from the observed linear relationship between the mean conditional sojourn time $\text{E}[T|s]$ and the file size s which was proven by Kleinrock [63]. This means if the file size is doubled, the expected download time is doubled, too. Due to [63]

$$\text{E}[T|s] = \kappa \cdot s . \tag{4.48a}$$

Now, the mean is computed over all file sizes s which follow an exponential distribution, $b(s) = \mu e^{-\mu s}$.

$$\text{E}[T] = \int_{s=0}^{\infty} \text{E}[T|s] \cdot b(s) ds = \int_{s=0}^{\infty} \kappa s \mu e^{-\mu s} ds = \frac{\kappa}{\mu}, \tag{4.48b}$$

where κ is a normalization constant.

Combining Equations (4.47) and (4.48b) leads to $\kappa = \frac{\mu}{C\mu - \lambda}$ and the final mean conditional sojourn time of an M/M/1-PS system.

$$E[T|s] = \frac{\mu}{C\mu - \lambda}s = \frac{s}{C(1 - \rho)} \qquad \textbf{mean conditional sojourn time} \quad (4.48c)$$

For an M/M/1-FIFO system, in contrast, the mean sojourn time can be easily derived, since the waiting time of a customer is independent of the service requirement. Download request arrivals follow a Poisson process with rate λ, while the download time in the FIFO system is s/C for a file of size s. The offered traffic is $\rho = \frac{\lambda}{C\mu}$. The mean waiting time is given in Equation (4.16) for the M/M/1-FIFO queue.

$$E[T|s] = E[W] + s/C = \frac{\rho}{C\mu - \lambda} + s/C . \qquad \text{M/M/1-FIFO} \quad (4.49)$$

Figure 4.30 compares the expected conditional download times in the PS and the FIFO system depending on the file size s. The offered load is varied from a highly loaded system ($\rho = 0.95$) to a slightly loaded system ($\rho = 0.25$). For the PS system, we observe the linear relationship also in the double-logarithmic scale of the figure. For higher load, $E[T|s]$ increases accordingly. In the FIFO system, the file size is dominating the download time for low load. For high load, however, the waiting time in the queue dominates the total sojourn time and we observe no significant impact of the file size up to a certain file size.

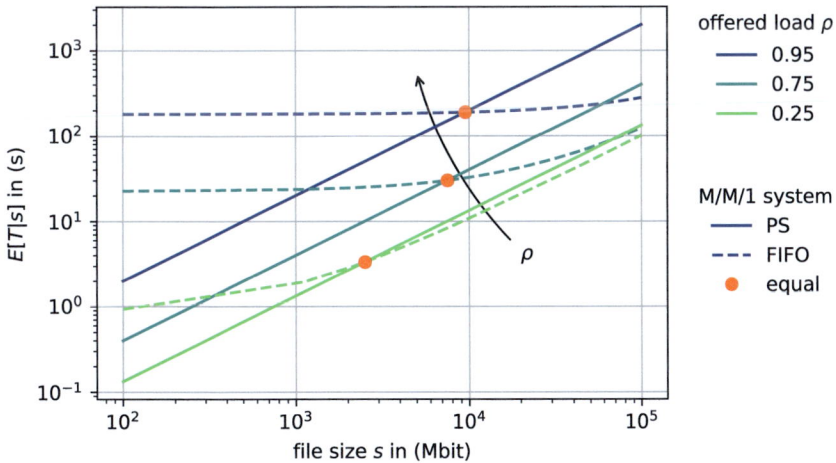

Figure 4.30: Mean conditional download time in the M/M/1-PS and the M/M/1-FIFO queue for a server capacity of $C = 1\,\text{Gbps}$ and different offered loads.

This behavior can also be seen for other load scenarios. The main interesting observation is that small files benefit from processor sharing compared to FIFO. On one hand, if the file size s is smaller than a threshold value s^*, i.e. $s < s^*$, the expected download time is smaller in PS than in FIFO. This threshold s^* is derived by comparing $E[T|s]$ for M/M/1-PS (Equation (4.48c)) and for M/M/1-FIFO (Equation (4.49)) and is marked with a dot in Figure 4.30:

$$s^* = \frac{C - \lambda/\mu}{C\mu - \lambda} .$$
(4.50)

On the other hand, FIFO is better for larger files $(s > s^*)$, but larger files cause long head-of-line (HOL) blocking for the other files. For exponentially distributed file sizes $(B \sim \text{EXP}(\mu))$, it is $P(B > s^*) = e^{-\mu \cdot s^*} = 1/e \approx 0.368$. As a consequence, many downloads suffer from HOL blocking in FIFO. If a system is preferred where downloads of single, large files is not causing congestion and large delays for smaller files, a processor sharing system is recommended.

4.5.4 Insensitivity Property: Generalization to M/GI/1-PS

An important and remarkable property of processor sharing systems is the insensitivity with respect to the actual service time distribution, i.e. the file size distribution. In particular, the following quantities are independent of the shape of the service time distribution and are also valid for the M/GI/1-PS queue:

- $x(i)$: distribution of the number of customers in the system in Equation (4.45)

- $E[X]$: mean number of downloads in the system in Equation (4.46)

- $E[T]$: mean download time in Equation (4.47)

- $E[T|s]$: mean conditional download time for files of size s in Equation (4.48c)

It should be noted that the insensitivity property does not apply to the sojourn time distribution. So far, the insensitivity property – also known as robustness property – was observed for the following systems, M/GI/n-0 in terms of $x(i)$ and p_B, Engset model in terms of $x(i)$ and p_B, and the M/GI/1-PS.

4.5.5 Fairness of PS in Comparison to FIFO Queues

Fairness in queueing systems may be defined in different ways which is nicely
summarized by Wierman [120] concerning different scheduling strategies including
processor sharing. Consider the notion of *temporal fairness* in terms of *seniority*. The
idea behind this fairness notion is that it is considered to be fair that jobs are served
in the order they arrive. The FIFO scheduling discipline is the only strictly temporally
fair policy. For the PS discipline, smaller files can overtake larger ones and therefore
decrease temporal fairness.

The notion of *proportional fairness* takes into account the file size. Perfect proportional fairness means that the expected download time is proportional to the file
size. As seen in Equation (4.48b), the PS discipline leads to perfect proportional
fairness which is, however, not the case for the FIFO system. However, the notion of
proportional fairness is discussed in expectation only.

Consider the variance of the download times in the PS and FIFO system for which
results are found in literature [83, 123, 4]. For the FIFO system, the download time
is $T = W + B/C$ with mean download time $\mathrm{E}[T] = \mathrm{E}[W] + \mathrm{E}[B]/C$ and variance
$\mathrm{VAR}[T] = \mathrm{VAR}[W] + \mathrm{VAR}[B]/C$ due to the independence of the waiting time W
and the file size B.

$$\mathrm{VAR}[T_{FIFO}] = \frac{1}{(C\mu)^2(1-\rho)^2}, \tag{4.51a}$$

$$\mathrm{VAR}[T_{PS}] = \frac{1}{(C\mu)^2(1-\rho)^2} \cdot \frac{2+\rho}{2-\rho} = \frac{2+\rho}{2-\rho} \cdot \mathrm{VAR}[T_{FIFO}]. \tag{4.51b}$$

Although both systems have the same mean download time $\mathrm{E}[T] = \frac{1}{C\mu-\lambda}$ (Equation (4.47)), the variance of the download time is larger in the PS system. The
coefficient of variation of the download times reveals this fact which is illustrated in
Figure 4.31. In the limit case of $\rho \to 1$, the coefficient of variation converges towards
$c_T^{PS} \to \sqrt{3}$. The higher variance and coefficient of variation of the download time in
the PS system can be explained by larger files for which the download times depend
on the subsequent arrivals of download requests and finished downloads.

$$c_T^{FIFO} = \frac{C\mu - \lambda}{(C\mu)(1-\rho)} = \frac{1}{1-\rho} - \frac{\rho}{1-\rho} = 1, \tag{4.52a}$$

$$c_T^{PS} = \sqrt{\frac{2+\rho}{2-\rho}} \cdot c_T^{FIFO} = \sqrt{\frac{2+\rho}{2-\rho}}. \tag{4.52b}$$

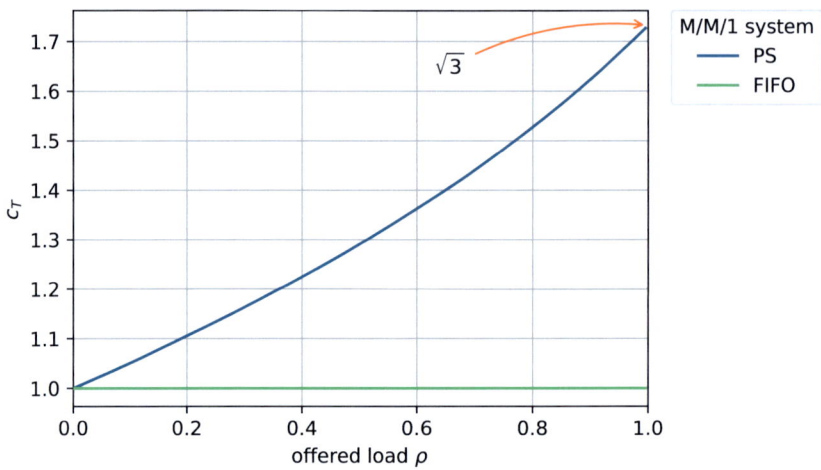

Figure 4.31: Coefficient of variation of the download time in the M/M/1-PS and the M/M/1-FIFO queue.

4.5.6 Example: Data Center Power Consumption

Looking at an example, where the power consumption of a data center is considered which is based on the work in [80]. First, the power consumption of a single server is computed. Then, the required number of servers for a certain quality of service requirement is derived.

Within the data center, there are n servers available, cf. Figure 4.32. A single server i in the data center is modeled as M/GI/1-PS system. In such a data center, the workload arrival is modeled as a Poisson process with rate λ_i. The Poisson process assumption is realistic due to the typical large number of sources for workload requests and independent workload arrival requests. The capacity of the server is shared among the present workload requests which is modeled by the processor sharing discipline.

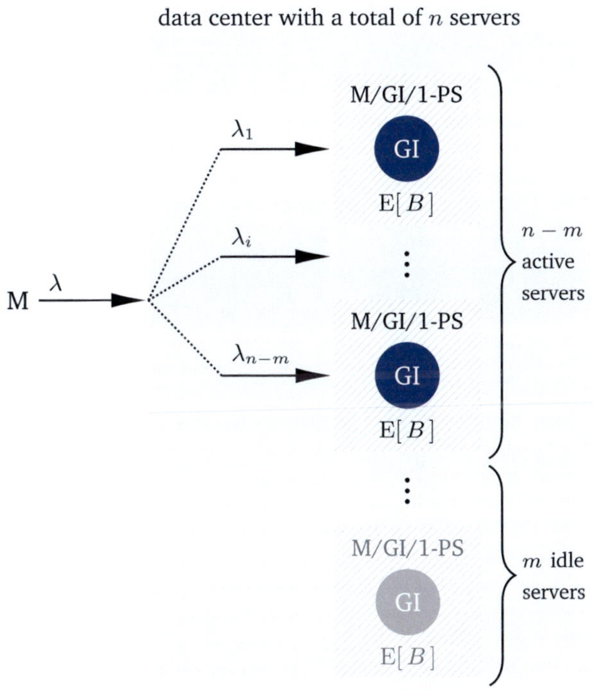

Figure 4.32: Data center with a total of n servers and m idle servers to reduce power consumption Ψ^*. The number m is adjusted such that QoS in terms of response time is still guaranteed: $\mathrm{E}[T|b_q] \leq T_{\max}$.

The mean *required service time* of a request to be processed in the data center follows a general distribution with a mean required service time $E[B]$. The response time for a request is identical to the required service time if the request is served alone. This means that the server capacity is 1. However, if there are k requests served in parallel, each request only obtains $1/k$-th of the server capacity and the actual response time of a request is larger than its required service time. The server utilization follows according to Little's law as $\rho_i = \lambda_i \cdot E[B]$. The expected power consumption Ψ_i of a single server i depends on the server utilization ρ_i, the idle power Ψ_{idle} and the peak power Ψ_{peak}.

$$\Psi_i = (1 - \rho_i)\Psi_{\text{idle}} + \rho_i(\Psi_{\text{peak}}) = \Psi_{\text{idle}} + \rho_i(\Psi_{\text{peak}} - \Psi_{\text{idle}}) \tag{4.53}$$

It should be noted that the server utilization and therefore the average power consumption is the same for all work-conserving strategies like PS, FIFO or LIFO and for GI/GI/1 in general. A work conserving strategy simply means that the server is working when there are requests available.

Within the data center, n servers are available. To reduce the total energy in the data center, up to m servers may be turned off. This will however increase the utilization ρ_i per server. The total arrival rate in the data center is λ and the requests may be distributed among the $n - m$ available servers:

$$\lambda_i = \frac{\lambda}{n - m} , \quad \rho_i = \lambda_i \cdot E[B] . \tag{4.54}$$

The expected total power consumption Ψ in the data center is

$$\Psi = (n - m)\Psi_i = (n - m)\Psi_{\text{idle}} + \lambda \cdot E[B](\Psi_{\text{peak}} - \Psi_{\text{idle}}) . \tag{4.55}$$

The maximum number m of servers which can be turned off is however also limited by the QoS requirement. The QoS requirement may be the maximum expected sojourn time $T_{\max}$ of the workload that can be tolerated. With the service rate $\mu = 1/E[B]$, the expected sojourn time follows from Equation (4.47):

$$E[T] = \frac{1}{\mu - \lambda_i} = \frac{1}{\mu - \frac{\lambda}{n-m}} \leq T_{\max} . \tag{4.56}$$

In practice, however, the QoS requirement may consider that the expected sojourn time for 99% of the workload requests are below a threshold $T_{\max}$. In that case, the useful property of the processor sharing system is utilized that the expected sojourn time is proportional to the service requirement – independent of the distribution of the service requirement. The 99%-quantile of the service requirements is denoted by b_q and $q = 0.99$. With the total offered load $a = \lambda E[B]$, Equation (4.48c) yields

$$E[T|b_q] = \frac{b_q}{1 - \rho_i} = \frac{b_q}{1 - \frac{\lambda}{(n-m)\mu}} = \frac{b_q}{1 - \frac{a}{n-m}} \leq T_{\max} . \tag{4.57}$$

It must be ensured that $T_{\max} > b_q/(1-\rho_i) > b_q$. The maximum number m^* of servers which can be turned off while fulfilling the QoS requirements is then

$$m^* = n - \left\lceil \frac{a}{1 - b_q/T_{\max}} \right\rceil \tag{4.58}$$

or

$$n^* = n - m^* = \left\lceil \frac{a}{1 - b_q/T_{\max}} \right\rceil > a \tag{4.59}$$

is the maximum number of servers which is turned on. The stability condition is satisfied for the data center when n^* servers are active, $n^* > a$. The expected power consumption Ψ^* when turning off m^* servers follows from Equation (4.55)

$$\Psi^* = \left\lceil \frac{a}{1 - \frac{b_q}{T_{\max}}} \right\rceil \Psi_{\text{idle}} + a \cdot (\Psi_{\text{peak}} - \Psi_{\text{idle}}) \tag{4.60}$$

with the total offered load in the system $a = \lambda \cdot \mathrm{E}[B]$.

Figure 4.33 shows the total power consumption Ψ^* of a data center with $n = 10$ available servers. The idle and peak power consumption is $\Psi_{\text{idle}} = 135\,\text{W}$ and $\Psi_{\text{peak}} = 270\,\text{W}$, respectively. The required service time B of a workload follows an exponential distribution with $\mathrm{E}[B] = 1.52\,\text{s}$. The 99%-quantile of the exponential distribution is $b_q = -\log(1 - 0.99)\mathrm{E}[B] = 7\,\text{s}$. The maximum threshold is assumed to be $T_{\max} = 8\,\text{s}$. The figure nicely shows the jumps when a new server needs to be activated to fulfill the QoS requirements.

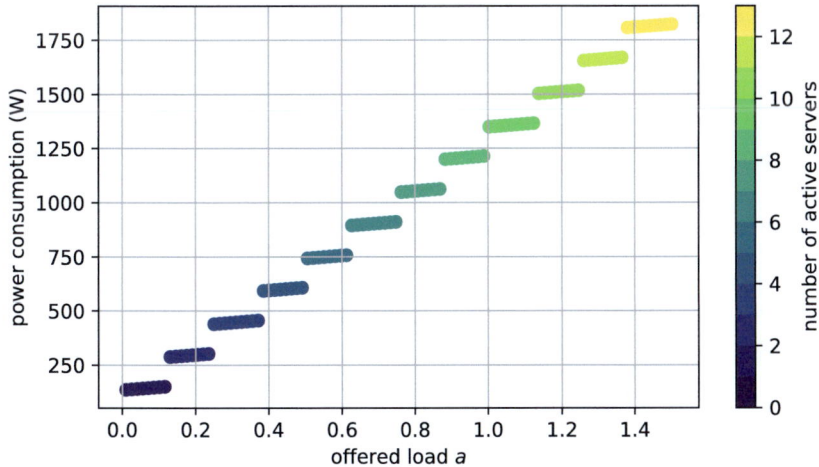

Figure 4.33: Expected power consumption Ψ^* in the data center when activating n^* servers to meet the QoS requirements.

4.5.7 Example: Virtualized Network Functions

Another example for a recent application of processor sharing is network function virtualization (NFV). Network functions and network services like firewalls or mobility management and session management were so far hosted on dedicated hardware. With the rise of the cloud computing paradigm and virtualization technologies, such network functions may be implemented within a cloud environment which offers virtual and physical resources of storage, computation, and network. The main idea of NFV is to decouple the network functions from the physical hardware that accommodates them. As a result, virtualized network functions (VNFs) are deployed on virtual resources provided within the NFV infrastructure.

Guillemin, Rodriguez and Simonian [42] consider a radio access network (RAN) whose functions are implemented in a cloud computing platform. This cloud RAN aims at improving the overall network performance and reducing cost. The cloud computing paradigm allows network operators to scale up their deployments more rapidly and according to the demand of arrival requests. Thereby, different radio access technologies can be implemented on the same physical infrastructure. In particular, the cloud RAN provides baseband processing of several distributed antennas of base stations which are implemented at a central cloud. The baseband processing includes several software defined sub-functions on the physical and data link layer, like fast Fourier transform (FFT) and inverse FFT, modulation and demodulation, or hybrid automatic repeat request (HARQ) management. The baseband processing VNF may be composed of several sub-functions which can be executed in parallel or in series within the computing system.

In [42], Guillemin, Rodriguez and Simonian model the parallel execution of requests for the baseband processing VNF as an $M^{[X]}/M/1$-PS system. Each VNF request is modeled as a batch of jobs reflecting the parallel execution of sub-functions. Batches arrive according to a Poisson process with rate λ. A batch contains X individual tasks and the batch size follows a discrete random variable X. The service requirement B of a single task follows an exponential distribution with $E[B] = 1/\mu$.

A key performance measure is the mean sojourn time of a batch, i.e. the total processing time of the VNF. For the *FIFO service discipline*, such a batch arrival system $M^{[X]}/M/1$-FIFO may be modeled as an M/GI/1-FIFO system. The batch arrival rate is λ. For the sake of simplicity, let us consider that the batch size is constant and contains k tasks to be executed. For an arriving batch, all k tasks of the batch are served in a row. Hence, the total service requirements B_X of the entire batch follows an Erlang-k distribution, $B_X = \sum_{i=1}^{k} B \sim E_k(\mu)$. The M/GI/1-FIFO allows to derive the sojourn time of the batches with $A \sim \text{EXP}(\lambda)$ and $B_X \sim E_k(\mu)$. The analysis of such systems is considered in Chapter 5.3.

For the VNF case, it is tempting to model the $M^{[X]}/M/1$-PS system as M/GI/1-PS system in a similar way. In the M/GI/1-PS system, the batches are processed in parallel and if there are n batches present, each *batch* gets $1/n$-th of the system capacity. However, in the $M^{[X]}/M/1$-PS, the system capacity is equally shared among all present *tasks* in the system. Consider two batches arriving in a short time. The first batch and second batch contain k_1 and k_2 tasks, respectively. The first batch gets $\frac{k_1}{k_1+k_2}$ of the server capacity and the second batch the remaining capacity. Now, consider constant batch sizes as discussed above. Then, $2k$ tasks are present and the capacity is equally shared among all tasks and also equally shared among the two batches. However, one of the tasks will be completed first, e.g. for batch 1. After the completion, the first batch will obtain $\frac{k-1}{2k-1}$ of the capacity which is thus not equally shared among batches. Figure 4.34 shows the difference of the system behavior between the $M^{[X]}/M/1$-PS system (labeled 'batches') and the corresponding M/GI/1-PS (labeled 'single job'). On the x-axis, the deterministic batch size is varied from 1 to 10. On the y-axis, the mean response time for the entire batch is depicted. As can be seen for increasing batch sizes the mean batch response time increases, too. The analysis of the batch processing time is beyond the scope of this text book but can be found in [42]. Practical measurements showed that the $M^{[X]}/M/1$-PS system models well the VNF response times in the cloud RAN.

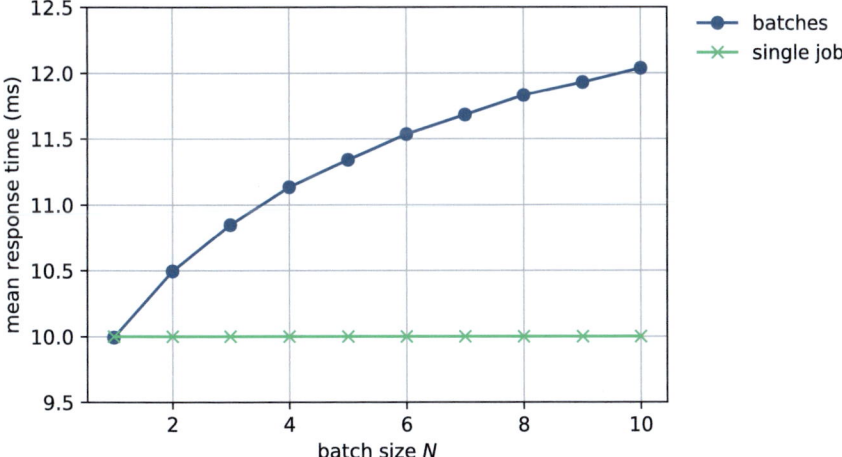

Figure 4.34: VNF example: The average batch response time of the $M^{[X]}/M/1$-PS system with batch arrivals is compared to the corresponding M/GI/1-PS system where the batch is modeled as a single large job. Deterministic batch sizes of size N are considered. The utilization is $\rho = 0.5$ in both systems.

Analysis of Non-Markovian Systems

In Chapter 4, traffic models with Markov property have been presented which, to be more precise, are continuous-time Markov chains (CTMC). In such Markov models, all model components are supposed to have the memoryless property. In case that some model components are non-Markovian, e.g. if the arrival or service process is generally distributed, the analysis methods presented for Markov traffic models, i.e. continuous-time Markov chains, cannot directly be used. Instead discrete-time instants are considered at which the system has the Markov property (embedded Markov chain). This leads to discrete-time Markov chains (DTMC).

Chapter 5 highlights some basic non-Markovian traffic models. These are models containing one component with non-Markovian behavior. First, the discrete-time Markov chain is defined and then the method of the embedded Markov chain is introduced. Fundamental delay models of type M/GI/1 and GI/M/1 and subsequently a more complex model with batch service and threshold control will be presented. Some results for continuous-time GI/GI/1 systems are shown.

5.1 Discrete-Time Markov Chain

A stochastic process $\{X(t), t > 0\}$ is considered which has the Markov property at discrete (not necessarily equidistant) points in time $\{t_n, n = 0, 1, \dots\}$. Thus, we obtain a sequence of random variables $\{X(t_0), X(t_1), \dots\}$. The value of the next random variable $X(t_{n+1})$ depends only on the current random variable $X(t_n)$, but not on other random variables in the past (Markov property). This discrete-time stochastic process is denoted by $\{X(t_n), n = 0, 1, \dots\}$ and called a *discrete-time Markov process*. Thereby, the random variables $X(t_n)$ may be discrete or continuous. For the analysis of M/GI/1 and GI/M/1, the considered state space is the number of customers and therefore discrete. Such a discrete-time Markov process with discrete values is called *discrete-time Markov chain*. For the analysis of a discrete-time GI/GI/1 system, a continuous random variable – which is the unfinished work – is considered, see Chapter 6.4, reflecting a discrete-time Markov process.

A discrete-time Markov chain is described by

- finite or countable state space S, e.g. $S = \{0, 1, 2, \dots\}$ is the number of customers in a system,

- transition probabilities $p_{ij} \geq 0$ for $i \neq j$ and $i, j \in S$,

- initial state $X(0)$, i.e. a probability distribution for the initial state.

The probability $x(i, n) = P(X(t_n) = i)$ for $i \in S$ and $n = 0, 1 \dots$ describes the system at time t_n which is the probability that the system is in state $[X_n = i]$ at time t_n. The Markov property is fundamental for the discrete-time Markov chain.

$$
\begin{aligned}
P(X(t_{n+1}) &= x_{n+1} | X(t_n) = x_n, \dots, X(t_0) = x_0) \\
&= P(X(t_{n+1}) = x_{n+1} | X(t_n) = x_n), \qquad t_0 < t_1 < \dots < t_n < t_{n+1}.
\end{aligned} \quad (5.1)
$$

The conditional probability $P(X(t_{n+1}) = j | X(t_n) = i)$ is called *transition probability* and depends on the previous system state.

$$
p_{ij} = P(X(t_{n+1}) = j | X(t_n) = i), \quad i, j \in S \qquad \textbf{transition probability} \quad (5.2)
$$

The transition probability matrix contains all transition probabilities. It is a quadratic matrix of size $|S| \times |S|$.

$$
\mathcal{P} = \{p_{ij}\} \qquad\qquad \textbf{transition probability matrix} \quad (5.3)
$$

Note that the rows of $\mathcal{P}$ sum up to 1, since the transition probabilities out of any state $i \in S$ sum up to 1. The matrix $\mathcal{P}$ is a *stochastic matrix*.

$$
\sum_{j \in S} p_{ij} = 1, \quad i \in S \qquad\qquad (5.4)
$$

Example: Bursty Channel (Gilbert-Elliot Model)   In communication channels, packet losses may occur. For modeling bursty losses, the Gilbert-Elliot model allows to distinguish two different states of the communication channel: a good state $[X = 0]$ with low packet loss probability q_0 and a bad state $[X = 1]$ with a high packet loss probability q_1. This burst-nose channel can be modeled as a discrete-time Markov chain of two states. The probability b and g reflect a change from good to bad conditions and vice versa, respectively. Figure 5.1 shows the state transition diagram of the DTMC as well as the transition matrix.

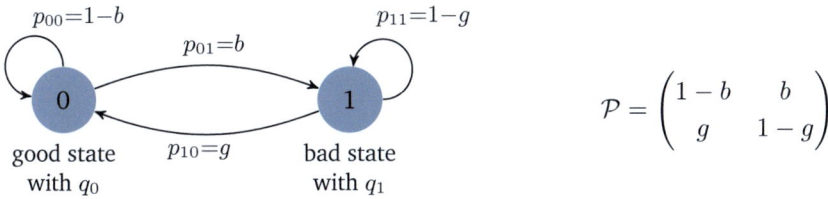

$$\mathcal{P} = \begin{pmatrix} 1-b & b \\ g & 1-g \end{pmatrix}$$

(a) Transition diagram. **(b)** Transition matrix.

Figure 5.1: Discrete-time Markov chain example: Gilbert-Elliot model for bursty channels.

Haßlinger and Hohlfeld sucessfully applied this model to fit packet loss processes of traffic traces measured in the IP backbone of an Internet provider [45]. It can also be extended to more states to reflect different state-dependent packet loss rates.

Example: DTMC of a CTMC   The continuous-time Markov chain was previously introduced in Chapter 3.5.1 and provided the state transition probabilities p_{ij} based on the transition rates q_{ij}. When the process leaves state i, the state $j \neq i$ is reached with probability p_{ij} in a CTMC, see Equation (3.24).

$$p_{ij} = \frac{q_{ij}}{q_i} = \frac{q_{ij}}{\sum_{i \neq j} q_{ij}} \tag{5.5}$$

Consider the embedded DTMC of a CTMC by looking at the transition time instances. To this end, we define the DTMC abstracting a CTMC by describing only the state transitions. Now, consider a birth-death process as discussed in Chapter 3.5.5 with four states, arrival rates λ_i, departure rates μ_i. Figure 5.2a provides the state transition diagram of the CTMC with the transition rates. Please note that for deriving the system states, it is not required to take into account the rate λ_3.

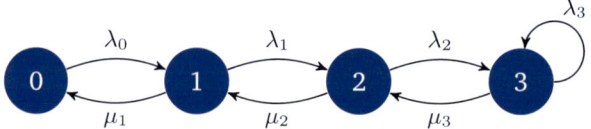

(a) Continuous-time Markov chain (CTMC) with transition rates.

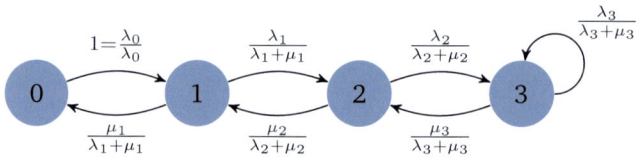

(b) Embedded discrete-time Markov chain (DTMC) with transition probabilities.

Figure 5.2: Birth-and-death process with four states.

As depicted in Figure 5.2b, the embedded DTMC or this CTMC has the same states as in the CTMC. However, the transition between states are the corresponding transition probabilities p_{ij} which relate the transition rate q_{ij} to the sum of rates for leaving state i, i.e. $\sum_{i \neq j} q_{ij}$, see Equation (5.5). The transition probability from state 0 to state 1 is $p_{01} = 1$, i.e., an arrival must occur as next transition event. In state 3, an arrival or a departure may occur. Therefore, the rate λ_3 needs to be taken into account.

5.2 Method of Embedded Markov Chain

In the next example consider a discrete-state stochastic process $\{X(t), t > 0\}$ which describes the state process of a performance model at time t. The process is thought of to be general, i.e. not necessarily memoryless. However, the process assumes that $\{X(t)\}$ has the Markov property at some particular instances $\{t_n, n = 0, 1, \ldots\}$:

$$
\begin{aligned}
P(X(t_{n+1}) &= x_{n+1}|X(t_n) = x_n, \ldots, X(t_0) = x_0) \\
&= P(X(t_{n+1}) = x_{n+1}|X(t_n) = x_n), \qquad t_0 < t_1 < \ldots < t_n < t_{n+1}. \quad (5.6)
\end{aligned}
$$

In other words: a discrete-time Markov chain is considered. Examine the process state at $X(t_n)$ at time instants t_n. From this point, the future development of the embedded process at times $t_{n+1}, t_{n+2}, \ldots$, depends only on the current process state $X(t_n)$. The complete development of the embedded process $X(t_0), X(t_1), \ldots, X(t_n)$ in the past, up to the time t_n, is completely contained in the state information

$[X(t_n) = x_n]$. Knowing the state x_n of the system at time t_n, the future development of the embedded process $X(t_{n+1})$, $X(t_{n+2}), \ldots$, can be determined out of $X(t_n)$.

Due to the Markov property of the process at times t_n, $n = 0, 1, \ldots$, the process $\{X(t_n) = x_n, n = 0, 1, \ldots\}$ is also a *Markov chain* embedded at times t_n. This chain is embedded in the original time-continuous process $\{X(t), t > 0\}$. The analysis method described here is therefore called the *method of embedded Markov chain*. The embedding times t_n are referred to as *regeneration points in time*, at which the state process is memoryless.

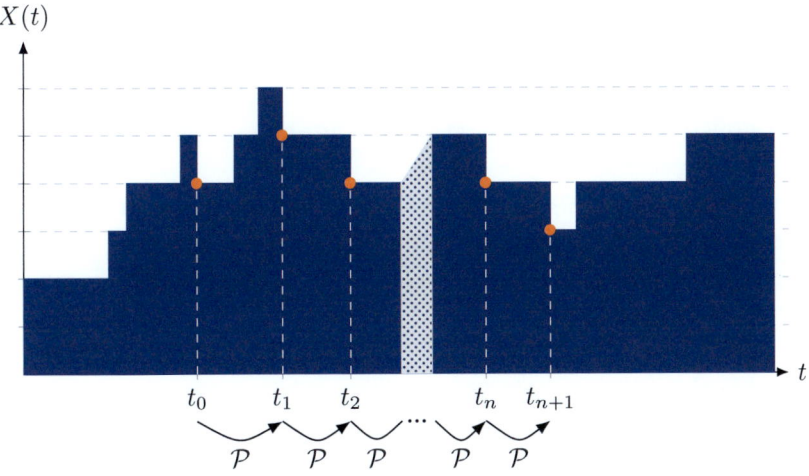

Figure 5.3: Regeneration points of the embedded Markov chain.

At each embedding time t_n the state probabilities form a state probability vector:

$$\mathbf{X}_n = \big(x(0,n), x(1,n), \ldots\big) , \tag{5.7a}$$
$$x(i, n) = P(X(t_n) = i) . \tag{5.7b}$$

If a performance model can be analyzed by means of the embedded Markov chain, a transition probability matrix exists which establishes the relationship between the state probability vectors at any two successive embedding times t_n and t_{n+1}, i.e.

$$\mathcal{P} = \{p_{ij}\} \tag{5.8a}$$

with

$$p_{ij} = P(X(t_{n+1}) = j | X(t_n) = i) , \quad i, j = 0, 1, 2, \ldots . \tag{5.8b}$$

This formulates a recursive equation which determines the state probability vector $\mathbf{X}_{n+1}$ of the next embedding point out of the current state probability vector $\mathbf{X}_n$:

$$\mathbf{X}_{n+1} = \mathbf{X}_n \cdot \mathcal{P} \ . \qquad\qquad \text{non-stationary analysis} \quad (5.9)$$

The elements of the matrix $\mathcal{P}$ are transition probabilities, and the transition probability matrix is a stochastic matrix. A matrix $\mathcal{P}$ with non-negative elements is called *stochastic* if $\mathcal{P}\,\mathbf{e} = \mathbf{e}$. If component-wise $\mathcal{P}\,\mathbf{e} \leq \mathbf{e}$ applies, the matrix $\mathcal{P}$ is called *substochastic*. Here $\mathbf{e}$ is the column vector of the corresponding dimension which contains only ones.

It should be noted here that the transition probability matrix $\mathcal{P}$ consists of *transition probabilities* as elements, where in the previous chapter the rate matrix $\mathcal{Q}$ contains *probability densities* (or rates) used for the analysis of continuous-time Markovian state processes.

Based on Equation (5.9) Markov chain probability vectors can successively be calculated if an initial (or starting) vector $\mathbf{X}_0$ is known. In the stationary state of the process, i.e. if the probability vector no longer varies over time or depends on the time index,

$$\mathbf{X}_{n+1} = \mathbf{X}_n = \mathbf{X} \ ,$$

the analysis is equivalent to an eigenvalue problem:

$$\mathbf{X} = \mathbf{X} \cdot \mathcal{P}. \qquad\qquad \text{stationary analysis} \quad (5.10a)$$

The stationary probability vector of the embedded Markov chain, according to Equation (5.10a), is hence the left-eigenvector of the transition probability matrix $\mathcal{P}$ with eigenvalue 1.

The embedded Markov chain method is suitable for the analysis of those traffic models, where only one model component is non-Markovian (not memoryless). The embedding times are expediently determined exactly where this non-Markovian model component becomes memoryless.

In an M/GI/1 system for example, the service time is the only non-Markovian model component. The state process in M/GI/1 has the Markov property at the end of each service time. The corresponding Markov chain is thus embedded at the service termination. In contrast, in a GI/M/1 system, the arrival process is not memoryless. The instants, at which customers arrive, are regeneration points of the embedded Markov chain. These systems will be discussed in this chapter.

5.2.1 Power Method for Numerical Derivation

A numerically robust method to derive the steady state probabilities $\mathbf{X}$ is the *power method*. Starting from an initial vector for state probabilities $\mathbf{X}_0$ and using the general state transition equation (5.27) to numerically determine the state vectors $\mathbf{X}_1, \ldots, \mathbf{X}_n, \mathbf{X}_{n+1}$ at the embedding times $t_1, \ldots, t_n, t_{n+1}$, until the steady state is reached.

In practice, the statistical equilibrium is considered as reached by a predefined termination condition (e.g. if $|\mathrm{E}[\,X(t_{n+1})\,] - \mathrm{E}[\,X(t_n)\,]| < \varepsilon = 10^{-6}$) which is checked after each iteration step. This *power method* is a numerically robust method for the analysis of state probabilities.

A requirement for the numerical computation in practice is a finite number of states. The pseudo-code of the algorithm is given in Python syntax and requires the initial state probability vector X0, the transition matrix P, the stopping condition stopFunction.

```
def powerMethod(X0, P, stopFunction):
    Z = P.shape[0]  # P is a quadratic matrix of size Z x Z
    X_old = numpy.zeros(Z)
    X1 = X0
    while stopFunction(X1, X_old): # test if steady state is reached
        X_old = X1
        X1 = X_old @ P # compute Xn+1 = Xn*P via matrix multiplication
    return X1
```

The steady state probabilities, with a proper definition of a stop function and an initial state, are obtained. The stop function returns true if the difference between means is still above the threshold epsilon.

```
def stopFunction_mean(X1, X_old, epsilon=1e-6):
    i = numpy.arange(len(X1)) # with i = (0, 1, ...,  len(X1)-1)
    EX_old = X_old @ i  # expected value E[X_n]
    EX1 = X1 @ i # expected value E[X_n+1]
    return abs(EX_old-EX1) > epsilon

Xmax = 6 # number of states 0, 1, ..., Xmax
X0 = numpy.zeros(Xmax+1)
X0[0] = 1 # initialization: empty system
X = powerMethod(X0, P, stopFunction_mean)
```

An implementation of the power method is provided at https://modeling.systems.

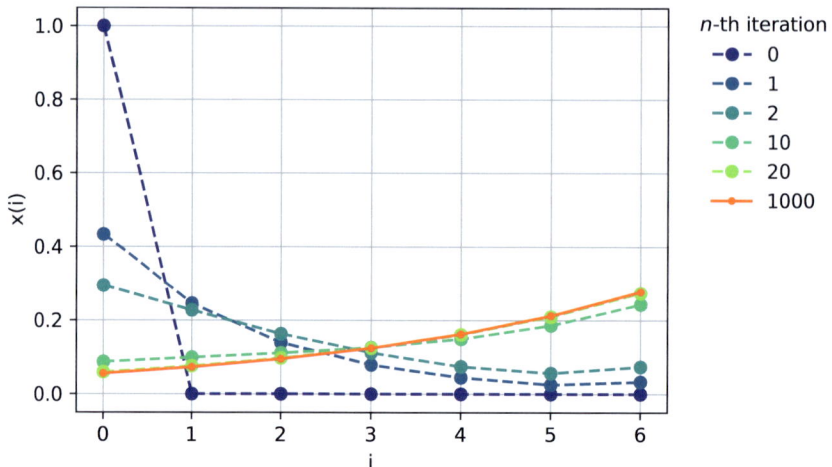

Figure 5.4: Illustration of the power method for an M/GI/1-5 with $\lambda = 1.7\,\mathrm{s}^{-1}$ and $\mu = 1.3\,\mathrm{s}^{-1}$. The probability distributions $P(X_n = i) = x(i, n)$ are plotted for the n-th iteration step. The initial system is empty, $x(1, 0) = 1$. The difference between $\mathrm{E}[\,X_{20}\,]$ and $\mathrm{E}[\,X_{1000}\,]$ is less than 3.8×10^{-4} and practically irrelevant.

5.2.2   Notion of Embedding Times

As previously mentioned, for the analysis of the M/GI/1 delay system and the GI/M/1 delay system, the method of the embedded Markov chain can be applied. The embedding times for M/GI/1 are immediately at the end of service; the number of customers X_n at time t_n at the n-th embedding point in time is a random variable. In order to highlight that the number of customers is considered at the departures, we use the notation $X_{D,n}$. Figure 5.5 illustrates the notation and the embedding times. Please note that the system is observed immediately *after* a departure – which is indicated by the black arrow pointing to the right side of t_n (after). We may also analyze the system by considering the system immediately *before* the departure. A proper selection immediately before or immediately after the embedding times simplifies the mathematical derivation, but both ways are acceptable. However, the embedding immediately after departure is more natural and intuitive, since the system state also includes zero. The steady state distribution X_D of the number of customers at departure times is obtained for $n \to \infty$.

$$X_D = \lim_{n \to \infty} X_{D,n} \tag{5.11}$$

For the analysis of a GI/M/1 system, the arrival times of customers are the embedding points in time. In order to highlight that the number of customers is considered at each arrival, we use the notation $X_{A,m}$ for the m-th arrival time. The steady state distribution X_A of the number of customers at the arrival times is obtained for $m \to \infty$.

$$X_A = \lim_{m \to \infty} X_{A,m} \tag{5.12}$$

Again, the system can be considered immediately *before* or *after* an arrival. Figure 5.5 illustrates the embedding immediately before an arrival – which is indicated by the black arrow pointing to the left side of t_m (before).

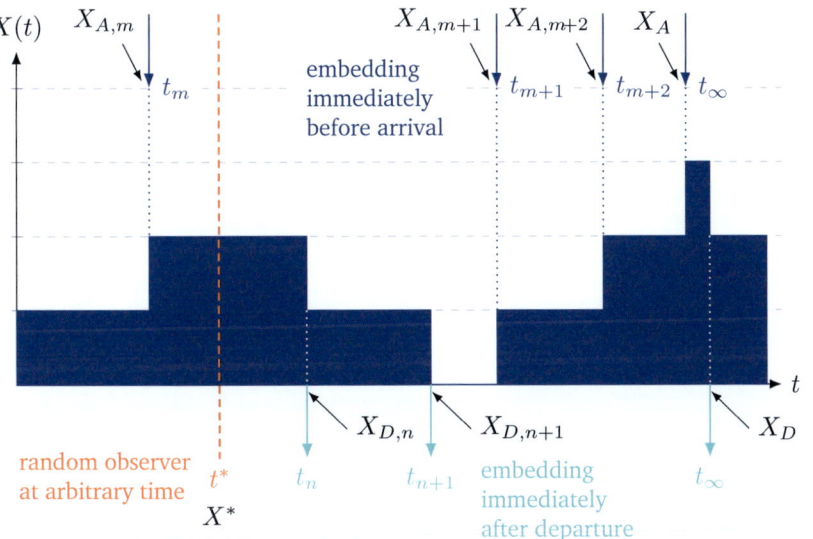

Figure 5.5: Notation of embedding times at arrivals and departure times.

Finally, in order to highlight that the system is observed at an arbitrary time by a random observer, we use the notation X^*. Let us summarize the notations for the steady state distributions of the number of customers in the system. The following random variables describe the system state.

X_A System state as seen by an arriving customer immediately before or after an arrival; the probability distribution is $x_A(i) = P(X_A = i)$.

X_D System state as seen by a departing customer immediately before or after service end; the probability distribution is $x_D(i) = P(X_D = i)$.

X^* System state as seen by a random observer, i.e., at an arbitrary time; the probability distribution is $x^*(i) = P(X^* = i)$.

X System state at embedding times; $X = X_D$ with embedding immediately after departure for M/GI/1; $X = X_A$ with embedding immediately before arrival for GI/M/1; $X = X^*$ for birth-and-death processes (Chapter 3.5.5).

In general, it is $X^* \neq X_A$. But in systems with Poisson arrivals, the PASTA property holds which means $X^* = X_A$.

In general, $X_A \neq X_D$. However, Kleinrock's result will provide some insights in which systems $X_A = X_D$ holds.

5.2.3 Kleinrock's Result

An important result will be used later for the analysis of an M/GI/1 delay system. The method of the embedded Markov chain provides the system state at the embedding times – which is immediately after the departure of a customer (X_D). However, we are interested in the system state when a customer arrives (X_A) in order to derive the waiting times.

Kleinrock's Result

For systems where the system state can change at most by $+1$ or -1, the system distribution as seen by an arriving customer will be the same as that seen by a departing customer.

$$x_A(i) = x_D(i) , \quad i = 0, 1, \ldots \tag{5.13}$$

However, the result cannot be applied to queues with batch arrivals or batch services.

We outline the proof of Kleinrock's result in the following. First, observe the state process during an interval of length T taking into account the segments of state $[X = i]$ (cf. Figure 5.6) with the following transitions marked:

- Transition from i to $i + 1$ (arrival of a customer). The total number of these transitions during the interval T is denoted by $n_A(i, T)$.

- Transition from $i + 1$ to i (departure of a customer). The total number of these transitions during the interval T is denoted by $n_D(i, T)$.

Since these two types of transitions are alternating during the evolution of the process, they differ during the observation period T maximal by 1, so that the following inequality holds

$$|n_A(i, T) - n_D(i, T)| \leq 1 . \tag{5.14}$$

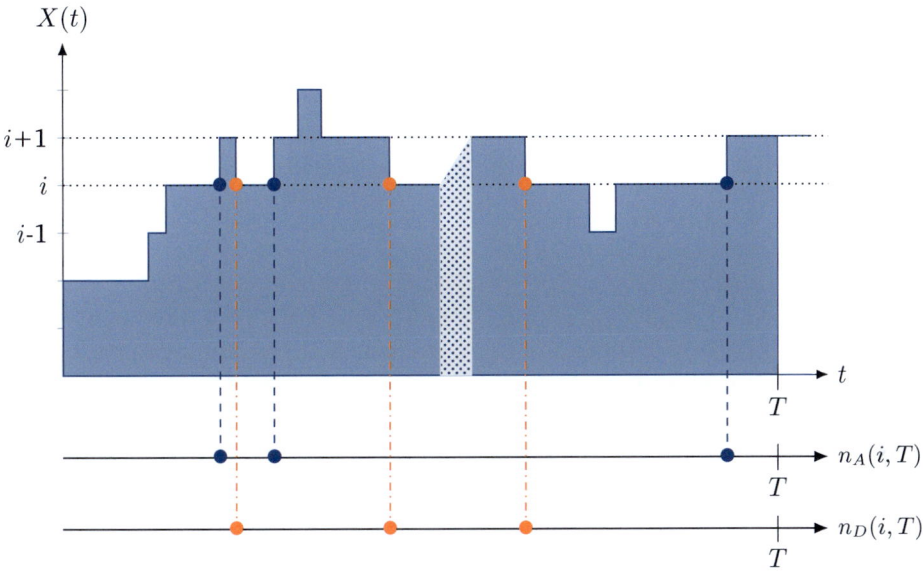

Figure 5.6: State probability at arbitrary observation time.

The total number of arrivals and departures during T are:

$$n_A(T) = \sum_{i=0}^{\infty} n_A(i, T),$$ (5.15a)

$$n_D(T) = \sum_{i=0}^{\infty} n_D(i, T).$$ (5.15b)

Taking into account the starting state $X(0)$ (integer value) at the beginning and the ending state $X(T)$ (integer value) at the end of the observation period T, the balance of the numbers of arrivals and departures delivers

$$n_D(T) = X(0) + n_A(T) - X(T).$$ (5.15c)

For stationary state probabilities at departure points:

$$x_D(i) = \lim_{T \to \infty} \frac{n_D(i, T)}{n_D(T)} = \lim_{T \to \infty} \frac{n_A(i, T) + n_D(i, T) - n_A(i, T)}{n_A(T) + X(0) - X(T)}$$

$$= \lim_{T \to \infty} \frac{\frac{n_A(i,T)}{n_A(T)} + \frac{n_D(i,T) - n_A(i,T)}{n_A(T)}}{1 + \frac{X(0) - X(T)}{n_A(T)}} \qquad i = 0, 1, \dots .$$ (5.16)

The *strong law of large numbers* for Markov chains (cf. Fisz [37]) was shown in Equation (3.63c) and yields

$$\lim_{T \to \infty} \frac{n_A(i, T)}{n_A(T)} = x_A(i), \quad i = 0, 1, \dots ,$$

(5.17a)

and insertion of Equation (5.14)

$$\lim_{T \to \infty} \frac{n_D(i, T) - n_A(i, T)}{n_A(T)} = 0$$

(5.17b)

and considering a steady state system

$$\lim_{T \to \infty} \frac{|X(0) - X(T)|}{n_A(T)} = 0,$$

(5.17c)

we finally arrive at

$$x_D(i) = x_A(i), \quad i = 0, 1, \dots .$$

(5.18)

5.3 Delay System M/GI/1

5.3.1 Model Structure and Parameters

The structure of the M/GI/1 delay system (M/GI/1-∞) is depicted in Figure 5.7. According to the Kendall notation the arrival process is Poisson, i.e. the interarrival time A is negative exponentially distributed:

$$A(t) = P(A \leq t) = 1 - e^{-\lambda t}, \qquad E[A] = \frac{1}{\lambda}.$$

The arrival rate λ stands for the mean number of arriving customers per time unit. The service time B is here generally distributed. The offered traffic, respectively the system load, is identical to the server occupancy or server utilization:

$$\rho = \frac{E[B]}{E[A]} = \lambda \cdot E[B].\qquad\qquad\text{server utilization}\quad(5.19)$$

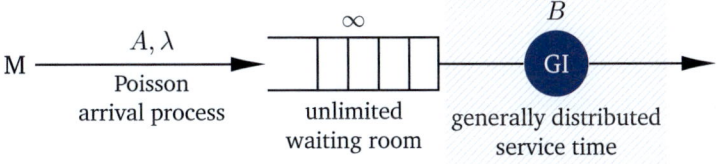

Figure 5.7: M/GI/1 delay system.

The queue capacity is assumed to be infinitely large, i.e. a pure delay system. A customer finding the server occupied upon arrival must wait until the current service terminates and the server becomes free. The server processes waiting requests from the queue according to a queueing discipline (or service discipline), e.g. FIFO (first-in, first-out) or FCFS (first-come, first-served), LIFO (last-in, first-out), RANDOM, etc.

Figure 5.8 illustrates a sample path of the state process of the M/GI/1 delay system. The n-th customer finds the server busy and waits in the first position of the queue. Here, at time t_{n-1} the observed customer will enter service. Its waiting time and service time are annotated in Figure 5.8.

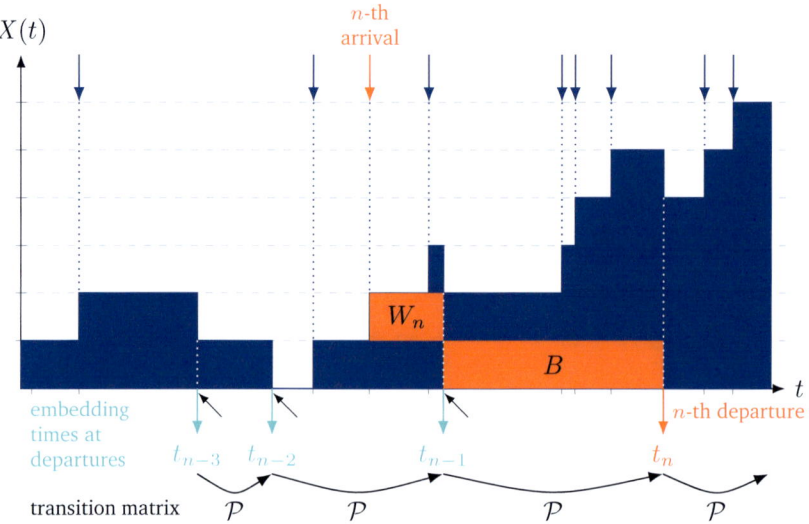

Figure 5.8: State process of delay system M/GI/1 (FIFO service discipline).

5.3.2 Markov Chain and State Transition

Embedded Chain and Regeneration Points In an M/GI/1 delay system, the service process is the only non-Markovian model component, i.e. it is *not* memoryless. This implies that the state process becomes memoryless at instances of service ends.

Therefore, a Markov chain can be embedded at the ends of service times, as marked in Figure 5.8. A regeneration point could principally be chosen either *immediately before* or *immediately after* a service termination. Here we deliberately chose instants *immediately after* service ends to constitute a Markov chain for the following M/GI/1 analysis, as depicted in Figure 5.8. One of the reasons for this choice is that in choosing instants *immediately before* service ends, the state "zero" doesn't exist and the state at embedding points would be quite artificial.

The regeneration points are at departures of customers. The time of the n-th regeneration point therefore corresponds to the n-th departure at t_n. The sequence $\{X(t_0), X(t_1), \ldots, X(t_n), X(t_{n+1}), \ldots\}$ of the system states forms an embedded Markov chain at these instances, at which the state probabilities will be analyzed below.

For the subsequent analysis it is useful to first look at the r.v. Γ for the number of arrivals during a service duration B and its distribution (see Chapter 3.3.3):

$$\gamma(i) = P(\Gamma = i) \tag{5.20a}$$

with the generating function

$$\Gamma_{GF}(z) = \sum_{i=0}^{\infty} \gamma(i) z^i, \tag{5.20b}$$

where the mean is

$$E[\Gamma] = \left.\frac{d\Gamma_{GF}(z)}{dz}\right|_{z=1} = \lambda E[B] = \rho. \tag{5.20c}$$

State Transition Probabilities Consider the transition between two successive regeneration points and the associated transition probability

$$p_{ij} = P(X(t_{n+1}) = j \mid X(t_n) = i) . \qquad \textbf{transition probability} \tag{5.21}$$

During the interval (t_n, t_{n+1}) the following state transitions can occur (cf. Figure 5.9):

- $i \neq 0$
  The system is not empty at regeneration time t_n (Figure 5.9a). The state development is as follows: At regeneration point t_n there are i customers in the system. Immediately after that, a service time starts. If after the termination of this service time, j customers are still in system, then $(j - i + 1)$ arrivals must have occurred during the observed service time, i.e.

$$p_{ij} = \gamma(j - i + 1), \quad i = 1, \ldots, \quad j = i - 1, i, \ldots . \tag{5.22}$$

- $i = 0$
  The system is empty at regeneration time t_n. When the first customer arrives, the initial service time of this customer starts, as shown in Figure 5.9b. If after this initial service time, j customers are still in system, then these j customers must have arrived during the initial service time, i.e.

$$p_{0j} = \gamma(j), \quad j = 0, \ldots . \tag{5.23}$$

In summary, the state transition matrix of the M/GI/1 delay system follows.

$$\mathcal{P} = \{p_{ij}\} = \begin{pmatrix} \gamma(0) & \gamma(1) & \gamma(2) & \gamma(3) & \cdots \\ \gamma(0) & \gamma(1) & \gamma(2) & \gamma(3) & \cdots \\ 0 & \gamma(0) & \gamma(1) & \gamma(2) & \cdots \\ 0 & 0 & \gamma(0) & \gamma(1) & \cdots \\ \vdots & \vdots & \vdots & \vdots & \ddots \end{pmatrix} \qquad \begin{array}{l} \textbf{state transition} \\ \textbf{matrix} \end{array} \tag{5.24}$$

In practice, $\gamma(i)$ can be derived by numerically computing the inverse transformation in Equation (3.20) or by numerically computing the integral in Equation (3.19c).

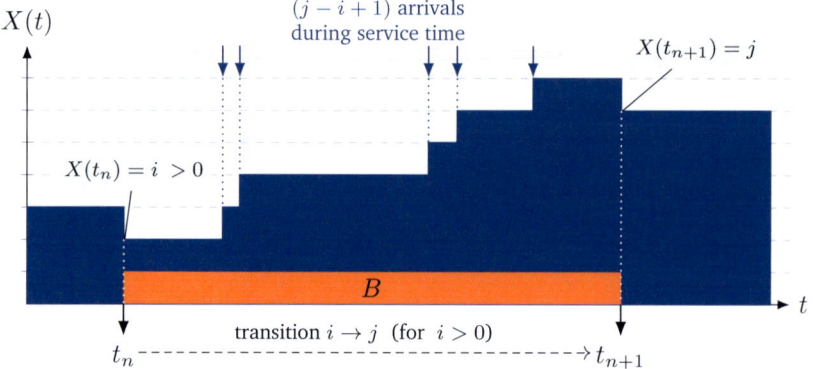

(a) Transition $[X(t_n) = i] \rightarrow [X(t_{n+1}) = j]$ for $(i > 0)$.

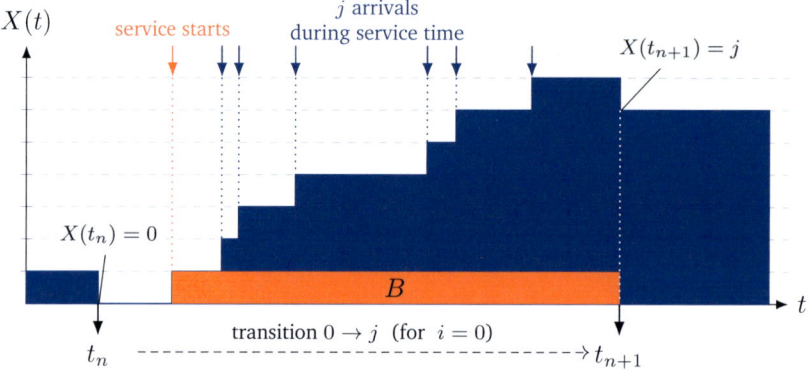

(b) Transition $[X(t_n) = 0] \rightarrow [X(t_{n+1}) = j]$ for $(i = 0)$.

Figure 5.9: Transition probabilities in the M/GI/1 delay system.

5.3.3   State Equation

State Transition Equation   The state probabilities at the regeneration point t_n

$$x(j, n) = P(X(t_n) = j) \quad j = 0, 1, \ldots \tag{5.25}$$

form the components of the state probability vector $\mathbf{X}_n$

$$\mathbf{X}_n = \left(x(0, n), x(1, n), \ldots, x(j, n), \ldots \right) . \tag{5.26}$$

The state probability vector at the next regeneration point t_{n+1} can be computed from the state probability vector at previous regeneration point t_n using the following state transition equation:

$$\mathbf{X}_n \cdot \mathcal{P} = \mathbf{X}_{n+1} . \qquad \text{\textbf{\color{blue}general state transition equation}} \tag{5.27}$$

Equation (5.27) generally applies to both stationary and transient – non-stationary – system states. From a start vector $\mathbf{X}_0$ at an initial regeneration point t_0, all future time-dependent state probability vectors $\mathbf{X}_n$, $n = 1, 2, \ldots$, can successively be computed. In doing so, process paths and subsequent characteristics of transient state processes can be analyzed, e.g. in investigations of transient processes in communication networks to assess their overload behavior.

Stationary State Transition Equation   Equation (5.27) provides the stationary system state probability vector

$$\mathbf{X}_n = \mathbf{X}_{n+1} = \ldots = \mathbf{X} , \tag{5.28a}$$
$$\mathbf{X} = \left(x(0), x(1), \ldots, x(j), \ldots \right) , \tag{5.28b}$$

and the stationary state transition equation

$$\mathbf{X} \cdot \mathcal{P} = \mathbf{X} . \qquad \text{\textbf{\color{blue}stationary state transition equation}} \tag{5.29}$$

5.3.4   State Probabilities

As seen in Equation (5.29) the steady state probability vector we are looking for is the left-eigenvector of the transition matrix $\mathcal{P}$ to the eigenvalue 1. This has already been pointed out in the discussion of the embedded Markov chain method in Chapter 5.2. The calculation of the state probabilities is reduced to the solution of an eigenvalue problem of an infinite matrix. Alternatively, the power method is a numerically robust method for deriving the steady state probabilities, as discussed in Chapter 5.2.1, which requires, however, to truncate the state space.

Analysis Using Generating Function The state transition equation (5.29) can be written in component notation as:

$$x(j) = x(0)\,\gamma(j) + \sum_{i=1}^{j+1} x(i)\,\gamma(j-i+1) \qquad j = 0, 1, \ldots \,. \tag{5.30}$$

And after multiplying each term with z^j and summing up for all j

$$\underbrace{\sum_{j=0}^{\infty} x(j)\,z^j}_{X_{GF}(z)} = x(0)\underbrace{\sum_{j=0}^{\infty}\gamma(j)\,z^j}_{\Gamma_{GF}(z)} + \sum_{j=0}^{\infty}\sum_{i=1}^{j+1} x(i)\,\gamma(j-i+1)\,z^j \tag{5.31a}$$

plus recognizing herein the corresponding generating functions

$$\Gamma_{GF}(z) = \sum_{j=0}^{\infty}\gamma(j)z^j \,,$$

$$X_{GF}(z) = \sum_{j=0}^{\infty} x(j)z^j \,. \tag{5.31b}$$

The double-sum in Equation (5.31a) can be rewritten as

$$\sum_{j=0}^{\infty}\sum_{i=1}^{j+1} x(i)\,\gamma(j-i+1)\,z^j = \sum_{i=1}^{\infty} x(i) \sum_{j=i-1}^{\infty}\gamma(j-i+1)\,z^j$$

$$\overset{j^*=j-i+1}{=} \sum_{i=1}^{\infty} x(i) \underbrace{\sum_{j^*=0}^{\infty}\gamma(j^*)\,z^{j^*}}_{\Gamma_{GF}(z)}\,z^{i-1}$$

$$= \Gamma_{GF}(z) \sum_{i=1}^{\infty} x(i)z^{i-1}$$

$$= \Gamma_{GF}(z)\,\frac{1}{z}\,(X_{GF}(z) - x(0)) \,. \tag{5.31c}$$

Obtained from Equation (5.31a) is

$$X_{GF}(z) = x(0)\Gamma_{GF}(z) + \frac{\Gamma_{GF}(z)}{z}(X_{GF}(z) - x(0)) \tag{5.32a}$$

or

$$X_{GF}(z) = x(0)\,\frac{\Gamma_{GF}(z)\,(1-z)}{\Gamma_{GF}(z) - z}\,. \tag{5.32b}$$

To determine $x(0)$ we apply the utilization law (Chapter 2.1.4) or consider the limit $z \to 1$ of the term

$$X_{GF}(z)\Big|_{z \to 1} = \frac{0}{0},$$

following the L'Hospital's rule and arrive at:

$$1 = \sum_{j=0}^{\infty} x(j) = X_{GF}(z)\Big|_{z \to 1} = x(0) \left. \frac{\frac{d}{dz}\Gamma_{GF}(z)(1-z) - \Gamma_{GF}(z)}{\frac{d}{dz}\Gamma_{GF}(z) - 1} \right|_{z \to 1}$$

$$= x(0) \frac{-1}{\frac{d}{dz}\Gamma_{GF}(z)\big|_{z \to 1} - 1},$$

with

$$\frac{d}{dz}\Gamma_{GF}(z)\Big|_{z \to 1} = \sum_{j=1}^{\infty} \gamma(j) \, j \, z^{j-1}\Big|_{z \to 1} = \mathrm{E}[\Gamma] = \lambda \, \mathrm{E}[B] = \rho,$$

i.e.

$$x(0) = 1 - \rho \tag{5.33a}$$

and finally arrive – with Equation (5.32b) – at

$$X_{GF}(z) = \frac{(1-\rho)(1-z)\Gamma_{GF}(z)}{\Gamma_{GF}(z) - z}. \tag{5.33b}$$

Recalling that the function $\Gamma_{GF}(z)$ is the generating function of the number of arrivals of a Poisson process during a service period B with distribution function $B(t)$ and LST $\Phi_B(s)$. From Equation (3.20) the term $\Gamma_{GF}(z)$ can be found:

$$\Gamma_{GF}(z) = \sum_{j=0}^{\infty} \gamma(j) \, z^j = \sum_{j=0}^{\infty} \int_0^{\infty} \frac{(\lambda t)^j}{j!} e^{-\lambda t} b(t) \, dt \, z^j$$

$$\underset{(3.20)}{=} \Phi_B(s)\Big|_{s = \lambda(1-z)} = \Phi_B(\lambda(1-z)). \tag{5.34}$$

Combining Equation (5.33b) and Equation (5.34) we obtain the generating function of the state probability distribution of the embedded Markov chain of the M/GI/1 delay system.

$$X_{GF}(z) = \frac{(1-\rho)\,(1-z)\,\Phi_B(\lambda(1-z))}{\Phi_B(\lambda(1-z)) - z} \quad \textbf{Pollaczek-Khintchine formula for system state} \tag{5.35}$$

5.3.5 Delay Distribution

The distribution function of the waiting time in M/GI/1 systems can be derived from the Pollaczek-Khintchine formula for state probabilities. The following derivation assumes that the queueing discipline is FIFO (first-in, first-out) or FCFS (first-come, first-served).

Consider in the following a sojourn time D of a test customer with probability density function $d(t)$, cumulative distribution function $D(t)$ and the corresponding Laplace-Stieltjes transform $\Phi_D(s)$. The sojourn time D is simply the sum of the waiting time W and the service time B of the test customer:

$$D = W + B \,, \tag{5.36a}$$

$$d(t) = w(t) * b(t) \,, \tag{5.36b}$$

$$\Phi_D(s) = \Phi_W(s) \cdot \Phi_B(s) \,. \tag{5.36c}$$

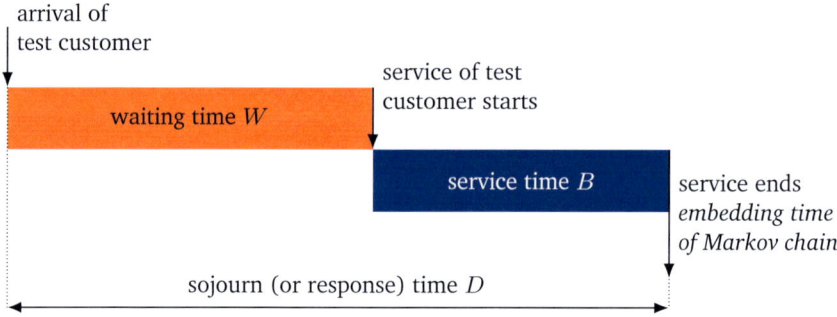

Figure 5.10: Sojourn time of a customer.

At departure time of the test customer we assume that there are still k customers in the system. According to the definition of the embedding time, $[X = k]$ is also the system state at the corresponding regeneration time of the Markov chain. Following the FIFO service discipline, these k customers left behind by the test customer must have arrived during the sojourn time D, i.e.

$$x(k) = P(\text{test customer left behind } X = k \text{ customers in system})$$
$$= P(k \text{ arrivals during the sojourn time of test customer}) \,.$$

According to this equation, $X = k$ is the number of Poisson arrivals during a sojourn time of length D, i.e. an interval with the distribution function $D(t)$ and

LST $\Phi_D(s)$. From Equation (3.20) the generating function $X_{GF}(z)$ can be derived:

$$X_{GF}(z) = \sum_{k=0}^{\infty} x(k)\, z^k \;=\; \sum_{k=0}^{\infty} \int_0^{\infty} \frac{(\lambda t)^k}{k!}\, e^{-\lambda t}\, d(t)\, dt\; z^k$$

$$\underset{(3.20)}{=}\; \Phi_D(s)\Big|_{s=\lambda(1-z)} \;=\; \Phi_D(\lambda(1-z))\,. \tag{5.37}$$

Inserting Equation (5.37) in Equation (5.35) we obtain

$$\Phi_D(\lambda(1-z)) = \frac{(1-\rho)\,(1-z)\,\Phi_B(\lambda(1-z))}{\Phi_B(\lambda(1-z)) \;-\; z} \tag{5.38a}$$

or after replacing $s = \lambda(1-z)$

$$\Phi_D(s) = \frac{s(1-\rho)}{s - \lambda + \lambda\Phi_B(s)}\, \Phi_B(s)\,. \tag{5.38b}$$

From Equation (5.38b) and Equation (5.36ac) the Laplace-Stieltjes transform of the waiting time in M/GI/1 system is obtained:

$$\Phi_W(s) = \frac{s\,(1-\rho)}{s - \lambda + \lambda\,\Phi_B(s)}\,. \qquad \textbf{\textcolor{blue}{Pollaczek-Khintchine}} \atop \textbf{\textcolor{blue}{formula for waiting time}} \tag{5.39}$$

In Figure 5.11 the complementary cumulative waiting time distribution function of an M/GI/1 system is depicted, for different values of the system utilization ρ and various types of service time distribution functions. It can be seen here that for service times with higher coefficients of variation c_B, the waiting time also has a higher variance, reflected in a flatter shape of the tail distribution functions.

5.3.6 Other System Characteristics

Waiting Probability With the Laplace transform of the *cumulative distribution function* of the waiting time and Equation (2.73a)

$$W(t) \quad \circ\!\!-\!\!\bullet \quad \frac{\Phi_W(s)}{s}$$

and the initial value theorem of the Laplace transform (cf. Equation (2.74a)), the Pollaczek-Khintchine formula (5.39) delivers the probability that a customer doesn't have to wait:

$$P(W = 0) = \lim_{t \to 0} W(t) = \lim_{s \to \infty} s \cdot \frac{\Phi_W(s)}{s} = 1 - \rho\,. \tag{5.40}$$

This may also be derived by utilizing the PASTA property $x_A(i) = x^*(i)$. The utilization law provides $x^*(0) = 1 - \rho$ and $P(W = 0) = x_A(0) = x^*(0) = 1 - \rho$.

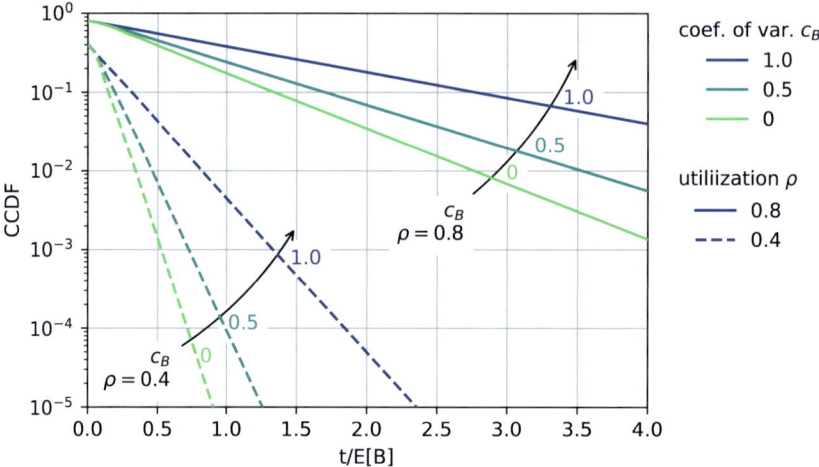

Figure 5.11: Complementary cumulative distribution function of the waiting time for M/GI/1 with various coefficient of variations of the service time.

This leads to the waiting probability

$$p_W = P(W > 0) = 1 - P(W = 0)$$
$$= 1 - W(t)\big|_{t\to 0} = \rho \,. \qquad \textbf{waiting probability} \text{ (5.41)}$$

Mean Waiting Times   Of importance is to distinguish between the mean waiting time $E[W]$ of all customers and the mean waiting time $E[W_1]$ of those customers who have to wait, i.e. their waiting time is non-zero. The mean waiting time of all customers $E[W]$ can be determined from Equation (5.39) and Equation (2.72):

$$E[W] = E[B] \cdot \frac{\rho(1 + c_B^2)}{2(1 - \rho)} = \frac{\lambda E[B^2]}{2(1 - \rho)} \,, \qquad (5.42a)$$

while the mean waiting time $E[W_1]$ of waiting customers is:

$$E[W_1] = \frac{E[W]}{p_W} = E[B] \cdot \frac{1 + c_B^2}{2(1 - \rho)} \,. \qquad (5.42b)$$

Following these expressions for the waiting times the mean delays in an M/GI/1 system depend only on the first two moments of the service time.

In Figure 5.12 the mean waiting time is shown as a function of the system occupancy. The set of curves depicts different coefficients of variation c_B of the service time. As expected, with increasing values of c_B the mean waiting time also increases. With larger values of the system load ρ, a relatively small increase of c_B can lead to a very large increase of the waiting time. The M/GI/1 delay system is hence very sensitive to load fluctuations when the system occupancy is high. This fact explains the dimensioning of technical systems operating in delay mode (switches, server, computing devices, etc.) choosing lower load ranges (e.g. $\rho < 0.7$).

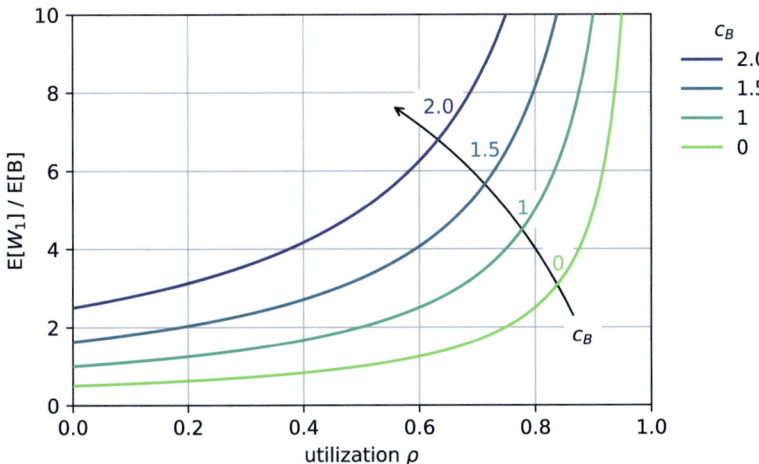

Figure 5.12: Normalized mean waiting time of waiting customer in M/GI/1 system.

Higher Moments of the Waiting Time In principle, higher moments of the customer waiting time can be obtained by means of the Pollaczek-Khintchine formula (Equation (5.39)). The expressions of these moments can however be more simply computed using the Takács recursion formula (cf. Kleinrock [61], Takács [102]):

$$E[W^k] = \frac{\lambda}{1-\rho} \sum_{i=1}^{k} \binom{k}{i} \frac{E[B^{i+1}]}{i+1} E[W^{k-i}] , \tag{5.43a}$$

$$E[W^0] = 1 . \qquad \qquad \text{Takács recursion formula} \tag{5.43b}$$

Especially for the two first moments:

$$E[W] = \frac{\lambda E[B^2]}{2(1-\rho)} , \tag{5.44a}$$

$$E[W^2] = 2E[W]^2 \frac{\lambda E[B^3]}{3(1-\rho)} . \tag{5.44b}$$

5.3.7 State Probabilities at Arbitrary Time

Up to now, the state probabilities $\{x(i),\ i = 0, 1, \ldots\}$ given in the Pollaczek-Khintchine formula (Equation (5.35)) hold at the regeneration points of the Markov chain. To be more precise, we have calculated $x(i) = x_D(i)$. However, for the M/GI/1 delay system, it can be shown that these state probabilities are also valid at any randomly selected time t^* by an independent outside observer. This property is detailed in the following.

According to notations in Chapter 5.2.2, $\{x^*(i),\ i = 0, 1, \ldots\}$ are the state probabilities at random observation time and $\{x_A(i),\ i = 0, 1, \ldots\}$ are the state probabilities seen by customers at arrival. For the M/GI/1 delay systems all three state probabilities are identical

$$x(i) = x_D(i) \underset{\text{Kleinrock Eq.(5.13)}}{=} x_A(i) \underset{\text{PASTA Eq.(4.4)}}{=} x^*(i), \qquad i = 0, 1, \ldots . \qquad (5.45)$$

Kleinrock's result can be applied (cf. Chapter 5.2.3), since the system state can change at most by $+1$ or -1 in the M/GI/1 queue. The system distribution as seen by an arriving customer will be the same as that seen by a departing customer: $x_A(i) = x_D(i)$, see Equation (5.13).

As the arrival process is a Poisson process, the positions of the arrival times are random. This implies that statistically, an arriving customer sees the state process upon arrival with the same view as an independent observer, i.e.

$$x^*(i) = x_A(i),\ i = 0, 1, \ldots . \qquad (5.46)$$

This corresponds to the PASTA property, see Chapter 3.3.2 and Equation (3.12). With Kleinrock's result in Equation (5.13) and the PASTA property in Equation (5.46) the validity of Equation (5.45) is proven. In particular, this shows that $x^*(0) = 1 - \rho$ (utilization law) and $p_W = 1 - x_A(0) = 1 - x^*(0) = \rho$.

5.4 Delay System GI/M/1

5.4.1 Model Structure and Parameters

The structure of the GI/M/1 delay system is shown in Figure 5.13. The arrival process is a renewal process. The random variable A of the interarrival time can be arbitrarily distributed. The service time B is negative exponentially distributed, i.e. it has the Markov property:

$$B(t) = P(B \leq t) = 1 - e^{-\mu t}, \qquad E[B] = \frac{1}{\mu}. \tag{5.47}$$

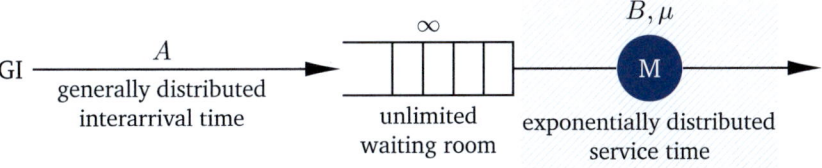

Figure 5.13: GI/M/1 delay system.

The system occupancy (or server utilization) is identical to the normalized offered traffic ρ defined by:

$$\rho = \frac{E[B]}{E[A]} = \frac{1}{\mu \cdot E[A]} . \qquad \text{utilization} \tag{5.48}$$

The random variable X represents the number of customers in the system. Figure 5.14 illustrates a sample path of the state process of the GI/M/1 delay system, where the time-dependent development $X(t)$ of the system state is depicted.

5.4.2 Markov Chain and State Transition

In GI/M/1 delay systems, the arrival process is the only non-Markovian model component, i.e. the interarrival time is *not* memoryless. This implies that the process becomes memoryless at arrival times of customers. Therefore, a Markov chain can be embedded at the customer arrival times, as marked in Figure 5.14. A regeneration point could principally be chosen either *immediately before* or *immediately after* a customer arrival. Here we deliberately chose instants *immediately before* customer arrivals to constitute a Markov chain for the GI/M/1 analysis, as depicted in Figure 5.14. One of the reasons for this choice is that choosing instants *immediately after* customer arrivals, the state "zero" doesn't exist and the states at embedding points become quite artificial.

Thus, the regeneration points are just before arrivals of customers (cf. Figure 5.14). The future development of the state process depends only on the system state at the embedding times. With $X(t_n)$ to be the system state immediately before the arrival time t_n of the n-th customer, and form $\{X(t_0), X(t_1), \ldots, X(t_n), X(t_{n+1}), \ldots\}$ an embedded Markov chain. The term *chain* refers to the discrete-state property of the process.

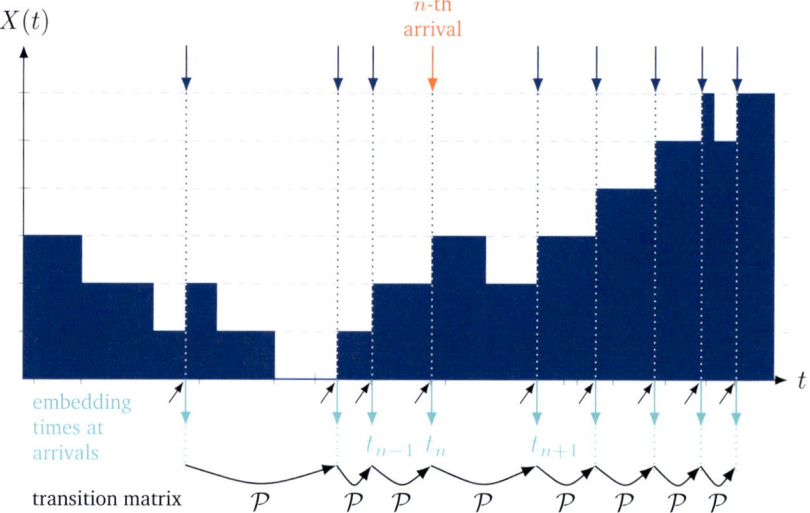

Figure 5.14: State process of GI/M/1 delay system.

For the following analysis it is convenient to first examine the random variable Γ which stands for the number of customers with service terminations during an interarrival time A. Think of the server as being in a busy period, i.e. it always has customers to serve in a back-to-back manner:

$$\gamma(i) = P(\Gamma = i) \tag{5.49}$$

with the generating function

$$\Gamma_{GF}(z) = \sum_{i=0}^{\infty} \gamma(i) z^i, \tag{5.50a}$$

where

$$E[\Gamma] = \left. \frac{d\Gamma_{GF}(z)}{dz} \right|_{z=1} = \mu \cdot E[A] = \frac{1}{\rho} .$$ (5.50b)

The state probabilities of the Markov chain are derived in the following. First, observe the transition probability between two successive regeneration points:

$$p_{ij} = P(X(t_{n+1}) = j \mid X(t_n) = i) .$$ (5.51)

Since there are no arrivals during the period (t_n, t_{n+1}), but only service terminations, the state process is solely a death process during this interval. Therefore, two types of transitions are distinguished:

- $j \neq 0$:
  The system is not empty at t_{n+1}. Since there are i customers in the system prior to t_n, there will be $i+1$ customers just after t_n. To have j customers in the system prior to t_{n+1}, the number $(i + 1 - j)$ of customers must have completed service during the observed interarrival time (t_n, t_{n+1}). The transition probability for this case is

$$p_{ij} = \gamma(i + 1 - j), \ i = 0, 1, \ldots, \ j = 1, \ldots, i + 1 .$$ (5.52)

- $j = 0$:
  The system is empty at t_{n+1}. There are i customers in the system prior to t_n, just after t_n there are $i + 1$. To have the system empty prior to t_{n+1}, all $i + 1$ customers in the system must have been served during (t_n, t_{n+1}). i.e. at least $i + 1$ service terminations must occur during (t_n, t_{n+1}). The transition probability for this case is

$$p_{i0} = \sum_{k=i+1}^{\infty} \gamma(k) = 1 - \sum_{k=0}^{i} \gamma(k), \ i = 0, 1, \ldots .$$ (5.53)

Finally, the state transition matrix results in

$$\mathcal{P} = \{p_{ij}\} = \begin{pmatrix} 1 - \gamma(0) & \gamma(0) & 0 & 0 & \cdots \\ 1 - \sum_{k=0}^{1} \gamma(k) & \gamma(1) & \gamma(0) & 0 & \cdots \\ 1 - \sum_{k=0}^{2} \gamma(k) & \gamma(2) & \gamma(1) & \gamma(0) & \cdots \\ \vdots & \vdots & \vdots & \vdots & \ddots \end{pmatrix} .$$ (5.54)

5.4.3 State Probabilities

At embedding time t_n, the probability for the system to be in state j is the state probability $x(j, n)$

$$x(j, n) = P(X(t_n) = j),$$ (5.55a)

and with the state probability vector $\mathbf{X}_n$

$$\mathbf{X}_n = \big(x(0, n), x(1, n), \ldots, x(j, n), \ldots\big),$$ (5.55b)

the following general state transition equation is obtained (the attribute "general" indicates that the non-stationary case is also included):

$$\mathbf{X}_n \cdot \mathcal{P} = \mathbf{X}_{n+1}.$$ **general state equation** (5.56)

Equation (5.56) holds thus for the stationary as well as for non-stationary, time-dependent system state evolution. Given a start vector $\mathbf{X}_0$ at time t_0, it is possible to successively compute the general case with customer-dependent, non-stationary state probability vectors $\mathbf{X}_n$. This enables the analysis of transient responses of technical systems and their overload behavior.

Is the process in stationary steady state condition (with $\rho < 1$), i.e.

$$\mathbf{X}_n = \mathbf{X}_{n+1} = \ldots = \mathbf{X} = \big(x(0), x(1), \ldots, x(j), \ldots\big),$$

the Equation (5.56) is just

$$\mathbf{X} \cdot \mathcal{P} = \mathbf{X}.$$ **stationary state equation** (5.57)

According to Equation (5.57) the steady state probability vector being searched for is the left-eigenvector of the transition matrix $\mathcal{P}$ to the eigenvalue 1, as already discussed in the derivation of the embedded Markov chain method.

5.4.4 State Analysis with Geometric Approach

The state equation (5.57) can be written in component notation as follows:

$$x(0) = \sum_{i=0}^{\infty} x(i) \left(1 - \sum_{k=0}^{i} \gamma(k)\right) = \sum_{i=0}^{\infty} x(i) \sum_{k=i+1}^{\infty} \gamma(k),$$ (5.58a)

$$x(j) = \sum_{i=j-1}^{\infty} x(i)\gamma(i+1-j) = \sum_{i=0}^{\infty} x(i+j-1)\gamma(i), \quad j = 1, 2, \ldots.$$ (5.58b)

To derive the state probabilities at regeneration points of the Markov chain we take the so-called *geometric approach* (cf. Gross and Harris [41], Kleinrock [61]). According to this approach we consider whether the following assumption would be valid and lead to a valid solution for σ

$$x(j+1) = \sigma x(j), \quad j = 0, 1, \ldots$$

or

$$x(j+1) = \sigma^{j+1} x(0) . \qquad\qquad \textbf{geometric assumption} \;\; (5.59)$$

We obtain from Equation (5.58b) for $j \geq 1$

$$x(j) - \left[x(j-1)\,\gamma(0) + x(j)\,\gamma(1) + x(j+1)\,\gamma(2) + \ldots \right] = 0$$

$$\sigma\, x(j-1) - x(j-1)\,\gamma(0) - \sigma\, x(j-1)\,\gamma(1) - \sigma^2\, x(j-1)\,\gamma(2) - \ldots = 0$$

$$x(j-1) \left[\sigma - \Big(\gamma(0) + \sigma\,\gamma(1) + \sigma^2\,\gamma(2) + \ldots \Big) \right] = 0$$

$$x(j-1)\ \left[\sigma - \sum_{i=0}^{\infty} \gamma(i)\,\sigma^i \right] = 0 . \qquad\qquad (5.60)$$

A non-trivial solution of Equation (5.60) is identical with a non-trivial root of $\sigma = \sum_{i=0}^{\infty} \gamma(i)\,\sigma^i$, i.e. a non-trivial root for $z = \sigma$ according to

$$z = \Gamma_{GF}(z) . \qquad\qquad \textbf{non-trivial root for } \sigma = z \;\; (5.61)$$

$\Gamma_{GF}(z)$ converges in $|z| \leq 1$, but the trivial solution $1 = \Gamma_{GF}(1)$ can be excluded. Instead, simply search for a solution σ for Equation (5.61) in the Interval $]0, 1[$. First of all, for real valued z ($z \geq 0$)

$$\frac{d\Gamma_{GF}(z)}{dz} = \sum_{i=1}^{\infty} i\gamma(i)z^{i-1} \geq 0 , \qquad\qquad (5.62a)$$

$$\frac{d^2\Gamma_{GF}(z)}{dz^2} = \sum_{i=2}^{\infty} i(i-1)\gamma(i)z^{i-2} \geq 0 , \qquad\qquad (5.62b)$$

i.e. the function $\Gamma_{GF}(z)$ is convex and monotonically increasing in the interval $]0, 1[$.

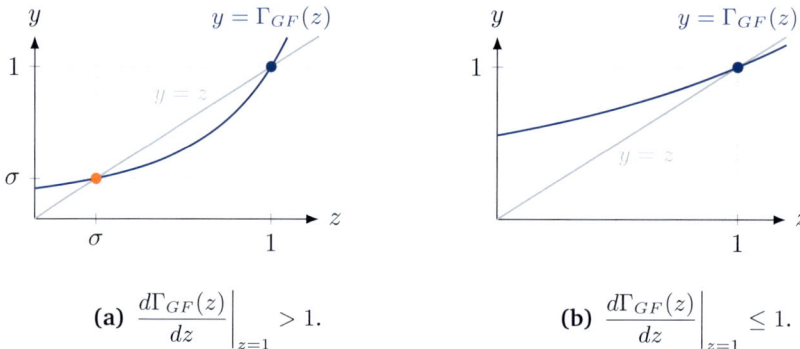

(a) $\dfrac{d\Gamma_{GF}(z)}{dz}\Big|_{z=1} > 1.$ (b) $\dfrac{d\Gamma_{GF}(z)}{dz}\Big|_{z=1} \leq 1.$

Figure 5.15: Analysis with geometric approach for GI/M/1. The numerical example uses a uniform distribution $A \sim U(0, 2/\lambda)$ with $E[A] = 1/\lambda$. It is $\mu = 1$ and (a) $\rho = 0.4$ and (b) $\rho = 1.5$, respectively.

As illustrated in Figure 5.15, σ is determined by the intersection of the two functions: $y = z$ and $y = \Gamma_{GF}(z)$. While it does not provide a non-trivial solution in case b), there is exactly one solution σ for case a) (cf. Figure 5.15), if

$$\frac{d\Gamma_{GF}(z)}{dz}\Big|_{z=1} = E[\Gamma] = \frac{1}{\rho} > 1 \qquad \text{or} \quad \rho < 1. \tag{5.63}$$

The condition in Equation (5.63) implies that a solution exists if the system is stable and a statistical equilibrium can be achieved. The state probabilities can be computed from Equation (5.59) and the normalization condition

$$x(j) = \sigma^j x(0), \tag{5.64a}$$

$$\sum_{j=0}^{\infty} x(j) = 1, \tag{5.64b}$$

together with the waiting probability σ to finally deliver

$$x(j) = (1 - \sigma)\,\sigma^j, \quad j \geq 0, \rho < 1. \qquad \textbf{\textcolor{blue}{state probability}} \tag{5.65}$$

Note that $X \sim \text{GEOM}(1 - \sigma)$, cf. Chapter 2.4.1.3. The key point of the computation of these probabilities and the corresponding performance measures is a sufficiently exact numerical calculation of σ according to Equation (5.61).

5.4.5 Waiting Time Distribution

The waiting time distribution function of the GI/M/1 delay system can be derived in the same way as the waiting time analysis of the M/M/n delay system (cf. Chapter 4.2.4). First, consider the conditional probability that an arriving customer experiences a positive (non-zero) waiting time:

$$P(W_1 > t) = P(W > t | W > 0) = \frac{P(W > t, W > 0)}{P(W > 0)} = \frac{P(W > t)}{P(W > 0)}, \quad (5.66a)$$

where

$$P(W > 0) = \sum_{i=1}^{\infty} x(i) = 1 - x(0) = \sigma. \quad (5.66b)$$

The waiting process of a randomly chosen test customer is taken into account. The test customer finds upon arrival X customers in system, where a positive waiting time exists only for $X > 0$, i.e.

$$P(W > t) = \sum_{i=1}^{\infty} P(W > t \,|\, X = i) \cdot P(X = i)$$

$$= \sum_{i=1}^{\infty} P(W > t | X = i) \cdot (1 - \sigma)\sigma^i. \quad (5.67)$$

Obtained from Equation (5.66b) and Equation (5.67) is:

$$P(W > t | W > 0) = \sum_{i=1}^{\infty} P(W > t | X = i)(1 - \sigma)\sigma^{i-1}. \quad (5.68)$$

Considering the queueing discipline FIFO (first-in, first-out), the conditional probability $P(W > t | X = i)$ can be derived. Let the test customer see $X = i$ customers upon arrival, i.e. there are $i - 1$ customers waiting in front and have to complete service.

The waiting time of the test customer consists of two components:

- the interval from arrival instant until the first service termination. This interval is a forward recurrence time of the service time B. Since B is memoryless, its forward recurrence time has the same distribution function.

- the interval from the first service termination until all remaining $i - 1$ customers in the queue have completed service. This interval consists of $i - 1$ service times of type B.

As a result, the waiting time for the test customer is made up of i service durations B. The conditional waiting time distribution function is hence an Erlang distribution function of i-th order:

$$P(W > t|X = i) = e^{-\mu t} \sum_{k=0}^{i-1} \frac{(\mu t)^k}{k!}$$

or from Equation (5.68)

$$P(W > t|W > 0) = e^{-\mu t} \sum_{i=1}^{\infty} \sum_{k=0}^{i-1} \frac{(\mu t)^k}{k!} (1 - \sigma) \sigma^{i-1}$$

$$= e^{-\mu t} \sum_{k=0}^{\infty} \frac{(\mu t)^k}{k!} \sum_{i=k+1}^{\infty} (1 - \sigma) \sigma^{i-1}$$

$$= e^{-\mu t} \sum_{k=0}^{\infty} \frac{(\sigma \mu t)^k}{k!} = e^{-(1 - \sigma) \mu t} \qquad (5.69)$$

by employing $\sum_{k=0}^{\infty} \frac{x^k}{k!} = e^x$. It is $W_1 \sim \text{EXP}((1 - \sigma)\mu)$. Then:

$$P(W > t) = P(W > t|W > 0) \cdot P(W > 0)$$
$$= \sigma e^{-(1-\sigma)\mu t} = 1 - W(t) .$$

Finally arriving at the waiting time distribution function $W(t)$ for customers in a GI/M/1 delay system with the waiting probability σ:

$$W(t) = 1 - \sigma\, e^{-(1 - \sigma)\,\mu\, t} . \qquad \textbf{\color{blue}{GI/M/1 waiting time}} \; (5.70)$$

Figure 5.16 shows the complementary cumulative distribution function of the waiting time for all customers in a scenario with low load ($\lambda = 0.4, \mu = 1, \rho = 0.4$) and high load ($\lambda = 0.4, \mu = 0.5, \rho = 0.8$), respectively. The higher the coefficient of variation c_A, the higher the probability $P(W > t)$. Please note that $c_A = 1$ corresponds to an M/M/1 system, while $c_A = 0$ represents an M/D/1 system which is analyzed in detail in Chapter 7.4.2 yielding a closed-form of the waiting time distribution function. For $c_A = 0.5$, an Erlang-k distribution is used for the interarrival time A with $k = 4$ and $E[A] = 1/\lambda$.

Figure 5.17 shows the waiting probability $p_W = P(W > 0) = \sigma$, cf. Equation (5.70), while σ is numerically derived by solving Equation (5.61). It can be seen that p_W depends on the system utilization ρ as well as the coefficient of variation c_A. For $c_A = 1$, we have an M/M/1 system with $p_W = \rho$. In general, for any M/GI/1 system, it is $p_W = \rho$, cf. Equation (5.41), which is independent of the coefficient of variation c_B of the service time.

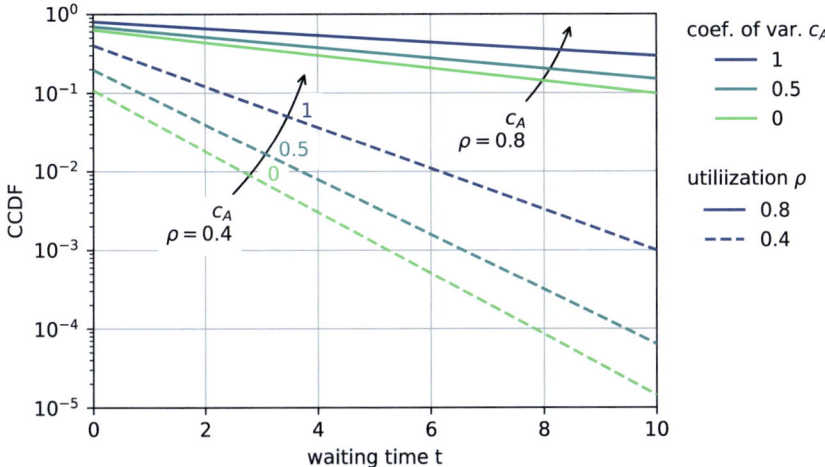

Figure 5.16: Waiting time distribution of all customers in GI/M/1 systems with varying system load ρ and coefficient of variation c_A of interarrival times on a logarithmic y-axis.

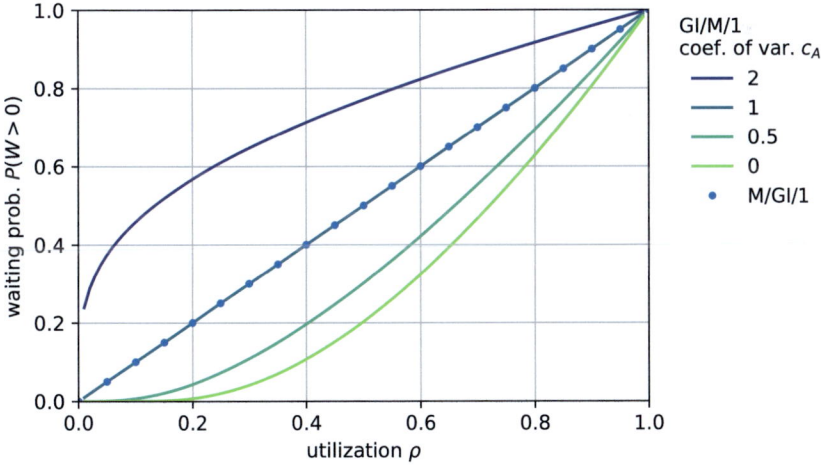

Figure 5.17: Waiting probability $p_W = P(W > 0)$ of customers in GI/M/1 systems with varying coefficient of variation c_A of interarrival times. Note that $p_W = \sigma$ for GI/M/1 depends on ρ and c_A, while $p_W = \rho$ is independent of c_B for M/GI/1.

5.5   Model with Batch Service and Threshold Control

This chapter examines a more complex model which can still be analyzed using the embedded Markov chain technique from Chapter 5.2. The model discussed here arises out of performance evaluation of manufacturing systems, especially in semiconductor manufacturing (cf. Gold and Tran-Gia [40]).

A work station processes a batch of jobs jointly (*batch service*). At most K jobs can be processed during batch service. However, the work station is first activated if there are enough jobs available to be processed (*threshold control*). This threshold Θ when to activate the service controls the efficiency of the system as well as the wait and response time for jobs. For manufacturing systems, it may be more cost-efficient to run the machine for a minimum number Θ of jobs, while the processing capacity K as well as the waiting space S are limited. The original model [40] may be applied and adapted to model various Internet services and applications.

In cloud computing, a pool of resources is provided to the users. Santhi and Saravanan [92] use a batch service queue to model access to a cloud database in batches of size K. In the full-batch service model, the batch size of requests to be processed may be less than K; the threshold control is not used, i.e., $\Theta = 1$. The partial-batch service model requires a constant batch size K in the system, i.e. $\Theta = K$. Both models are included in the batch service model with threshold control as described in this chapter.

Data backup processes to a cloud infrastructure are another example for the batch service model and threshold control. There is a trade-off between backing up frequently and reducing resource usage e.g. for power consumption. According to Saxena, Claeys, Zhang, and Walraevens [94] the basic model of the storage process considers incoming data packets waiting for storage in the cloud; the service corresponds to data packets being stored on the cloud infrastructure. A batch service is implemented for efficiency, while the threshold allows controlling the trade-off.

Smart city applications and services represent another application domain. Data is collected from IoT sensors and stored in a smart city database, cf. Chapter 7.2. The incoming data is processed and aggregated, e.g. for a specific geographic region or over a period of time. This processed and aggregated information is then published and accessible in the smart city application. The smart city system is modeled as a queue of incoming sensor data. The service corresponds to the batch processing of the data coming from several sensors. Concerning the quality of aggregated information, it may be reasonable to update the aggregated information only if there is information of at least Θ sensors. However, this threshold also affects the timeliness of the published information. The batch processing may be limited by K, e.g. due to increased batch service computation times or memory usage.

5.5.1 Model Structure and Parameters

The general model structure is shown in Figure 5.18. The server stage consists of a single batch server containing a group of K service places. The server can also be activated even if not all service places are occupied. Once it is started, the service time has to be continued to the end. If there are too many empty places in the server in a service time, the system operation can become inefficient. The service time B is arbitrarily distributed with the distribution function $B(t)$, regardless of the size of the group that is processed during an operation. All customers in a batch, which are simultaneously served, will experience exactly the same service duration. There is no possible additional reloading during an operation. Those servers can often be found in operating units e.g. in semiconductor manufacturing.

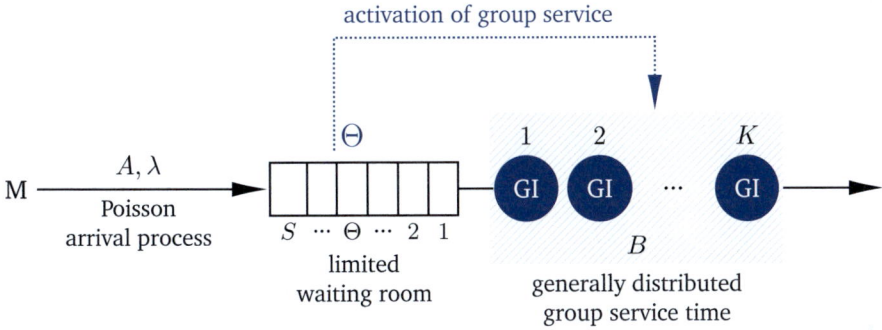

Figure 5.18: Batch server with starting threshold: $M/GI^{[\Theta,K]}/1$-S.

Customers arrive according to a Poisson process with rate λ, i.e. for the assumed interarrival time

$$A(t) = P(A \le t) = 1 - e^{-\lambda t}, \qquad E[A] = \frac{1}{\lambda}.$$

The queue has a capacity of S waiting places. Customers finding upon arrival the queue fully occupied are considered to be blocked. The batch server is controlled by the following trigger mechanism using a starting threshold Θ as follows: At the end of an operation, the server is loaded and started immediately if at least Θ customers are waiting to be processed. If there are fewer than Θ customers in the queue, the system waits until the starting threshold Θ is reached, before the next operation begins.

Using the short-hand notation M/GI$^{[\Theta,K]}$/1-S, we denote with the random variable $X(t)$ the number of customers in the queue at time t. The random variable $X(t)$ is also referred to as system state. Figure 5.19 shows a sample of the state process.

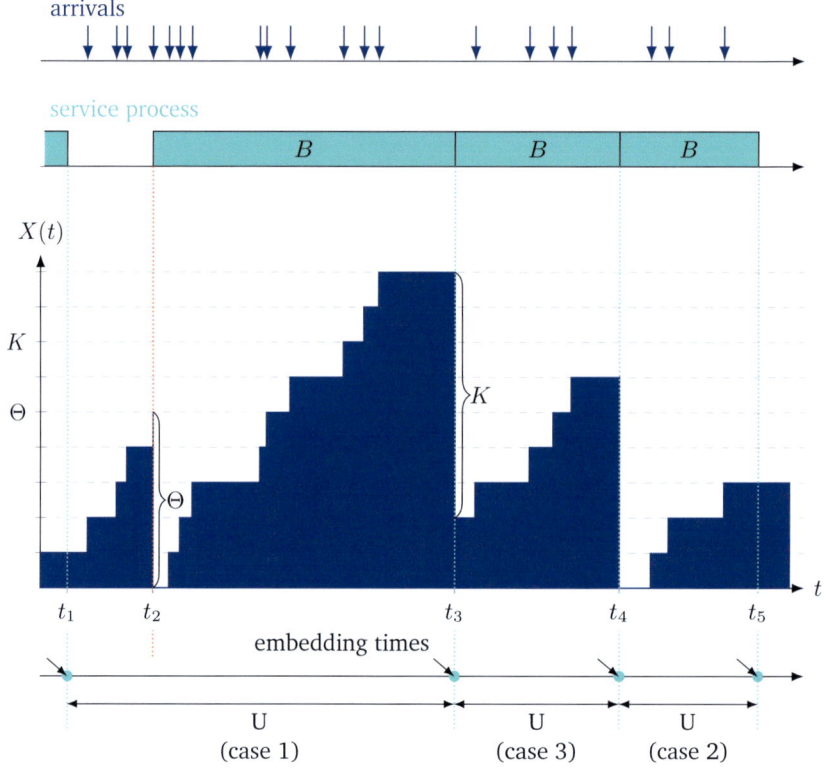

Figure 5.19: State process of an M/GI$^{[\Theta,K]}$/1-S system.

5.5.2 Markov Chain and State Transition

The only non-Markovian model component of the system described above is the service time. Thus, a Markov chain can be embedded at the ends of service times, as seen in Figure 5.19. A regeneration point could principally be chosen either immediately before or immediately after a service termination. Here we deliberately chose instants *immediately before* service ends to constitute a Markov chain for the analysis, as depicted in Figure 5.19. Note that we chose instants immediately after service ends for the analysis of the M/GI/1 system in Chapter 5.3.

Let the random variable Γ be the number of customers arriving during a service time B with the probability mass function $\gamma(k)$, $k = 0, 1, \ldots$. With $X(t_n)$ denoting the system state immediately *before* the n-th service termination t_n, the sequence $\{X(t_0), X(t_1), \ldots, X(t_n), X(t_{n+1}), \ldots\}$ constitutes an embedded Markov chain.

To compute the state probabilities at embedding points in the following, the transition probabilities between two consecutive embedding points must first be determined:

$$p_{ij} = P(X(t_{n+1}) = j | X(t_n) = i) \, . \tag{5.71}$$

The duration of the interval U between the successive embedding points t_n and t_{n+1} and the transition probability p_{ij} can be obtained from the state $[X(t_n) = i]$:

- (*Case 1*, time t_1 in Figure 5.19): $i < \Theta$
  Since the minimum number Θ of customers to start the server is not yet reached, further $\Theta - i$ customers still have to arrive before the server can be started. This interval is denoted by $E_{\Theta-i}$ and is Erlang-($\Theta - i$) distributed. If there are a total of Θ customers in the queue, the server is activated (time t_2 in Figure 5.19). During this service time (duration from t_2 to t_3) the number j of customers arrive. The transition time U is $U = E_{\Theta-i} + B$, and the corresponding transition probability is:

$$p_{ij} = \gamma(j) \, , \qquad j = 0, \ldots, S - 1 \, ,$$
$$p_{iS} = \sum_{k=S}^{\infty} \gamma(k) \, , \quad j = S \, .$$

- (*Case 2*, time t_4 in Figure 5.19): $\Theta \le i \le K$
  There are more than Θ customers waiting in the queue. The queue will then be emptied immediately after the service termination, starting a new service period of length B. During this service period, j customers arrive. The transition time U is identical to the service time, i.e. $U = B$, and the transition probability is identical to that in Case 1.

- (*Case 3*, time t_3 in Figure 5.19): $K < i \le S$
  Immediately after the service termination, K requests from the queue are transferred to the server stage, the remaining customers will stay in the queue and wait for the next service. The server starts then again. The transition time U is identical to the service time, i.e. $U = B$. Immediately after the start of the new service period there are still $i - K$ requests in the queue.

To ensure that there are j customers in the queue at the next embedding time, there must be $j - i + K$ customers arriving during the service time. The corresponding transition probability is:

$$p_{ij} = \gamma(j - i + K) , \qquad j = 0, \ldots, S - 1 ,$$

$$p_{iS} = \sum_{k=S-i+K}^{\infty} \gamma(k) , \qquad j = S .$$

Taking all cases into account, the state transition matrix can be given as follows.

$$\mathcal{P} =
\begin{matrix}
 & 0 & 1 & 2 & & S-1 & S & \\
\end{matrix}
\left(
\begin{matrix}
\gamma(0) & \gamma(1) & \gamma(2) & \cdots & \gamma(S-1) & \sum_{k=S}^{\infty} \gamma(k) \\
\gamma(0) & \gamma(1) & \gamma(2) & \cdots & \gamma(S-1) & \sum_{k=S}^{\infty} \gamma(k) \\
\vdots & \vdots & \vdots & \ddots & \vdots & \vdots \\
\gamma(0) & \gamma(1) & \gamma(2) & \cdots & \gamma(S-1) & \sum_{k=S}^{\infty} \gamma(k) \\
0 & \gamma(0) & \gamma(1) & \cdots & \gamma(S-2) & \sum_{k=S-1}^{\infty} \gamma(k) \\
0 & 0 & \gamma(0) & \cdots & \gamma(S-3) & \sum_{k=S-2}^{\infty} \gamma(k) \\
\vdots & \vdots & \vdots & \vdots & \vdots & \vdots \\
0 & 0 & 0 & \cdots & \gamma(K-1) & \sum_{k=K}^{\infty} \gamma(k)
\end{matrix}
\right)
\begin{matrix}
0 \\ 1 \\ \\ K \\ K+1 \\ K+2 \\ \\ S
\end{matrix}
\tag{5.72}$$

5.5.3 State Probabilities and System Characteristics

Following the definition of state probabilities at embedding point t_n

$$x(j, n) = P(X(t_n) = j) \tag{5.73a}$$

and the state probability vector $\mathbf{X}_n$,

$$\mathbf{X}_n = \big(x(0, n), x(1, n), \ldots, x(S, n)\big) , \tag{5.73b}$$

the general state equation is

$$\mathbf{X}_n \cdot \mathcal{P} = \mathbf{X}_{n+1} . \qquad \text{state equation for general case} \tag{5.74}$$

The general state equation (5.74) is valid for both cases, stationary (steady state) as well as for non-stationary system system states. When a start vector $\mathbf{X}_0$ is known, the state probability vector $\mathbf{X}_n$ can be successively determined.

For the stationary case, i.e.

$$\mathbf{X}_n = \mathbf{X}_{n+1} = \ldots = \mathbf{X} = \big(x(0), x(1), \ldots, x(S)\big) \,,$$

we obtain from Equation (5.74):

$$\mathbf{X} \cdot \mathcal{P} = \mathbf{X} \,. \qquad\qquad\qquad\qquad \text{stationary state equation} \quad (5.75)$$

According to Equation (5.75) the steady state probability vector is the left-eigenvector of the transition matrix $\mathcal{P}$ to the eigenvalue 1, as already discussed in the derivation of the embedded Markov chain method (Chapter 5.2).

Performance Measures   The state probability vector at arbitrary observation instants can be derived from the state probability vector at embedding points.

$$\mathbf{X}^* = \big(x^*(0), x^*(1), \ldots, x^*(S)\big)$$

The derivation is presented in detail in Gold and Tran-Gia [40]. Another approach is provided by Chaudhry and Gupta in [19] which is outlined in the following.

We define the random variable $X_y^*(i) = P(X^* = i, Y = y)$ with X^* reflecting the number of customers in the waiting queue at an arbitrary time, while Y indicates if the server is active and serving a batch of customers ($Y = 1$) or if the server is idle ($Y = 0$). The steady state probabilities are then as follows. A proof for this relationship is provided in [19].

$$x_0^*(i) = \frac{\sum_{j=0}^{i} x(j)}{\lambda \mathrm{E}[\,B\,] + \sum_{k=0}^{i} (\Theta - i)x(k)}, \quad 0 \le i \le \Theta - 1 \qquad (5.76a)$$

$$x_1^*(i) = \frac{\sum_{j=i+1}^{\min(K+i,S)} x(j)}{\lambda \mathrm{E}[\,B\,] + \sum_{k=0}^{i} (\Theta - i)x(k)}, \quad 0 \le i \le S - 1 \qquad (5.76b)$$

$$x_1^*(S) = 1 - \sum_{i=0}^{\Theta-1} x_0^*(i) - \sum_{i=0}^{S-1} x_1^*(i) \qquad (5.76c)$$

Further system characteristics are obtained from the probabilities in vector $\mathbf{X}^*$. The arbitrary-time state probabilities are then $x^*(i) = x_0^*(i) + x_1^*(i)$. The blocking probability is

$$p_B = x^*(S) \,. \qquad (5.77a)$$

The mean waiting time in the system is

$$\mathrm{E}[\,W\,] = \frac{\mathrm{E}[\,X^*\,]}{\lambda(1 - p_B)} \quad \text{with} \quad \mathrm{E}[\,X^*\,] = \sum_{k=0}^{S} k \cdot x^*(k) \,. \qquad (5.77b)$$

Numerical Results   In the following some numerical results are presented for the system M/GI$^{[\Theta, K]}$/1-S for the server with $K = 32$ service positions and a finite queue size of $S = 64$. Fixing $E[B] = 1\,\text{s}$.

In Figure 5.20 the mean waiting time is depicted in dependency of the offered traffic $\rho = \lambda\,E[B]/K$. The parameters are the starting threshold Θ and the service time coefficient of variation c_B, where especially two cases are selected, deterministic ($c_B = 0$) and negative exponentially distributed service time ($c_B = 1$). At lower traffic intensity ρ the waiting time is long, since the system has to wait for at least Θ customers to arrive before a service period can start. The extent of this effect depends on the choice of the starting threshold Θ. At higher traffic intensity ($0.3 < \rho < 1$), the mean waiting time depends rather more on the type of service (c_B). Service times with a larger coefficient of variation c_B correspond to longer waiting times.

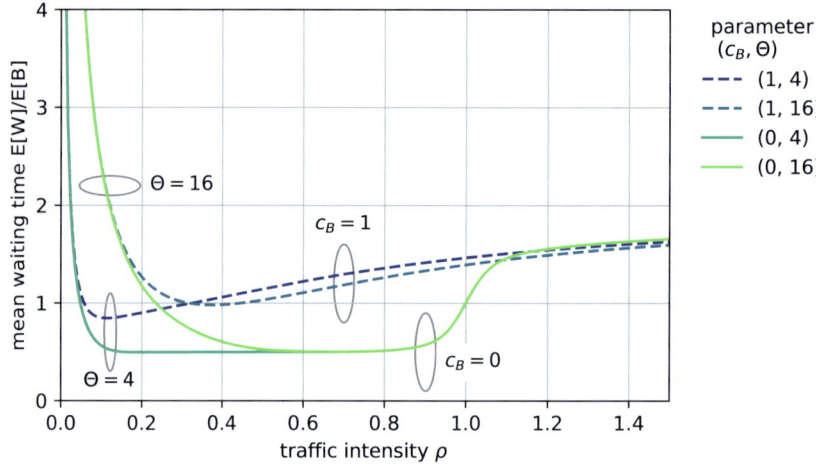

Figure 5.20: Impact of threshold Θ on mean waiting time for $S = 64$ and $K = 32$.

The choice of the starting threshold Θ is illustrated in Figure 5.21, where the mean waiting time is shown as a function of Θ. Although an optimal choice of the starting threshold with regard to the mean waiting time exists, the respective minimum is very parameter-sensitive. For dimensioning purposes of system operation, a precise calculation of the optimal starting threshold must be carried out individually for each system.

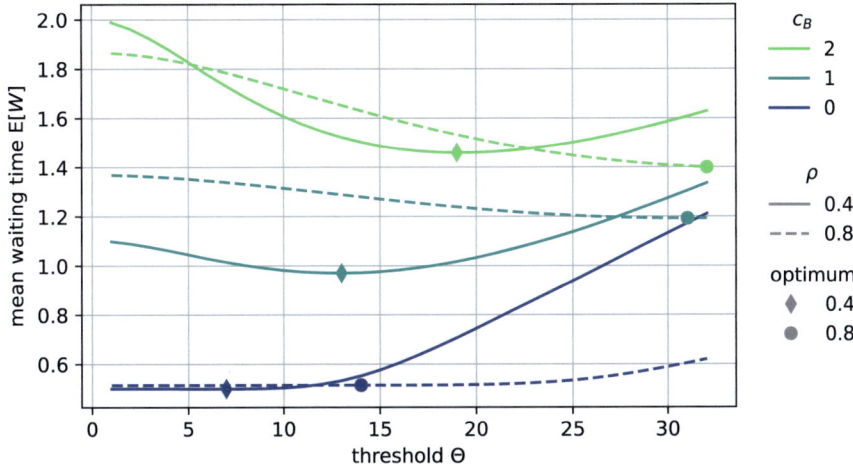

Figure 5.21: On dimensioning of the threshold value Θ for the batch service queue. The optimal threshold for a parameter setting is depicted with a marker.

Figure 5.21 also shows the optimal threshold for a parameter setting which is plotted as a diamond marker ($\rho = 0.4$) and circle marker ($\rho = 0.8$), respectively. An algorithm for deriving the optimum is provided by Zeng and Xia in [124] and given here as pseudo-code in Python syntax.

```
def optimalTheta(lam, EB, cB, S, K):
    a = 1 # initialize threshold
    while True:
        # compute expected waiting time for Theta=a
        EWa  = calc_M/GI[ab]/1-S (Theta=a, lam, EB, cB, S, K)
        if a == min( ceil(lam*EWa), K): return a
        a = min( ceil(lam*EWa), K)
```

An implementation of the M/GI$^{[\Theta,K]}$/1-S model and the computation of the optimal threshold can be found online at https://modeling.systems.

5.6 Results for Continuous-Time GI/GI/1 Delay Systems

The GI/GI/1 delay system has two components with non-Markovian behavior. Observing a continuous-time, non-negative r.v. A for the interarrival time and B for the service time. The according cumulative distribution functions are $A(t)$ and $B(t)$, the probability density functions are $a(t)$ and $b(t)$ accordingly. We provide some fundamental characteristics and the Lindley integral equation as functional relationship for the waiting time W.

5.6.1 Characteristics of GI/GI/1 Delay Systems

The GI/GI/1 delay system requires the stability condition, cf. Equation (2.9) for GI/GI/n. This means that the number of arrivals during the mean service time $E[B]$ must be less than the number of available servers ($n = 1$). The arrival rate is $\lambda = 1/E[A]$ and the number of arrivals during $E[B]$ is $\lambda E[B]$.

$$\rho = \frac{E[B]}{E[A]} = \lambda E[B] < 1 \tag{5.78}$$

Applying Little's law and in particular the law of utilization (Chapter 2.1.4) leads to the utilization $\rho = \lambda E[B]$ of the server. Hence, the probability that the server is idle, i.e. the system is empty at an arbitrary point in time, is

$$x(0) = P(X = 0) = 1 - \rho = \frac{E[A] - E[B]}{E[A]} \tag{5.79}$$

for a single server queue which is illustrated in Figure 5.22.

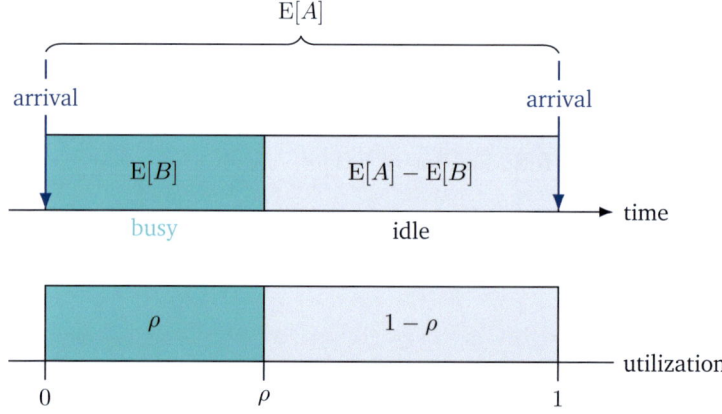

Figure 5.22: Illustration of the utilization and idle probability $x(0)$ in a GI/GI/1 delay system.

This relates to the length of an idle period I which is a random variable. In the queueing system, idle periods and busy periods alternate. Note that the mean idle time $E[I]$ is not the fraction of idle time of the server, but depicts the average over all idle period lengths, see Cohen [21]. Consider the system state X_A from the perspective of arrivals. The probability that an arrival finds the system empty is $x_A(0)$. It relates the server's idle time fraction (during mean interarrival time $E[A]$) to the mean idle time length, see Chapter 6.4.8 for the derivation of the mean idle time in a discrete-time GI/GI/1 delay system.

$$x_A(0) = P(X_A = 0) = \frac{(1-\rho)E[A]}{E[I]} = \frac{E[A] - E[B]}{E[I]} \tag{5.80}$$

It is $E[I] \geq E[A] - E[B]$; equality holds for a deterministic system (D/D/1) with $x_A(0) = 1$ (otherwise the D/D/1 system would be overloaded). Therefore, the waiting probability for GI/GI/1 is

$$p_w = 1 - x_A(0) = \frac{E[I] - (E[A] - E[B])}{E[I]} . \tag{5.81}$$

The mean number of customers in the system follows from Little's law and the sojourn time $T = W + B$.

$$E[X] = \lambda(E[W] + E[B]) \tag{5.82}$$

The mean waiting time is therefore

$$E[W] = E[X] \cdot E[A] - E[B] . \tag{5.83}$$

Note that there are no simple equations available for $x_A(0), E[I]$ or $E[X]$ which only depend on $E[A]$ and $E[B]$.

For the analysis of waiting times, an embedded Markov process $\{W_n, n = 0, 1, 2, \ldots\}$ is used with W_n being a continuous random variable of the waiting time for the n-th arriving customer. Note that this is not a Markov chain, since W_n is continuous instead of discrete.

$$W_{n+1} = \max(W_n + B_n - A_n, 0) \tag{5.84}$$

In the steady state, i.e. for $n \to \infty$, we obtain

$$W = \max(W + B - A, 0) = \max(W + C, 0) \tag{5.85}$$

with $C = B - A$ which leads to the Lindley integral equation of continuous-time GI/GI/1 delay systems. More results and details are provided for discrete-time GI/GI/1 in Chapter 6.4 which also illustrates and explains the iterative computation of W_n. Note that there is no simple embedded Markov chain $\{X_n\}$ of the number of customers in the system at arrival or departure times; this requires additional efforts.

▤ *Further reading:* Yang and Chaudhry (1996) "On steady-state queue size distributions of the discrete-time GI/G/1 queue" [122].

5.6.2 Lindley Integral Equation of Continuous-Time GI/GI/1 Systems

Given a GI/GI/1 system under stationary conditions, the following functional relationship for the waiting time distribution function are obtained $W(t)$

$$W(t) = \begin{cases} 0 & t < 0 \\ W(t) * c(t) & t \geq 0 \end{cases} \quad , \qquad \textbf{Lindley integral equation} \quad (5.86a)$$

where

$$c(t) = b(t) * a(-t) \tag{5.86b}$$

and "$*$" denotes the continuous-time convolution operator. The probability density function $c(t)$ of the r.v. $C = B - A$ contains all parameters of stochastic processes of the GI/GI/1 system, it is called the *system function*.

Equation (5.86a) is the integral form of the Lindley integral equation for determining the waiting time distribution function $W(t)$ in a GI/GI/1 delay system in the continuous-time domain. It is a slightly modified version of the well-known Wiener-Hopf integral equation often employed in mathematical physics and stochastic system theory. Taking the derivatives of both sides of Equation (5.86a), the form for the probability density function $w(t)$ of the waiting time is derived:

$$w(t) = \begin{cases} 0 & t < 0 \\ \delta(t) \int\limits_{-\infty}^{0^+} \Big(w(u) * c(u) \Big) du & t = 0 \\ w(t) * c(t) & t > 0 \end{cases} \tag{5.87}$$

or in a more compact notation (cf. Kleinrock [61])

$$w(t) = \pi_0 \Big(w(t) * c(t) \Big) , \tag{5.88}$$

where the operator π_0 in continuous-time domain is defined as follows:

$$\pi_0 \Big(f(t) \Big) = \begin{cases} 0 & t < 0 \\ \delta(t) \int\limits_{-\infty}^{0^+} f(u) du & t = 0 \\ f(t) & t > 0 \end{cases} . \tag{5.89}$$

The Dirac delta function $\delta(t)$ defined in Equation (2.27) ensures $\int_{-\infty}^{\infty} w(t) = 1$.

The solution of the Lindley integral equation may cause numerical issues. In Chapter 6.4, the Lindley integral equation is derived and modified to an algorithm for discrete-time GI/GI/1 systems with robust numerical solutions [11].

5.6.3 Kingman's Approximation of Mean Waiting Times

An accurate and computationally manageable analysis of GI/GI/1 queues with general distributions is difficult. However, there are approximate solutions in the literature. In practice, an important system characteristic is the mean waiting time. Thereby, operators may not require very accurate results, but rather an approximation of the expected waiting time or bounds of the waiting times in order to dimension the system. Kingman [59] provides an approximation $\widetilde{W}$ for the mean waiting time $E[W]$ as well as bounds.

$$E[W] \approx \left(\frac{\rho}{1-\rho}\right)\left(\frac{c_A^2 + c_B^2}{2}\right)E[B] \stackrel{\text{def}}{=} \widetilde{W} \qquad \textbf{Kingman's formula} \quad (5.90)$$

In case of a Poisson process, i.e. M/GI/1 queues, the Kingman approximation is exact and yields the same result as in Equation (5.42).

$$E[W] = \left(\frac{\rho}{1-\rho}\right)\left(\frac{1+c_B^2}{2}\right)E[B] = \widetilde{W} \qquad \text{M/GI/1} \quad (5.91)$$

A tighter upper bound $\widehat{U}$ of the mean waiting time is provided by Daley [27].

$$E[W] \leq \frac{(2-\rho)c_A^2 + \rho c_B^2}{2(1-\rho)} \cdot E[B] \stackrel{\text{def}}{=} \widehat{U} \qquad \text{upper bound} \quad (5.92)$$

By computing the difference between the upper bound and the approximated mean waiting time, we observe that

$$\widehat{U} - \widetilde{W} = E[B] \cdot c_A^2 \qquad (5.93)$$

which is independent of c_B. From that relation, we can also see that the upper bound and the approximation are identical for D/GI/1 queues with $c_A = 0$. Figure 5.23 illustrates the mean waiting time (normalized by $E[B]$) for different combinations of c_A and c_B. Observe that the approximation $\widetilde{W}$ is close to the upper bound $\widehat{U}$ for high load. The approximations $\widetilde{W}$ are the same for identical sums, i.e., $c_A^2 + c_B^2 = 1$. However, we observe different upper bounds $\widehat{U}$. The relative distance between the upper bound and the approximation (normalized by the approximated mean waiting time)

$$\frac{\widehat{U} - \widetilde{W}}{\widetilde{W}} = \frac{2c_A^2}{c_A^2 + c_B^2} \cdot \left(\frac{1-\rho}{\rho}\right) \qquad (5.94)$$

is given in Figure 5.24 and shows this more clearly.

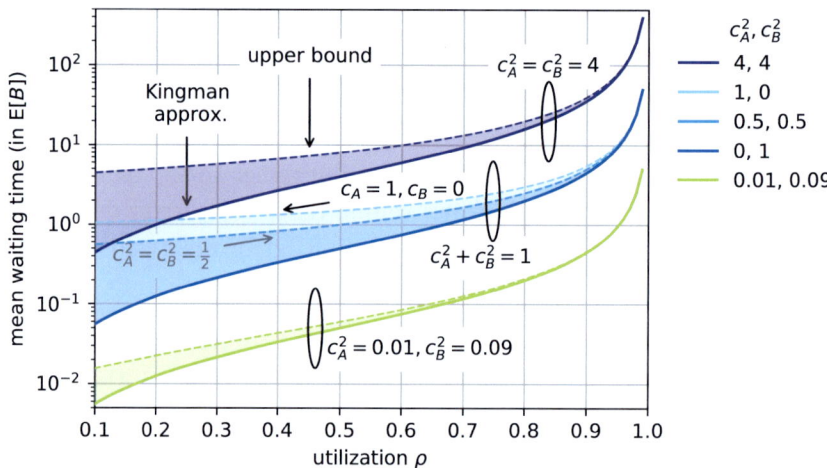

Figure 5.23: Approximation of the mean waiting times $\widetilde{W}$ (solid lines) and the upper bound $\widehat{U}$ (dashed lines) for GI/GI/1 queues with $E[B] = 1$. Note that the curves for the Kingman approximation overlap for $c_A^2 + c_B^2 = 1$.

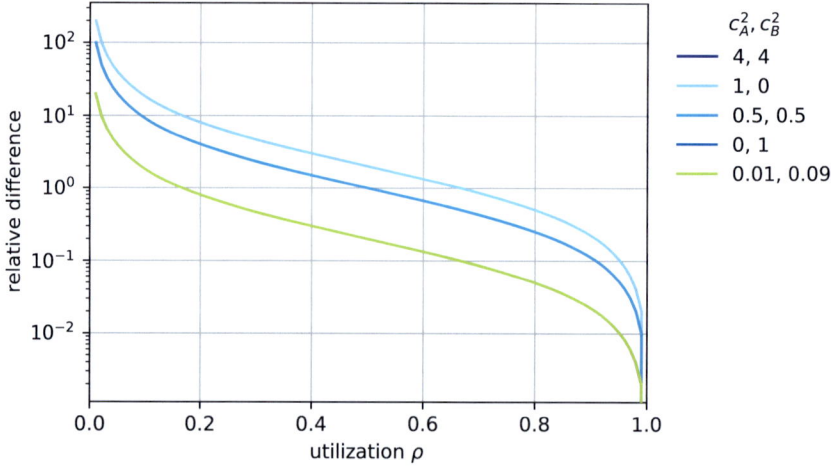

Figure 5.24: Relative distance $\frac{\widehat{U} - \widetilde{W}}{\widetilde{W}}$ for GI/GI/1 queues with $E[B] = 1$. For $c_A = 0$ the relative difference diminishes, since $\widehat{U} = \widetilde{W}$ (cf. Equation (5.94)). Note that the curves for $c_A^2 = c_B^2$ overlap.

▱ *Further reading:* A dedicated chapter on GI/GI/1 and approximations is provided in the book by Bhat (2015) *An Introduction to Queueing Theory: Modeling and Analysis in Applications* [10]. Approximations for the delay in GI/GI/1 queues and closer bounds with respect to the Kingman's formula are discussed by Krämer and Langenbach-Belz (1976) "Approximate formulae for the delay in the queueing system GI/G/l" [68] and Ciucu and Poloczek (2018) "Two extensions of Kingman's GI/G/1 bound" [20].

Advanced solutions for the Lindley integral equation are provided by: Boxma, Löpker, Mandjes, and Palmowski (2021) "A multiplicative version of the Lindley recursion" [13]. Lipilina (2020) "The spectral decomposition method for solving the Lindley integral equation and related numerical methods" [72]. Sumita and Kijima (1987) "Numerical Exploration of a bivariate Lindley process via the bivariate Laguerre transform" [99]. Ackroyd (1980) "Computing the waiting time distribution for the G/G/1 queue by signal processing methods" [1].

6

Discrete-time Models and Analysis

Contents

For the traffic models in this chapter, we assume that the time axis is discretized in intervals of constant length Δt and we observe discrete time instants – or time ticks. The resulting equidistant points in time form the index set of the stochastic processes under consideration. The state processes in this model environment are therefore *discrete in time and state*. The models are referred to as *discrete-time models*.

Why are discrete-time models used in practice? First, communication networks may be time-slotted or have packets of fixed size. In that case, discrete-time models are the natural choice and provide exact results. Second, discrete-time analysis is a numerically robust method allowing users to overcome numerical issues when solving continuous models; e.g., GI/GI/1 means solving integral equations (Chapter 5.6). Discrete-time analysis is a robust approximation method, see [3, 16, 101].

Third, discrete-time analysis provides efficient algorithms for time-dependent analysis [115], e.g. GI(t)/GI(t)/1, or correlated arrival and service processes. Examples include a discrete-time priority queue [117, 116], discrete-time multiserver queueing model that includes time-correlated processes for the server availability process and the arrival process [113]. In this book, we analyze overload phenomena using discrete-time queueing systems in Chapter 7.6.

This chapter begins with important prerequisites for discrete-time models. Then, required transformation methods are discussed, which later find application in the discrete-time analysis of queueing systems. In particular, the GEOM/GI/1 and GI/GI/1 waiting queues are analyzed.

6.1 Discrete-time Random Processes

6.1.1 Prerequisites and Parameters

In the analysis of discrete-time models, random variables (e.g. interarrival or service times) are taken into account, whose realizations are integer multiples of a model-wide unit of time Δt. This assumption means that occurrences or events in those models (e.g. customer arrival, service termination, clock-driven operation, etc.) can only occur at the instants on the discretized time axis. The discretized time axis is perceived to be comprised of time ticks, at which all events and occurrences take place. If arrivals and service terminations occur at the same time, i.e. at the same time tick, it is assumed that service terminations are processed first. The sequence of processing within an event type depends however on the respective model definition.

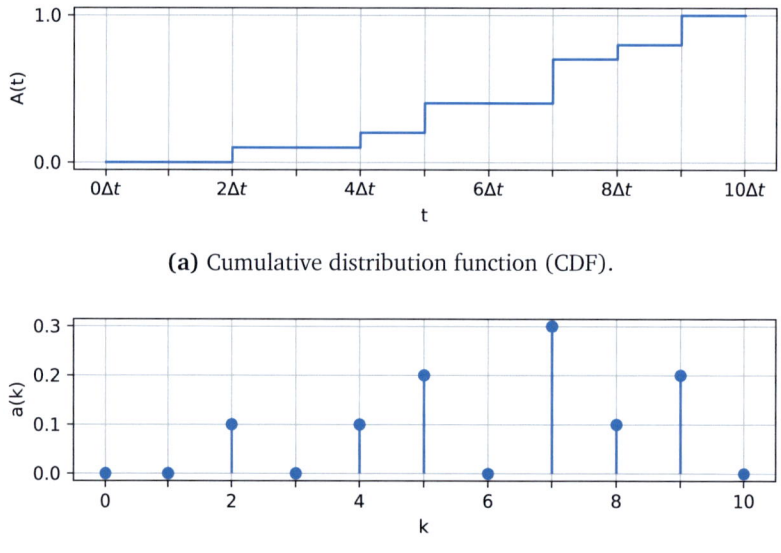

(a) Cumulative distribution function (CDF).

(b) Probability mass function (PMF).

Figure 6.1: Characterization of discrete-time random variables.

When modeling real systems, the choice of the time discretization constant Δt is often motivated or predetermined by the system's own parameters. In models of modern communication networks that operate with packets of constant length, it is expedient to choose the transmission duration of a slot or packet to be the discretization constant Δt.

In previous chapters some explanations on discrete random variables were discussed and are recalled here. As illustrated in an example in Figure 6.1, such a discrete-time random variable (r.v.) A can be characterized in different forms:

- Cumulative distribution function $A(t)$ in (Figure 6.1a): The function

$$A(t) = P(A \leq t) \tag{6.1a}$$

  is here step-wise; the step heights correspond to the probability values.

- Probability distribution $a(k)$ in (Figure 6.1b): Since the realizations of A are integer multiples of Δt, the r.v. A can be characterized using the probability mass function

$$a(k) = P(A = k \cdot \Delta t), \quad k = -\infty, \ldots, +\infty. \tag{6.1b}$$

To simplify the notation, all time-related variables used in this chapter are normalized to Δt. E.g. $A = k$ instead of $A = k \cdot \Delta t$. Hence, A is considered as a discrete random variable with the cumulative distribution function

$$A(k) = P(A \leq k) = \sum_{i=-\infty}^{k} a(k), \quad k = -\infty, \ldots, +\infty, \tag{6.2a}$$

and the probability mass function, i.e. the probability distribution of the discrete r.v.,

$$a(k) = P(A = k), \quad k = -\infty, \ldots, +\infty. \tag{6.2b}$$

6.1.2 Discrete-Time Renewal Processes

6.1.2.1 Definition and Examples

A point process in discrete-time domain is a sequence of occurrences lying on the discretized time axis. In general, the interarrival times A_i (interval between the event times t_{i-1} and t_i) are accordingly discrete-time with the associated distributions $a_i(k)$, $k = 0, 1, \ldots$.

A discrete-time point process is called *ordinary* discrete-time renewal process, if the intervals A_i are independent and identically distributed, i.e.

$$a_i(k) = a(k), \quad i = 0, 1, \ldots, \quad k = 0, 1, \ldots. \tag{6.3}$$

Since $a(0)$ can assume non-zero values, the approach discussed here includes cases in which several events occur at a discrete point in time. For example, in an arrival process with $a(0) = 0.3$, the next arrival will occur with probability 0.3 at the same time. Therefore, the class of processes considered here also include batch arrival processes with a geometrically distributed batch size.

It can be shown that the following two discrete-time renewal processes P_1 and P_2 are identical:

- Process P_1:
  Single-arrival renewal process with the interarrival time A_1 having the following probability mass function:

$$a_1(k) = P(A_1 = k) , \qquad k = 0, 1, \dots . \tag{6.4a}$$

- Process P_2:
  Batch-arrival process with the with the interarrival time A_2 and the following modified probability mass function:

$$a_2(k) = P(A_2 = k) = \frac{a_1(k)}{1 - a_1(0)} , \qquad k = 1, 2, \dots , \tag{6.4b}$$

and the geometrically distributed batch size G with probability distribution:

$$g(i) = P(G = i) = \left(1 - a_1(0)\right) a_1(0)^{i-1} , \qquad i = 1, 2, \dots . \tag{6.4c}$$

6.1.2.2 Recurrence Time Distribution of Discrete-Time Renewal Processes

Analogous to the definition in the continuous-time renewal processes, the forward recurrence time R of discrete-time renewal processes is defined as the time interval from a random observation time t^* to the next arrival. The observation instant lies also at the equidistant time instants on the discretized time axis. Here we distinguish between two cases: the observation instant is considered to be immediately *before* or *after* a discretized time instant.

In principle, both specifications are possible for the construction of the recurrence time of a discrete-time renewal process: The observation time can be immediately *before* or *after* the time instant on the discretized time axis. These two alternative approaches lead to different recurrence time distributions, which are used depending on the application.

Observation prior to discretized time instants   Figure 6.2 illustrates a discrete-time renewal process that is viewed from a random time t^* by an independent outside observer. It is assumed that the observation time t^* is immediately before a time instant of the discretized time axis. If an arrival occurs at the same time as the observation, the forward recurrence time is zero.

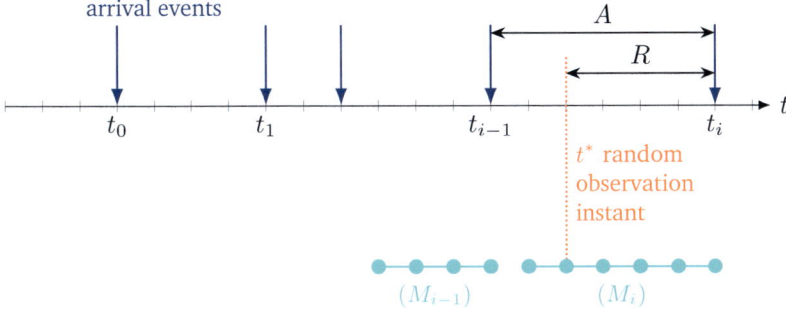

Figure 6.2: Discrete-time renewal processes with random observation instant t^*. The set of possible observation instants, for which the next arrival occurs at time instant t_i is M_i.

The distribution of the discrete-time forward recurrence time $r(k)$ is subsequently derived. First, we formulate $r(k)$ using the law of total probability as:

$$r(k) = \sum_{n=k+1}^{\infty} r(k \mid n)\, p(n) , \qquad (6.5a)$$

with

$p(n)$ probability that an interarrival interval of length n is observed,

$r(k|n)$ conditional probability that the random observation time t^* lies in an interarrival interval of length n:

$$r(k|n) = P(R = k|t^* \text{ lies in interarrival interval } A = n) . \qquad (6.5b)$$

The probability $p(n)$ is determined from the following considerations:

- $p(n)$ is proportional to the probability $a(n)$ of (the occurrence of) an interarrival time of length n;

- $p(n)$ is proportional to the length n itself, since from the perspective of an independent outside observer, a long interval is more likely to be encountered than a short one.

These observations lead to

$$p(n) = K \cdot n \cdot a(n) , \qquad (6.6a)$$

where the constant K can be calculated using the normalization condition:

$$1 = \sum_{n=0}^{\infty} p(n) = K \sum_{n=0}^{\infty} n\,a(n) = K \cdot \mathrm{E}[A], \quad \text{i.e.} \quad K = \frac{1}{\mathrm{E}[A]} \tag{6.6b}$$

or

$$p(n) = \frac{n \cdot a(n)}{\mathrm{E}[A]}. \tag{6.6c}$$

Consider now an interarrival length of n. The observer can only be in one of the time instants in the set M_i as shown in Figure 6.2. Each of the time instants in M_i can host the observer with the same probability, i.e.

$$r(k|n) = \begin{cases} \dfrac{1}{n} & k = 0, 1, \ldots, n-1, \\ 0 & \text{otherwise}. \end{cases} \tag{6.7}$$

Combining the Equations (6.5a), (6.6c) and (6.7) the distribution of the discrete-time forward recurrence time

$$r(k) = \frac{1}{\mathrm{E}[A]} \left(1 - \sum_{i=0}^{k} a(i) \right), \quad k = 0, 1, \ldots, \tag{6.8a}$$

is obtained and its Z-transform is

$$R_{ZT}(z) = \sum_{k=0}^{\infty} r(k) \cdot z^{-k} = \frac{1 - A_{ZT}(z)}{\mathrm{E}[A](1 - z^{-1})}. \tag{6.8b}$$

The mean recurrence time is

$$\mathrm{E}[R] = \frac{\mathrm{E}[A]}{2} \cdot (c_A^2 + 1) - \frac{1}{2}. \tag{6.9}$$

For a discrete-time renewal process with interarrival time distribution $a(k)$, the distribution $r(k)$ of the recurrence time can be recursively calculated as follows:

$$r(0) = \frac{1}{\mathrm{E}[A]} \cdot (1 - a(0)),$$
$$r(k) = r(k-1) - \frac{1}{\mathrm{E}[A]} \cdot a(k), \quad k = 1, 2, \ldots. \tag{6.10}$$

Observation just after discretized time instants   Now the observation time t^* is located immediately after a time instant of the discretized time axis. The distribution of the forward recurrence time is derived analogously to the previous section.

The conditional distribution from Equation (6.7) is

$$r(k|n) = \begin{cases} \dfrac{1}{n} & k = 1, \ldots, n \,, \\ 0 & \text{otherwise} \,. \end{cases} \tag{6.11}$$

Now the forward recurrence time distribution

$$r(k) = \sum_{n=k}^{\infty} r(k|n) \cdot p(n) = \frac{1}{\mathrm{E}[A]} \left(1 - \sum_{i=0}^{k-1} a(i)\right), \quad k = 1, 2, \ldots \tag{6.12a}$$

is obtained and its Z-transform is

$$R_{ZT}(z) = \frac{z^{-1}(1 - A_{ZT}(z))}{\mathrm{E}[A](1 - z^{-1})} \,. \tag{6.12b}$$

The mean recurrence time is

$$\mathrm{E}[R] = \frac{\mathrm{E}[A]}{2}(c_A^2 + 1) + \frac{1}{2} \,. \tag{6.13}$$

A comparison of Equation (6.12a) with Equation (6.8a) shows that the forward recurrence time in Equation (6.12a) is shifted with the discretization interval Δt. This can be also seen when comparing the mean recurrence times in Equation (6.13) and Equation (6.9), respectively.

6.1.2.3 Discrete-Time Renewal Processes with Memoryless Property

A renewal process is memoryless (M: Markov) if the interarrival time A has the same distribution as the forward recurrence time R. This also applies to discrete-time renewal processes. Depending on whether the observation time is immediately *before* or *after* a discrete time instant, two process types with Markov property can be specified.

Observation just before discretized time instants From Equation (6.8b) it can be shown that a renewal process with an interarrival distribution of type GEOM(0) is memoryless:

$$R_{ZT}(z) = \frac{1 - A_{ZT}(z)}{\mathrm{E}[A](1 - z^{-1})} = \frac{1 - \dfrac{1-q}{1 - q \cdot z^{-1}}}{\dfrac{q}{1-q} \cdot (1 - z^{-1})} = A_{ZT}(z) \,. \tag{6.14}$$

Observation just after discretized time instants In this case, it is obvious from Equation (6.12b) that a Bernoulli arrival process is memoryless. The interarrival distribution is here of type GEOM(1):

$$R_{ZT}(z) = \frac{z^{-1}(1 - A_{ZT}(z))}{\mathrm{E}[A](1 - z^{-1})} = \frac{z^{-1}\left(1 - \dfrac{1 - q}{1 - q \cdot z^{-1}}\right)}{\dfrac{q}{1 - q} \cdot (1 - z^{-1})} = A_{ZT}(z) . \qquad (6.15)$$

The Bernoulli arrival process is used for memoryless discrete-time traffic processes and has the BASTA property (Bernoulli Arrivals See Time Averages) similar to PASTA.

6.2 Transform Methods for Discrete-Time Analysis

In the analysis and the numerical evaluation of analytical results for discrete-time models in the chapters to follow, transform methods for discrete-time functions play an important role, e.g. the *Discrete Fourier Transform* (DFT) and the associated *Fast Fourier Transform* (FFT) as well as the *Cepstrum* concept. These methods are summarized below.

6.2.1 Discrete Fourier Transform

6.2.1.1 Definition of Discrete Fourier Transform

The Discrete Fourier Transform (DFT) of a finite time sequence $x(k)$ of length N for $k = 0, 1, \ldots, N - 1$, is defined as follows

$$X_{DFT}(n) = \mathrm{DFT}\{x(k)\} = \sum_{k=0}^{N-1} x(k)e^{-(i\frac{2\pi}{N}n)k} , \qquad (6.16a)$$

$$n = 0, ..., N - 1, \; i^2 = -1 .$$

Although the sequence $x(k)$ in the time domain and the transform $X_{DFT}(n)$ can in principle be complex functions, the time sequences considered here are often probability distributions and have accordingly real values. The inverse transform is

$$x(k) = \mathrm{DFT}^{-1}\{X_{DFT}(n)\} = \frac{1}{N} \sum_{n=0}^{N-1} X_{DFT}(n) \cdot e^{+(i\frac{2\pi}{N}k)n} , \qquad (6.16b)$$

$$k = 0, ..., N - 1, \; i^2 = -1 .$$

Analogous to Equation (2.69b), the convolution theorem also applies to the DFT concerning the sum X of two independent, discrete random variables X_1 and X_2:

$$\begin{aligned}
X_{DFT}(n) &= \mathrm{DFT}\{x(k)\} = \mathrm{DFT}\{x_1(k) * x_2(k)\} \\
&= X_{1,DFT}(n) \cdot X_{2,DFT}(n) .
\end{aligned} \qquad (6.17)$$

6.2.1.2 Relationship between DFT and Z-Transform

Consider a finite distribution $x(k)$, $k = 0, ..., N-1$. It can be shown (cf. Oppenheim and Schafer [82]) that the Z-transform

$$X_{ZT}(z) = \sum_{k=0}^{N-1} x(k) z^{-k} \tag{6.18}$$

can be fully described by means of the samples lying on the unit circle:

$$X_{ZT}(z_n) = X_{ZT}\left(e^{n \cdot \frac{2\pi i}{N}}\right), \qquad n = 0, 1, ..., N-1, \; i^2 = -1 . \tag{6.19}$$

A comparison with the definition of the Discrete Fourier Transform shows that for the class of finite distributions, the Discrete Fourier Transform can be used instead of the Z-transform.

Accordingly, the inverse Z-transform can be replaced by the inverse Discrete Fourier Transform (DFT^{-1}). This allows the use of efficient methods and algorithms for evaluating the Discrete Fourier Transform like the Fast Fourier Transform, which were developed in the context of signal processing.

6.2.1.3 Fast Fourier Transform and Algorithms

The definitions of the Discrete Fourier Transforms DFT or DFT^{-1} show that the numerical effort to evaluate a DFT corresponds to the order of magnitude $O(N^2)$. The quadratic runtime is thereby dictated by the number of required multiplications of complex numbers. To reduce this effort, efficient algorithms for DFT evaluation and its inverse have been developed, primarily in signal processing technology. This class of algorithms, which started with the groundbreaking work by J.W. Cooley and J.W. Tukey [22] and reduces the numerical effort from $O(N^2)$ to $O(N \log N)$, is the Fast Fourier Transform (FFT). A classic overview of applications of FFT algorithms can be found e.g. in Henrici [48].

6.2.2 Concept of Complex Cepstrum

In the analysis of discrete-time systems in the transform domain, e.g. in GI/GI/1 systems, the concept of complex Cepstrum which originates from the theory of signal processing is applied (see Ackroyd [1], Tran-Gia [107]). This concept can be systematically described using elements of homomorphic system theory (cf. Oppenheim and Schafer [82]). Before introducing the Cepstrum concept, it is important to first discuss some properties of homomorphic systems which will be relevant later in this chapter and related transforms.

6.2.2.1 Homomorphic Systems and Transforms

Definition   Consider a system that carries out a transform T (cf. Figure 6.3a). The operators $[I]$ and $[O]$ are defined for the set of input signals $\{x_i\}$ and output signals $\{y_i\}$. Furthermore, a scalar variable c is linked to the input signals by the operator $[i]$ and to the output signals by the operator $[o]$. The system or the transform is called *homomorphic* if

$$T\{x_1 \, [I] \, x_2\} = T\{x_1\} \, [O] \, T\{x_2\} = y_1 \, [O] \, y_2 \, , \tag{6.20a}$$

$$T\{c \, [i] \, x_1\} = c \, [o] \, T\{x_1\} = c \, [o] \, y_1 \, . \tag{6.20b}$$

As suggested from Equations (6.20a) and (6.20b), the homomorphic property is a generalization of the concept of linearity in classical systems theory. If homomorphic systems are connected in series, the entire system is also homomorphic. This property plays an important role in signal processing and leads to canonical structures of homomorphic systems.

Homomorphic System and Convolution   A special homomorphic system for the convolution operation is shown in Figure 6.3b, where:

- Input- and Output-Signals:
  $\{x_i\}$ and $\{y_i\}$ are vectors of complex numbers.

- Transform T:
  Discrete Fourier Transform (DFT, cf. Equation (6.16a)).

- Input Operator:
  $[I]$ is here the discrete convolution with the operator symbol $*$.

- Output Operator:
  $[O]$ is here the component-wise multiplication of vectors.

- Input- and Output-operation with scalar values:
  $[i]$ and $[o]$ are multiplication.

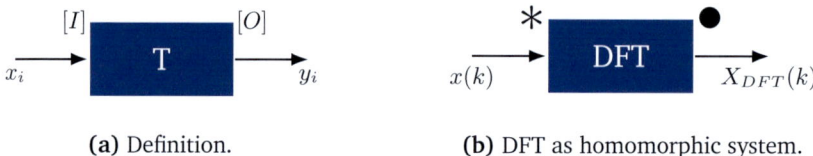

(a) Definition.   (b) DFT as homomorphic system.

Figure 6.3: Homomorphic systems. The DFT as homomorphic system shown here converts the convolution operation of input signals in multiplication of output signals.

6.2.2.2 The Complex Cepstrum

With transform methods like LT (Laplace transform), GF (generating function), ZT (Z-transform) and DFT (Discrete Fourier Transform), the convolution operation at the input of the considered homomorphic system is converted into a simple multiplication at the output.

The concept of the complex Cepstrum goes one step further: The convolution operation at input is converted by the Cepstrum homomorphic system into an addition. The canonical structure of the Cepstrum and inverse Cepstrum forming depicted in Figure 6.4 has the following basic features:

- The discrete-time input signals $\{x(k)\}$ as well as the discrete-time output signals $\{y(k)\}$ (e.g. sampling values in digital transmission systems, probability distributions, etc.) interoperate via the discrete convolution operator.

- The homomorphic transform T converts convolution operations into additions. The input signal $x(k)$ is converted into the so-called *complex Cepstrum* $X_{CEP}(k)$.

- The inner system carries out transformations in the cepstrum domain, in which the addition is retained as operation.

- The inverse transformation T^{-1} carries out the inverse mapping from the Cepstrum domain to the time domain.

As can be seen, the aim of the structure presented is to use the homomorphic transform to convert the convolution operation in time domain at the input side into addition in Cepstrum domain at the output side. The construction of the complex Cepstrum (transform T) and the associated inverse transform T^{-1} are schematically depicted in Figure 6.4b and Figure 6.4c.

The Cepstrum construction operator T consists of three steps:

- Z-transform (convert the convolution operation into multiplication)

$$X_{ZT}(z) = ZT\left\{x(k)\right\} . \tag{6.21a}$$

- Compute the complex logarithm (convert the multiplication into addition)

$$X_{LN}(z) = \ln\left(X_{ZT}(z)\right) . \tag{6.21b}$$

The attribute "complex" of the Cepstrum refers to the use of the complex logarithm and does not mean that the complex Cepstrum must in principle be complex.

- Inverse Z-transform

$$X_{CEP}(k) = ZT^{-1}\left\{X_{LN}(z)\right\}. \tag{6.21c}$$

Equation (6.21c) assumes that $X_{LN}(z)$ is a valid Z-transform.

The inverse Cepstrum construction operator T^{-1} consists also of three steps:

- Z-transform

$$Y_{ZT}(z) = ZT\left\{Y_{CEP}(k)\right\}. \tag{6.22a}$$

- Compute the complex exponential function

$$Y_{EXP}(z) = e^{Y_{ZT}(z)}. \tag{6.22b}$$

- Compute the inverse Z-transform

$$y(k) = ZT^{-1}\left\{Y_{EXP}(z)\right\}. \tag{6.22c}$$

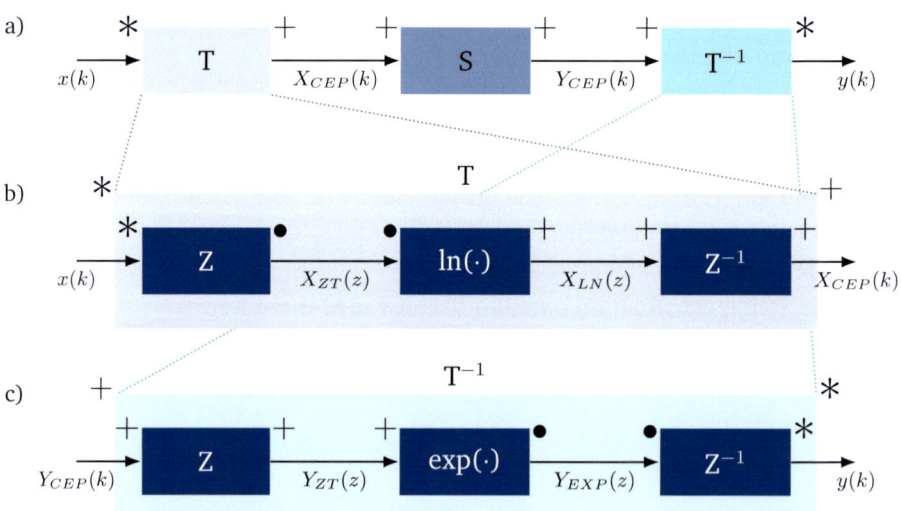

Figure 6.4: Canonical form of a homomorphic system for signal convolution.
a) Entire system [Time to Cepstrum] and [Cepstrum to Time].
b) Subsystem for [Time to Cepstrum] transform.
c) Subsystem for [Cepstrum to Time] inverse transform.

Complex Cepstrum for Minimum-Phase and Non-Minimum-Phase Sequence

Some properties of the complex Cepstrum are explained below. These explanations especially take into account the class of signals or time sequences which have rational functions as Z-transforms:

$$X_{ZT}(z) = \frac{A \cdot z^r \cdot \prod_{n=1}^{n_i} (1 - z^{-1} q_{in}) \cdot \prod_{n=1}^{n_o} (1 - \frac{z}{q_{on}})}{\prod_{n=1}^{m_i} (1 - z^{-1} p_{in}) \prod_{n=1}^{m_o} (1 - \frac{z}{p_{on}})}, \tag{6.23}$$

where

- q_{in} and q_{on} are zeros (roots) inside and outside the unit circle,

- p_{in} and p_{on} are poles inside and outside the unit circle, respectively.

From Equation (6.21) the complex Cepstrum is obtained in the following form:

$$X_{CEP}(k) = \begin{cases} \sum_{n=1}^{n_o} \frac{q_{on}^k}{k} - \sum_{n=1}^{m_o} \frac{p_{on}^k}{k} & k < 0, \\ \ln |A| & k = 0, \\ \sum_{n=1}^{m_i} \frac{p_{in}^k}{k} - \sum_{n=1}^{n_i} \frac{q_{in}^k}{k} & k > 0. \end{cases} \tag{6.24}$$

From Equation (6.24) the following properties of the complex Cepstrum can be derived:

- In case that $x(k)$ is a so-called *minimum-phase sequence*, i.e.. if all poles and zeros of $X_{ZT}(z)$ are inside the unit circle, then the Cepstrum $X_{CEP}(k)$ exists only for $k \geq 0$.

- In case that $x(k)$ is a *non-minimum-phase sequence*, i.e., if all poles and zeros of $X_{ZT}(z)$ are outside the unit circle, then the Cepstrum $X_{CEP}(k)$ exists only for $k \leq 0$.

- The complex Cepstrum decreases with increasing number of k; the decay is at least as fast as the function $1/k$.

- The complex Cepstrum of finite time sequences is not necessarily finite.

These features allow the separation of the minimum-phase from the non-minimum-phase parts in the Cepstrum domain. It plays an important role in the analysis of discrete-time GI/GI/1 delay systems, as will be discussed later in this chapter.

Separation of Minimum-Phase and Maximum-Phase Sequences Consider the convolution of a non-minimum-phase sequence $x_{MAX}(k)$ with a minimum-phase sequence $x_{MIN}(k)$

$$x(k) = x_{MAX}(k) * x_{MIN}(k) , \tag{6.25a}$$

with the Z-transform:

$$X_{ZT}(z) = X_{MAX,ZT}(z) \cdot X_{MIN,ZT}(z) . \tag{6.25b}$$

The separation can be done in Cepstrum domain as follows:

$$X_{CEP}(k) = \begin{cases} X_{MAX,CEP}(k) & k < 0 \\ X_{MAX,CEP}(0) + X_{MIN,CEP}(0) & k = 0 \\ X_{MIN,CEP}(k) & k > 0 . \end{cases} \tag{6.25c}$$

In Equation (6.25c) it can be seen that the Cepstra of the non-minimum-phase sequence and the minimum-phase sequence can be separated. In the Cepstrum domain, there is only an overlap at the zero point, the overlapping portions being merely a multiplication factor. This separation property can therefore be used to separate those sequences in Cepstrum domain. The algorithm is schematically shown in Figure 6.5.

As shown in Figure 6.5, after the separation in the Cepstrum domain and the inverse transform to time domain, a factor K remains which arises from the overlap of the Cepstra at the zero point, as discussed above. If $x_{MIN}(k)$ represents, e.g. the distribution of a discrete-time random variable, the factor K can simply be determined using normalization. This separation technique will later be applied in the analysis of the discrete-time GI/GI/1 delay system using the Cepstrum concept.

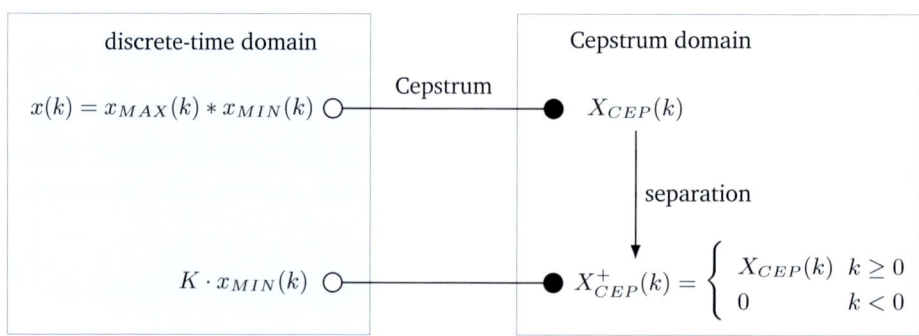

Figure 6.5: Cepstrum separation of non-minimum-phase and minimum-phase sequences.

6.3 Discrete-Time Delay System GEOM(1)/GI/1

Similar to the case of continuous-time systems, in the analysis of discrete-time performance models, in which the state process has the memoryless property at certain points in time, the method of embedded Markov chain can also be applied. This is the case in systems in which only one model component is non-Markovian, e.g.

GEOM(0)/GI/1 or GEOM(1)/GI/1 (Bernoulli arrival process),

GI/GEOM(0)/1 or GI/GEOM(1)/1 (Bernoulli service process).

In this chapter we use the example of the GEOM(1)/GI/1 system to illustrate this method. It should be noted here that the GEOM(1)/GI/1 system is the discrete-time counterpart of the continuous-time M/GI/1 system.

6.3.1 Model Structure and Parameters

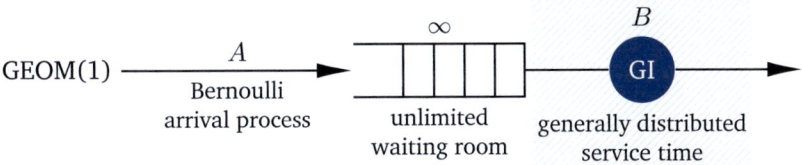

Figure 6.6: Discrete-time GEOM(1)/GI/1 delay system.

The structure of the GEOM(1)/GI/1 delay system (or GEOM(1)/GI/1-∞) is depicted in Figure 6.6. The arriving customer stream is modeled by a Bernoulli process with Parameter $p = (1 - \alpha)$, i.e. at each point on the discrete time line an arrival occurs with probability $p = (1 - \alpha)$. Hence, the interarrival time A is GEOM(1) distributed:

$A \sim \text{GEOM}_1(p)$ with $p = 1 - \alpha$

$$a(k) = (1 - p)^{k-1} \cdot p = \alpha^{k-1} \cdot (1 - \alpha), \quad k = 1, 2, \ldots, \tag{6.26a}$$

$$\text{E}[A] = \frac{1}{p} = \frac{1}{1 - \alpha},$$

where $\text{E}[A]$ is given in multiples of Δt. The associated Z-transform of $a(k)$ is

$$A_{ZT}(z) = \frac{1 - \alpha}{z - \alpha}. \tag{6.26b}$$

The queue size is assumed to be infinite, i.e. the system operates as a pure delay system. A customer who finds the server busy upon arrival has to wait. The service time B is arbitrarily distributed. The offered traffic is identical to the system occupancy or server utilization:

$$\rho = \frac{\mathrm{E}[\,B\,]}{\mathrm{E}[\,A\,]} = (1 - \alpha) \cdot \mathrm{E}[\,B\,] = p \cdot \mathrm{E}[\,B\,] \,. \qquad\qquad \text{server utilization} \quad (6.27)$$

6.3.2 Markov Chain and State Transition

A sample path of the state process development is illustrated in Figure 6.7. The number $X(t)$ of customers in the system at time t on the discretized time axis describes the system state. Clearly, the process $X(t)$ is memoryless at the end of a service period.

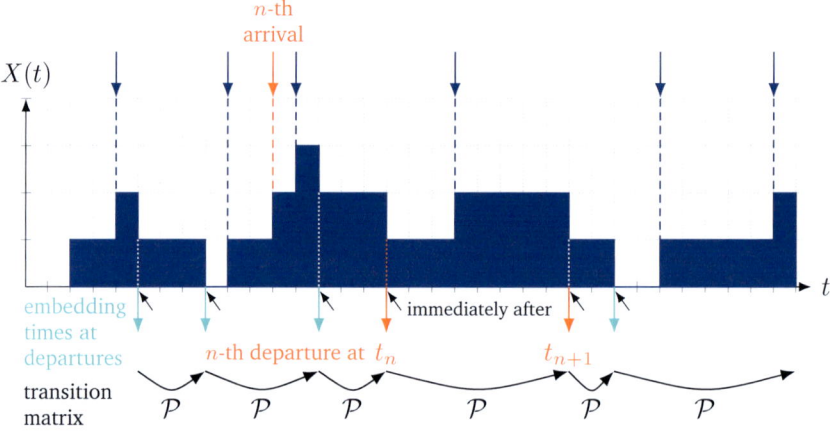

Figure 6.7: Sample path of state process in GEOM(1)/GI/1 delay system.

A Markov chain is now embedded at times t_n, where X_n is the r.v. of the number of customers immediately after the n-th service (cf. Figure 6.7). The analysis with embedded Markov chain technique is analogous to the continuous-time M/GI/1 system in the previous Chapter 5.3.

6.3.3 State Probabilities

Continuing the derivation the distribution $\gamma(k)$ of the number Γ of arriving customers during a service time B with the distribution $b(k)$ is introduced. Taking into account the properties of the Bernoulli arrival process,

$$\gamma(k) = \sum_{m=k}^{\infty} b(m) \binom{m}{k} (1-\alpha)^k \alpha^{m-k} , \quad k = 0, 1, \ldots \quad (6.28a)$$

results, or after the Z-transform

$$\Gamma_{ZT}(z) = B_{ZT}\left(\frac{z}{1-\alpha+\alpha z}\right) = B_{ZT}\left(\frac{\mathrm{E}[A]\cdot z}{1+(\mathrm{E}[A]-1)z}\right) . \quad (6.28b)$$

Furthermore by taking the derivative of Equation (6.28b) we obtain

$$\mathrm{E}[\Gamma] = -\left.\frac{d\Gamma_{ZT}(z)}{dz}\right|_{z=1} = \rho . \quad (6.28c)$$

By observing two consecutive system states X_n and X_{n+1} with the corresponding state probabilities

$$x(j, n) = P(X_n = j) , \quad (6.29a)$$
$$x(j, n+1) = P(X_{n+1} = j) , \quad j = 0, 1, \ldots, \quad (6.29b)$$

the transition behavior of the system is fully characterized by the transition matrix

$$\mathcal{P} = \{p_{ij}\} , \quad i, j = 0, 1, \ldots ,$$
$$p_{ij} = P(X_{n+1} = j | X_n = i). \quad (6.30a)$$

Using the distribution $\gamma(k)$ in Equation (6.28a) the transition probabilities p_{ij} are given as

$$p_{ij} = \begin{cases} \gamma(j) & i = 0 , \\ \gamma(j-i+1) & i > 0, \ j \geq i-1 , \\ 0 & \text{otherwise.} \end{cases} \quad (6.30b)$$

The state probabilities $\{x(j, n+1), \ j = 0, 1, \ldots\}$ can accordingly be calculated from the state probabilities at the previous embedding time using the following state equations:

$$x(j, n+1) = x(0, n) \cdot \gamma(j) + \sum_{i=1}^{j+1} x(i, n) \cdot \gamma(j-i+1) , \quad j = 0, 1, \ldots . \quad (6.31)$$

For a stationary system ($\rho < 1$) with the equilibrium state probabilities

$$x(j) = \lim_{n \to \infty} x(j, n), \quad j = 0, 1, \dots, \tag{6.32}$$

is obtained from Equation (6.31) an equation system to compute the state probabilities of the GEOM(1)/GI/1 queueing system at Markov chain embedding points:

$$x(j) = x(0) \cdot \gamma(j) + \sum_{i=1}^{j+1} x(i) \cdot \gamma(j - i + 1), \quad j = 0, 1, \dots. \tag{6.33}$$

Solution with Z-Transform The Z-transformation of Equation (6.33) yields

$$X_{ZT}(z) = x(0) \frac{\Gamma_{ZT}(z)(1 - z)}{1 - z \cdot \Gamma_{ZT}(z)}. \tag{6.34a}$$

The remaining term $x(0)$ can be determined by setting $z = 1$ in Equation (6.34a) taking into account the mean $E[\Gamma] = \rho$ in Equation (6.28c):

$$x(0) = 1 - \rho. \tag{6.34b}$$

Putting together Equations (6.28b), (6.34a) and (6.34b), the Markov chain state probabilities in the Z-domain is obtained as follows:

$$X_{ZT}(z) = (1 - \rho) \frac{(1 - z) \cdot B_{ZT}\left(\dfrac{z}{1 - \alpha + \alpha z}\right)}{1 - z \cdot B_{ZT}\left(\dfrac{z}{1 - \alpha + \alpha z}\right)}. \qquad \textbf{GEOM(1)/GI/1} \tag{6.35}$$

It should be noted here that Equation (6.35) represents the discrete-time form of the Pollaczek-Khintchine formula for state probabilities as derived for the continuous-time M/GI/1 system in Equation (5.35).

Initially, this relationship applies at the Markov chain regeneration times (see Figure 6.7). However, it can be proven for the GEOM(1)/GI/1 system (cf. Kobayashi [64]) that the steady state probabilities given in Equation (6.35) apply to any observation times on the discretized time axis. With $x_D(j) = x(j)$ and Kleinrock's result, it is $x_A(j) = x_D(j)$. The BASTA property means $x_A(j) = x^*(j)$. Finally, $x(j) = x^*(j)$.

6.3.4 Waiting Time Distribution

The waiting time distribution is derived in the following from the state probabilities. Let W and D denote the r.v. for the waiting time and the sojourn time of customers in the system, with:

$$D = W + B \ , \tag{6.36a}$$

$$d(k) = w(k) * b(k) \ , \tag{6.36b}$$

$$D_{ZT}(z) = W_{ZT}(z) \cdot B_{ZT}(z) \ . \tag{6.36c}$$

Assuming now the queueing discipline FIFO (first-in, first-out), so the number of arriving customers during the sojourn time of the test customer is exactly the system population just after the test customer leaves the system. This number of customers is the system state at the embedding points of the Markov chain.

Thus, the distribution of the number of customers during a sojourn time can be given as follows (cf. Equation (6.28a))

$$x(k) = \sum_{m=k}^{\infty} d(m) \binom{m}{k} (1-\alpha)^k \alpha^{m-k} \ , \quad k = 0, 1, \dots \ , \tag{6.37a}$$

or with Z-transform

$$X_{ZT}(z) = D_{ZT}\left(\frac{z}{1-\alpha+\alpha z}\right) \ . \tag{6.37b}$$

A comparison of Equation (6.37b) and Equation (6.35) yields

$$D_{ZT}(z) = (1-\rho) \cdot \frac{(1-z) \cdot B_{ZT}(z)}{1 - \alpha z - (1-\alpha) \cdot z \cdot B_{ZT}(z)} \ . \tag{6.38}$$

Taking together Equation (6.36c) and Equation (6.38) the Z-transform of the waiting time distribution in GEOM(1)/GI/1 system is obtained:

$$W_{ZT}(z) = \frac{(1-\rho) \cdot (1-z)}{1 - \alpha z - (1-\alpha) z \ B_{ZT}(z)} \ . \qquad \textbf{GEOM(1)/GI/1} \tag{6.39}$$

Equation (6.39) can be seen as the discrete-time form of the Pollaczek-Khintchine formula, which has been derived in Chapter 5.3.5 for the continuous-time M/GI/1 queueing system in Equation (5.39).

6.4   Discrete-Time Delay System GI/GI/1

6.4.1   Model Structure and Parameters

Figure 6.8 shows the basic structure of the delay system GI/GI/1 (or GI/GI/1-∞).
The interarrival time A and the service time B can be arbitrarily distributed:

$$a(k) = P(A = k \cdot \Delta t) \quad k = 0, 1, \ldots ,$$
$$b(k) = P(B = k \cdot \Delta t) \quad k = 0, 1, \ldots .$$

In the model discussed here, assume both interarrival and service times to be non-
negative. The offered traffic is identical to the system occupancy or server utilization:

$$\rho = \frac{E[B]}{E[A]} .$$
server utilization   (6.40)

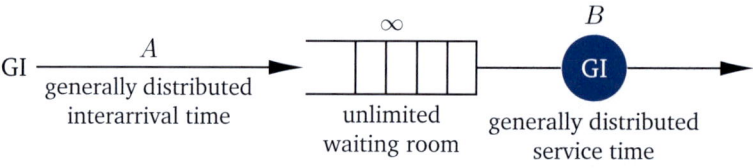

Figure 6.8: Discrete-time delay system GI/GI/1.

The waiting space is assumed to be infinite, as in a pure delay system. A customer
finding the server busy has to wait until the server becomes available. The server
operates according to a queueing discipline, e.g. FIFO (first-in first-out), FCFS
(first-come first-served), LIFO (last-in first-out), RANDOM, etc.

The analysis of GI/GI/1 systems is normally done based on the amount $U(t)$ of
unfinished work in the system, in contrast to the *number of customers* $X(t)$ as used
in previous chapters. The difference between the two state description concepts is
as follows: assuming the FIFO queueing discipline (i) the system state $X(t)$ at an
observation time t seen from a test customer stands for the number of customers in
the system at time t, and $X(t)$ services have to be finished prior to the test customer
service, where (ii) the unfinished work $U(t)$ is the sum of all amounts of unfinished
works of the $X(t)$ customers, and $U(t)$ remaining work has to be processed by the
server before it can serve the test customer. For the FIFO queueing discipline, the
unfinished work $U(t)$ is identical to the waiting time of the test customer.

The analysis of continuous-time GI/GI/1 queueing systems (see Chapter 5.6) generally leads to an integral equation introduced by Lindley [71], which plays a central role in the analysis of the GI/GI/1 delay system in the continuous-time domain. As for this class of GI/GI/1 models no closed-form analytical solution exists, therefore, the focus is on discrete-time GI/GI/1 delay systems and looking at discrete-time algorithms using well-known concepts and transform methods in signal processing.

6.4.2 Modified Lindley Integral Equation of Discrete-Time GI/GI/1

In principle, the Lindley integral equation for continuous-time systems in Equation (5.86a) allows also to derive corresponding equations for discrete-time systems. To explain the expressions for discrete-time GI/GI/1 systems, we will directly derive the modified form of the Lindley integral equation.

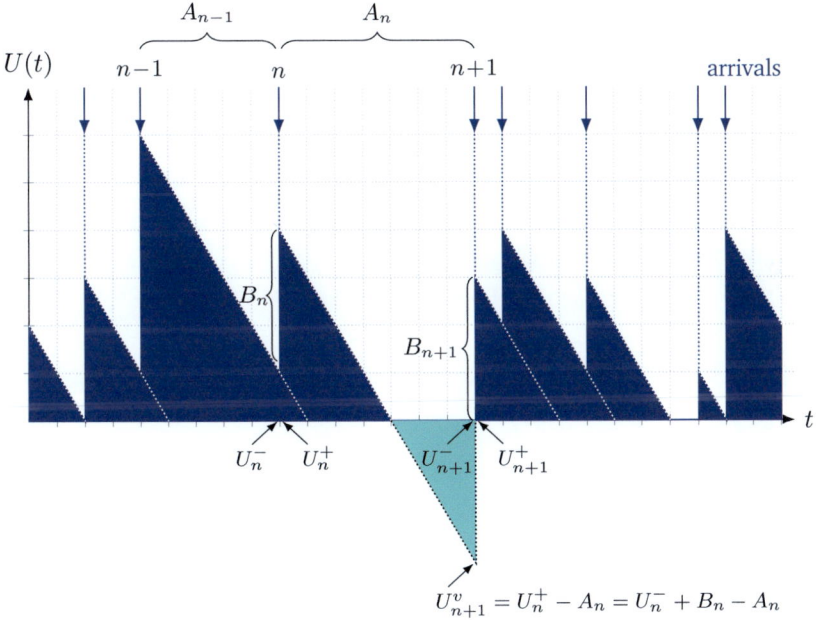

Figure 6.9: Sample path of unfinished work in GI/GI/1 system.

Figure 6.9 shows a sample development of the unfinished work process in the GI/GI/1 system. Again, the amount of unfinished work $U(t)$ is the sum of service times of all waiting customers plus the remaining time – the recurrent time – of the customer in service at time t. Since the distribution of service time is assumed to be discrete-time, the unfinished work $U(t)$ is also discrete-time, consisting of an integer number of work units Δt. If the server is busy, exactly one work unit is processed per discretized time unit Δt. Thus, the linear gradual declines of the unfinished works are in principle step functions, but for the sake of visibility they are depicted with straight lines in Figure 6.9.

Observe the following random variables, as depicted in Figure 6.9:

A_n r.v. for the interarrival time between customer n and customer $n + 1$,

B_n r.v for the service time of the n-th customer,

U_n^- r.v. for the unfinished work immediately *before* the arrival of the n-th customer,

U_n^+ r.v. for the unfinished work immediately *after* the arrival of the n-th customer,

U_{n+1}^v r.v. for the *virtual unfinished work* immediately before the arrival of the customer $n + 1$.

The virtual unfinished work U_{n+1}^v is introduced here just to simplify the derivation. For U_{n+1}^v it is assumed that the server would continue to operate during an interarrival time, even if the system is empty. Accordingly, the virtual unfinished work can assume negative values (see Figure 6.9).

The unfinished work U_{n+1}^- should now be calculated out of the unfinished work U_n^-. This is done in the following three steps $U_n^- \rightarrow U_n^+ \rightarrow U_{n+1}^v \rightarrow U_{n+1}^-$.

$U_n^- \rightarrow U_n^+$: after the arrival of the n-th customer, the service time is added to the unfinished work, i.e.

$$U_n^+ = U_n^- + B_n , \tag{6.41a}$$
$$u_n^+(k) = u_n^-(k) * b_n(k) , \tag{6.41b}$$

where the relationship for the distribution of the sum of random variables presented in an earlier chapter is used

$U_n^+ \rightarrow U_{n+1}^v$: as shown in Figure 6.9:

$$U_{n+1}^v = U_n^+ - A_n , \tag{6.42a}$$
$$u_{n+1}^v(k) = u_n^+(k) * a_n(-k) , \tag{6.42b}$$

where the relationship for the distribution of the difference of two independent r.v. is taken into account.

$U_{n+1}^v \to U_{n+1}^-$: An interrelation between the unfinished work and the virtual unfinished work is such that if the system is empty, the virtual unfinished work continues to decrease, while the unfinished work remains zero:

$$U_{n+1}^- = \max(0, \, U_{n+1}^v) \, , \tag{6.43a}$$

$$u_{n+1}^-(k) = \pi_0\left(u_{n+1}^v(k)\right) \, , \tag{6.43b}$$

whereby π_m is a discrete operator which is defined analogously to the definition in Equation (5.89):

$$\pi_m\left(x(k)\right) = \begin{cases} 0 & k < m \, , \\ \displaystyle\sum_{i=-\infty}^{m} x(i) & k = m \, , \\ x(k) & k > m \, . \end{cases} \tag{6.44}$$

Putting together these equations ($U_n^- \to U_n^+ \to U_{n+1}^v \to U_{n+1}^-$) the general discrete form of the Lindley integral equation given in (5.86a) is obtained:

$$u_{n+1}^-(k) = \pi_0\left(u_n^-(k) * b_n(k) * a_n(-k)\right)$$
$$= \pi_0\left(u_n^-(k) * c_n(k)\right) \, , \tag{6.45a}$$

where

$$c_n(k) = b_n(k) * a_n(-k) = (b_n * -a_n)(k) \tag{6.45b}$$

stands for the so-called *discrete-time system function*.

Taking the service discipline FIFO (first-in, first-out) into account, it is obvious that the unfinished work U_n^- is identical with the waiting time W_n of the n-th customer. This equation delivers a recursive algorithm for the computation of the waiting time in GI/GI/1 systems:

$$W_{n+1} = \max(0, W_n + B - A) \qquad \textbf{Lindley recursion for} \quad \tag{6.46a}$$
$$w_{n+1}(k) = \pi_0(w_n(k) * c_n(k)) \, . \qquad \textbf{non-stationary GI/GI/1} \tag{6.46b}$$

It should be noted that the relationship in Equation (6.46b) between the distribution of waiting times of two successive customers generally holds for customer-dependent interarrival and service length distributions in a GI/GI/1 system. The algorithm in the time domain resulting from this property is discussed later in this chapter.

Assuming now that interarrival and service times are statistically independent and identically distributed, i.e.

$$A_n = A , \quad B_n = B \quad \text{for all } n ,$$ (6.47a)

and further that the system is stationary, with

$$W = \lim_{n \to \infty} W_n ,$$ (6.47b)

a relationship similar to the Lindley integral equation for stationary, discrete-time GI/GI/1 delay systems follows from Equation (6.46b), (6.47a), and (6.47b):

$$w(k) = \pi_0\Big(w(k) * c(k)\Big) \quad \text{with} \quad c(k) = b(k) * a(-k) . \quad \textbf{stationary GI/GI/1}$$ (6.48)

From Equation (6.48), which is derived for the waiting time distribution $w(k)$, a relationship for the waiting time distribution function can be obtained – which does not require the π_0-operator. For $k \geq 0$ yields:

$$W(k) = \sum_{i=0}^{k} w(i) = \sum_{i=-\infty}^{k} c(i) * w(i) = \sum_{i=-\infty}^{k} \sum_{j=-\infty}^{\infty} c(j) \cdot w(i - j)$$

$$= \sum_{j=-\infty}^{\infty} c(j) \sum_{i=-\infty}^{k} w(i - j) = \sum_{j=-\infty}^{\infty} c(j) \cdot W(k - j) , \quad k = 0, 1, \ldots$$ (6.49a)

or

$$W(k) = \begin{cases} 0 & k < 0 \\ c(k) * W(k) & k \geq 0 \end{cases} . \quad \textbf{discrete-time Lindley equation}$$ (6.49b)

The waiting probability p_W for customers is

$$p_W = P(\text{a customer has to wait prior to enter service})$$
$$= P(W > 0) = 1 - W(0) = 1 - w(0) .$$ (6.50)

6.4.3 Analysis Algorithm in Time Domain

From the general form of Lindley's integral equation in discrete-time domain according to Equation (6.45b) and Equation (6.46b)

$$w_{n+1}(k) = \pi_0 \Big(w_n(k) * b_n(k) * a_n(-k) \Big) = \pi_0 \Big(w_n(k) * c_n(k) \Big) \tag{6.51}$$

the waiting time distribution of the $(n+1)$-st customer can be successively calculated from the waiting time distribution of the n-th customer. The interarrival and service time distributions can be chosen in a customer-dependent manner. This leads to an iterative algorithm for calculating the waiting time distribution of the GI/GI/1 system in time domain (see Ackroyd [1]).

The algorithm is depicted in Figure 6.10 with a computational diagram:

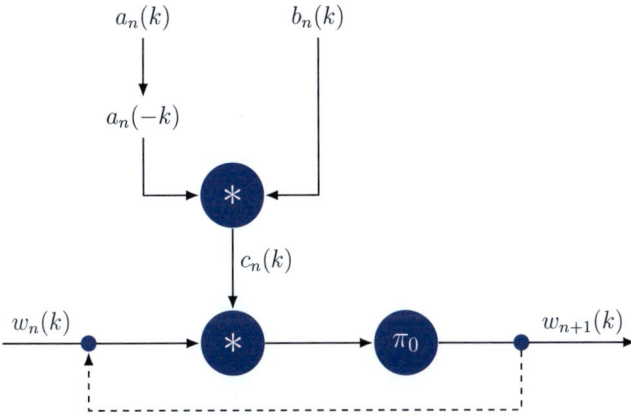

Figure 6.10: Analysis algorithm of discrete-time GI/GI/1 system in time-domain.

(i) Initializing the waiting time distribution $w_0(k)$. In principle, this can be done with any distribution. It can be initiated with an empty system when the 0-th request arrives:

$$w_0(k) = \delta(k) = \begin{cases} 1, & k = 0, \\ 0, & \text{otherwise.} \end{cases}$$

(ii) Computing of the system function $c_n(k)$.

(iii) Executing the convolution operation to calculate the waiting time distribution of the $(n+1)$-st customer from the n-th customer according to Equation (6.51).

(iv) Performing the π_0 operation (Equation (6.44)).

(v) Repeating the steps ii), iii) and iv) until the waiting time distribution converges. As convergence criterion, e.g. the difference between the mean values of two successively determined waiting time distributions, can be taken (cf. power method in Chapter 5.2.1).

The convolution operations contained in the algorithm can e.g. be efficiently carried out with the help of the Discrete Fourier Transform or with the corresponding Fast Fourier Transform.

If the interarrival and service times are chosen individually customer-by-customer, two convolution operations are required per iteration cycle. In contrast, with GI/GI/1 systems where the interarrival and service times are the same for all customers, the system function $c(k)$ has to be calculated only once. In this case there is only one convolution operation needed per iteration cycle.

Compared to the algorithm in transform domain, the discrete-time domain algorithm presented here requires relatively more computing time, especially if the system function $c(t)$ is lengthy. However, the advantage of the time-domain algorithm is that the convergence behavior is very robust with regard to different types of distribution functions. As mentioned, the algorithm in time domain, in contrast to the methods in the transformed domain, can be used for systems with customer-dependent interarrival and service times.

6.4.4 Characteristic Equation in Transform Domain

Figure 6.11 illustrates the composition of the waiting time distribution function $W(k)$ in Equation (6.49b): this function arises out of the discrete convolution $c(k) * W(k)$, where the so-called disturbance components on the negative time axis are omitted. Denoting this disturbance term by $W^-(k)$, $k < 0$, we arrive at

$$W^-(k) + W(k) = c(k) * W(k) .$$ (6.52)

Note that the addition of probabilities $(W^-(k) + W(k))$ results in a mixture distribution, not to be confused with the addition of r.v.s, resulting in a convolution.

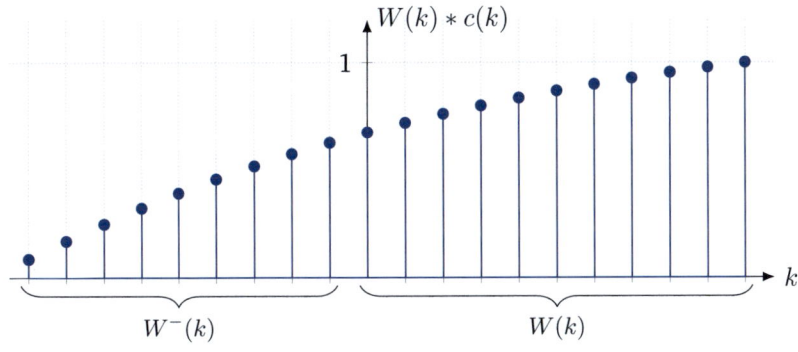

Figure 6.11: Waiting time distribution function $W(k)$ and disturbance term $W^-(k)$.

Take a closer look at the Z-transforms $W_{ZT}(z)$ of the distribution $w(k)$, $\mathcal{W}_{ZT}(z)$ of the distribution function $W(k)$ and $\mathcal{W}_{ZT}^-(z)$ of the disturbance term $W^-(k)$. These terms are related as follows:

$$w(k) \ \overset{\text{ZT}}{\circ\!\!-\!\!\bullet} \ W_{ZT}(z) = \sum_{k=0}^{\infty} w(k) z^{-k}$$

$$\Big\downarrow \Sigma$$

$$W(k) = \sum_{i=0}^{k} w(i), \quad k = 0, 1, \dots \ \overset{\text{ZT}}{\circ\!\!-\!\!\bullet} \ \mathcal{W}_{ZT}(z) = \sum_{k=0}^{\infty} W(k) z^{-k}$$

$$W^-(k), \quad k = -\infty, \dots, -1 \ \overset{\text{ZT}}{\circ\!\!-\!\!\bullet} \ \mathcal{W}_{ZT}^-(z) = \sum_{k=-\infty}^{-1} W^-(k) z^{-k} .$$

Examine first the Z-transform:

$$W_{ZT}(z) = \sum_{k=0}^{\infty} W(k)z^{-k} = \sum_{k=0}^{\infty} \sum_{i=0}^{k} w(i)z^{-k} = \frac{W_{ZT}(z)}{1 - z^{-1}} . \tag{6.53a}$$

From (6.52) and (6.53a) is obtained

$$W_{ZT}^{-}(z) + W_{ZT}(z) = C_{ZT}(z) \cdot W_{ZT}(z) \tag{6.53b}$$

and the characteristic equation for the analysis of the waiting time of the discrete-time GI/GI/1 system:

$$W_{ZT}^{-}(z) \cdot \frac{1}{W_{ZT}(z)} = \frac{C_{ZT}(z) - 1}{1 - z^{-1}} . \qquad \textbf{characteristic equation} \tag{6.54}$$

The right side of Equation (6.54) is called the *characteristic function*, since it contains all parameters of the GI/GI/1 system under consideration:

$$S_{ZT}(z) = \frac{C_{ZT}(z) - 1}{1 - z^{-1}} . \qquad \textbf{characteristic function} \tag{6.55}$$

The characteristic equation (6.54) is often given in form of a generating function (cf. Kobayashi [64]), and plays a central role in algorithms and analysis methods in discrete-time solutions of the Lindley integral equation. Some interesting properties of the characteristic equation are:

- The disturbance term $W_{ZT}^{-}(z)$ is the Z-transform of a time sequence which has positive, non-increasing coefficients on the negative time axis. According to the Eneström-Kakeya theorem (cf. Ackroyd [1]), all zeros of this function lie outside the unit circle. Since $W^{-}(k)$ is a left-hand sequence (see Figure 6.11) with finite, non-negative values $0 \leq W^{-}(k) < 1$, $k < 0$, it can also be shown (see Oppenheim and Schafer [82]) that the function $W_{ZT}^{-}(z)$ converges within and on the unit circle, i.e. all its poles must lie outside the unit circle. The function $W_{ZT}^{-}(z)$ is therefore the Z-transform of a non-minimum-phase sequence.

- The function $W_{ZT}(z)$ is the Z-transform of a distribution. Hence, this function converges outside and on the unit circle, i.e. all poles of $W_{ZT}(z)$ or all zeros of the term $\frac{1}{W_{ZT}(z)}$ of the characteristic equation lie within the unit circle.

- Following the stability condition $\rho < 1$ and the limit theorem of the Z-transform we have

$$0 < \lim_{z \to \infty} W_{ZT}(z) \leq 1 . \tag{6.56}$$

These properties are used later in the algorithm for the GI/GI/1 delay system in transform domain (Chapter 6.4.5).

Example: Closed-Form Solution for GEOM(m)/GEOM(m)/1 Delay System   For some special cases, closed-form expressions of the waiting time distribution can directly be derived from the characteristic equation. Outlined below is the example of the GEOM(m)/GEOM(m)/1 delay system.

Both interarrival and service distributions are shifted geometric distributions, where the shift m is chosen to be the same for both processes, i.e.

$$a(k) = (1 - \alpha)\alpha^{k-m}, \quad k \geq m, \quad \mathrm{E}[A] = m + \frac{\alpha}{1 - \alpha},$$

$$b(k) = (1 - \beta)\beta^{k-m}, \quad k \geq m, \quad \mathrm{E}[B] = m + \frac{\beta}{1 - \beta},$$

or in Z-domain

$$A_{ZT}(z) = \frac{(1 - \alpha)z^{-m}}{1 - \alpha z^{-1}},$$

$$B_{ZT}(z) = \frac{(1 - \beta)z^{-m}}{1 - \beta z^{-1}}.$$

The stability condition is thus

$$\rho = \frac{\mathrm{E}[B]}{\mathrm{E}[A]} < 1 \quad \text{or} \quad \frac{\beta}{\alpha} < 1.$$

From Equation (6.45b) the system function yields

$$C_{ZT}(z) = A_{ZT}(z^{-1}) \cdot B_{ZT}(z) = \frac{(1 - \alpha)(1 - \beta)}{(1 - \alpha z)(1 - \beta z^{-1})}. \tag{6.57}$$

Hence, the characteristic function of the GEOM(m)/GEOM(m)/1 system according to Equation (6.55) is

$$S_{ZT}(z) = \frac{\alpha z - \beta}{(1 - \alpha z)(1 - \beta z^{-1})} \tag{6.58a}$$

and can be reformulated to simplify the localization of poles and zeros (cf. Equation (6.23))

$$S_{ZT}(z) = \alpha \cdot \frac{z(1 - \frac{\beta}{\alpha} \cdot z^{-1})}{(1 - \alpha z) \cdot (1 - \beta z^{-1})} = W_{ZT}^-(z) \cdot \frac{1}{W_{ZT}(z)}. \tag{6.58b}$$

Thus $1/\alpha$ is the pole of $W_{ZT}^-(z)$, the Z-transform of the non-minimum-phase sequence $W^-(k)$. From Equation (6.58b) the waiting time distribution can be given:

$$W_{ZT}(z) = K_0 \cdot \frac{1}{\alpha} \cdot z^{K_1 - 1} \cdot \frac{1 - \beta z^{-1}}{1 - \frac{\beta}{\alpha} \cdot z^{-1}}. \tag{6.59}$$

Using the normalization condition $W_{ZT}(1) = 1$, K_0 can be determined

$$K_0 = \frac{\alpha - \beta}{1 - \beta} ,$$
(6.60a)

and from Equation (6.56)

$$\lim_{z \to \infty} W_{ZT}(z) > 0$$
(6.60b)

yields

$$K_1 = 1 .$$
(6.60c)

Assembling the equations (6.59), (6.60a) and (6.60c) we arrive at the Z-transform of the waiting time distribution of the GEOM(m)/GEOM(m)/1 system:

$$W_{ZT}(z) = \frac{\alpha - \beta}{1 - \beta} \cdot \frac{z - \beta}{z\alpha - \beta} .$$
(6.61)

6.4.5 Analysis Algorithm in Transform Domain

6.4.5.1 Basic Principle

Algorithms for the calculation of the waiting time distribution of time-discrete GI/GI/1 systems in the transform domain are based almost exclusively on the characteristic equation according to Equation (6.54) of Z-transforms

$$W_{ZT}^-(z) \cdot \frac{1}{W_{ZT}(z)} = \frac{C_{ZT}(z) - 1}{1 - z^{-1}}$$
(6.62a)

or formulated in generating functions

$$W_{GF}^-(z) \cdot \frac{1}{W_{GF}(z)} = \frac{C_{GF}(z) - 1}{1 - z} .$$
(6.62b)

Taking into account the position of poles and zeros of the terms on the right side of the characteristic equation, the waiting time distribution $W_{ZT}(z)$ can be extracted from the left side by separating the disturbance term $W_{ZT}^-(z)$. There are two basic possibilities for separation in the transform domain:

- *Polynomial factorization:*
  Separation method by explicit calculation of zeros and poles using polynomial factorization (see Konheim [67], Tijms [105]);

- *Cepstrum-based separation:*
  Separation in Cepstrum domain under consideration of the phase-based property of the terms in the characteristic function with the help of the Cepstrum concept (cf. Ackroyd [1], Tran-Gia [107]).

Assume that in the following algorithms the interarrival and service time distributions are of finite length n_A and n_B, respectively:

$$a(k) = P(A = k) , \qquad k = 0, 1, \ldots, n_A - 1 , \quad n_A < \infty , \qquad (6.63a)$$

$$b(k) = P(B = k) , \qquad k = 0, 1, \ldots, n_B - 1 , \quad n_B < \infty . \qquad (6.63b)$$

6.4.5.2 Algorithm Using Polynomial Factorization

The generating function of the characteristic equation is now considered. The algorithm by Konheim [67] also assumes that the interarrival process is a single arrival process, i.e. $a(0) = 0$. With

$$C_{GF}(z) - 1 \Big|_{z=1} = 0 ,$$

$$\frac{d}{dz}(C_{GF}(z) - 1)\Big|_{z=1} = \mathrm{E}[B] - \mathrm{E}[A] < 0$$

the root $z = 1$ of the numerator polynomial of the characteristic function

$$S_{GF}(z) = W_{GF}^-(z) \cdot \frac{1}{W_{GF}(z)} = \frac{C_{GF}(z) - 1}{1 - z} \qquad (6.64)$$

is a single zero. Since the distributions $a(k)$ and $b(k)$ are finite, the characteristic function can be written as a polynomial. This leads to the factorization approach

$$S_{GF}(z) = S_{GF}^+(z) \cdot S_{GF}^-(z) \qquad (6.65a)$$

with

$$S_{GF}^+(z) = K_1 \prod_{n=1}^{n_o} (z - q_{on}) , \qquad |q_{on}| > 1 \qquad (6.65b)$$

and

$$S_{GF}^-(z) = K_2 \, z^{-K_3} \prod_{n=1}^{n_i} (z - q_{in}) , \qquad |q_{in}| < 1 , \qquad (6.65c)$$

where q_{in}, $n = 1, \ldots, n_i$ and q_{on}, $n = 1, \ldots, n_o$, are the roots of the polynomial $S_{GF}(z)$ within and outside the unit circle.

The constants K_1 and K_2 must fulfil the normalization condition for distributions:

$$S_{GF}^+(1) = 1 .$$

In Konheim [67] it is shown that the generating function of the waiting time distribution can be specified as:

$$W_{GF}(z) = \frac{1}{S_{GF}^+(z)} . \tag{6.66}$$

The application of this method requires an explicit calculation of zeros of the characteristic function, e.g. with help of algorithms for polynomial factorization. For GI/GI/1 systems with relatively large interarrival and service time distributions, the associated numerical effort is quite high. Another disadvantage of the method is that the solution according to Equation (6.66) is given in transform domain. If the waiting time distributions in the time domain, the mean value or coefficient of variation of the distribution, are required, further numerical efforts have to be added (cf. Henrici [48]). For systems with relative small distributions, however, the algorithm with polynomial factorization offers quite an efficient way to analyze the discrete-time GI/GI/1 system.

6.4.5.3 Algorithm Using Cepstrum Concept

The separation method in Cepstrum domain is based on the characteristic equation:

$$S_{ZT}(z) = W_{ZT}^-(z) \cdot \frac{1}{W_{ZT}(z)} = \frac{C_{ZT}(z) - 1}{1 - z^{-1}} . \tag{6.67}$$

The waiting time distribution $W_{ZT}(z)$ is now to be extracted from the characteristic function $S_{ZT}(z)$. For the separation approach in Cepstrum domain it should first be shown that the two terms $W_{ZT}^-(z)$ and $\dfrac{1}{W_{ZT}(z)}$ are the Z-transforms of a non-minimum-phase sequence and a minimum-phase sequence.

- $C_{ZT}(z)$ is a polynomial in z^{-1}:
  If the distributions of the interarrival and service time are of finite length, these distributions as well as the system function can be written as polynomials in Z-transforms:

  $$A_{ZT}(z) = \sum_{k=0}^{n_A - 1} a(k) z^{-k} , \qquad B_{ZT}(z) = \sum_{k=0}^{n_B - 1} b(k) z^{-k} , \tag{6.68a}$$

  $$C_{ZT}(z) = A_{ZT}(z^{-1}) \cdot B_{ZT}(z) = \sum_{k=-(n_A - 1)}^{n_B - 1} c(k) z^{-k} . \tag{6.68b}$$

- $S_{ZT}(z)$ is a polynomial in z^{-1}:
  Similar to the polynomial factorization in the previous section, it can be shown that the function $C_{ZT}(z) - 1$ has a single zero at location $z = 1$. The characteristic function $S_{ZT}(z)$ has no poles and can therefore be formulated as a polynomial in z^{-1}.

- $\mathcal{W}_{ZT}^{-}(z)$ is the Z-transform of a non-minimal phase sequence:
  With Equation (6.52) (cf. Figure 6.11):

$$W^{-}(k) + W(k) = c(k) * W(k)$$

  and taking into account the finite length of the system function $c(k)$ according to Equation (6.68b) the Z-transform $\mathcal{W}_{ZT}^{-}(z)$ can also be written as polynomial of the form

$$\mathcal{W}_{ZT}^{-}(z) = \sum_{k=-(n_A-1)}^{-1} W^{-}(k)z^{-k} = \sum_{k=1}^{n_A-1} W^{-}(-k)z^{k} \ . \tag{6.69}$$

This means that $\mathcal{W}_{ZT}^{-}(z)$ has no poles. Since $\mathcal{W}_{ZT}(z)$ in Equation (6.52) is a sequence with non-decreasing coefficients (cf. Figure 6.11), it can also be shown (cf. Ackroyd [1]) that all zeros of $\mathcal{W}_{ZT}^{-}(z)$ are outside the unit circle. This means that $\mathcal{W}_{ZT}^{-}(z)$ is the Z-transform of a non-minimum-phase sequence.

- $\dfrac{1}{W_{ZT}(z)}$ is the Z-transform of a minimum-phase sequence:
  Since $W_{ZT}(z)$ is the Z-transform of a distribution and converges in $|z| > 1$, all poles of $W_{ZT}(z)$ are inside the unit circle. This means that the term $\frac{1}{W_{ZT}(z)}$ only has zeros inside the unit circle.

  As shown above, $S_{ZT}(z)$ and $\mathcal{W}_{ZT}^{-}(z)$ have no poles. According to Equation (6.67) it is obvious that $\frac{1}{W_{ZT}(z)}$ also has no poles. The term $\frac{1}{W_{ZT}(z)}$ is hence the Z-transform of a minimum-phase sequence.

To derive the waiting time distribution $w(k)$, the separation method of maximum-phase and minimum-phase sequences can now be carried out in Cepstrum domain (see Equation (6.25a), (6.25b) and (6.25c)) applied on the characteristic function in Equation (6.67). The Z-transform and Z-inverse-transform required for the Cepstrum computation can be accomplished with the Discrete Fourier Transform or the Fast Fourier Transform.

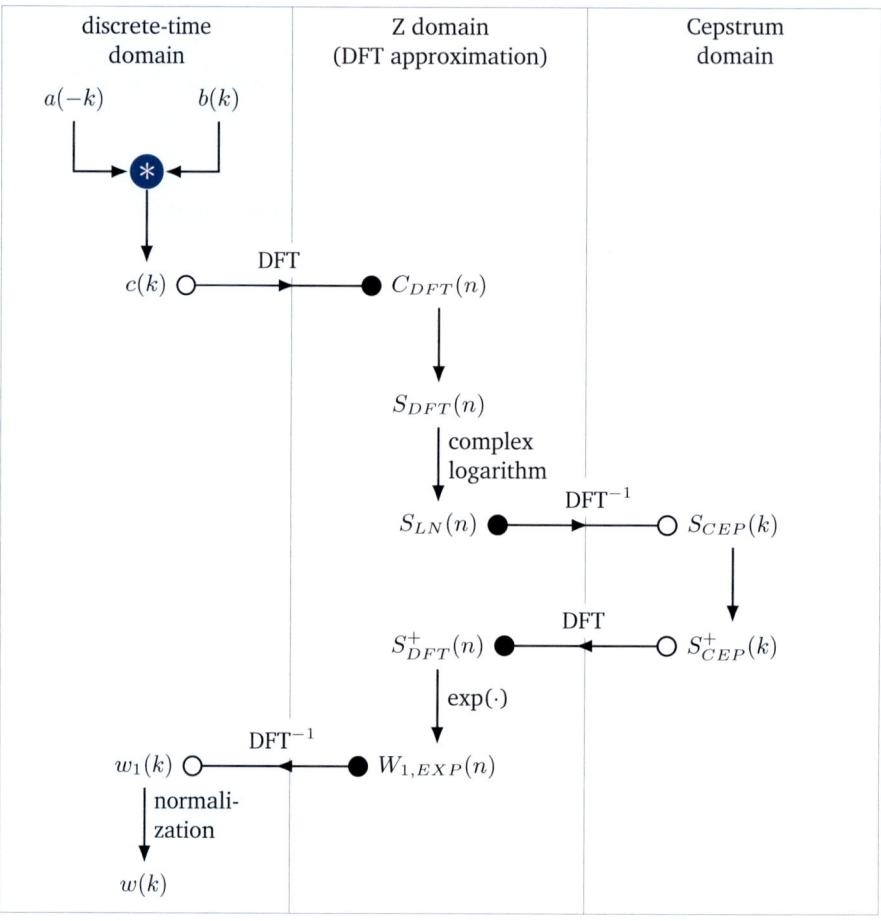

Figure 6.12: Analysis algorithm for discrete-time GI/GI/1 system using Cepstrum concept.

As schematically shown in Figure 6.12, the basic steps of the algorithm using Cepstrum concept (cf. Ackroyd [1]) can be summarized as follows:

(i) Compute the Discrete Fourier Transform (DFT) of the characteristic function $S_{DFT}(n)$.

(ii) Calculate the complex logarithm

$$S_{LN}(n) = \ln S_{DFT}(n)$$

and the complex Cepstrum of the characteristic function

$$S_{CEP}(k) = \text{DFT}^{-1}\{S_{LN}(n)\}\,.$$

(iii) Separation of non-minimum-phase and minimum-phase parts of $S_{CEP}(k)$. The part of the Cepstrum

$$S_{CEP}^{+}(k) = \begin{cases} S_{CEP}(k) & k \geq 0 \\ 0 & k < 0 \end{cases}$$

is belonging to the term $\frac{1}{W_{ZT}(z)}$ which, however, is still not normalized due to the overlap of the amplitude parts of the maximum- and minimum-phase-sequences at the point $k = 0$.

(iv) Calculation of the (still) unnormalized distribution $w_1(k)$ using inverse Cepstrum algorithm according to Equation (6.22a), (6.22b) and (6.22c):

$$S_{DFT}^{+}(n) = \mathrm{DFT}\{S_{CEP}^{+}(k)\} \,,$$
$$W_{1,EXP}(n) = \frac{1}{S_{EXP}^{+}(n)} = e^{S_{DFT}^{+}(n)} \,,$$
$$w_1(k) = \mathrm{DFT}^{-1}\{W_{1,EXP}(n)\} \,.$$

(v) Normalization of $w_1(k)$ to finally obtain $w(k)$.

With this algorithm, some numerical problems arise when calculating the complex Cepstrum, e.g. the overlap of Cepstrum components (aliasing) or the phase unwrapping (see Oppenheim and Schafer [82]). The algorithm presented here using Cepstrum concept is an efficient method for calculating the waiting time distribution of the time-discrete GI/GI/1 system. The algorithm is particularly well-suited for systems with large numbers of distribution values of interarrival and service times. This advantage is based on the use of efficient algorithms for the Fast Fourier Transform.

◨ *Further reading:* Haßlinger (1995) "A polynomial factorization approach to the discrete time GI/G/1/(N) queue size distribution" [44].

6.4.6 Numerical Examples

Example 1: A System with Arbitrarily Distributed Interarrival and Service Times
In many applications of time-discrete analysis, distributions are obtained from measurements and given in the form of histograms. The following distributions for interarrival and service times are considered to illustrate the use of the algorithm:

$$a(4) = 0.4, \quad a(8) = 0.5, \quad a(20) = 0.1, \quad a(k) = 0 \text{ otherwise,}$$
$$b(4) = 0.2, \quad b(5) = 0.1, \quad b(6) = 0.7, \quad b(k) = 0 \text{ otherwise.}$$

The random variables have the following characteristics.
$$\mathrm{E}[A] = 7.6, \quad \mathrm{E}[B] = 5.5, \quad \rho = 0.724, \quad c_A = 0.598, \quad c_B = 0.147.$$

Figure 6.13 shows the cumulative distribution functions of the interarrival time, the service time and the waiting time, whereby the step functions of the results are depicted. The mean waiting time is low ($\mathrm{E}[W] = 1.415$) due to the small variations in the processes. Kingman's approximation in Equation (5.90) is overestimating here, $\widetilde{W} = 2.728$.

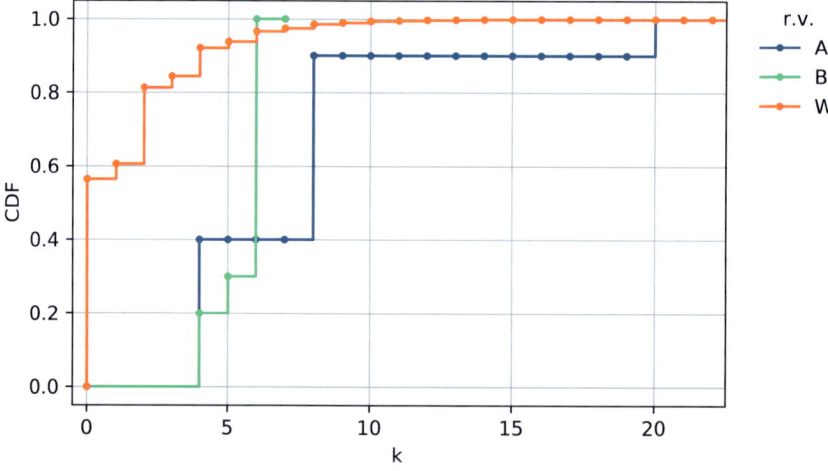

Figure 6.13: Cumulative waiting time distribution function of a discrete-time GI/GI/1 system with arbitrarily distributed interarrival and service times.

Please note the following trivial situation: consider the maximum potential service time $b_{\max}$, i.e., the greatest k for which $b(k) > 0$ is positive. Then consider the minimum potential interarrival time $a_{\min}$, i.e., the smallest k for which $a(k) > 0$ is positive. If the interarrival time is larger than the maximum service time, customers never have to wait in the steady state.

$$a_{\min} = \underset{k \in \{0,1,\dots\}}{\arg\min} \ (a(k) > 0)$$

$$b_{\max} = \underset{k \in \{0,1,\dots\}}{\arg\max} \ (b(k) > 0)$$

$$a_{\min} > b_{\max} \quad \implies \quad W = 0$$

Example 2: NEGBIN/D/1 Delay System A NEGBIN/D/1 system is considered. The interarrival time follows the two-parametric negative binomial distribution (NEGBIN), and the service time is deterministic. The negative binomial distribution is limited in length to enable numerical calculations; typically, distribution values $a(k)$ smaller than $\varepsilon = 10^{-9}$ are neglected and the remaining distribution is re-standardized. Another typical way is to determine the inverse k_q of the complementary cumulative distribution function, $P(A > k_q) < q$, e.g. for $q = 10^{-6}$, which we follow in the numerical example. Hence, the distribution is cut at point k_q and the remaining distribution is normalized. We are using a conditional r.v. $A^* = A|A \le k_q$ with $a^*(k) = a(k)/\sum_{k=0}^{k_q} a(k)$ for $k \le k_q$ and $a^*(k) = 0$ otherwise. Thus, A^* has a finite length and is used instead of A. Figure 6.14 shows the cumulative distribution function $A(k)$ for $E[A] = 5$ and $c_A \in \{0.5, 1.0, 1.5\}$ which have the cutoff points k_q at $22, 65, 128$, respectively.

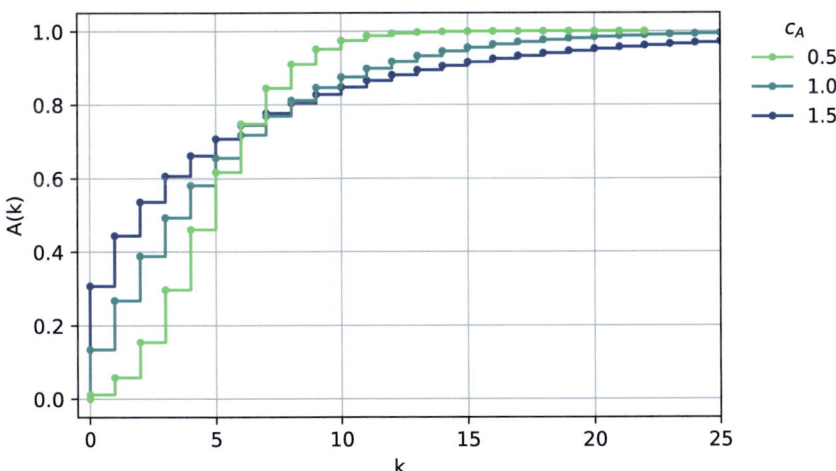

Figure 6.14: Cumulative distribution function $A(k)$ of the interarrival time A of a discrete-time NEGBIN/D/1 system with $E[A] = 5$.

The stationary cumulative distribution functions of the waiting times of the discrete-time NEGBIN/D/1 system are shown in Figure 6.15 using A^*. The coefficients of variation are chosen such that the interarrival time corresponds to the continuous-time distribution of types Erlang-4-th order E_4 ($c_A = 0.5$), negative exponential M ($c_A = 1$) and hyper-exponential H_2 ($c_A = 1.5$).

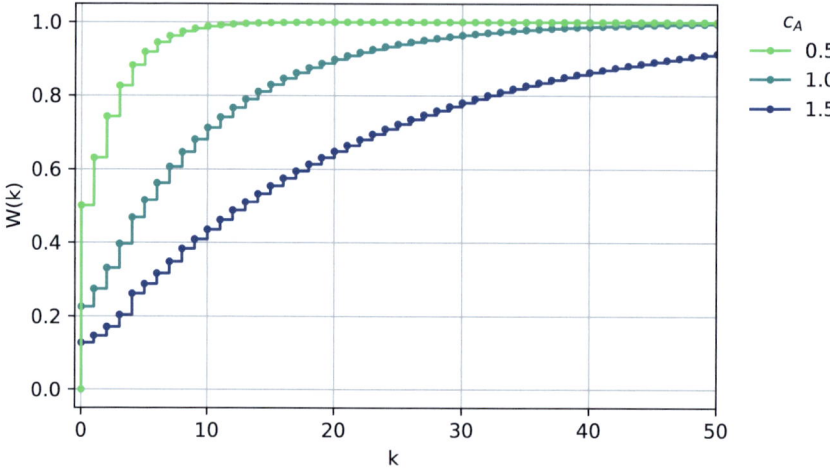

Figure 6.15: Cumulative distribution function of the waiting time of a discrete-time NEGBIN/D/1 system. The system load is $\rho = 0.8$, $E[B] = 4$, $E[A] = 5$.

6.4.7 Other Performance Measures

Some system characteristics of interest can be derived from the waiting time distribution $w(k)$ of a GI/GI/1 system in equilibrium.

6.4.7.1 Waiting Probability

As already discussed in Equation (6.50), the probability that an arriving customer has to wait is identical to the probability that the server is occupied immediately before the arrival time of the request, i.e.

$$p_W = \sum_{k=1}^{\infty} u^-(k) \;=\; 1 - u^-(0) \;=\; 1 - w(0) \,. \qquad \textbf{waiting probability} \quad (6.70)$$

6.4.7.2 Waiting Time for Waiting Customers

The distribution $w_1(k)$ of the waiting time W_1 of waiting customers can be calculated from the waiting time distribution $w(k)$ of the r.v. W for the waiting time of all customers:

$$w_1(k) = P(W_1 = k) = \begin{cases} 0 & k \leq 0 \\ \frac{w(k)}{p_W} & k > 0 \end{cases}. \tag{6.71}$$

6.4.7.3 System Occupancy and Mean Queue Length

The mean queue length Ω and the system occupancy $E[X]$ can be calculated from the mean waiting time using the Little theorem. For the GI/GI/1 system with the mean sojourn time $E[W] + E[B]$ and the mean interarrival time $E[A]$ results to the mean system occupancy $E[X]$ according to the Little formula:

$$E[X] = \frac{E[W] + E[B]}{E[A]} = \frac{E[W]}{E[A]} + \rho. \tag{6.72}$$

Now, the Little theorem is applied only to the queue which is considered as system. The mean sojourn time is $E[W_1]$ and the mean interarrival time $\frac{E[A]}{p_W}$. The mean queue length is, according to the Little formula, as

$$\Omega = E[X_W] = \frac{E[W_1] \cdot p_W}{E[A]} = \frac{E[W]}{E[A]}. \tag{6.73}$$

Alternatively: $E[X_W] = E[X] - E[X_B]$ with $E[X_B] = \rho$ due to the utilization law.

6.4.8 Idle Times, Busy Times, Interdeparture Times

In a GI/GI/n queueing system, the long-term average fraction of idle time for any server is $(1 - \rho)$, cf. Chapter 2.1.6. Consider here the duration of an idle period for the GI/GI/1 queue which is denoted by the random variable I. It is tempting to assume that (a) the long-term average fraction of idle time $(1 - \rho)$ during two arrivals with mean interarrival time $E[A]$ and (b) the expected idle time $E[I]$ are identical, see Figure 6.16. However, this relation is not valid, since the idle time only manifests after the end of a busy period (composed of several service times and smaller interarrival times; a larger interarrival time ends the busy period and yields an idle period). In fact, the following inequality holds, see Marshall and Evans [75] and Chapter 5.6:

$$E[I] \geq E[A] - E[B] = (1 - \rho)E[A], \tag{6.74}$$

while equality holds for the D/D/1 queue.

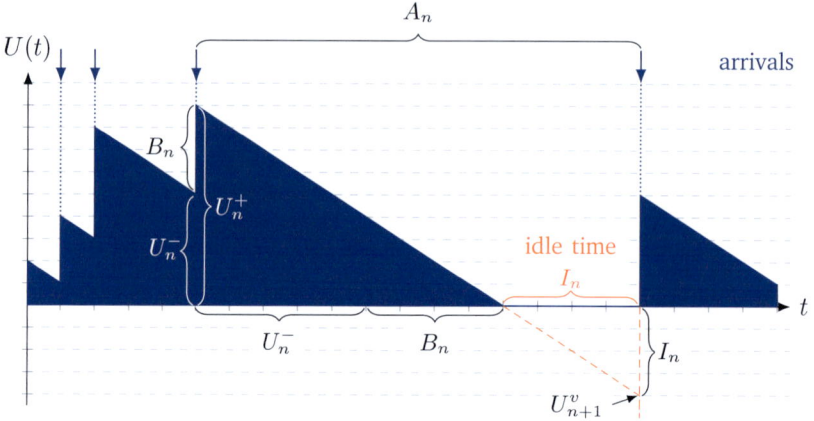

Figure 6.16: Derivation of idle time distribution I for a GI/GI/1 delay system.

The distribution of the idle times I can be derived by taking a closer look at Figure 6.16. The idle time I_n after the completion of the n-th customer is a conditional r.v. which is simply the negative part ($k < 0$) of the virtual unfinished work U^v_{n+1} immediately before the arrival of the customer $n + 1$. Let us define Y_{n+1} as the difference between the interarrival time A_n and the unfinished work U^+_n immediately after arrival of customer n. Then the idle time I_n is the conditional r.v. that there is a positive idle time (otherwise, for $Y_n \leq 0$, the system is in a busy period). Hence, $I_n = Y_n | Y_n > 0$.

$$U^v_{n+1} = U^+_n - A_n = U^-_n + B_n - A_n \tag{6.75a}$$

$$Y_n = -U^v_{n+1} = A_n - (U^-_n + B_n) \tag{6.75b}$$

$$I_n = Y_n | Y_n > 0 \tag{6.75c}$$

$$i_n(k) = \begin{cases} \dfrac{a_n(k) * u_n(-k) * b_n(-k)}{P(Y_n > 0)} & \text{for } k > 0 \\ 0 & \text{otherwise} \end{cases} \tag{6.75d}$$

In a queueing system, idle periods and busy periods are alternating. Consider the busy period is composed of j individual service times. Then, the duration V_j of the busy period is a conditional r.v. and is the sum of those j service times, $V_j = \sum_{i=1}^{j} B$.

The output process of the GI/GI/1 queue considers the departure points of customers. In general, the output process of a GI/GI/1 queue is not a renewal process. Nevertheless, the output process is often characterized by the interdeparture time distribution D. The discrete-time analysis allows to numerically derive the interdeparture time D_n of the n-th customer.

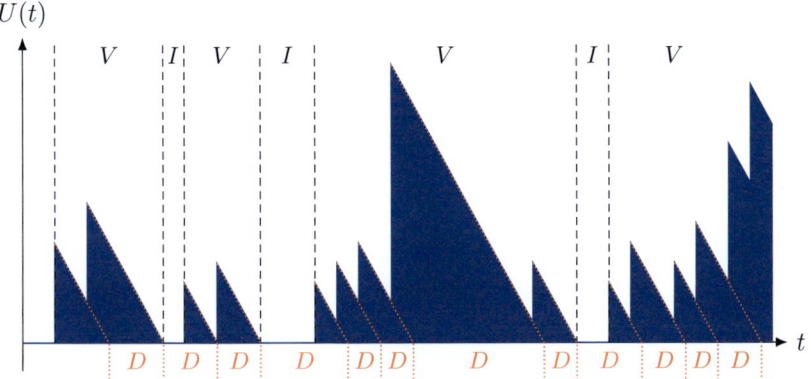

Figure 6.17: Idle and busy periods of length I and V are alternating in a GI/GI/1 queue.

Consider a large time interval T_0. The duration of a busy period and an idle period is V and I, respectively. Then the number of busy periods during T_0 is

$$n_v = \frac{T_0}{\mathrm{E}[V] + \mathrm{E}[I]} \, , \tag{6.76a}$$

while the number of arriving customers during T_0 is

$$n_a = \frac{T_0}{\mathrm{E}[A]} \, . \tag{6.76b}$$

Due to Kleinrock's principle (Chapter 5.2.3), the number of arrival events and departures events is the same in the long term. Hence, the mean number of departure events during a busy period is

$$n_d^v = \frac{n_a}{n_v} = \frac{\mathrm{E}[V] + \mathrm{E}[I]}{\mathrm{E}[A]} \, . \tag{6.76c}$$

The probability p_I that the departure happens at the end of a busy period (i.e. one departure out of n_d^v) is

$$p_I = \frac{1}{n_d^v} = \frac{\mathrm{E}[V] + \mathrm{E}[I]}{\mathrm{E}[A]} = \frac{\mathrm{E}[B]}{\mathrm{E}[V]} \, . \tag{6.77a}$$

The long-term average fraction of busy time can also be expressed in terms of the mean idle and busy period durations.

$$\rho = \frac{\mathrm{E}[V]}{\mathrm{E}[V] + \mathrm{E}[I]} = \frac{\mathrm{E}[B]}{\mathrm{E}[A]} \tag{6.77b}$$

This leads to

$$p_I = \frac{\mathrm{E}[A]}{\mathrm{E}[I] + \mathrm{E}[V]} = \frac{\mathrm{E}[A] - \mathrm{E}[B]}{\mathrm{E}[I]}. \tag{6.77c}$$

Hence, the following mixture distribution is obtained to characterize the interdeparture time D_n, see Figure 6.17:

$$D_n = \begin{cases} I_n + B_n & \text{with probability } p_I \\ B_n & \text{with probability } 1 - p_I \end{cases} \tag{6.78}$$

with probability mass function

$$d_n(k) = p_I(i_n(k) * b_n(k)) + (1 - p_I)b_n(k). \tag{6.79}$$

6.4.9   Queue Size and Distributional Little's Law

Finally, the system size X^* at an arbitrary point in time for the discrete-time GI/GI/1 queue is derived by utilizing an extended version of Little's law: the distributional Little's law which was first discussed in [43]. A discrete-time version of the distributional Little's law was proposed by Kim and Chaudhry in [58].

The assumptions for the distributional Little's law are as follows and are fulfilled for the discrete-time GI/GI/1. (a) Customers arrive according to a discrete-time renewal process (Chapter 6.1.2) with single arrivals and no batch arrivals. (b) All customers remain in the system until they are served (no blocking, balking or reneging). (c) The customers leave the system (or the queue) in the order of arrival (FIFO). (d) New arriving customers do not affect the time in the system (or the queue) for previous customers. Thus, the waiting time of a customer is independent of the arrival process after its arrival.

The system size X^* is the number of arrivals $\Lambda(T)$ during the sojourn time $T = W + B$ of a customer. This relation is written in form of r.v.s.

$$X^* = \Lambda(T) \qquad\qquad \textbf{distributional Little's law} \tag{6.80}$$

The probability distribution $x^*(k) = P(X^* = k)$ for $k = 0, 1, \ldots$ can be derived using the law of total probability and the conditional r.v. Λ_i with $\Lambda_i = \Lambda | T = i$. The number of arrivals is conditioned on a sojourn time of length $T = i$.

$$x^*(k) = \sum_{i=0}^{\infty} P(\Lambda = k | T = i) \cdot P(T = i) = \sum_{i=0}^{\infty} P(\Lambda_i = k) \cdot P(T = i) \tag{6.81}$$

The probability $P(\Lambda_i \geq k)$ that there are at least k arrivals during time $T = i$ means that the sum τ_k of the forward recurrence time R of the interarrival time A and $k - 1$ interarrival times A is equal or smaller than i.

$$P(\Lambda_i \geq k) = P(\tau_k \leq i) = P(R + \sum_{j=1}^{k-1} A \leq i) \tag{6.82}$$

with

$$\tau_k = \begin{cases} R, & k = 1 \\ R + \sum_{j=1}^{k-1} A, & k > 1 \end{cases}. \tag{6.83}$$

The recurrence time R of the interarrival time A has the following distribution, as derived in Equation (6.12a), when observing after the discrete time instants.

$$r(k) = \frac{1}{\mathrm{E}[A]}(1 - \sum_{i=0}^{k-1} a(i)), \quad k = 1, 2, \dots \tag{6.84}$$

Per definition it is $\Lambda_0 = 0$ and $P(\tau_0 \leq i) = P(\Lambda_i \geq 0) = 1$. Together with

$$P(\Lambda_i = k) = P(\Lambda_i \geq k) - P(\Lambda_i \geq k + 1) = P(\tau_k \leq i) - P(\tau_{k+1} \leq i) \tag{6.85}$$

we finally obtain:

$$\begin{aligned} x^*(k) &= \sum_{i=0}^{\infty} P(\Lambda_i = k) \cdot P(T = i) \\ &= \sum_{i=0}^{\infty} (P(\tau_k \leq i) - P(\tau_{k+1} \leq i)) \cdot P(W + B = i). \end{aligned} \tag{6.86}$$

The distributional Little's law is valid for various other systems, e.g. for both the number in the system and the number in the queue – similar to Little's law – for a continuous GI/GI/1 system [9]. There are also transient laws provided and their application by Bertsimas and Mourtzinou in [8].

📖 *Further reading:* Discrete-time version of distributional Little's law by Kim and Chaudhry (2008) "The use of the distributional Little's law in the computational analysis of discrete-time GI/G/1 and GI/D/c queues" [58]. Bertsimas and Nakazato (1995) "The distributional Little's law and its applications" [9]. Bertsimas and Mourtzinou (1997) "Transient laws of non-stationary queueing systems and their applications" [8].

7

Advanced Models and Applications in Telecommunication Networks

We have already introduced some modeling examples for recent applications in telecommunication networks and the Internet in Chapter 1.3. Those models are advanced and extend the basic queueing theory models from the previous chapters. The first advanced model considers QoS and QoE of video streaming and represents a Markovian System. In particular, the M/M/1 queue with N-policy is analyzed which allows derivation of QoS parameters. A non-linear QoS-QoE mapping function is applied on the resulting random variables which requires the use of Jensen's inequality. The next advanced models are related to the Internet of Things (IoT). Thereby, the superposition of periodic traffic from several sensors is analyzed and compared to the corresponding Poisson process due to the Palm-Khintchine theorem.

An IoT cloud platform is then analyzed and, in particular, the IoT load balancer as a potential performance bottleneck is modeled with an nD/D/1 delay system. The performance is compared to an M/D/1 delay system. Other applications are random access schemes of IoT sensor nodes which may suffer from message collisions on the air interface between IoT sensor and IoT gateway, but also from the energy consumption of those mechanisms. This use case nicely demonstrates the application of fundamental non-Markovian queueing models to analyze different random access mechanisms: pure ALOHA (M/D/∞), slotted ALOHA (M/C/∞), perfect CSMA/CA (M/D/1-∞), and energy-aware CSMA/CA with restricted accessibility (M/D/1-S).

Finally, two use cases are discussed where discrete-time analysis is employed. Spacers in communication networks are used for traffic shaping and overload prevention in networks, since the spacer reduces the variance of interarrival times of packets. Discrete-time analysis methods are used to obtain exact computational algorithms for numerical results. The discrete-time analysis allows derivation results for stationary and non-stationary load conditions. In particular, the evaluation of the overload control strategy under short-term overloads is of interest in practice.

7.1 Video Streaming QoS and QoE

Video streaming over HTTP (Hypertext Transfer Protocol) is currently responsible for the majority of Internet traffic. Video service provider platforms offer videos in a variety of quality settings and deploy different mechanisms to provide high video quality without any video playout interruptions, which may happen due to insufficient network resources or variations in network conditions. For a smooth playout, the video client at the end-user site implements a video buffer to iron out jitters, which might occur during the transmission. The player fills up the video buffer, e.g. until a certain amount of video data is available, before the video playout is started. If the video buffer empties at some point in time, then the video freezes or stalls until the video buffer is filled again. This buffering strategy allows the client to overcome network dynamics, in particular variances of the download data rate.

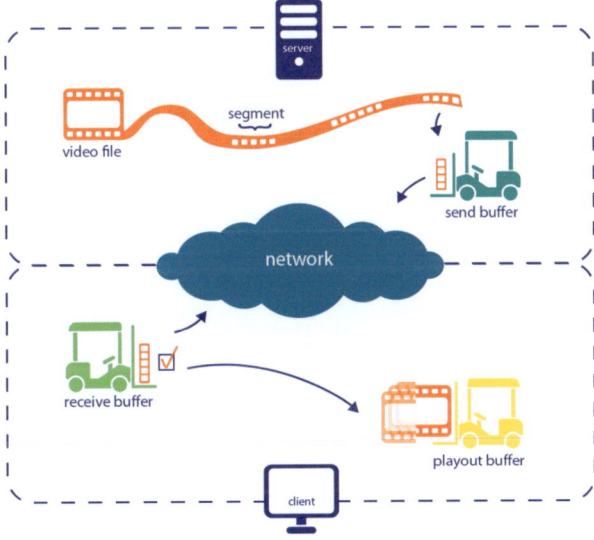

Figure 7.1: Illustration of video streaming buffer (M/M/1 system with N-policy).

HTTP-based video streaming suffers from insufficient network data rates or video server capacity as well as varying network conditions when the video contents are not delivered fast enough to the video client, such that the video stalls for some intervals until the video buffer is filled again and the video playout can be restarted. While HTTP adaptive streaming adjusts the video quality to the available network resources, a user might insist on watching a certain video in a particular quality like High Definition (HD) even though the network does not provide enough bandwidth to stream the whole video without stalling, which is modeled in this chapter.

The notion of quality of experience emerged which provides quantifiable QoE models for the user perceived quality depending on network or application-level quality of service parameters. For HTTP-based video streaming, the key QoE influence factors on the application layer are the number of video interruptions or stalls during the playout, and the total stall duration.

We develop a queueing model of the video buffer in [51] which allows analysis of the impact of the video playout strategy and its parameters. The model provides the status of the video buffer for a given network data rate and the video bit rate and allows various performance parameters to be derived: stall ratio, average stall duration, and the stall frequency. These parameters are input for the QoE model, such that we may derive the QoE-optimal video buffer parameter.

7.1.1 Model Structure and Parameters: Video Buffer

The video buffer is modeled as M/M/1 queue with a trigger mechanism called N-policy, which allows study of the stalling behavior of HTTP video streaming.

The video contents are downloaded as HTTP segments which contain a certain video play time B. This video play time per HTTP segment is assumed to follow an exponential distribution with parameter $\mu = 1/\mathrm{E}[B]$.

$$B \sim \mathrm{EXP}(\mu) \qquad B(t) = 1 - e^{-\mu t} \qquad b(t) = \mu e^{-\mu t} \qquad (7.1)$$

Consider that the playback of a video consists of multiple HTTP segments. The HTTP segments are downloaded in-order and arrive at the client with rate λ. Assuming the interarrival times of HTTP segments at the video buffer follow an exponential distribution with rate λ.

$$A \sim \mathrm{EXP}(\lambda) \qquad A(t) = 1 - e^{-\lambda t} \qquad a(t) = \lambda e^{-\lambda t} \qquad (7.2)$$

In order to reduce the number of stalling events during playback, the video player uses a playback buffer. Video playback stops, if the buffer empties and is only, but immediately resumed, if the video buffer grows and reaches the level containing N HTTP segments again. In the queueing literature, this strategy is referred to as N-policy.

The resulting system model is an M/M/1 system with N-policy. The interest here is to analyze the steady state system behavior depending on the parameter N. If the server is busy, the video, i.e. the video content of a particular HTTP segment, is currently played out. However, if the server is idle, i.e. the video buffer is empty, the video stalls until the video buffer reaches N HTTP segments.

7.1.2 System Model: M/M/1 with N-Policy

The state of the video buffer is described by a two-dimensional Markov process (X, Y). The discrete random variable X captures the current number of HTTP segments in the video buffer, while the random variable Y indicates whether the player is idle, i.e. stalling $(Y = 0)$, or is busy, i.e. the video is playing out, $(Y = 1)$. The information on the number X of segments in the buffer alone is not sufficient, since for $X < N$ it is unclear whether the video is stalling or playing. Therefore, the second dimension is required to describe the system status.

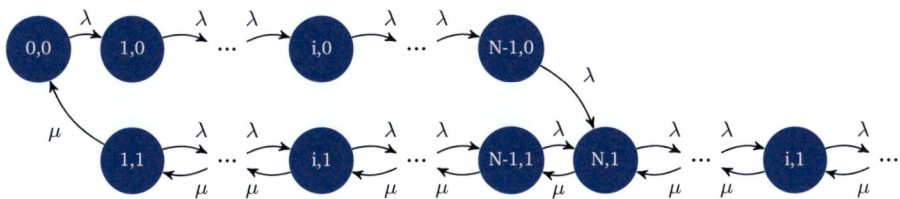

Figure 7.2: State transition diagram of an M/M/1 system with N-policy.

7.1.2.1 Micro State Equations

In principle, the steady state probabilities can be derived by solving the micro state equations. For each state, the incoming rates must equal the outgoing rates. This results in the following equation system.

$$outgoing\ flow = incoming\ flow$$

$$\lambda \cdot x(0,0) = \mu \cdot x(1,1) \tag{7.3a}$$

$$(\lambda + \mu) \cdot x(1,1) = \mu \cdot x(2,1) \tag{7.3b}$$

$$(\lambda + \mu) \cdot x(N,1) = \lambda \cdot x(N-1,0) + \lambda \cdot x(N-1,1) + \mu \cdot x(i+1,1) \tag{7.3c}$$

for $i = 1, \dots, N-1$:

$$\lambda \cdot x(i,0) = \lambda \cdot x(i-1,0) \tag{7.3d}$$

for $i \neq N$, $i = 2, \dots, \infty$:

$$(\lambda + \mu) \cdot x(i,1) = \lambda \cdot x(i-1,1) + \mu \cdot x(N+1,1) \tag{7.3e}$$

Together with the normalization condition, the equation system can be solved.

$$1 = \sum_{i=0}^{N-1} x(i,0) + \sum_{i=0}^{\infty} x(i,1) \tag{7.3f}$$

7.1.2.2 Macro State Balance Equations

The steady state probabilities $x(i, 0)$ and $x(i, 1)$ can be derived in a more elegant way using an appropriate choice of macro states. The definition of the macro states is thereby key for an elegant solution.

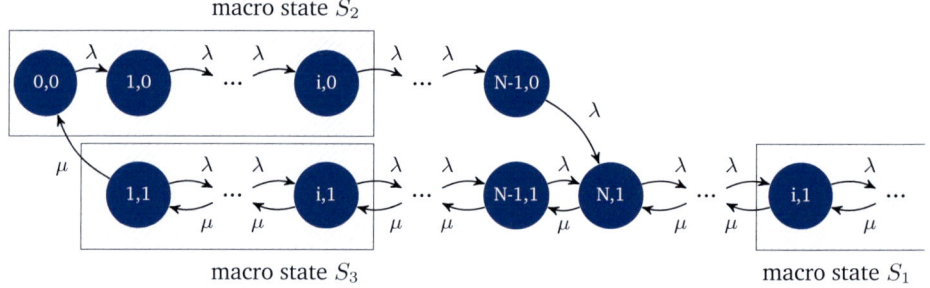

Figure 7.3: Macro states of an M/M/1 system with N-policy.

- Macro state S_1 for $i = N+1, \ldots, \infty$
  The macro state S_1 contains the states $\{x(i, 1), x(i+1, 1), \ldots\}$.

$$\mu \cdot x(i, 1) = \lambda \cdot x(i-1, 1)$$

$$\Longrightarrow x(i, 1) = \frac{\lambda}{\mu} \cdot x(i-1, 1) \qquad\qquad i = N+1, \ldots, \infty \qquad (7.4a)$$

- Macro state S_2 for $i = 0, \ldots, N - 1$
  The macro state S_2 contains the states $\{x(0, 0), \ldots, x(i, 0)\}$.

$$\lambda \cdot x(i, 0) = \mu \cdot x(1, 1)$$

$$\Longrightarrow x(i, 0) = \frac{\mu}{\lambda} \cdot x(1, 1) \qquad\qquad i = 0, \ldots, N - 1 \qquad (7.4b)$$

- Macro state S_3 for $i = 2, \ldots, N$
  The macro state S_3 contains the states $\{x(1, 1), \ldots, x(i-1, 1)\}$.

$$\mu \cdot x(1, 1) + \lambda \cdot x(i-1, 1) = \mu \cdot x(i, 1)$$

$$\Longrightarrow x(i, 1) = x(1, 1) + \frac{\lambda}{\mu} \cdot x(i-1, 1) \qquad\qquad i = 2, \ldots, N \qquad (7.4c)$$

The macro state equations can be solved depending on the probability $x(1, 1) = \sigma$. Then, the macro state equations are expressed for S_2 depending on σ, then for S_3, and finally for S_1. Together, with the normalization condition, we obtain σ and hence all steady state probabilities based on the parameter N and $\rho = \lambda/\mu$.

$$x(1,1) = \sigma \tag{7.5a}$$

$$S_2: \quad x(i,0) = \frac{\mu}{\lambda} \cdot \sigma = \frac{\sigma}{\rho} \qquad\qquad i = 0,\ldots,N-1 \tag{7.5b}$$

$$S_3: \quad x(i,1) = \sigma + \frac{\lambda}{\mu} \cdot x(i-1,1) = \sigma \cdot \frac{1-\rho^i}{1-\rho} \qquad i = 2,\ldots,N \tag{7.5c}$$

$$S_1: \quad x(i,1) = \frac{\lambda}{\mu} \cdot x(i-1,1) = \sigma \cdot \frac{1-\rho^N}{1-\rho} \cdot \rho^{i-N} \qquad i = N+1,\ldots,\infty \tag{7.5d}$$

The normalization condition finally leads to the computation of $x(1,1) = \sigma$ and thus the solution of the equation system.

$$1 = \sum_{i=0}^{N-1} x(i,0) + \sum_{i=0}^{\infty} x(i,1)$$

$$= \sum_{i=0}^{N-1} \frac{\sigma}{\rho} + \sum_{i=1}^{N} \sigma \cdot \frac{1-\rho^i}{1-\rho} + \sum_{i=N+1}^{\infty} \sigma \cdot \frac{1-\rho^N}{1-\rho} \cdot \rho^{i-N}$$

$$= \sigma \left(\frac{N}{\rho} + \frac{\rho(\rho^N - 1) - N\rho + N}{(1-\rho)^2} + \frac{\rho(1-\rho^N)}{(1-\rho)^2} \right)$$

$$= \sigma \left(\frac{N}{\rho(1-\rho)} \right)$$

$$\implies \sigma = \frac{\rho(1-\rho)}{N} = x(1,1) \tag{7.6}$$

As a result of the solution of the macro state equations, steady state probabilities are obtained for the M/M/1 system with N-policy and utilization $\rho = \lambda/\mu$.

$$x(i,0) = \frac{1-\rho}{N} \qquad\qquad i = 0,1,\ldots,N-1 \tag{7.7a}$$

$$x(i,1) = \frac{\rho(1-\rho^i)}{N} \qquad\qquad i = 1,2,\ldots,N-1 \tag{7.7b}$$

$$x(i,1) = \frac{\rho^{i-N+1} \cdot (1-\rho^N)}{N} \qquad\qquad i = N, N+1,\ldots \tag{7.7c}$$

Note that for $N = 1$, a regular M/M/1 system with $x(i) = \rho^i(1-\rho)$ is obtained.

$$x(i,0) = x(0) = 1 - \rho \qquad\qquad i = 0 \tag{7.8a}$$

$$x(i,1) = x(i) = \rho^i \cdot (1-\rho) \qquad\qquad i = 1,2,\ldots \tag{7.8b}$$

7.1.3 Mean Value Analysis: Stalling Measures

The utilization of the system equals the offered load according to the utilization law (cf. Chapter 2.1.4)

$$\rho = \frac{\lambda}{\mu} \qquad (7.9a)$$

which corresponds to the ratio of the time when the video player (server) is busy. The video player cycles through two phases: a) the idle period when the video stalls for the duration T_I and b) the busy period when the video is played out for the duration T_B. Hence, the utilization reflects the busy fraction of the video player; the mean busy period divided by the mean cycle length is equal to the fraction of time the server is working.

$$\rho = \frac{\mathrm{E}[T_B]}{\mathrm{E}[T_B] + \mathrm{E}[T_I]} \qquad (7.9b)$$

Due to the memoryless property of the Poisson arrival process, the duration of the idle period is the sum of N exponentially distributed phases with parameter λ which follows an Erlang-N distribution, $T_I \sim E_N(\lambda)$. The average idle time, i.e. the average stall duration, is therefore

$$\mathrm{E}[T_I] = \frac{N}{\lambda}. \qquad (7.10)$$

Hence, the mean duration of the busy period which is the mean video playout time without interruption can be derived from Equations (7.9a) – (7.10).

$$\mathrm{E}[T_B] = \frac{N}{\mu - \lambda} = \frac{N \cdot \mathrm{E}[B]}{1 - \rho} \qquad (7.11a)$$

The mean video playout time equals N HTTP segments with average video duration $\mathrm{E}[B]$ per segment normalized by the idle fraction of the player. Equation (7.11a) can also be understood as follows. A busy period starts when N segments are in the buffer which have an average duration of $N \cdot \mathrm{E}[B]$. In addition to these N service times, the busy period consists of all the segments arriving while the busy period is ongoing which contain $(\lambda \cdot \mathrm{E}[T_B]) \cdot \mathrm{E}[B] = \rho \cdot \mathrm{E}[T_B]$ video time.

$$\mathrm{E}[T_B] = N \cdot \mathrm{E}[B] + \rho\mathrm{E}[T_B] \qquad (7.11b)$$

Subsequently, QoE relevant parameters can be derived: stall ratio, average stall duration, and stall frequency. The stall ratio ψ is the fraction of time the video player is idle.

$$\psi = 1 - \rho = 1 - \frac{\lambda}{\mu} \qquad (7.12)$$

The average stall duration L is the average idle duration – which is independent of the video play time per HTTP segment $E[B]$.

$$L = E[T_I] = \frac{N}{\lambda} \tag{7.13}$$

The stall frequency F is the number of interruptions per video playout time. This stall frequency can also be seen as the probability that the system is idle ($x_A(0) = x(0) = 1 - \rho$ for Poisson process) and the reciprocal of the buffered video time when the video playout starts ($N \cdot E[B]$).

$$F = \frac{1}{E[T_B]} = \frac{\mu - \lambda}{N} = \frac{1 - \rho}{N \cdot E[B]} \tag{7.14}$$

Doesn't Jensen's inequality apply here? Do we need to consider $E[\frac{1}{T_B}]$*?* In fact, we are deriving the following limit distribution V which observes the average video playtime per stall event. The entire video playtime is the sum of all k busy periods with duration $T_{B,i}$ for $i = 1, \ldots, k$. For steady state characteristics, the limit $k \to \infty$ needs to be considered. Due to the central limit theorem, a normal distribution is obtained which converges in the limit towards a deterministic distribution, i.e. a real number.

$$V = \lim_{k \to \infty} \frac{1}{k} \sum_{i=1}^{k} T_{B,i} \sim \lim_{k \to \infty} N(E[T_B], \frac{\sigma}{\sqrt{k}}) = D(E[T_B]) \tag{7.15}$$

Hence, $F = E[1/V] = 1/E[V] = 1/E[T_B]$ for a deterministic distribution V.

Figure 7.4 visualizes the buffer status over time. On average, the cycle starts with an idle (stalling) phase of length $L = t_1 = N/\lambda$ followed by a busy (playout) phase of length $t_2 - t_1 = N/(\mu - \lambda)$. The system characteristics in the steady state reflects the long-term performance of the video buffer and are utilized in Chapter 7.1.4 to derive the QoE-optimal value for N.

Figure 7.5 presents some measurement results from literature on the YouTube video streaming platform [53]. In the experiments, the network bandwidth is throttled such that the finite video content cannot be delivered without stalling. The *reception ratio* is thereby defined as the ratio of the network download data rate and the video encoding rate, which is the offered load ρ in the M/M/1 system. For $\rho < 1$, then network capacity is not sufficient. An 'overload' situation ($\rho > 1$) means that the download data rate is higher than the video bit rate, such that the video buffer fills and no interruption is expected. It can be seen that the theoretical results from the M/M/1 system with N-policy predict the stall frequency very well. There are some outliers (about 15 %); however, the majority of the downloaded videos (85 %) are close to the M/M/1 results for which $N \cdot E[B] = 2\,s$ was found. It should be mentioned that Internet video platforms are, however, adapting their services and system configuration frequently to improve QoE.

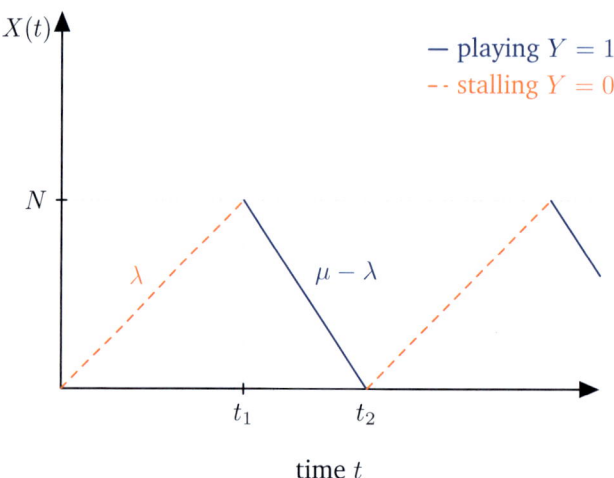

Figure 7.4: Video buffer status evolving over time for a deterministic $D/D/1$ system with N-policy and constant video bitrate and network bandwidth.

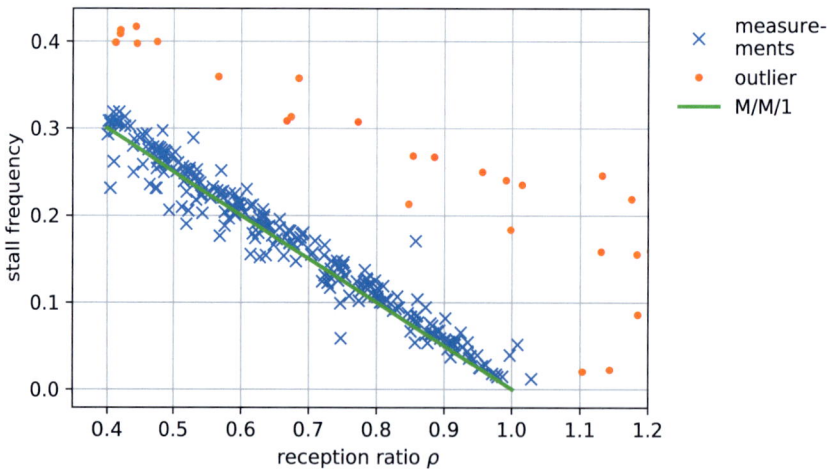

Figure 7.5: Measurement results of the stall frequency in experiments with the YouTube video streaming platform [53] compared to the M/M/1 model with N-policy for $N \cdot \mathrm{E}[B] = 2\,\mathrm{s}$ in Equation (7.14).

7.1.4 QoE-optimal Threshold for the N-Policy

For the implementation of the video player the question arises how to select the threshold N of the segments in the video buffer initiating the video playout. To this end, existing QoE models can be utilized which map stalling as experienced by the user to QoE on a scale from 1 to 5. The numerical indication of the QoE scores is interpreted as follows: 1 – 'bad', 2 – 'poor', 3 – 'fair', 4 – 'good', and 5 – 'excellent'.

The QoE model in [52] takes into account the stall frequency F and the average duration L per stall based on subjective experiments. An exponential relationship according to the IQX hypothesis [35] is observed, see Equation (7.16). The parameter γ reflects the minimum observed QoE value as measured in the subjective tests. Thereby, the video with the same stall characteristics is shown to several users who rate the QoE on the above mentioned 5-point rating scale. For quantifying QoE, the mean opinion score (MOS) is used by averaging over the subjects. The QoE model [52] found $\gamma = 1.5$. In case no stalling occurs, the maximum QoE score of 5 is obtained, leading to the scale parameter $\alpha = 3.5$.

The crucial parameters of the IQX model are the sensitivity parameters β_L and β_F in the exponent which are weighting the influence of the average stall duration L per interruption and the stall frequency F. Using the parameters that Hoßfeld, Schatz, Biersack, and Plissonnea [52] obtained via non-linear regression of subjective tests: $\beta_L = 0.15\,\mathrm{s}^{-1}, \beta_F = 0.19 \cdot 30\,\mathrm{s}$ with units $[L] = \mathrm{s}, [F] = \mathrm{s}^{-1}$.

$$f(L,F) = \alpha e^{-\beta_F \cdot F - \beta_L \cdot L} + \gamma \tag{7.16}$$

Now, the results for the average stall duration L in Equation (7.13) and the stall frequency F in Equation (7.14) are used in the QoE model $f(L,F)$. As a result, a function $g(N)$ is obtained which depends on the threshold N, while the system parameters λ and μ and the QoE model parameters $\alpha, \beta_L, \beta_F, \gamma$ are constant.

$$g(N) = \alpha e^{-\beta_F \cdot \frac{\mu - \lambda}{N} - \beta_L \cdot \frac{N}{\lambda}} + \gamma \tag{7.17}$$

The QoE-optimal threshold N is derived by finding the maximum $g(N)$. To this end, $\frac{d}{dN} g(N) = 0$ has to be solved which leads to the QoE-optimal threshold N:

$$N = \sqrt{(\mu - \lambda) \cdot \lambda \cdot \frac{\beta_F}{\beta_L}} \, . \tag{7.18}$$

It should be noted that in practice N needs to be an integer value and $N \geq 1$. Hence, $N^* = \max\left(\lfloor N + \frac{1}{2} \rfloor, 1\right)$. Figure 7.6 shows the optimal value of N depending on the reception ratio ρ and the segment duration $\mathrm{E}[B]$. Measurements indicate that prominent video streaming platforms have segment durations in the order of $2\,\mathrm{s} - 10\,\mathrm{s}$. For example, measurements on Netflix [54] show that Netflix segments have a constant duration of $4\,\mathrm{s}$. Recent measurements [74] for YouTube indicate a constant duration of $5\,\mathrm{s}$. For larger segments as used in practice, $N = 1$ leads to the optimal QoE, see Figure 7.6. For $N = 1$, the resulting system is an ordinary M/GI/1 system.

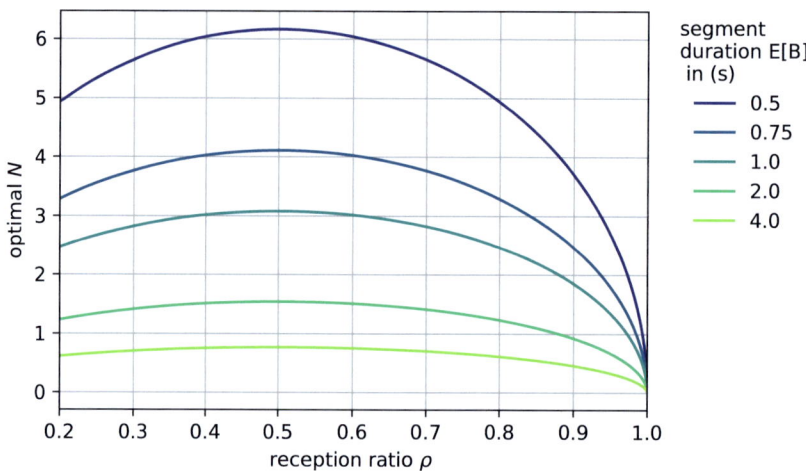

Figure 7.6: Optimal number N of segments for maximum QoE depending on the video segment duration $\mathrm{E}[\,B\,]$ and the reception ratio ρ.

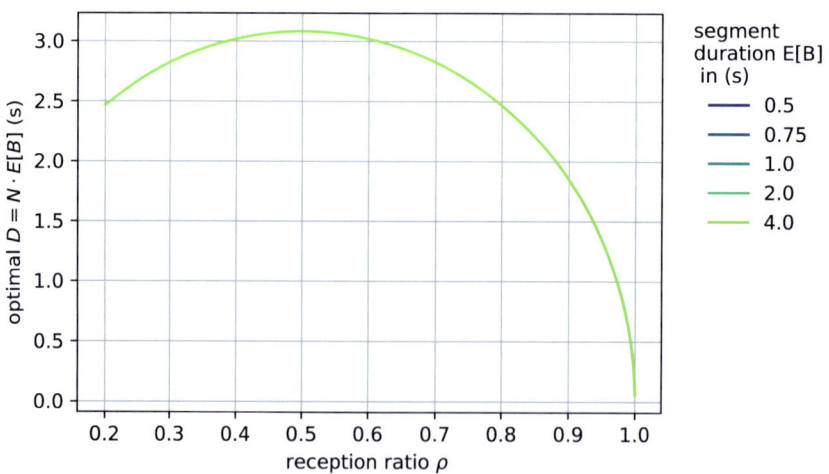

Figure 7.7: Optimal video buffer time $D = N \cdot \mathrm{E}[\,B\,]$ when the video playout starts.

The optimal threshold N of segments means that the video time $D = N \cdot \mathrm{E}[B]$ is on average available in the buffer when the playout starts again after a video interruption. Figure 7.7 shows the video buffer time D for the optimal threshold N. It can be seen that the curves are overlapping. Thus, the buffered video amount is the crucial component for the optimal playout. The D-policy is a different scheduling policy which works as follows. Again, the server (i.e. video player) is turned off at the end of a busy period and turned on when the cumulative amount of work (i.e. video play time) reaches the threshold D. Recent developments in Internet video delivery allow to start the playout, even if the entire segment is not completely downloaded, thus allowing an implementation of the D-policy.

7.1.5 Impact of Network Variances for GI/M/1

Results on the optimal number of video segments show that for segment duration of $4\,\mathrm{s}$ the playout should immediately start when $N = 1$ segments are in the buffer, see Figure 7.6. Recent measurements also confirm that the video playout starts when one segment is available in the buffer. In that case, the N-policy is a regular GI/GI/1 system. The mean idle time and the mean busy time for GI/GI/1 can be derived as follows:

$$a_0 \mathrm{E}[T_I] = \mathrm{E}[A] - \mathrm{E}[B] \tag{7.19}$$

with the probability $a_0 = x_A(0) = P(X_A = 0)$ that an arriving customer finds the system empty. In that case, the arriving customer starts the busy period. In a stable system, it is $\mathrm{E}[A] > \mathrm{E}[B]$ and in the case of arriving customer finds an empty system, the average idle time is $\mathrm{E}[A] - \mathrm{E}[B]$.

For GI/M/1, it is

$$a_0 = x_A(0) = 1 - \sigma \tag{7.20a}$$

with σ as root of the equation (see Equation (5.61) in Chapter 5.4.4)

$$\sigma = \Gamma_{GF}(\sigma) = \Phi_A(\mu(1 - \sigma)) \tag{7.20b}$$

which can be determined numerically. Hence, the entire distribution of A affects σ and therefore the average idle time.

$$L = \mathrm{E}[T_I] = \frac{\mathrm{E}[A] - \mathrm{E}[B]}{a_0} = \frac{\mathrm{E}[A] - \mathrm{E}[B]}{1 - \sigma} \tag{7.21}$$

The utilization ρ of the system can be expressed in terms of the mean idle time and the mean busy time:

$$\rho = \frac{\mathrm{E}[T_B]}{\mathrm{E}[T_B] + \mathrm{E}[T_I]} = \frac{\mathrm{E}[B]}{\mathrm{E}[A]}. \tag{7.22a}$$

As a result, the mean busy time follows:

$$E[T_B] = \frac{\rho}{1-\rho} \cdot E[T_I] = \frac{\rho}{1-\rho} \cdot \frac{E[A] - E[B]}{1-\sigma} = \frac{E[B]}{1-\sigma} \, . \tag{7.22b}$$

The stall frequency F is the inverse of the mean busy time and we finally obtain for the GI/M/1 system:

$$F = \frac{1}{E[T_B]} = \frac{1-\sigma}{E[B]} \, . \tag{7.23}$$

The impact of the network variances is analyzed by varying the coefficient of variation c_A of the interarrival time of video segments in the video buffer. For $c_A < 1$, the Erlang distribution is used. For $c_A > 1$, the hyperexponential distribution under the symmetry condition is used. Figure 7.8 shows the average stall duration for different reception ratios ρ. The higher c_A the higher is the mean stall duration L. At the same time, the stall frequency F decreases with increasing reception ratio ρ, but also with increasing coefficient of variation c_A. Higher variances in the network will result into longer stall durations which appear less frequently. Mapping the stall parameters to QoE shows that the QoE decreases for increasing network variances and lower reception ratio.

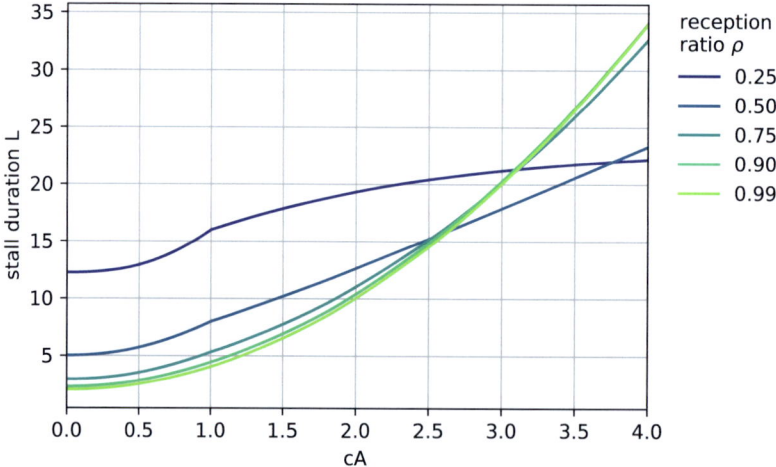

Figure 7.8: Average stall duration L for the GI/M/1 queue depending on the coefficient of variation c_A reflecting various network dynamics and the reception ratio ρ indicating the available network capacity.

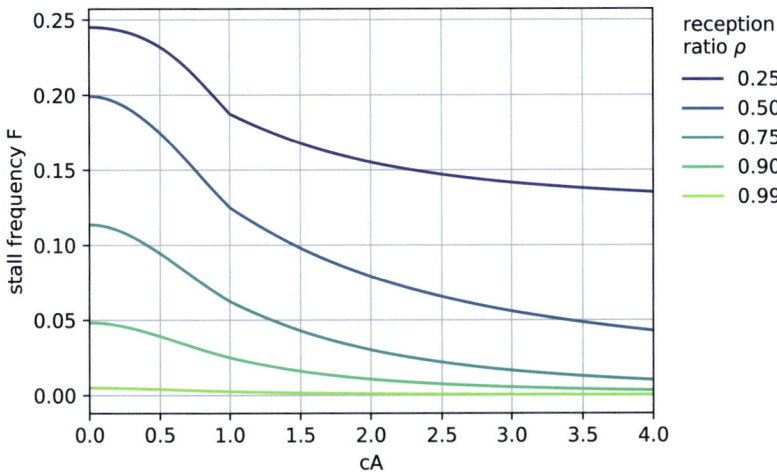

Figure 7.9: Stall frequency F for the GI/M/1 queue depending on the coefficient of variation c_A reflecting various network dynamics and the reception ratio ρ indicating the available network capacity.

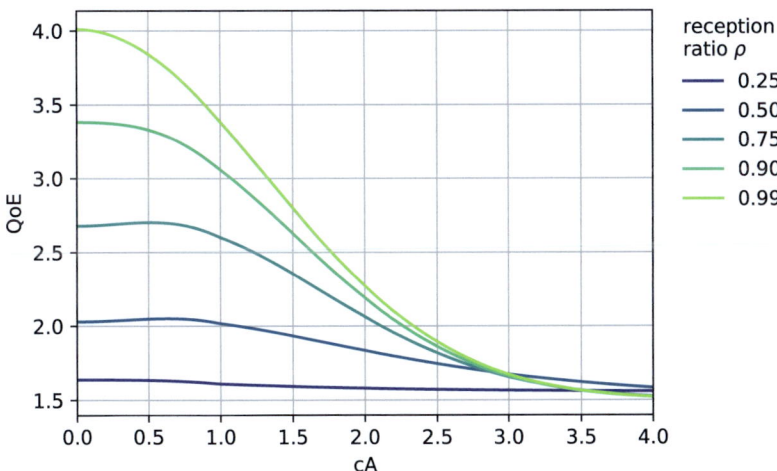

Figure 7.10: QoE for the GI/M/1 queue depending on the coefficient of variation c_A reflecting various network dynamics and the reception ratio ρ indicating the available network capacity.

7.2   Traffic Modeling in the Internet of Things

The Internet of Things (IoT) is becoming ever more important in the emerging societal operation and offers a variety of online services based on data from networked IoT sensors. The range of services include typical smart city applications such as environmental sensing of air quality, road traffic conditions, free parking lots, or for bike fleet management. Sensors are monitoring the environment and are sending the IoT data for further processing e.g. to a central IoT cloud. In general, IoT traffic can be roughly partitioned into periodic and event-based modes of communication. In the case of periodic sensor traffic, sensors are periodically monitoring the environment in fixed intervals. Prominent examples are water, gas, or electricity metering. In smart grids, the measurement and collection of current power usage values from residential and industrial smart meters may be done once per day. As a result, aggregated periodic IoT traffic stemming from a large number of sensors is arriving in the IoT cloud.

The second class of IoT traffic is event-based with sensors reacting on events in the environment, e.g. when an alarm is triggered in a smart home equipped with motion detection sensors. Such random events may be described properly with random variables and standardization bodies like 3GPP suggest to assume a Poisson process for event-based IoT traffic due to the Palm-Khintchine theorem. *But how to model aggregated periodic IoT traffic?* Section 7.2.1 investigates the superposition of periodic traffic from n sensor nodes. Again the Palm-Khintchine theorem may be applied. But the question arises, how large must n be such that the aggregated IoT traffic may be properly (i.e. with negligible bias) approximated by a Poisson process?

IoT will bring a very large number of devices that collect data, connect to the Internet, and send the data, e.g., to a central cloud which provides a certain online service. Most IoT networks exhibit such a centralized structure. A number of simple IoT devices connect to one IoT gateway forwarding the traffic to a central cloud processing platform via the Internet. Often there are multiple hierarchical levels of aggregation (from the edge to the cloud) to combine different regional hubs together. This basic architecture is illustrated in Figure 7.11 for periodic sensor traffic. Hence, IoT traffic is aggregated in the IoT architectures at different points, such as the IoT gateways or the IoT load balancer at an IoT cloud. The IoT load balancer is the first point of the cloud architecture where the individual traffic flows become aggregated. Due to the large number of IoT devices, the load balancer is required to distribute the workload across back-end servers. *But how to dimension such an IoT load balancer?* Section 7.3 models such an IoT load balancer which may be the crucial component in the architecture and may be a potential performance bottleneck. Data arrives from sensor nodes and is aggregated at the load balancer which forwards the data

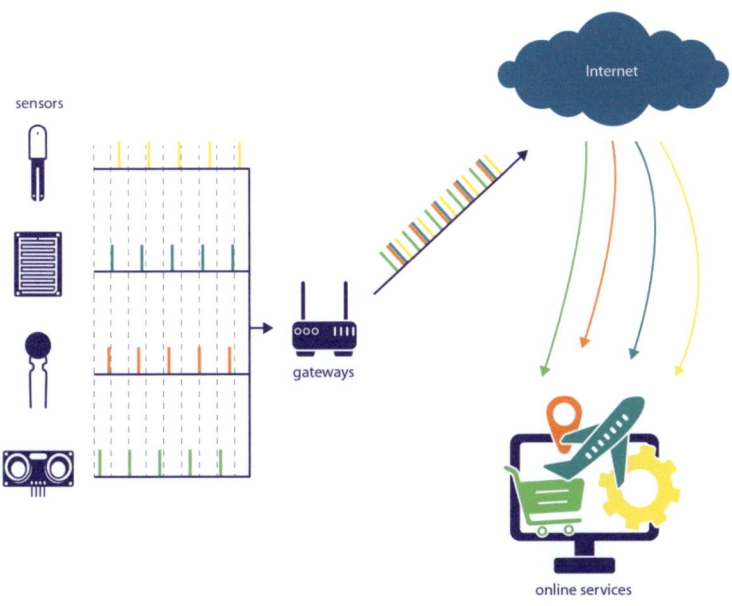

Figure 7.11: Illustration of the IoT cloud for periodic traffic.

to back-end cloud servers. The performance measure for dimensioning the load balancer is the waiting time of IoT data. In particular, we consider small sensor messages of constant size which are periodically sent from n asynchronous sensors to the IoT cloud. The system is modeled as a non-Markovian nD/D/1 queue and compared to an approximating M/D/1 queue.

Finally, the transmission of the sensor nodes to the IoT gateway is modeled and different transmission schemes are compared: pure and slotted ALOHA, perfect CSMA/CA as well as energy-aware CSMA/CA with restricted accessibility. Thereby, LoRaWAN (Long Range Wide Area Network) is considered as smart city infrastructure. Recently, LoRaWAN has received public interest through provider-backed installations, but also community-operated or smart city-operated gateway networks. LoRaWAN operates in the unlicensed radio spectrum and offers a projected range of up to 20 km in rural areas. Such LoRaWAN gateways can aggregate the traffic from thousands of devices which is of particular interest in dense urban environments with up to 10,000 households per km^2. *What is the performance and the energy efficiency of basic channel access mechanisms for LoRaWAN?* Section 7.4 analyzes the performance (throughput, packet loss) and the energy efficiency of the different channel access mechanisms in a simplified LoRaWAN system. Again, we consider small IoT data messages encapsulated in LoRaWAN packets of constant size. Particularly, the LoRaWAN IoT devices are kept inexpensive and extremely resource-saving for enabling suggested runtimes of ten years on one reasonably sized battery charge. Thus, energy efficiency is of major interest in this context.

7.2.1 Superposition of Aggregated Periodic IoT Data

There are n IoT nodes which are periodically sending IoT data packets in fixed intervals of length Δt. At a certain aggregation point in the IoT system, e.g. the IoT gateway, or the IoT load balancer, the traffic from the sensor devices is aggregated. The scope of this chapter is to model the arrival process of the aggregated traffic, which is later used as input arrival process for queueing models.

The Palm-Khintchine theorem (Chapter 3.4.2) suggests that the aggregated arrival process emerging from the n IoT nodes can be modeled as a Poisson process, if a large number of nodes are sending independently and no single node is dominating the rate of the aggregated traffic. The interarrival process of an individual node is a renewal process, i.e., the interarrival time between the arrivals of two consecutive data packets from a particular node is described by a random variable A. In the case of periodic traffic, $A \sim D(\Delta t)$. The question arises how large must n be such that the Poisson process approximation only leads to a practically negligible error ε.

If the n nodes are synchronized, then all nodes send the data at the same time. The aggregated traffic is a batch arrival of n packets at time $i\Delta t$ for $i = 0, 1, \ldots$. In Kendall's notation, the batch arrival process of the aggregated traffic is described as $D^{[n]}$. Due to the synchronization, the requirements of the Palm-Khintchine theorem are not fulfilled and the aggregated process obviously cannot be modeled as a Poisson process.

Assume that the n IoT nodes are not synchronized. The n nodes are sending asynchronously and independently but periodically in fixed intervals Δt. This is a valid assumption for many real-world scenarios. A single node i will randomly start to send at time t_i. Hence, the arrival time t_i of node i for $(i = 1, \cdots, n)$ is uniformly randomly distributed in the interval $[0, \Delta t]$, i.e. $t_i \sim U(0, \Delta t)$. The node i will then send packets at times $t_i + k\Delta t$ for $k \in \mathbb{N}_0$. The interarrival times A_i between the i-th and the $(i+1)$-st data packet from node i and node $i+1$ are identical in each period. Figure 7.12 illustrates the asynchronous aggregated IoT traffic and the notation of variables.

Remarks on modeling and merging of several periodic traffic sources: In models of a vast number of technical systems, i.e. a large number of sensors emitting traffic or multiplexing systems, there is often the case where it is necessary to choose

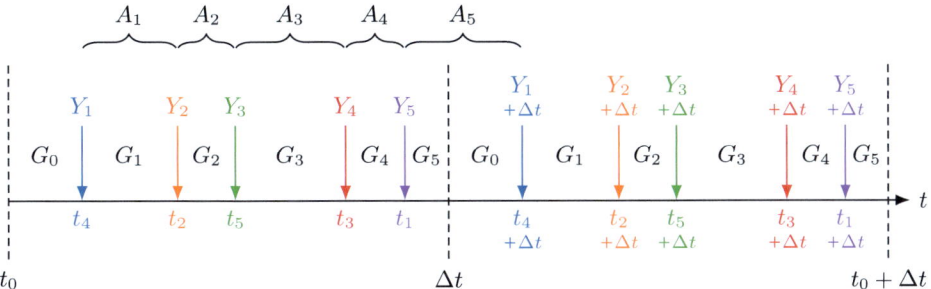

Figure 7.12: Asynchronous periodic system with $n = 5$ IoT nodes and identical period Δt is depicted for two periods.

a traffic source model to describe the traffic behavior and the reaction of the technical system, where these parameters are the major ones:

- The number n of traffic sources to be merged or superimposed.

- The period Δt of the traffic process.

- The observation interval τ, during which we want to investigate the behavior of the system or subsystem under consideration.

In general, the superposition of more than two periodic sources result in a periodic arrival process which as such is a non-renewal process. Each superposition delivers a specific pattern, the larger the number of sources and the smaller the observation interval, the more random the resulting process from the view of an independent observer, who randomly sees a pattern out of many.

The main approaches in the literature are i) using a renewal process to describe the superimposed (resulting) process or ii) simply take the easy-to-use Poisson process with its many available mathematically tractable Markovian models. The major questions arising are:

- Can the superimposed (resulting) process be approximately modeled using a renewal process to sufficiently describe its stochastic behavior? The appropriateness can be judged e.g. by comparing the interaction of the approximating process with a system in terms of performance measures like mean waiting times.

- What kind of error do we make if we take a simple renewal process based on two parameters $(\mathrm{E}[A], c_A)$ – or in some cases Poisson process based on a single parameter $(\mathrm{E}[A])$ – as approximating process?

We examine three parameters n, Δt and τ, to further discuss this issue.

- First consider that if n is "sufficiently large", the component processes will be merged in a rather random way to form the resulting process. The periodicity is maintained, but for a smaller τ (compared to Δt) the resulting process can be approximated with a renewal process during τ. It is possible to observe the system at a random point t^* from outside and derive the next arrival using *recurrence times* R^*. The approximating process (described by the interarrival time A^* of the superposition) assumes a renewal process. This observation is illustrated by Wamser, Tran-Gia, Geißler, and Hoßfeld [118] and discussed in Chapter 7.2.3. In the limit when n goes to ∞, a Poisson process is observed.

- In a similar way, a "sufficiently large" n is considered such that the component processes will be merged in a rather random way to form the resulting superposition process. We can derive the distribution of arrival and interarrival times of the n sensors within a single interval of length Δt based on *order and gap statistics*. This was investigated by Hoßfeld, Metzger, and Heegaard [50] and is discussed in Chapter 7.2.2. The approximating process (described by the interarrival time A of the superposition) assumes that the patterns in subsequent intervals Δt are independent. Again, the approximating process (described by the interarrival time A in Chapter 7.2.2) assumes a renewal process. In the limit when n goes to ∞, a Poisson process is observed.

- In case the period Δt is very long compared to the observation interval τ and the number n is large enough (e.g. a number of 100 sensors), the resulting process can also be approximated with a renewal process, or – in some cases – even with a Poisson process.

7.2.2 Distribution of Interarrival Times: Order and Gap Statistics

The derivation of the distribution of the interarrival times A_i between two consecutive arrivals requires sorting the random samples t_i in increasing order. This provides the following random variables Y_i for $i = 1, \ldots, n$ by considering the order of the random variables t_i.

Y_1 is the time of the first arrival: $Y_1 = \min\left(\{t_1, t_2, \ldots, t_n\}\right)$

Y_2 is the time of the second arrival: $Y_2 = \min\left(\{t_1, t_2, \ldots, t_n\} \setminus Y_1\right)$

$\ldots$

Y_n is the time of the last arrival: $Y_n = \max\left(\{t_1, t_2, \ldots, t_n\}\right)$

Y_i is called the *i-th order statistic* and it is $Y_1 < Y_2 < \cdots < Y_n$. The distribution function Y_i is derived as follows. $Y_i \leq t$ means that there at least i arrivals at $\{t_1, \ldots, t_n\}$ that are less than or equal to t. The arrival times t_i follow the same distribution X which is in this case a uniform distribution $X \sim U(0, \Delta t)$ with $X(t) = P(X \leq t) = t/\Delta t$.

$$Y_i(t) = P(Y_i \leq t) = \sum_{k=i}^{n} \binom{n}{k} P(X \leq t)^k \cdot P(X > t)^{n-k} \tag{7.24a}$$

The distribution of the first arrival and the last arrival follows easily from the minimum and maximum of random variables, Equation (2.65) and Equation (2.63), respectively.

$$Y_1(t) = P(Y_1 \leq t) = 1 - P(t_1 > t, \ldots, t_n > t) = 1 - (1 - t/\Delta t)^n \tag{7.24b}$$
$$Y_n(t) = P(Y_n \leq t) = P(t_1 \leq t, \ldots, t_n \leq t) = (t/\Delta t)^n \tag{7.24c}$$

In the context of order statistics, the distribution between two consecutive arrivals is referred to as the *spacing distribution* or *gap distribution*, $G_i = Y_i - Y_{i-1}$. The joint probability density function $f_i(x, y)$ of two consecutive arrivals at time $Y_{i-1} = x$ and $Y_i = y$ is as follows. There are $i - 2$ arrivals before x with probability $(x/\Delta t)^{i-2}$ and $n - i$ arrivals after y with probability $(1 - y/\Delta t)^{n-i}$. The density for an arrival at time x or y in this case is the density of the uniform distribution, $1/\Delta t$. The number of combinations for this event ($i - 2$ before x, $n - i$ after y) is $\frac{n!}{(i-2)!(n-i)!}$. Due to the independence of the arrival events, the joint PDF is the product of the probabilities and densities.

$$
\begin{aligned}
f_i(x, y) &= \frac{n!}{(i-2)!(n-i)!} \left(\frac{x}{\Delta t}\right)^{i-2} \left(1 - \frac{y}{\Delta t}\right)^{n-i} \left(\frac{1}{\Delta t}\right)^2 \\
&= \frac{n!}{(i-2)!(n-i)!} (x)^{i-2} (\Delta t - y)^{n-i} (\Delta t)^{-n}
\end{aligned}
\tag{7.25}
$$

for $i = 2, \ldots, n$. The probability density function $g_i(t)$ of the gap distribution is obtained by solving the integral.

$$
\begin{aligned}
g_{i-1}(t) &= \int_0^{\Delta t - t} f_i(x, x + t) dx \\
&= \int_0^{\Delta t - t} \frac{n!}{(i-2)!(n-i)!} (x)^{i-2} (\Delta t - x - t)^{n-i} (\Delta t)^{-n} dx \\
&= n(\Delta t)^{-n} (\Delta t - t)^{n-1} = \frac{n}{\Delta t} \left(1 - \frac{t}{\Delta t}\right)^{n-1} \quad \text{for } 0 \leq t \leq \Delta t
\end{aligned}
\tag{7.26}
$$

The PDF is independent of i. The cumulative distribution function $G_i(t)$ for $i = 1, \ldots, n-1$ follows accordingly and is also independent from i.

$$G_i(t) = \int_0^t g_i(\tau)d\tau = 1 - \left(1 - \frac{t}{\Delta t}\right)^n \quad \text{for } 0 \leq t \leq \Delta t \tag{7.27}$$

We define $G_0 = Y_1$ and with Equation (7.24b), $G_0(t) = 1 - (1 - t/\Delta t)^n$. The distribution of the last gap is the distance between Y_n and Δt, i.e. $G_n = \Delta t - Y_n$.

$$G_n(t) = P(\Delta t - Y_n \leq t) = P(Y_n > \Delta t - t) = 1 - \left(1 - \frac{t}{\Delta t}\right)^n \tag{7.28}$$

In summary, the gaps $G_0, \ldots, G_n$ follow the same distribution which is a scaled Beta distribution with parameters 1 and n

$$G \sim \Delta t \cdot \text{BETA}(1, n), \quad G(t) = 1 - \left(1 - \frac{t}{\Delta t}\right)^n, \quad g(t) = \frac{n}{\Delta t}\left(1 - \frac{t}{\Delta t}\right)^{n-1} \tag{7.29}$$

for which the mean, variance, and coefficient of variation are

$$\text{E}[G] = \frac{\Delta t}{n+1}, \quad \text{VAR}[G] = \frac{n\Delta t^2}{(n+1)^2(n+2)}, \quad c_G = \sqrt{\frac{n}{n+2}}. \tag{7.30}$$

The interarrival times $A_i \sim G$ for $i = 1, \ldots, n-1$, while $A_n = G + G$. Note that the distributions A_i are *not independently distributed*, but the A_i are correlated.

Next, the difference between the distribution G and the interarrival time A of the corresponding approximating Poisson process is considered. This provides guidelines when the Poisson approximation is close enough, i.e. when the number of IoT devices n is large enough. The arrival rate of the aggregated traffic is $\lambda = n/\Delta t$, since the n IoT devices are sending once per period Δt.

$$A \sim \text{EXP}(n/\Delta t), \quad A(t) = 1 - e^{-nt/\Delta t}, \quad a(t) = \frac{n}{\Delta t}e^{-nt/\Delta t} \tag{7.31}$$

It is $c_G < 1$ and $\lim_{n \to \infty} c_G = 1 = c_A$. *For which n is the difference between the coefficient of variations below ε?* Note that the absolute error $c_A - c_G$ and the relative error $1 - c_G/c_A$ are identical due to $c_A = 1$.

$$c_A - c_G = 1 - \sqrt{\frac{n}{n+2}} < \varepsilon \quad \Longrightarrow \quad n > \frac{2(1-\varepsilon)^2}{(2-\varepsilon)\varepsilon} \approx \frac{1}{\varepsilon} \quad \text{since } \varepsilon \ll 1 \tag{7.32}$$

Thus, for $n > 1/\varepsilon$, the error regarding the coefficient of variation of the interarrival times of the approximating Poisson process is smaller than ε. For $\varepsilon = 1\%$ this holds for $n > 100$. Figure 7.13 shows the CDF of the interarrival times of the aggregated period traffic for different number n of IoT. Thereby, the sending interval is chosen to be $\Delta t = n$, such that $\lambda = 1$.

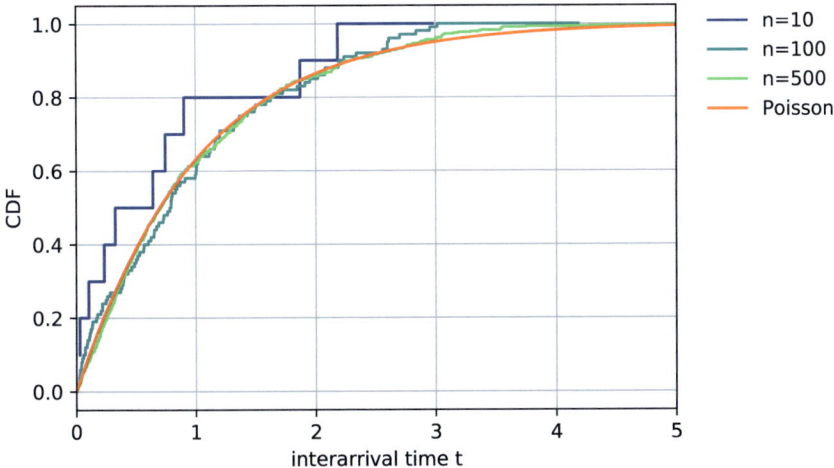

Figure 7.13: CDF of interarrival times of aggregated periodic traffic vs Poisson process approximation.

7.2.3 Renewal Approximation for Interarrival Time Distribution

An alternative method to approximate the distribution of the interarrival times uses renewal theory. Each sensor starts at a random point in time and periodically sends the next data packet after time Δt. Hence, the interarrival time D_i between packets of a sensor i is a deterministic distribution, $D_i \sim D(\Delta t)$, which has the following cumulative distribution function $(i = 1, \ldots, n)$.

$$D_i(t) = \begin{cases} 0 & , \ t < \Delta t \\ 1 & , \ t \geq \Delta t \end{cases} \tag{7.33}$$

The residual time or forward recurrence time R_i of the deterministic distribution follows according to Equation (3.5).

$$r_i(t) = \frac{1}{E[D_i]}(1 - D_i(t)) = \frac{1}{\Delta t} \qquad \text{for } 0 \leq t \leq \Delta t \tag{7.34a}$$

$$R_i(t) = \int_0^t r_i(\tau)d\tau = \frac{t}{\Delta t} \qquad \text{for } 0 \leq t \leq \Delta t \tag{7.34b}$$

287

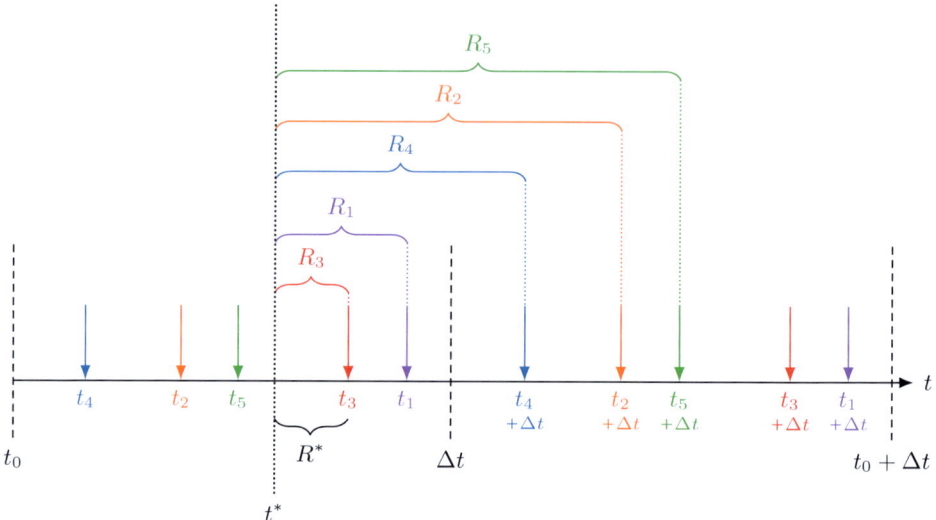

Figure 7.14: Asynchronous periodic system with $n = 5$ IoT nodes and identical period Δt is depicted for two periods.

Now, consider an observer looking at the system at a random time t^* within the interval $[0; \Delta t]$, see Figure 7.14. The residual time R^* to the next arrival is the minimum of the n residual times R_i, i.e. $R^* = \min\{R_1, \dots, R_n\}$.

$$R^*(t) = P(R^* \leq t) = 1 - P(R^* > t)$$

$$= 1 - P(R_1 > t, \dots, R_n > t) = 1 - (1 - \frac{t}{\Delta t})^n \quad \text{for } 0 \leq t \leq \Delta t \quad (7.35a)$$

$$r^*(t) = \frac{d}{dt} R^*(t) = \frac{n}{\Delta t}(1 - \frac{t}{\Delta t})^{n-1} \qquad \text{for } 0 \leq t \leq \Delta t \quad (7.35b)$$

The interarrival time A^* is derived from the fundamental renewal theory relationship in Equation (3.5) together with the mean interarrival time $\mathrm{E}[A^*]$. The arrival rate follows from n sensors sending once during the interval Δt, i.e. $\lambda^* = n/\Delta t$ and $\mathrm{E}[A^*] = \Delta t/n$.

$$r^*(t) = \frac{1}{\mathrm{E}[A^*]}(1 - A^*(t))$$

$$\Longrightarrow A^*(t) = 1 - \mathrm{E}[A^*]r^*(t) = 1 - \left(1 - \frac{t}{\Delta t}\right)^{n-1} \qquad (7.36a)$$

$$a^*(t) = \frac{d}{dt} A^*(t) = \frac{n-1}{\Delta t}\left(1 - \frac{t}{\Delta t}\right)^{n-2} \qquad (7.36b)$$

The variance and coefficient of variation of the interarrival time A^* based on the renewal approximation follow.

$$E[A^*] = \frac{\Delta t}{n} \qquad\qquad E[A^{*2}] = \frac{2(\Delta t)^2}{n(n+1)} \qquad (7.37a)$$

$$VAR[A^*] = \frac{(\Delta t)^2 (n-1)}{n^2(n+1)} \qquad\qquad STD[A^*] = \frac{\Delta t}{n}\sqrt{\frac{n-1}{n+1}} \qquad (7.37b)$$

$$c_{A^*} = \sqrt{\frac{n-1}{n+1}} \qquad (7.37c)$$

For the derivation of a guideline, when n is large enough such that the Poisson process approximates the aggregated periodic traffic, the difference between the coefficient of variations is considered again, as in the previous section using order statistics (Equation (7.32)).

$$c_A - c_{A^*} = 1 - \sqrt{\frac{n-1}{n+1}} < \varepsilon \qquad\Longrightarrow\qquad n > \frac{(1-\varepsilon)^2 + 1}{\varepsilon(2-\varepsilon)} \approx \frac{1}{\varepsilon} \qquad \text{since } \varepsilon \ll 1$$

$$(7.38)$$

Comparing the guidelines derived from the gap statistics (Equation (7.32)) and the renewal approximation (Equation (7.38)), it can be seen that the same guideline for $n > \frac{1}{\varepsilon}$ is derived such that the Poisson approximation leads to a small bias concerning the coefficient of variation. In particular, the coefficient of variation of the gap distribution c_G considers $n + 1$ gaps, as illustrated in Figure 7.12, when the period of length Δt is cut into n pieces reflecting the arrival times. The renewal approximation considers that the n interarrival times correspond to n gaps (instead of $n + 1$ gaps). In fact, for $n' = n - 1$, it is $c_{G'} = \sqrt{\frac{n'}{n'+2}} = \sqrt{\frac{n-1}{n+1}} = c_{A^*}$.

7.2.4 Autocorrelation of Periodic Traffic

We emphasize that the Poisson process is only an approximation of the aggregated periodic traffic. The autocorrelation $r(k) = COR[A_i, A_{i+k}]$ in a Poisson process is 0 for any lag $k > 0$ since the interarrival times are iid (independent and identically distributed). However, in an aggregated periodic process, the autocorrelation is $r(k) = 1$ for multiples of n (i.e. $k = n \cdot i$, $i = 1, 2, \ldots$), due to the deterministic periodic pattern of arrivals. Thus, a Poisson approximation is not able to properly capture any autocorrelation characteristics of the aggregated traffic. When, for example, considering the waiting times of a queue where the offered traffic is periodic, then the nodes will always observe the same waiting times in every period. For many scenarios, this may not be relevant, e.g. when dimensioning an IoT load balancer.

7.3 Dimensioning of an IoT Load Balancer

The guidelines derived in the previous Section 7.2.1 indicate when n is large enough to use a Poisson process instead of the aggregated periodic traffic. This approximation is now used for dimensioning an IoT load balancer which is the first point of the IoT cloud architecture where the individual traffic flows become aggregated. Such a load balancer is required to distribute the workload across the back-end servers.

The waiting time of packets at the IoT load balancer is used for dimensioning the required processing capabilities. Consider periodic traffic from n asynchronous IoT sensors sending every time Δt. The processing times B of the load balancer are constant, e.g. for computing hashes of the incoming packets. The deterministic service times have the following Laplace transform.

$$B \sim D(b) \text{ with } \mathrm{E}[B] = b \qquad\qquad \Phi_B(s) = e^{-sb} \qquad (7.39)$$

The IoT load balancer is modeled as $nD/D/1 - \infty$ delay system. For large n, this can be approximated as an M/D/1-∞ delay system.

7.3.1 M/D/1 Waiting Time

Equation (5.39) provides the Laplace transform of the waiting time for the M/G/1 waiting queue which is applied here for constant service times.

$$\Phi_W(s) = \frac{s(1-\rho)}{s - \lambda + \lambda\Phi_B(s)} = \frac{s(1-\rho)}{s - \lambda + \lambda e^{-st_0}} \qquad (7.40)$$

The inverse Laplace transform can be used to numerically derive the waiting time probability density function efficiently. However, the numerical Laplace transform is not straightforward due to discontinuities of the PDF at multiples of the service time, see the kink in the CCDF at $t = 1$ in Figure 7.17 for $b = 1$. This results in numerical issues when solving the inverse Laplace transform. Alternatively, the approach by Iversen [57] or Virtamo [114] can be used for fast numerical computation of the CDF of the waiting times for M/D/1.

For the M/D/1 system, the CDF of the waiting time W can also be derived directly according to the Beneš approach [7]. To this end, the unfinished work U at an arbitrary time t^* when the system is stationary is considered. Applying the Poisson arrival process, it is $U = W$. To be more precise, the unfinished work is the same for an arriving user (U_a) and a user observing the system at a random time (U). Hence, $U = U_a = W$.

The basic idea is to look backwards in time at time t_{-1} when the system is empty and the unfinished work is $U_{-1} = 0$. If at time t^*, the unfinished work $U > t$, then

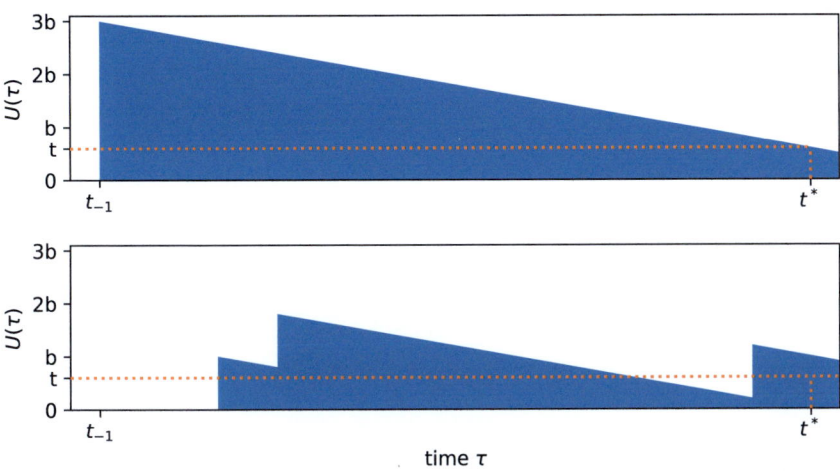

Figure 7.15: Illustration of the unfinished work in the M/D/1 system for $k = 3$ arrivals within the interval $[t_{-1}; t^*]$ which has length $kb - t$.

there may be k arrivals within time $t^* - t_{-1} = k \cdot b - t$. The arriving workload increases the unfinished work by $k \cdot b$ which decreases over time $t^* - t_{-1}$. With $U_{-1} = 0$ and k arrivals, it is

$$U > k \cdot b - (t^* - t_{-1}) = k \cdot b - (k \cdot b - t) = t, \tag{7.41}$$

as illustrated in Figure 7.15. In the upper sub-figure, all k arrivals happen at time t_{-1}, such that $U = t$ at time t^*. The lower sub-figure shows that $U > t$, if the k arrivals happen within the interval $[t_{-1}; t^*]$ which has length $kb - t$.

The number of arrivals N_a in the interval of length $t^* - t_{-1} = k \cdot b - t$ follows a Poisson distribution with mean $\mathrm{E}[N_a] = \lambda(k \cdot b - t)$. The probability that the system is empty is $1 - \rho$ for a GI/GI/1 system which represents the probability that there is no unfinished work. Here, $\rho = \lambda b$. Due to the independence of the number of arrivals N_a and $U_{-1} = 0$, the CCDF of the waiting time is

$$P(W > t) = P(U > t) = \sum_{k=\lceil t/b \rceil}^{\infty} P(N_a = k, U_{-1} = 0)$$

$$= 1 - \sum_{k=0}^{\lfloor t/b \rfloor} P(N_a = k) \cdot P(U_{-1} = 0) \tag{7.42}$$

$$= 1 - \sum_{k=0}^{\lfloor t/b \rfloor} \frac{(\lambda(k \cdot b - t))^k}{k!} e^{-(\lambda(k \cdot b - t))} \cdot (1 - \lambda b) \, .$$

The CDF of the waiting time in an M/D/1 system is

$$W(t) = (1 - \lambda b) \sum_{k=0}^{\lfloor t/b \rfloor} \frac{(\lambda(k \cdot b - t))^k}{k!} e^{-(\lambda(k \cdot b - t))}. \tag{7.43}$$

The mean of the waiting time follows from Takacs recursion (Equation (5.43)) with $E[B^2] = b^2$ or the Laplace transform $E[W] = -\frac{d}{ds} \Phi_W(s)|_{s=0}$.

$$E[W] = \frac{\lambda E[B^2]}{2(1 - \rho)} = \frac{\rho b}{2(1 - \rho)} \tag{7.44}$$

📗 *Further reading:* An excellent explanation of the M/D/1 system and the numerical computation of the waiting time distribution is provided by Iversen [57] and Virtamo [114].

7.3.2 nD/D/1 Waiting Time

The waiting time for the nD/D/1 system is derived in a similar way as for the M/D/1 system. There are n nodes sending asynchronously periodically with a sending interval Δt. The service time is constant $B = b$. The unfinished work U at a time t^* is considered. Along the same argumentation of the M/D/1 system, the unfinished work at time t^* is $U > t$, when there are k arrivals within time $t^* - t_{-1} = k \cdot b - t$ and the system is empty at time t_{-1}, i.e. $U_{-1} = 0$, cf. Figure 7.16.

$$P(U > t) = \sum_{k=\lceil t/b \rceil}^{n} P(N_a = k, U_{-1} = 0)$$

$$= \sum_{k=\lceil t/b \rceil}^{n} P(N_a = k) \cdot P(U_{-1} = 0 | N_a = k) \tag{7.45}$$

The number N_a of arrivals in the interval of length $k \cdot b - t$ follows a binomial distribution with success probability p which is the ratio between the length of this interval and the length of the period Δt.

$$N \sim \text{BINOM}\left(n, \frac{kb - t}{\Delta t}\right), \quad P(N_a = k) = \binom{n}{k}\left(\frac{kb - t}{\Delta t}\right)^k \left(1 - \frac{kb - t}{\Delta t}\right)^{n-k} \tag{7.46}$$

If there are k arrivals in the interval $[t_{-1}; t^*]$, then there are $(n - k)$ arrivals in the interval $[t^*; t_{-1} + \Delta t]$. This interval has the length $\Delta t - kb + t$, as depicted in Figure 7.16. In this periodic system, the unfinished work at time t_{-1} and at time $t_{-1} + \Delta t$ is the same. The probability that the system is empty at time $t_{-1} + \Delta t$ when there are $(n - k)$ arrivals can be derived as follows. For a stable system, it is

$$t + (n - k)b < \Delta t - kb + t \quad \Longrightarrow \quad nb < \Delta t \tag{7.47}$$

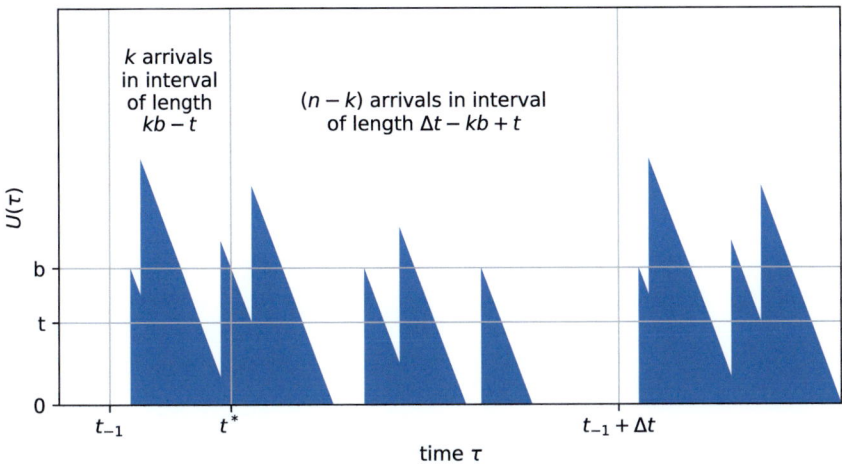

Figure 7.16: Illustration of the unfinished work in the nD/D/1 system for $k = 3$ arrivals within the interval $[t_{-1}; t^*]$ which has length $kb - t$.

and there must be a time instant after t^* when the unfinished work is zero. Hence, only the $(n - k)$ arrivals need be considered to derive the probability that the system is idle at time $t_{-1} + \Delta t$. Finally, the probability that the unfinished work is zero given k arrivals in the interval $[t_{-1}; t^*]$ is obtained.

$$P(U_{-1} = 0 | N_a = k) = 1 - \frac{(n-k)b}{\Delta t - k \cdot b + t} = \frac{\Delta t - n \cdot b + t}{\Delta t - k \cdot b + t} \tag{7.48}$$

Combining Equations (7.45)–(7.48) yields the complementary cumulative distribution function of the unfinished work at an arbitrary time for the nD/D/1 queue.

$$P(U > t) = \sum_{k=\lceil t/b \rceil}^{n} \binom{n}{k} \left(\frac{kb - t}{\Delta t} \right)^k \left(1 - \frac{kb - t}{\Delta t} \right)^{n-k} \frac{\Delta t - n \cdot b + t}{\Delta t - k \cdot b + t} \tag{7.49}$$

The arrival theorem, as introduced for the Engset system (Chapter 4.3), is applied here. Upon arrival at the system, the message sent by a node observes the system as if in steady state at an arbitrary instant for the system without that node. A formal proof for the nD/D/1 waiting time $W(t) = P(W \le t)$ is given in references [89, 90, 29].

$$W(t) = 1 - \sum_{k=\lceil t/b \rceil}^{n-1} \binom{n-1}{k} \left(\frac{kb - t}{\Delta t} \right)^k \left(1 - \frac{kb - t}{\Delta t} \right)^{n-1-k} \frac{\Delta t - (n-1) \cdot b + t}{\Delta t - k \cdot b + t}$$

$$\tag{7.50}$$

293

We provide the mean waiting time without deriving it explicitly, see Eckberg [30]. For the computation of the Erlang-B formula $B(n, a)$, the iterative method is used.

$$\mathrm{E}[W] = \frac{(n-1)\rho b}{2n \cdot B(n-2, n/\rho)} \tag{7.51a}$$

$$B(0, a) = 1, \quad B(n, a) = \left(1 + \frac{n}{a \cdot B(n-1, a)}\right)^{-1} \tag{7.51b}$$

Thereby, $\mathrm{E}[W]$ converges towards the mean value of the corresponding $M/D/1$ system with $\lambda = n/\Delta t$ for increasing number of nodes n.

$$\lim_{n \to \infty} \mathrm{E}[W] = \frac{\rho b}{2(1-\rho)} \qquad \lim_{n \to \infty} B(n-2, n/\rho) = 1 - \rho \tag{7.52}$$

7.3.3 Difference of M/D/1 and nD/D/1 Waiting Time Distributions

The difference of the waiting time distributions for the nD/D/1 and the approximating M/D/1 system are now quantified. To this end, the earth mover's distance (EMD) δ is used to compute the difference. It is $W_1(t) \geq W_2(t)$ with $\lambda = n/\Delta t$, $\rho = \lambda b < 1$, see Figure 7.17. The EMD then simplifies to the difference of two integrals.

$$\delta(W_1, W_2) = \int_{t=0}^{\infty} |W_1(t) - W_2(t)| \, dt = \int_{t=0}^{\infty} W_1(t) - W_2(t) dt$$

$$= \int_{t=0}^{\infty} (1 - W_2(t)) - (1 - W_1(t)) dt \tag{7.53}$$

$$= \int_{t=0}^{\infty} P(W_2 > t) dt - \int_{t=0}^{\infty} P(W_1 > t) dt$$

The expected value of a random value can also be derived by integrating over the complementary cumulative distribution function.

$$\mathrm{E}[W] = \int_{t=0}^{\infty} P(W > t) dt = \int_{t=0}^{\infty} 1 - W(t) dt = \int_{t=0}^{\infty} \int_{\tau=t}^{\infty} w(\tau) d\tau dt$$

$$= \int_{\tau=0}^{\infty} \int_{t=0}^{\tau} w(\tau) dt d\tau = \int_{\tau=0}^{\infty} [tw(\tau)]_0^{\tau} d\tau = \int_{\tau=0}^{\infty} \tau w(\tau) d\tau \tag{7.54}$$

Hence, Equation (7.53) simplifies to the difference of means, as $W_1(t) \geq W_2(t)$ for any t and thus $\mathrm{E}[W_2] \geq \mathrm{E}[W_1]$.

$$\delta(W_1, W_2) = \mathrm{E}[W_2] - \mathrm{E}[W_1] \quad \text{for } W_1(t) \geq W_2(t) \tag{7.55}$$

We have already obtained the expected values for nD/D/1 and M/D/1.

$$\mathrm{E}[W_{nD/D/1}] = \frac{(n-1)\rho b}{2n \cdot B(n-2, n/\rho)} \qquad \mathrm{E}[W_{M/D/1}] = \frac{\rho b}{2(1-\rho)} \tag{7.56}$$

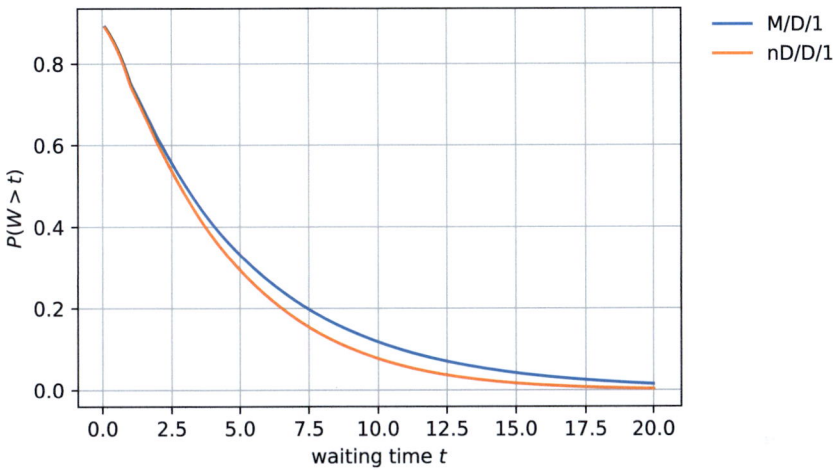

Figure 7.17: Complementary cumulative distribution function of the waiting times for $n = 500$, $b = 1$, $\rho = \lambda b = 0.9$, $\Delta t = n/\rho$ for an nD/D/1 and the corresponding M/D/1 system.

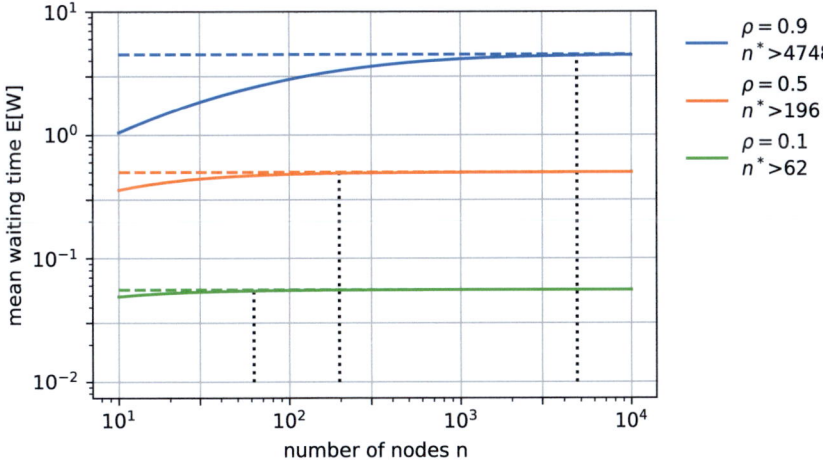

Figure 7.18: The mean waiting times are depicted for the nD/D/1 system depending on the number of nodes n for different offered loads ρ and $b = 1$. The dashed lines indicate the corresponding M/D/1 system. The legend indicates which is the minimal number n^* of nodes resulting in a relative error $r_W(\rho)$ between the mean waiting times smaller than $\varepsilon = 2\%$.

Figure 7.18 shows the mean waiting times for the nD/D/1 system depends on the number of nodes n for different offered loads ρ and $b = 1$. Hence, $\lambda = \rho = n/\Delta t$ and $\Delta t = n/\rho$. The dashed line indicate the corresponding M/D/1 system. For heavy load, there are significant differences between the nD/D/1 and the M/D/1 system. The higher the number of nodes the closer the nD/D/1 system approaches M/D/1. The relative error between the mean waiting times (which is identical to the difference of both corresponding distributions) is defined as follows, whereby $E[W_{nD/D/1}] < E[W_{M/D/1}]$, and $r_W(\rho)$ is obtained from the mean values in Equation (7.56).

$$r_W(\rho) = 1 - \frac{E[W_{nD/D/1}]}{E[W_{M/D/1}]} = 1 - \frac{(n-1)(1-\rho)}{n \cdot B(n-2, n/\rho)} > 0 \tag{7.57}$$

This allows to derive the minimum number n^* of nodes for which the relative error is below a threshold ε.

$$n^* = \underset{n \in \mathbb{N}}{\arg \min} \; \{r_W(\rho) < \varepsilon\} \tag{7.58}$$

Figure 7.18 indicates n^* for $\varepsilon = 2\%$. For low load, this is already achieved for a small number of nodes in the order of tens. For high load, n^* is in the order of thousands. An intuitive explanation of the differences between the mean waiting times of M/D/1 and nD/D/1 is the boundedness of individual waiting times. In nD/D/1, the individual waiting time is bounded by $b(n-1)$ which happens if all n arrivals occur simultaneously. Ramamurthy [88] explains it with the busy period: "*In the M/D/1 queue both the waiting time and the busy period is unbounded as the utilization gets close to one [i.e. heavy load]. On the other hand, in our [nD/D/1] model the busy period (and consequently the waiting time) is always upper bounded by one. For this reason, it is not surprising that the M/D/1 results overestimate those of our [nD/D/1] model.*" The dimensioning of the system needs to take this into account.

7.3.4 Guideline and Comparison

Figure 7.19 provides a simple approximation of the required number n^* of nodes for the relative error between the mean waiting times in Equation (7.58). The solid lines correspond to n^* for various thresholds ε, while the dashed lines show the approximated number of nodes $\tilde{n}$ which simply depends on the load ρ and the threshold ε.

$$\tilde{n} > \frac{1}{\varepsilon(1-\rho)^2} \tag{7.59}$$

It can be seen that the approximation $\tilde{n}$ is close to the exact value n^*. The ratio behind this approximation is that the waiting time in a system is sensitive to the system load ρ. The higher the load ρ is, the higher the number of required nodes is. As a result, the numerical approximation in Equation (7.59) is found which can be also obtained by approximating the Erlang-B loss formula in Equation (7.57).

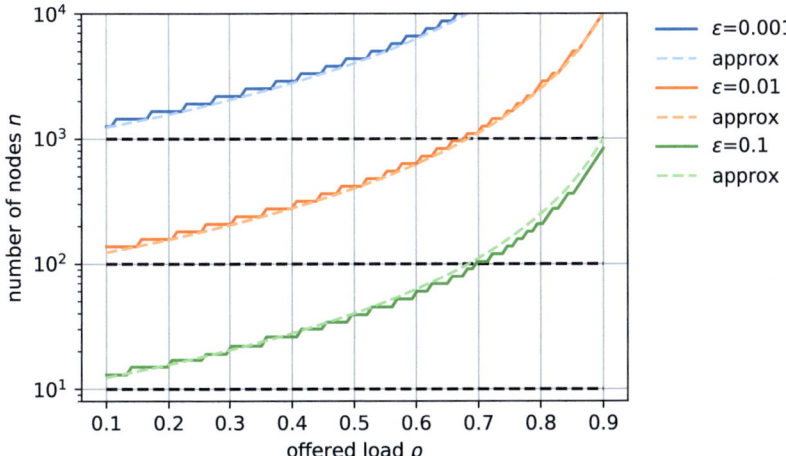

Figure 7.19: Required number of IoT nodes such that the nD/D/1 system can be approximated by an M/D/1 system when comparing the mean waiting times with a bias smaller than ε. The black dashed horizontal line corresponds to the guideline for n_A based on interarrival times (Equation (7.60)). The solid lines show the exact values n^* (Equation (7.58)), while the dashed colored lines show the load-based approximation $\tilde{n}$ (Equation (7.59)).

Figure 7.19 also shows the required number n_A of nodes when considering the coefficient of interarrival times, either based on the renewal assumption in Equation (7.38) or on the order statistics in Equation (7.32). This relation is independent of the offered load ρ and plotted as a horizontal dashed black line which illustrates a lower bound.

$$n_A > \frac{1}{\varepsilon} \tag{7.60}$$

The dimensioning of the IoT load balancer may consider that the mean waiting time is below a certain value $k \cdot b$. The guideline above is utilized by using the approximating M/D/1 system.

$$\mathrm{E}[W_{M/D/1}] = \frac{\rho b}{2(1 - \rho)} < k \cdot b \qquad \Longrightarrow \qquad \rho = \frac{n}{\Delta t} b < \frac{2k}{1 + 2k} \tag{7.61}$$

For example, $k = 2$ requires that the system load $\rho < 0.8$. This can be ensured in three different ways by modifying the IoT load balancer, the entire IoT system, or the sensing behavior of the IoT sensors.

- Reduce the processing time b using a high performance server: $b < \frac{2k\Delta t}{(1+2k)n}$

- Assign only a maximum number of IoT nodes to the server: $n < \frac{2k\Delta t}{(1+2k)b}$

- Increase the sending period of the IoT nodes: $\Delta t > \frac{(1+2k)bn}{2k}$

📰 *Further reading:* Analysis of the nD/D/1 queue [89, 90, 29, 77, 79]. Numerical computation for M/D/1 queue by Iversen and Staalhagen (1999) "Waiting time distribution in M/D/1 queueing systems" [57] and Baek, Lee, Ahn, and Bae (2016) "Exact time-dependent solutions for the M/D/1 queue" [6].

7.4 Modeling Random Access Schemes of IoT Sensors

The transmission of the sensor nodes to the IoT gateway is modeled in this chapter. The goal is to show how appropriate queueing models can be used to model various transmission schemes. The intention is not to model the schemes as detailed as possible, but to highlight the different system behaviors which are relevant for IoT systems. In particular, the different transmission schemes are compared in terms of the performance (throughput, success probability, response time) and the energy consumption.

The IoT nodes are independently sending messages over the air interface. The aggregated arrival process is modeled as a Poisson process with rate λ. The messages are assumed to have constant size which requires time b on the air interface (time on air, ToA) for the transmission from the IoT node to the IoT gateway, see Figure 7.11. Note that the time on air depends on the configuration of the channel, e.g. the used spreading factor in case of LoRa, the payload of the message, the preamble length of messages, cyclic redundancy checks for error detection, etc. The time on air b subsumes the effects in this model.

Depending on the transmission scheme, messages may get lost or have to wait until they are delivered. Of interest are the following performance measures.

- Success probability ψ: probability that an arbitrary message is successfully transmitted to the IoT gateway.

- Throughput Θ: mean number of successful transmissions per time; it is $\Theta = \psi\lambda$.

- Mean response time $\mathrm{E}[T]$: sum of the mean waiting time $\mathrm{E}[W]$ and the processing time b, i.e., $\mathrm{E}[T] = \mathrm{E}[W] + b$.

The energy consumption depends on the response time T for sending a message. To be more precise, the energy consumption is the integral of the power consumption over the time needed to send the message. We may differentiate between the power consumption (1) for sending the message (γ_b) which takes time b and (2) for waiting before sending (γ_w) which takes time W. Different values γ_b and γ_w for the power use (in Watt) are used. The energy consumption (in Joule = Watt · second) for a single message is then $\gamma_b b + \gamma_w W$, which is a linear function f of the random variable W. Therefore, it is $E[f(W)] = f(E[W])$.

- Mean energy consumption for single sent message: $\Omega = \gamma_b b + \gamma_w E[W]$.

It is however more relevant to quantify the mean consumed energy per successfully received message, which is denoted by w. There are m messages sent in total, from which $\psi \cdot m$ messages are successfully received. The energy consumption for m messages is $m \cdot \Omega$ on average. Then w is the mean energy consumption per received message, i.e., $w = \frac{m\Omega}{m\psi}$.

- Energy consumption per received message: $w = \dfrac{\Omega}{\psi}$.

Energy efficiency can be described as the ratio between the total number of packets received at the destination node (i.e. the IoT gateway) and the total energy consumption spent by the network to deliver these packets (i.e. the sensor nodes), see [14]. In that sense, energy efficiency means how many messages are carried per joule. In this chapter, we normalize the amount of consumed energy by the energy consumption of a single message. Energy efficiency is then the ratio between *'How many messages are received?'* and *'How many messages could have been received regarding the total energy consumption?'*. The energy efficiency η takes values in the interval $[0; 1]$. Maximum energy efficiency is reached ($\eta = 1$), if all messages are received and require the minimum amount of energy $\gamma_b b$. A value $\eta = 1/2$ may be interpreted in two ways: (a) 50% of the messages are received, but all messages require the minimum energy consumption or (b) all messages are received, but additional energy consumption is required for the successful delivery, e.g. due to waiting times.

- Energy efficiency: $\eta = \dfrac{\psi}{\Omega/(\gamma_b b)} = \dfrac{\gamma_b b}{w}$.

The medium access control (MAC) schemes of the IoT nodes consider pure and slotted ALOHA as random access mechanism, perfect carrier-sense multiple access with collision avoidance (CSMA/CA) as well as energy-aware CSMA/CA with restricted accessibility. These mechanisms can be modeled as (1) M/D/∞ for ALOHA, (2) M/D/1-∞ for a perfect carrier-sense mechanism with collision avoidance, (3) M/D/1-S for energy-aware CSMA/CA with restricted accessibility.

7.4.1 Pure and Slotted ALOHA: M/D/∞ and M/C/∞

Pure ALOHA. The simplest MAC protocol is pure ALOHA. If a node has a message to send, the node accesses the channel and sends the message. There is no coordination among the nodes and the nodes are independently and randomly sending. If two nodes are sending at the same time, there is a message collision and the message is not received correctly at the IoT gateway. However, the IoT nodes do not retransmit messages in case of collisions. This would require extra efforts (like acknowledgments and time-outs) and energy consumption of the IoT nodes. Besides the energy consumption, the key quantity of interest is the success probability and the throughput of the system. The system includes the air interface (the server) and the IoT nodes sending messages (the customers).

The system can be modeled as: The arrival process corresponds to the arrival of messages to be sent over the air interface. A Poisson process with rate λ is assumed. The service time of messages is the constant time on air b. Messages are always "accepted" by the air interface, although the partly simultaneous transmission of messages results in a collision. Kendall's notation of the system is M/D/∞.

The random variable X denotes the current number of simultaneous transmissions over the air interface. The system state probability $x(i) = P(X = i)$ is derived by considering the limiting process for the M/GI/n loss system for $n \to \infty$ for the Erlang formula for loss systems, cf. Equation (4.5). Due to the robustness property of the Erlang formula the result is also valid for M/GI/∞.

$$x(i) = P(X = i) = \lim_{n \to \infty} \frac{\dfrac{a^i}{i!}}{\displaystyle\sum_{k=0}^{n} \dfrac{a^k}{k!}} = \frac{a^i}{i!} e^{-a} \tag{7.62}$$

with the denominator representing the power series of the exponential function

$$\sum_{k=0}^{\infty} \frac{a^k}{k!} = e^a \tag{7.63}$$

for the offered load

$$a = \lambda b . \tag{7.64}$$

Note that the system state X follows a Poisson distribution with parameter $a = \lambda b$. It is $X \sim \text{POIS}(a)$.

Due to the PASTA property, the steady state probability $x(i)$ is the same as for an arriving customer, $x_A(i) = x(i)$. Here an arriving customer means an IoT node which wants to send a message over the air interface.

A message is successfully delivered if the customer arrives to an empty system *and* the next arrival happens after the time on air b, i.e., $A > b$ and $P(A > b) = e^{-\lambda b}$.

$$\psi = P(X_A = 0, A > b) = x(0) \cdot P(A > b) = e^{-a} \cdot e^{-a} = e^{-2a} \tag{7.65}$$

The throughput is the mean number of successful transmissions per time. With an arrival rate λ and the success probability ψ, we obtain $\Theta = \psi\lambda$ (in successfully received messages per time). Since there is no waiting time for the ALOHA system, the following performance measures are obtained.

- Success probability $\psi = e^{-2a}$
- Throughput $\Theta = \lambda e^{-2a}$
- Mean response time $\mathrm{E}[T] = b$
- Mean energy consumption per sent message $\Omega = \gamma_b b$
- Mean energy consumption per received message $\omega = \Omega/\psi = \gamma_b b e^{2a}$
- Energy efficiency $\eta = \gamma_b b/\omega = e^{-2a}$

Slotted ALOHA. For increasing the throughput of the system, slotted ALOHA was introduced. The time is discretized into slots of length b. A node can start a transmission only at the beginning of a time slot. This helps to reduce the collision probability. However, in practice the system requires a synchronization mechanism, such that all IoT nodes have a common understanding of the beginning of a time slot. The required efforts in terms of signaling overhead and energy consumption are neglected in the analysis here.

Literature suggests to denote the clocked service in Kendall's notation by using 'C' for the service process . The "clocked service" means that the service only starts at the beginning of a time slot and the service time is the duration of the time slot. Again, all arrivals are accepted by the system meaning an infinite number of servers. The suggested Kendall's notation is M/C/∞.

Now, consider an arriving customer in a time slot. This means a node wants to send a message. Then, the node has to wait until the beginning of the next time slot. Since the arrival process is a Poisson process, the arrival times are randomly distributed within a time slot of length b, cf. Chapter 3.3.2. The waiting time W follows a uniform distribution. Please note that a uniform distribution $U \sim U(0, b)$ has the cumulative distribution function $U(t) = t/b$ and that the transformed random variable $b - U$ follows the same distribution, $b - U \sim U(0, b)$. It is $P(b - U \leq t) = P(U \geq b - t) = 1 - \frac{b-t}{b} = t/b$. The waiting time W of a message in slotted ALOHA before sending is $W = b - U$.

$$W \sim U(0, b) \qquad\qquad \mathrm{E}[W] = b/2 \tag{7.66}$$

The node successfully sends the message if there are no other arrivals within that time slot. Again, $N \sim \text{POIS}(a)$ with $a = \lambda b$.

$$\psi = P(N = 0) = e^{-a} \tag{7.67}$$

The throughput follows accordingly, $\Theta = \psi \lambda$. The throughput can also be derived in the following manner. The number N_s of successful transmissions in a time slot is $N_s = 1$, if there is exactly a single arrival within the time slot. In all other cases, there are collisions and $N_s = 0$. The number N of arrivals within a time slot of length b follows a Poisson distribution with $a = \lambda b$.

$$N \sim \text{POIS}(a) \qquad\qquad P(N = i) = \frac{a^i}{i!} e^{-a} \tag{7.68}$$

The throughput is the mean number of successful transmissions per time and a time slot has length b.

$$\Theta = \frac{1}{b}(1 \cdot P(N = 1) + 0 \cdot P(N \neq 1)) = \frac{ae^{-a}}{b} = \lambda e^{-a} \tag{7.69}$$

The mean energy consumption for a single message needs to take into account the waiting time and the sending time.

$$\Omega = \gamma_b b + \gamma_w \text{E}[W] = b(\gamma_b + \gamma_w/2) \tag{7.70}$$

The energy consumption regarding successfully received messages follows.

$$\omega = \frac{\Omega}{\psi} = b(\gamma_b + \gamma_w/2)e^a \tag{7.71}$$

The energy efficiency relates the energy consumption for a single message to the mean energy consumption per received message.

$$\eta = \frac{\gamma_b b}{\omega} = \frac{\gamma_b}{\gamma_b + \gamma_w/2} \cdot e^{-a} \tag{7.72}$$

In summary, the following performance measures are obtained for slotted ALOHA. It can be seen that the performance of slotted ALOHA is increased in terms of throughput and success probability compared to pure ALOHA. The costs are increased energy consumption. In practice, synchronization mechanisms need to be deployed resulting in additional overhead and additional energy consumption.

- Success probability $\psi = e^{-a}$
- Throughput $\Theta = \lambda e^{-a}$
- Mean response time $\text{E}[T] = b/2 + b$
- Mean energy consumption for sent message: $\Omega = b(\gamma_b + \gamma_w/2)$
- Mean energy consumption per received message $\omega = b(\gamma_b + \gamma_w/2)e^a$
- Energy efficiency $\eta = \dfrac{\gamma_b}{\gamma_b + \gamma_w/2} e^{-a}$

7.4.2 Perfect CSMA/CA: M/D/1-∞

The pure and slotted ALOHA approaches suffer from the collision of messages. In order to avoid collisions, assume now perfect carrier-sense multiple access with collision avoidance. The IoT nodes sense the communication channel and are only sending if the channel is free, i.e., the server is idle. When the channel is occupied by another message transmission, the IoT nodes have to wait until the channel is free again. In practice, carrier sensing alone does not guarantee the avoidance of collisions due to the hidden node problem or hidden terminal problem. Collision avoidance may be approached with common approaches like RTS-CTS. When an IoT node wants to transmit a message, a very small Request-to-Send (RTS) message is sent to the IoT gateway which may reply with a Clear-to-Send (CTS). The RTS and CTS messages include the reservation time for the channel. Even for LoRaWAN, this MAC protocol improves the success probability. ◪ *Further reading:* survey on IoT and especially LoRaWAN and LoRaWAN MAC layer [46, 81].

In the system model, perfect CSMA/CA is assumed, such that no collisions occur. The nodes are served in a FIFO way, i.e., messages are sent in order over the air interface. There is a single server (the air interface). The customers in the system (the messages from the IoT nodes to the IoT gateways) arrive according to a Poisson process with rate λ. The processing time is the time on air b. The nodes are waiting until they are able to transmit which means an unlimited waiting room. The system is an M/D/1-∞ delay system.

The waiting time distribution and the mean waiting time for M/D/1 were derived in Chapter 7.3.1. The stability condition must be fulfilled, i.e. $\rho = \lambda b < 1$.

$$E[W] = \frac{\rho b}{2(1 - \rho)} \tag{7.73}$$

There are no blocked customers. Hence, all messages are eventually transmitted over the air interface and the success probability is $\psi = 1$. The throughput is $\Theta = \lambda$.

The mean energy consumption of a message directly follows from the mean waiting time. Since all messages are delivered, the mean energy consumption Ω per sent message is identical to the energy consumption ω per received message. Energy efficiency follows directly.

$$\Omega = \gamma_b b + \gamma_w E[W] = \gamma_b b + \gamma_w \frac{\rho b}{2(1 - \rho)} \tag{7.74}$$

$$\eta = \frac{\gamma_b b}{\Omega} = \frac{\gamma_b}{\gamma_b + \gamma_w \frac{\rho}{2(1-\rho)}} \tag{7.75}$$

In summary, perfect CSMA/CA is modeled as M/D/1-∞ with those performance measures.

- Success probability $\psi = 1$
- Throughput $\Theta = \lambda$
- Mean response time $\mathrm{E}[T] = \frac{b(2-\rho)}{2(1-\rho)}$
- Mean energy consumption for sent message: $\Omega = \gamma_b b + \gamma_w \dfrac{\rho b}{2(1-\rho)}$
- Mean energy consumption per received message $\omega = \Omega$
- Energy efficiency $\eta = \dfrac{\gamma_b}{\gamma_b + \gamma_w \frac{\rho}{2(1-\rho)}}$

7.4.3 Perfect CSMA/CA with Restricted Accessibility: M/D/1-S

In high load situations, the perfect CSMA/CA suffers from large waiting times and high energy consumption. To this end, restricted accessibility is introduced which provides a control knob between blocked messages and energy efficiency. Again, we are investigating a perfect mechanism without modeling the impact of signaling. In practice, the IoT nodes may send an RTS-CTS like mechanism to inform the gateway about their transmission requests. If there are already S messages waiting, the IoT gateway rejects the requests and informs the IoT nodes that their request is blocked. If there are less than S transmission requests waiting at the server, the IoT gateway accepts the request. The requests are served in order. The IoT nodes with accepted requests are waiting until the IoT gateway informs them. Then, the message will be sent over the air interface. There are no message collisions, but messages may be blocked which differs the system from the previous one.

The system can be modeled as a finite capacity queue and is denoted as M/D/1-S in Kendall's notation. The transmission requests (the customers) arrive according to a Poisson process with rate λ. The air interface represents the server and processes the requests in a FIFO manner. The processing time is constant and is the time on air b for sending the message from the IoT node to the IoT gateway. The waiting room has finite capacity S. The main interest for the analysis of the system are the mean waiting time to compute the energy efficiency as well as the success probability ψ which is the counter probability of the blocking probability, $\psi = 1 - p_B$.

The random variable X is the total number of requests in the system, i.e. in the waiting room and currently served. The embedded Markov chain approach (Chapter 5.2) is used to derive the steady state probabilities $x(i)$ for $i = 0, \ldots, S+1$. The embedding time is immediately after service. Similar to the derivation of the M/GI/1 system, the state transition matrix $\mathcal{P} = \{p_{ij}\}$ is developed. Then, the state probabilities at embedding times are obtained as Eigenvector of $X\mathcal{P} = X$ or by means of the power method, i.e., iterating $X_n = X_{n-1}\mathcal{P}$ until X converges.

State Transition Matrix   The state state transition matrix $\mathcal{P} = \{p_{ij}\}$ summarizes the state transition probability between two embedding times t_n and t_{n+1}. The embedding times are immediately after service and there are at most S customers in the system at an embedding time. The state space is $\{0, 1, \ldots, S\}$ and the quadratic matrix $\mathcal{P}$ has the dimensions $(S + 1) \times (S + 1)$.

$$p_{ij} = P(X(t_{n+1}) = j | X(t_n) = i) , \quad i, j = 0, 1, \ldots, S \tag{7.76}$$

If the system is empty at time t_n, i.e. $i = 0$ and $[X(t_n) = 0]$, the arrival of the next request immediately starts the service process. To have $j < S$ requests after finishing the first request, j arrivals are required during the service time b. To have $j = S$ requests at time t_{n+1}, there are at least S arrivals from which some requests may be blocked due to finite capacity S. The number Γ of arrivals during one service time follows a Poisson distribution with parameter $\lambda b = \rho$.

$$\Gamma \sim Pois(\lambda b) \tag{7.77}$$

The state transition probabilities p_{0j} follows.

$$p_{0j} = \gamma(j) \qquad\qquad\qquad j = 0, 1, \ldots, S - 1 \tag{7.78a}$$

$$p_{0S} = \sum_{k=S}^{\infty} \gamma(k) = 1 - \sum_{k=0}^{S-1} \gamma(k) \qquad j = S \tag{7.78b}$$

If the system is not empty at time t_n, $i > 0$, the service process immediately starts at t_n. If there are $j <$ requests in the system immediately after the service of this request at time t_{n+1}, there are $(j - i + 1)$ arrivals during the service process. If there are $j = S$ requests at time t_{n+1}, then, there must be at least $(S - i + 1)$ arrivals.

$$p_{ij} = \gamma(j - i + 1) \qquad i = 1, \ldots, S , \qquad j = i - 1, i, \ldots, S - 1 \tag{7.79a}$$

$$p_{iS} = \sum_{k=S-i+1}^{\infty} \gamma(k) \qquad i = 1, \ldots, S , \qquad j = S \tag{7.79b}$$

The state transition matrix is $\mathcal{P} = \{p_{ij}\}$. It is a truncated matrix of the M/D/1-∞ system, cf. Equation (5.24).

$$\mathcal{P} = \begin{pmatrix} \gamma(0) & \gamma(1) & \gamma(2) & \gamma(3) & \cdots & \gamma(S-1) & 1 - \sum_{i=0}^{S-1} \gamma(i) \\ \gamma(0) & \gamma(1) & \gamma(2) & \gamma(3) & \cdots & \gamma(S-1) & 1 - \sum_{i=0}^{S-1} \gamma(i) \\ 0 & \gamma(0) & \gamma(1) & \gamma(2) & \cdots & \gamma(S-2) & 1 - \sum_{i=0}^{S-2} \gamma(i) \\ 0 & 0 & \gamma(0) & \gamma(1) & \cdots & \gamma(S-3) & 1 - \sum_{i=0}^{S-3} \gamma(i) \\ \vdots & \vdots & \vdots & \vdots & \ddots & \vdots & \vdots \\ 0 & 0 & 0 & 0 & \cdots & \gamma(0) & 1 - \gamma(0) \end{pmatrix} \tag{7.80}$$

The state probabilities at embedding times $x(k)$ for $k = 0, \ldots, S$ are derived by numerically solving $X\mathcal{P} = X$ (Eigenvector) or by iterating $X_n = X_{n-1}\mathcal{P}$ until X converges (power method).

Steady State Probabilities   The steady state probabilities $x^*(k)$ at arbitrary times are resulting from Kleinrock's principle (Chapter 5.2.3) and the PASTA property (Chapter 3.3.2). The steady state probabilities $x(k) = x_D(k)$ immediately after a departure are derived with the method of embedded Markov chain. The PASTA property means that the probability $x^*(k)$ of the state k as seen by a *random observer* is the same as the probability $x_A(k)$ of the state seen by an *arriving customer*, if arrivals follow a Poisson process, cf. Equation (4.4). The PASTA property only requires Poisson arrivals as an assumption.

Kleinrock's principle means that for systems where the system state can change at most by +1 or -1, the system distribution as seen by an accepted arriving customer will be the same as that seen by a departing customer. Kleinrock's principle can therefore be applied for $GI/GI/n$ queues, but not for bulk service or batch arrival queues. Hence, the state distribution $x_A^1(k)$ at the *arrival instants of accepted customers* will be the same as the state distribution at the departure instants $x_D(k)$. Kleinrock's result yields $x_D(k) = x_A^1(k)$. Take care here, since arrivals may be blocked due to the finite capacity of the system. Therefore, $x_A^1(k) \neq x_A(k)$.

$$x_A^1(k) = P(X_A^1 = k) = P(X_A = k | X_A \leq S) = \frac{P(X_A = k, X_A \leq S)}{P(X_A \leq S)}$$
$$= \frac{P(X_A = k)}{P(X_A \leq S)} = \frac{x_A(k)}{1 - p_B} \tag{7.81}$$

The random variable X^* is the number of customers at arbitrary times, while X_A is the number of customers at arrival times. X^* and X_A are independent of whether the arriving customer is accepted or blocked. X_A^1 is the number of customers at arrival times when the arriving customer is accepted. $X = X_D$ is the number of customers immediately after departure of a customer (embedding time). For the finite M/D/1-S system (and for the general M/GI/1-S system), we obtain the following fundamental relationship for $k = 0, \ldots, S$.

$$x^*(k) \underset{\text{PASTA}}{=} x_A(k) \underset{(7.81)}{=} (1 - p_B)x_A^1(k) \underset{\text{Kleinrock}}{=} (1 - p_B)x_D(k) \tag{7.82}$$

The unknown variable is the blocking probability p_B which is derived by comparing the effective arrival rate $(1 - p_B)\lambda$ and the effective departure rate $(1 - x^*(0))/b$. The term $(1 - x^*(0))$ indicates the probability that the server is busy which is valid for any GI/GI/1 system, see Chapter 5.6. The offered load is $\rho = \lambda b$.

$$(1 - p_B)\lambda = \frac{1 - x^*(0)}{b} \quad \Longrightarrow \quad p_B = \frac{\rho - 1 + x^*(0)}{\rho} \tag{7.83}$$

Now, apply Equation (7.82) for $k = 0$ yielding $x^*(0) = (1 - p_B)x_D(0)$ which is inserted into Equation (7.83).

$$p_B = \frac{\rho - 1 + (1 - p_B)x_D(0)}{\rho} \quad \Longrightarrow \quad p_B = \frac{\rho - 1 + x_D(0)}{\rho + x_D(0)} \tag{7.84}$$

Equation (7.82) provides the steady state probabilities for $k = 0, \ldots, S$.

$$x^*(k) = \frac{x_D(k)}{\rho + x_D(0)} \qquad\qquad x^*(S + 1) = p_B \tag{7.85}$$

📑 *Further reading:* Analytical solution of finite capacity M/D/1 queues [15, 56].

Performance Measures The blocking probability p_B is provided in Equation (7.84) and requires the numerical derivation of $x(k) = x_D(k)$ based on the state transition matrix in Equation (7.80). The success probability is $\psi = 1 - p_B$. The throughput of the system is $\Theta = (1 - p_B)\lambda$.

The mean sojourn time $\mathrm{E}[T]$ in the system follows from Little's theorem. The mean number of customers $\mathrm{E}[X^*]$ is derived numerically.

$$\mathrm{E}[X^*] = \sum_{i=0}^{S+1} x^*(i) = (1 - p_B)\lambda \mathrm{E}[T] \tag{7.86}$$

The mean waiting time $\mathrm{E}[W] = \mathrm{E}[T] - b$ is used to quantify the mean energy consumption $\Omega = \gamma_b b + \gamma_w \mathrm{E}[W]$ for sent messages. Finally, the energy consumption per received message $\omega = \Omega/\psi$ and energy efficiency follow.

- Success probability $\psi = 1 - p_B$
- Throughput $\Theta = (1 - p_B)\lambda$
- Mean response time $\mathrm{E}[T] = \dfrac{\mathrm{E}[X^*]}{(1 - p_B)\lambda}$
- Mean energy consumption for sent message: $\Omega = \gamma_b b + \gamma_w(\mathrm{E}[T] - b)$
- Mean energy consumption per received message $\omega = \frac{\Omega}{1 - p_B}$
- Energy efficiency $\eta = \dfrac{\gamma_b b}{\omega} = \dfrac{\gamma_b(1 - p_B)}{\gamma_b + \gamma_w(\mathrm{E}[T]/b - 1)}$

7.4.4 Numerical Results: Success Probability and Energy Efficiency

Success Probability The success probability ψ of the different IoT channel access mechanism are compared in Figure 7.20. The offered load is given on the x-axis which ranges from low load scenarios (a close to zero) to high load scenarios ($a > 1$). Pure ALOHA has the lowest success probability ψ of the considered mechanisms. Slotted ALOHA significantly improves probability ψ. Perfect CSMA/CA with restricted accessibility further improves ψ. It can be seen that even for an M/D/1-0 system there is a significant improvement compared to slotted ALOHA when $a > 1$. For M/D/1-0, the Erlang-B formula can be used to derive the blocking probability p_B and the success probability $\psi = 1 - p_B$. Although increasing the number S of waiting places leads to an increased success probability ψ, the gain gets smaller and smaller. Therefore, the impact of S on the energy efficiency may be used to derive practical guidelines for S.

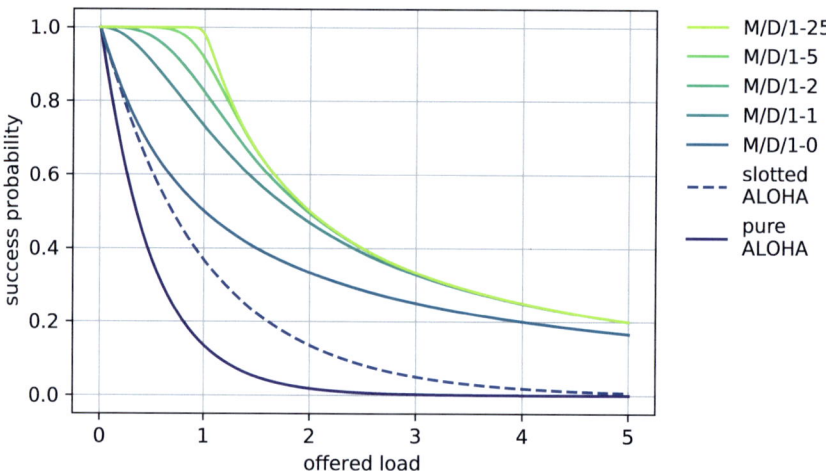

Figure 7.20: Success probability ψ of IoT messages for different MAC mechanisms. M/D/1-S represents perfect CSMA/CA with restricted accessibility.

Energy Efficiency Figure 7.21 compares the energy efficiency η of the MAC mechanisms depending on the offered load a. Observe that for very low load, pure ALOHA
is more energy efficient than slotted ALOHA due to the waiting times in slotted
ALOHA. CSMA/CA with restricted accessibility outperforms the ALOHA approaches
if the number of waiting slots is not too high. If the offered load approaches $a = 1$,
the waiting times are dominating if S is large. Note that $\gamma_w = \gamma_b/2$ was used. Hence,
there is a trade-off between the success probability and the energy efficiency for
M/D/1-S.

Figure 7.22 visualizes this trade-off for various loads. Each dot in the figure
corresponds to one particular choice of S. The larger S is the higher the success
probability ψ is. The figure indicates that for low loads $(a < 0.5)$, the parameter S
has no significant impact on energy efficiency. However, for $a = 0.5$, larger values of
S yield into higher success probabilities. For high load situations, e.g. $a = 2.0$, an
increase in S results into a strong decrease of the energy efficiency η. This is due to
the fact that the success probability cannot be increased significantly anymore, once
a certain threshold of S is reached. But further increasing of S negatively affects
the energy efficiency due to waiting times. A good trade-off is reached for $S = 3$.
In practice, however, adaptive mechanisms would be recommended. In low load
situations, S can be selected higher. In medium load situations $(0.7 < a \leq 1.5)$, a
good trade-off is reached for $S = 5$. For high load $a > 1.5$, small values of S are
sufficient.

Table 7.1 provides a summary of the performance and energy measures.

Performance Measure	Pure ALOHA	Slotted ALOHA	Perfect CSMA/CA	Restricted Accessibility
Success probability ψ	e^{-2a}	e^{-a}	1	$1 - p_B$
Throughput Θ	λe^{-2a}	λe^{-a}	λ	$(1 - p_B)\lambda$
Response time $E[T]$	b	$b/2 + b$	$\frac{b(2-\rho)}{2(1-\rho)}$	$\frac{E[X^*]}{(1-p_B)\lambda}$
Energy consumption Ω	$b\gamma_b$	$b(\gamma_b + \gamma_w/2)$	$\gamma_b b + \gamma_w \frac{\rho b}{2(1-\rho)}$	$\gamma_b b + \gamma_w E[W]$
Consump. rcvd msg. ω	$\gamma_b b e^{2a}$	$b(\gamma_b + \gamma_w/2)e^a$	$\gamma_b b + \gamma_w \frac{\rho b}{2(1-\rho)}$	$\frac{\Omega}{1-p_B}$
Energy efficiency η	e^{-2a}	$\frac{\gamma_b}{\gamma_b+\gamma_w/2}e^{-a}$	$\frac{\gamma_b}{\gamma_b+\gamma_w \frac{\rho}{2(1-\rho)}}$	$\frac{\gamma_b(1-p_B)}{\gamma_b+\gamma_w(E[T]/b-1)}$

Table 7.1: Performance comparison of MAC protocols for IoT nodes.

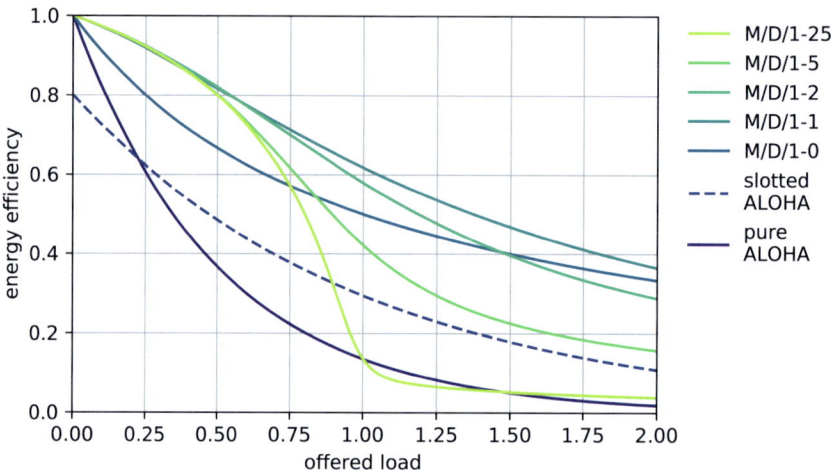

Figure 7.21: Energy efficiency for different MAC mechanisms. M/D/1-S represents perfect CSMA/CA with restricted accessibility. Here, it is $\gamma_w = \gamma_b/2$.

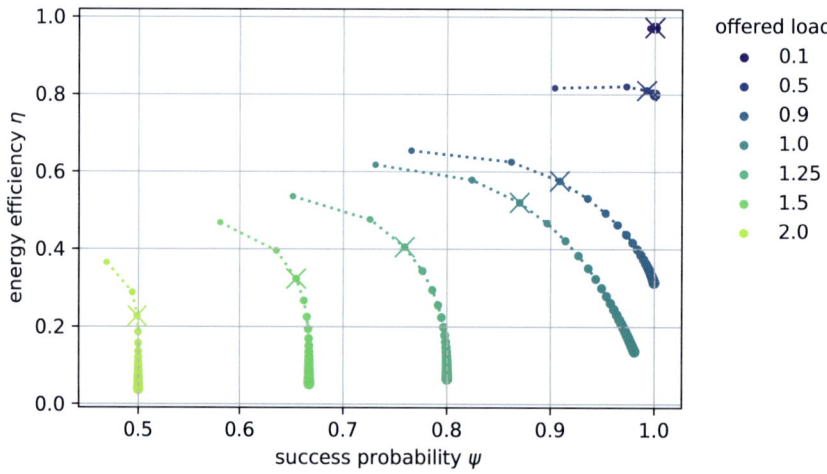

Figure 7.22: Trade-off between success probability ψ and energy efficiency ψ for perfect CSMA/CA with restricted accessibility (M/D/1-S). Here, it is $\gamma_w = \gamma_b/2$. The crosses ($\times$) indicate $S = 3$.

Kleinrock's Approach for Deriving the Operational Point   For the identification of the operational point, which is the number of waiting places S for the M/D/1-S queueing system, we follow an approach by Kleinrock [60]. He suggests the *Power* metric in queueing systems as optimization metric to identify the knee of the curve. The power metric is the ratio of 'goodness' divided by 'badness'. Then, the optimization of power leads to a trade-off between maximizing 'goodness' while minimizing 'badness'. In his original work, a single server system is considered with 'goodness' being the relative efficiency $G = \rho$ of the server, i.e., the fraction of time the server is being used. 'Badness' refers to the normalized response time $B = T/\mathrm{E}[B]$ which should be minimal. The maximum value of the power metric G/B is then the operational point. For the IoT system and CSMA/CA with restricted accessibility, consider the ratio between energy efficiency η and the counter success probability $(1 - \psi)$. The maximum of the ratio $G/B = \eta/(1 - \psi)$ corresponds to the operational point. Figure 7.23 shows the ratio G/B which is normalized with the maximum observed ratio per offered load a, depending on S.

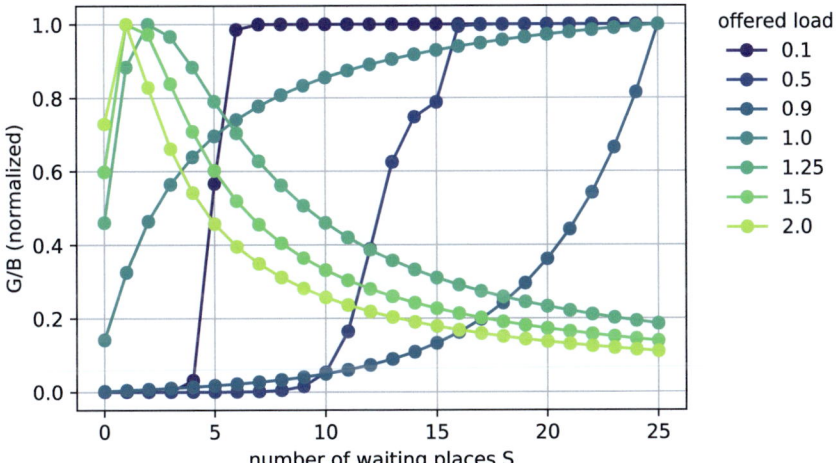

Figure 7.23: Kleinrock's power metric G/B [60] is modified to identify the operational point (which is the number of waiting places S) for the M/D/1-S system. G/B is the normalized ratio between energy efficiency η and the counter success probability $(1 - \psi)$.

7.5 Spacing Function: Discrete-time GI/GI/1 Queue with Bounded Delay

In this modeling example we will discuss spacing – or policing – functions in communication systems and related analytical issues. Spacing functions can often be found in traffic shaping and overload prevention in networks. It is shown that a spacer can be analyzed using a GI/D/1 queue with bounded delay. This is a special case of the GI/GI/1 system with bounded delay, where a modified time-domain discrete-time algorithm is derived [109].

The discrete-time delay-loss system presented here differs from the regular GI/GI/1 queueing system in Chapter 6.4 with the assumption that new customers are blocked if the expected waiting time exceeds a maximum threshold waiting time at the time of arrival. Before going further to the detailed analysis steps, it is important to first describe the main components of a spacer and point out why a spacing device can be modeled using a GI/D/1 queue with bounded delay.

Spacing in Communication Networks   The spacing concept is often found in the traffic shaping, access control at the edge interface of communication networks. The spacer is mainly used to smooth burst-like traffic flows for overload avoidance purposes. The concept of the spacer has been intensively investigated, starting in the context of ATM (Asynchronous Transfer Mode) networks , but also in IP (Internet Protocol) networks.

The main function of a spacer is to ensure that two successive customers or data packets of an arrival process are at least a time-span T apart. This corresponds to a maximum (instantaneous) arrival rate of $1/T$. This peak arrival rate is e.g. negotiated and given in service level agreements (SLAs) between users and network operators or service providers. The inbound traffic is shaped or smoothed by the spacer in such a way that compliance with the agreed SLA is guaranteed. The spacer works like a "distance keeper" for arrivals before they enter the communication network.

Spacer Model using a GI/D/1 Queue with Bounded Delay Figure 7.24 depicts the basic structure of a spacer with

A_1 random variable for the interarrival time of the input process of packets

T minimum interarrival time (in Δt) which corresponds to the maximum instantaneous arrival rate $1/T$

A_2 random variable for the interdeparture time of the packet output process (departure process)

τ_{max} maximum spacer delay (in Δt); as the customers have to be buffered due to the spacing operation, an intermediate finite-capacity spacer buffer has to be implemented with a predefined maximum delay

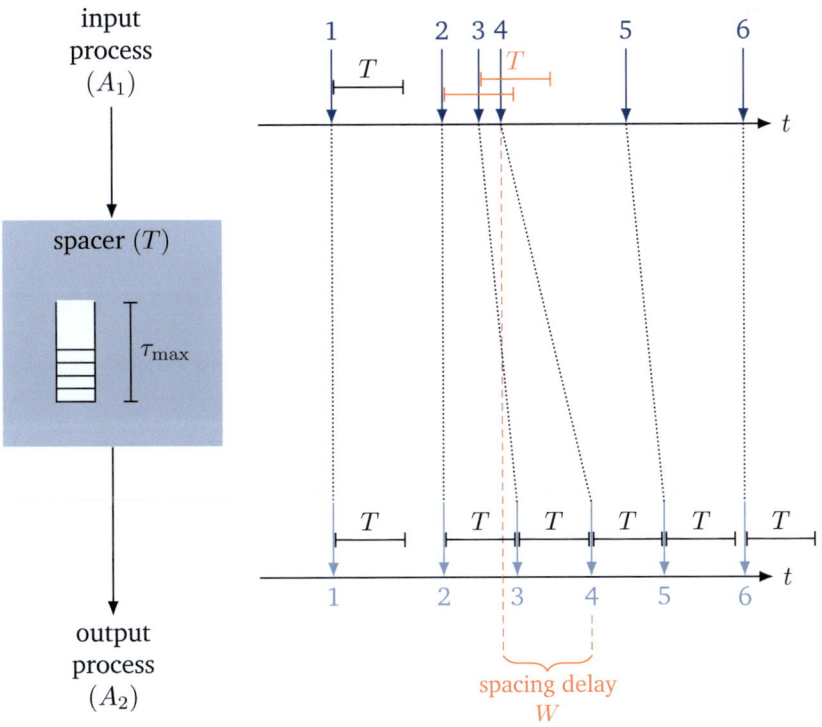

Figure 7.24: Mode of operation and structure of a spacer with maximum spacer delay.

The analysis of the spacer can be carried out using a discrete-time GI/D/1 system with bounded delay and is illustrated below. This would be the case if the reaction of both models to the same arrival process in terms of blocking behavior and output process are identical. As shown below, for the same input process i) both models have the same blocking behavior and ii) the output processes are identical except for a shift of length T. For this purpose, the state developments in the spacer and in the GI/D/1 delay-loss system (with service time T and maximum spacing delay $\tau_{\max}$) are inspected in Figure 7.25, where the blocking behavior and the output processes are particularly compared.

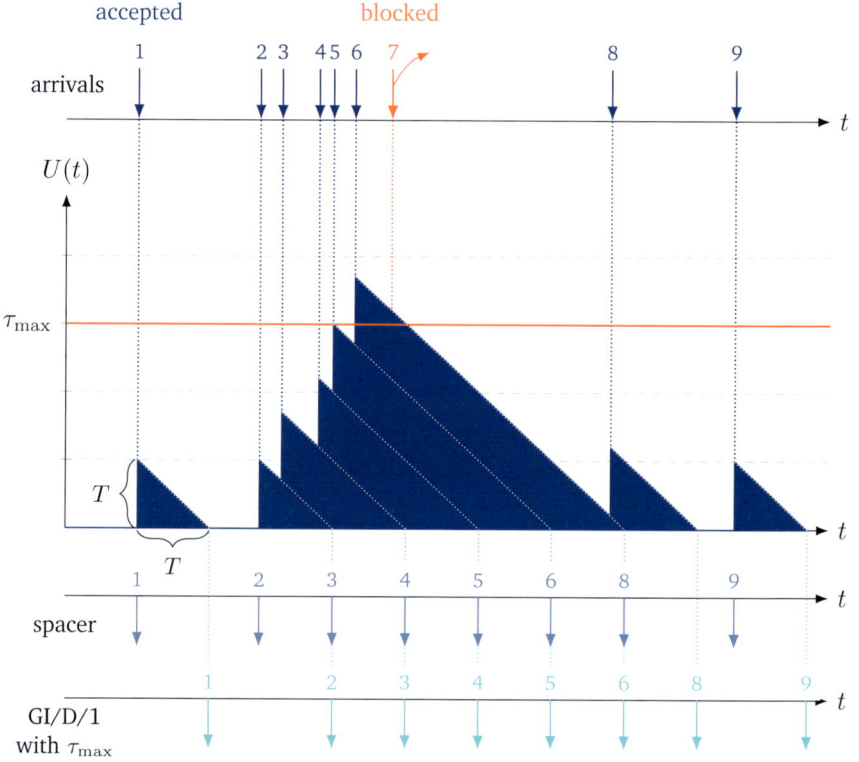

Figure 7.25: Comparison of the output process of a spacer and the corresponding GI/D/1 system with bounded delay $\tau_{\max}$ and minimum spacing time T.

The unfinished work $U(t)$ (cf. Figure 7.25) is now interpreted for the two models, where we refer to customers or packets likewise.

1. Spacer: Here, $U(t)$ is the time until the arrival of the next accepted packet (since the minimum interarrival distance is kept). Packets 1 and 2 in Figure 7.25 find an empty spacer and and pass it without suffering any delay. Upon arrival, packets 3, 4, 5, 6 see the spacer with positive unfinished work $U(t)$ and have

to wait the duration $U(t)$ until they can pass the spacer. Each accepted packet increases the unfinished work $U(t)$ by the amount of minimum inter-packet time T. Packet 7 would have to wait longer than the delay bound τ_{max}. It is therefore rejected by the spacer and does not increment the unfinished work $U(t)$.

2. GI/D/1 system with bounded delay: $U(t)$ describes here as usual the unfinished work in the system, including the customer in service.

The delays of packets in both systems are identical. The only difference is that in the case of the spacer, no additional service time is counted. The comparison of the output processes shows that due to this effect, the output processes differ just by the service time T. The blocking behaviors are identical. This implies that it is possible to analyze a spacer using a GI/D/1 system with bounded delay.

7.5.1 General GI/GI/1 Queue with Bounded Delay

The analysis is derived for the general case of GI/GI/1 queueing system with bounded delay. A GI/GI/1 delay system with FIFO service discipline and the following modification is considered. Customers will be accepted – or are allowed to enter the waiting room – if the expected waiting time upon arrival is less than a threshold value $\tau_{max} = L \cdot \Delta t$, i.e., if the unfinished work in the system does not exceed the threshold value L at the time of arrival. The Kendall notation can be modified to denote this GI/GI/1 system with bounded delay: GI/GI/1-L with bounded delay L. It should be noted here that the system with bounded delay is *not* identical with a GI/GI/1-S delay-loss system with limited waiting space S, where the limitation is based on the *number* of customers waiting in the system upon arrival.

7.5.2 Analysis of the GI/GI/1 Queue with Bounded Delay

The analysis is carried out in the same way as in the time-domain analysis of the regular GI/GI/1 system. The time axis is again discretized in Δt. We consider the following discrete random variables (r.v.)

A_n r.v. for the interarrival time, i.e. the time between the n-th and the $(n + 1)$-st arrival

B_n r.v. of the service time of the n-th customer

U_n unfinished work in the system immediately upon the arrival of the n-th customer

We take into account the system state $U(t)$ with a sample path depicted in Figure 7.26.

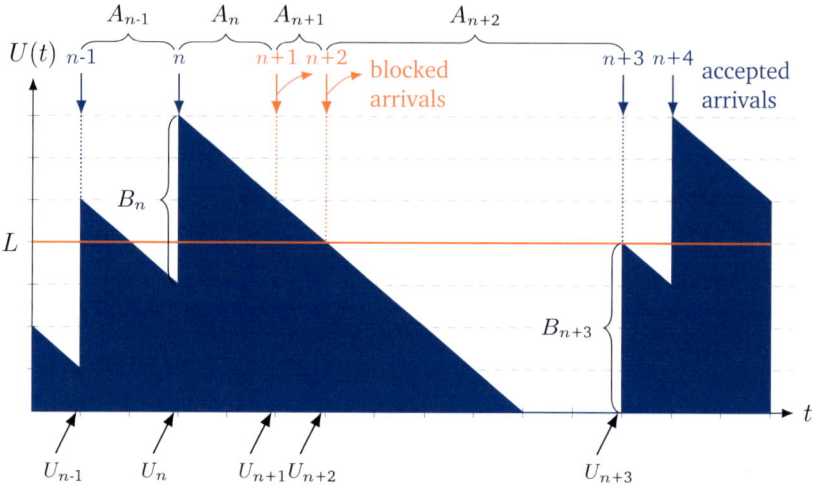

Figure 7.26: Unfinished work in a GI/D/1 system with bounded delay $L = 4$ and $B_n = 4$.

Observing the n-th customer (test customer) encountering an amount U_n of unfinished work upon arrival, where U_n would be exactly the waiting time, if the test customer is accepted to enter the system, we can distinguished between two cases, as carried out in the following.

Case 1: Customer Acceptance $(U_n < L)$ In case of customer acceptance, the amount of unfinished work is defined by the conditional random variable $U_{n,0} = U_n|U_n < L$ which has the following distribution.

$$u_{n,0}(k) = \frac{\sigma^L \left[u_n(k)\right]}{P(U_n < L)} = \frac{\sigma^L[u_n(k)]}{\sum_{i=0}^{L} u_n(i)} \tag{7.87a}$$

The σ^m operator truncates parts of a probability distribution. In particular, the operator $\sigma^m [x(k)]$ takes the lower part $(k < m)$ of a distribution $x(k)$ and suppresses the rest.

$$\sigma^m[x(k)] = \begin{cases} x(k) & k < m \\ 0 & k \geq m \end{cases} \tag{7.87b}$$

The result of this operation is an unnormalized distribution. The normalization (division by $P(U_n < L)$) in Equation (7.87a) leads to the conditional random variable $U_{n,0} = U_n|U_n < L$.

316

Observing the development of the process in the case of an accepted customer $(U_n < L)$, the following relationship between the random variables and their distributions are obtained.

$$U_{n+1,0} = \max(U_{n,0} + B_n - A_n, 0) \tag{7.87c}$$

$$u_{n+1,0}(k) = \pi_0 \left[u_{n,0}(k) * b_n(k) * a_n(-k) \right] \tag{7.87d}$$

Case 2: Customer Rejection, i.e. Blocking $(U_n \geq L)$ In case of a rejected customer, the unfinished work upon arrival of the blocked customer is defined as conditional random variable $U_{n,1} = U_n | U_n \geq L$. The probability distribution is as follows

$$u_{n,1}(k) = \frac{\sigma_L \left[u_n(k) \right]}{P(U_n \geq L)} = \frac{\sigma_L \left[u_n(k) \right]}{\sum_{i=L}^{\infty} u_n(i)} . \tag{7.88a}$$

The σ_m operator truncates the lower part of a probability distribution. In particular, the operator $\sigma_m \left[x(k) \right]$ takes the upper part $(k \geq m)$ of a distribution $x(k)$ and suppresses the rest.

$$\sigma_m[x(k)] = \begin{cases} 0 & k < m \\ x(k) & k \geq m \end{cases} \tag{7.88b}$$

The normalization with $P(U_n \geq L)$ results in the conditional random variable $U_{n,1} = U_n | U_n \geq L$. The relationships for the state process development in case of blocking $(U_n \geq L)$ are as follows.

$$U_{n+1,1} = \max(U_{n,1} - A_n, 0) \tag{7.88c}$$

$$u_{n+1,1}(k) = \pi_0 \left[u_{n,1}(k) * a_n(-k) \right] \tag{7.88d}$$

Combining Case 1 and Case 2   The combination of both cases, i.e. acceptance and blocking, results in the development of the unfinished work for the $(n + 1)$-st customer.

$$u_{n+1}(k) = P(U_n < L) \cdot u_{n+1,0}(k) + P(U_n \geq L) \cdot u_{n+1,1}(k) \tag{7.89a}$$

We finally arrive at a recursive relation to calculate the unfinished work at arrival epochs of customers which means immediately before the arrival of a customer.

$$\begin{aligned} u_{n+1}(k) &= \pi_0 \left[\sigma^L \left[u_n(k) \right] * b_n(k) * a_n(-k) \right] + \pi_0 \left[\sigma_L \left[u_n(k) \right] * a_n(-k) \right] \\ &= \pi_0 \left[\left(\sigma^L \left[u_n(k) \right] * b_n(k) + \sigma_L \left[u_n(k) \right] \right) * a_n(-k) \right] \end{aligned} \tag{7.89b}$$

Finally, the customer rejection probability in statistical equilibrium is

$$p_B = \sum_{k=L}^{\infty} u(k).$$ (7.90)

This equation leads to an algorithm (cf. Figure 7.27) to compute the distribution of the unfinished work prior to customer arrival and thus, the rejection probability. The algorithm can be used for stationary and non-stationary traffic conditions. Under steady state conditions, the subscripts n and $(n+1)$ can be omitted.

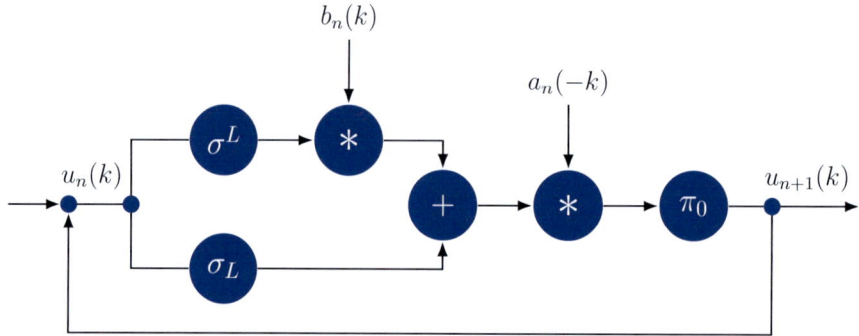

Figure 7.27: Computational diagram of a GI/GI/1 system with bounded delay.

7.5.3 Spacer Dimensioning Example

A dimensioning example of the spacer is shown below for GI/D/1 with $E[B] = T$. While it is clear that the function of the spacer is to smooth the input process, two opposing dimensioning goals are taken into consideration: i) the blocking probability should be kept small (i.e. large buffer size of the spacer or τ_{max}) and ii) small spacer delay which should not exceed predefined QoS value, i.e. small buffer size.

Figure 7.28 illustrates how the spacer affects and forms the packet process (with $E[A] = 20$ and $c_A = 0.5$) where the distribution functions of the input and the output processes of the spacer are compared. This is done for different values of the maximum spacer delay τ_{max}). The shape of the output process distribution function shows a jump at $T = 15$ due to the spacing process (service time T) as well as a truncation due to the bounded delay.

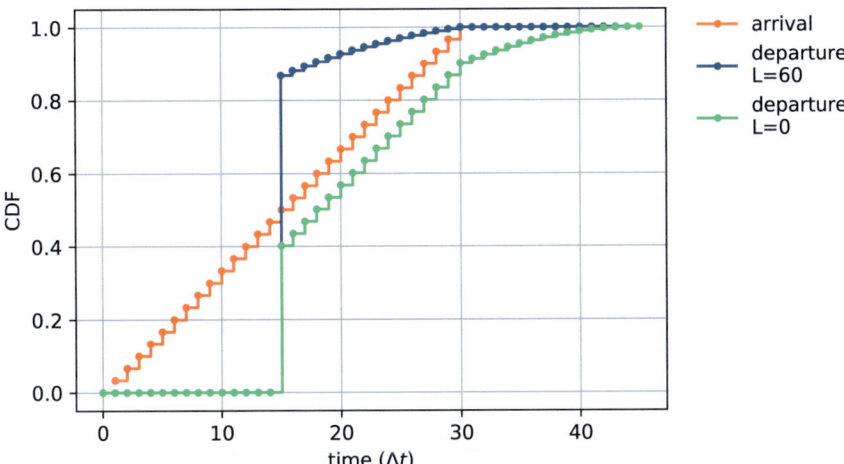

Figure 7.28: Change of the input process due to spacing for different bounded delays.

The main function of the spacer – to smooth out bursty, high-variance packet traffic streams and make them smoother – is presented in Figure 7.29. For the case of $E[A_I] = 6$, the coefficient of variation c_D of the output process is drawn as a function of the coefficient of variation c_A of the input process. A proper spacer makes the traffic variation smaller; this effect is observed for all values of the maximum spacer delay (τ_{max}). Figure 7.30 shows the so-called damping factor c_D/c_A for various values of the threshold L. We observe that the damping factor is less than 1. Thus, the arrival process is smoothed by the spacer and leads to lower coefficient of variation of the interdeparture times and thus $c_D/c_A < 1$.

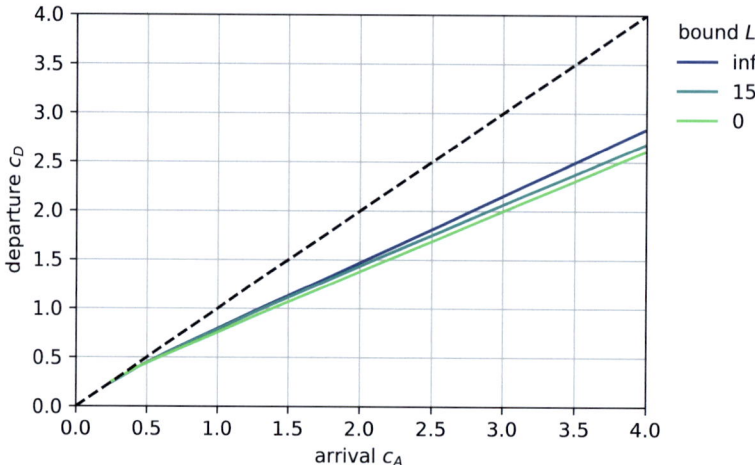

Figure 7.29: Influence of the maximum spacing delay on the interdeparture time. The computation of the interdeparture time D is provided in Chapter 6.4.8.

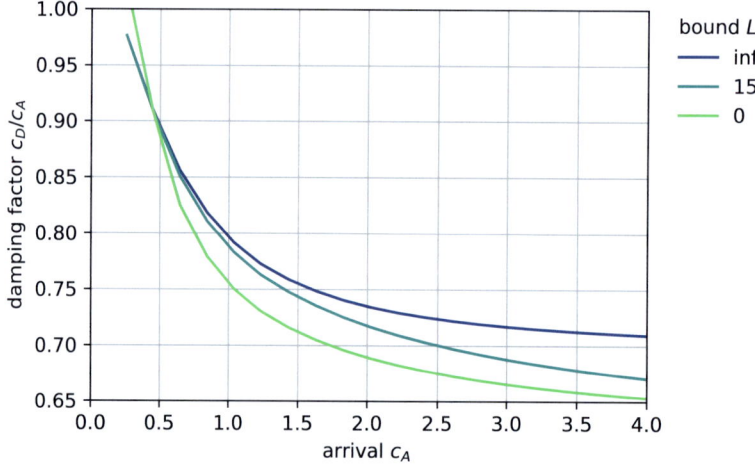

Figure 7.30: The arrival process (coefficient of variation of interarrival times c_A) is smoothed by the spacer and leads to lower coefficient of variation of the interdeparture times c_D.

7.6 An Overload Control Model

Modeling of overload situations and control processes are often required in assessments of robust communication systems. This chapter examines an example of an overload control model, following the studies in [106].

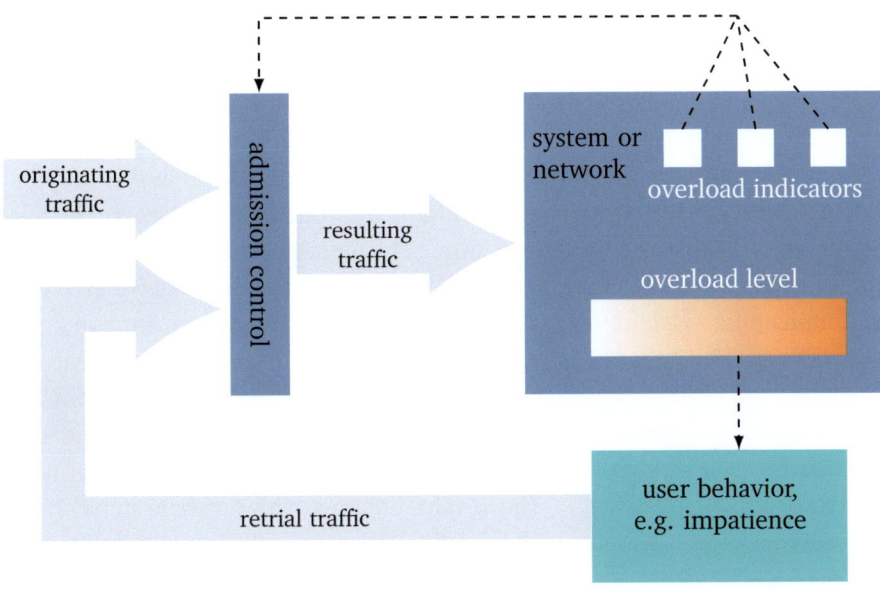

Figure 7.31: Anatomy of an overload situation and related control loop.

In general the operation of an overload control mechanism can be seen as a feedback control loop, as depicted in Figure 7.31. The overload situation is often initiated by a traffic burst (i.e. a non-stationary flash-crowd) which can be a result of incorrect dimensioning of systems or unforeseen high traffic situations. Blocking phenomenon due to (temporary) resource shortage will increase, which in turn leads to additional traffic caused by customer impatience and larger incomplete tasks. The workload then cannot be properly processed by the system, backlog of works increases, etc.

An overload situation often corresponds to a control loop with positive feedback mechanisms. Such an overload situation may be caused by some external events (increased number of arrivals) or internal events (increased service times within a server). An example for such an external event is the failure of another server; the requests (to the failed server) are redirected to the server under investigation causing a temporary overload until the failed server recovers. Another example is an IoT system where an event triggers sensors to send data to an IoT cloud (event-based IoT traffic, see Chapter 7.2). Internal events are for example a temporary failure of the single server under consideration which leads to increased service times. In all situations, the traffic load to the system increases.

The system monitors the load level using an overload indicator (tasks waiting to be processed, packet queue length, etc.) to estimate the actual overload level. The overload situation will affect – with some delay – the traffic level according to the user behavior (e.g. task abandonment, retrials, etc.) leading to e.g. a higher traffic level. Some overload control mechanisms result in traffic admission control and admit only a reduced level of resulting traffic to resolve the overload situation.

The basic model of the overload control strategy considered in this chapter is of type (discrete-time) GI/GI/1 with a feedback-controlled input process. The analysis is done with an discrete-time algorithm. This generic model leads to a modified form of the Lindley integral equation (5.86a), when the analysis is derived in the continuous-time domain. In this case, solutions are only given for some specific systems or as approximations, e.g. [10]. To provide a generally applicable exact calculation algorithm, analysis methods operating in the discrete-time domain are used in this subchapter. The algorithm provided to calculate system characteristics (e.g. customer blocking probability) is developed to estimate the performance of the overload control strategy. The results obtained show system behavior under stationary and non-stationary traffic conditions.

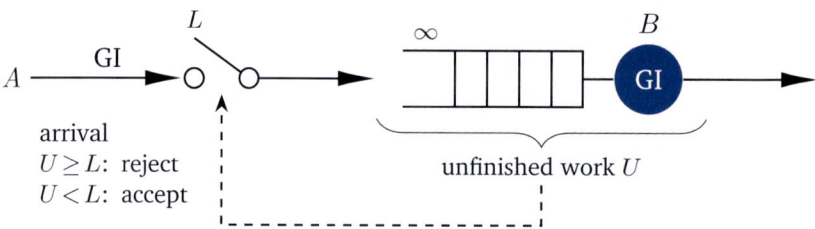

Figure 7.32: The basic model for load-driven overload control for a GI/GI/1 queue with threshold L.

7.6.1 Basic Model for Load-driven Overload Control

The basic structure and related parameters of the overload control model are illustrated in Figure 7.32. In principle, the model has the structure of a GI/GI/1 system with a feedback control path. The input process models the customer arrival stream and the service time models the computation time for an accepted customer. An assumption made for these two processes is that they can be customer-dependent, i.e., the interarrival time and the service time can be individually chosen for each customer. Reasoning for this general assumption is useful e.g., in the modeling of realistic customer mixes in systems with mixed services and in the construction of non-stationary overload patterns offered to a system.

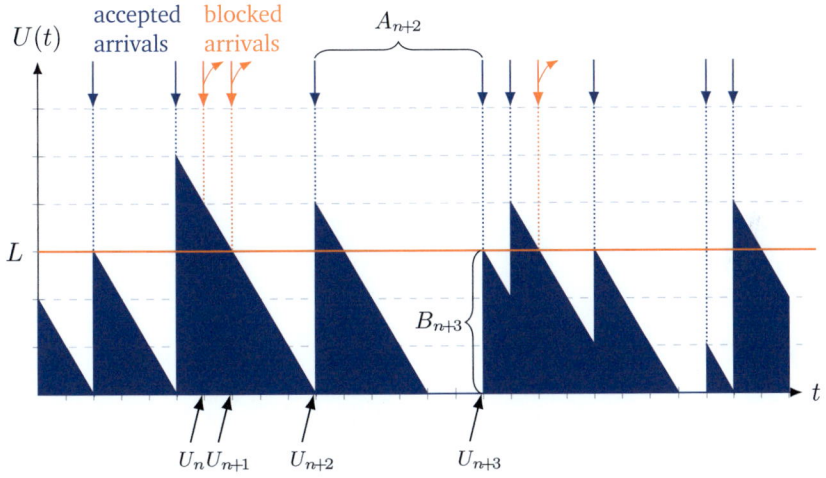

Figure 7.33: Sample path of unfinished work in the system.

As indicated in Figure 7.33, the following symbols and random variables are used:

A_n r.v. for the interarrival time between the n-th and the $(n + 1)$-st customer.

B_n r.v. for the service time of the n-th customer.

U_n r.v. for the amount of unfinished work (workload) which remains in the system (e.g., the number of tasks to be executed, not the number of customers) immediately prior to the arrival instant of the n-th customer. This measure is used as overload indicator.

L threshold value of the overload control mechanism.

The main mechanism of the overload control strategy discussed is based on the following workload-driven customer acceptance scheme:

$U_n < L$ the arriving customer will be accepted

$U_n \geq L$ the arriving customer will be rejected

7.6.2 Analysis in Discrete-Time Domain

The analysis is identical as for the GI/GI/1 queue with bounded delay in Chapter 7.5.2. However, in this subchapter we explicitly use different A_n and B_n depending on the n-th customer arrival, while the results for the spacer example considered the same interarrival and service times for all customers. For the sake of completeness, we also provide a brief analysis for the overload scenario in this chapter. In the context of discrete-time analysis, consider the random variables to be of discrete-time nature, i.e., the time axis is divided into intervals of unit length Δt. As a consequence, samples of those random variables are integer multiples of Δt.

A sample of the state process development in the system is shown in Figure 7.33. Observing the n-th customer in the system and the condition for customer acceptance upon arrival instant, the following conditional r.v. for the workload is introduced:

$$U_{n,0} = U_n | U_n < L \qquad\qquad U_{n,1} = U_n | U_n \geq L \qquad (7.91a)$$

$$U_{n+1,0} = U_{n+1} | U_n < L \qquad\qquad U_{n,1} = U_{n+1} | U_n \geq L \qquad (7.91b)$$

Thus, the probability mass function of these random variables can be obtained:

$$u_{n,0}(k) = \frac{\sigma^L[u_n(k)]}{P(U_n < L)} = \frac{\sigma^L[u_n(k)]}{\sum_{i=0}^{L-1} u_n(i)} \qquad (7.91c)$$

$$u_{n,1}(k) = \frac{\sigma_L[u_n(k)]}{P(U_n \geq L)} = \frac{\sigma_L[u_n(k)]}{\sum_{i=L}^{\infty} u_n(i)} \qquad (7.91d)$$

where σ^m and σ_m are operators which truncate a part of a probability distribution function. σ^m sweeps away the upper part $(k \geq m)$ and takes the lower part $(k < m)$. σ_m sweeps away the lower part $(k < m)$ and takes the upper part $(k \geq m)$. The results of these operations are unnormalized distributions as follows:

$$\sigma^m[x(k)] = \begin{cases} x(k) & k < m \\ 0 & k \geq m \end{cases} \qquad (7.92a)$$

$$\sigma_m[x(k)] = \begin{cases} 0 & k < m \\ x(k) & k \geq m \end{cases} \qquad (7.92b)$$

Taking into account the development of the process (cf. Figure 7.33) with the overload control scheme discussed above, the following relationships between the random variables and their distributions are obtained.

(Case 1) Customer Acceptance: $U_n < L$

$$U_{n+1,0} = \max(U_{n,0} + B_n - A_n, 0) \tag{7.93a}$$

$$u_{n+1,0}(k) = \pi_0[u_{n,0}(k) * b_n(k) * a_n(-k)] \tag{7.93b}$$

where the operator π_m is defined as

$$\pi_m(x(k)) = \begin{cases} 0 & k < m \\ \sum_{i=-\infty}^{m} x(i) & k = m \\ x(k) & k > m \end{cases} \tag{7.94}$$

and the $*$-symbol denotes the discrete convolution operation. For the sum of random variables, $A_3 = A_1 + A_2$, the distribution is

$$a_3(k) = a_1(k) * a_2(k) = \sum_{j=-\infty}^{\infty} a_1(k - j) \cdot a_2(j) . \tag{7.95}$$

For the difference of random variables, $A_3 = A_1 - A_2$, the distribution is

$$a_3(k) = a_1(k) * a_2(-k) = \sum_{j=-\infty}^{\infty} a_1(k + j) \cdot a_2(j) . \tag{7.96}$$

(Case 2) Customer Rejection: $U_n \geq L$

$$U_{n+1,1} = \max(U_{n,1} - A_n, 0) \tag{7.97a}$$

$$u_{n+1,1}(k) = \pi_0[u_{n,1}(k) * a_n(-k)] \tag{7.97b}$$

The distribution of the workload seen by the $(n + 1)$-st customer is

$$u_{n+1}(k) = P(U_n < L) \cdot u_{n+1,0}(k) + P(U_n \geq L) \cdot u_{n+1,1}(k) . \tag{7.98}$$

Hence, U_{n+1} is a mixture distribution composed of $U_{n+1,0}$ and $U_{n+1,1}$:

$$U_{n+1} = \begin{cases} U_{n+1,0} & \text{with probability } P(U_n < L) \\ U_{n+1,1} & \text{with probability } P(U_n \geq L) \end{cases} \tag{7.99}$$

or in a compact way

$$U_{n+1} \sim \text{MIX}\big((U_{n+1,0}, U_{n+1,1}), (P(U_n < L), P(U_n \geq L))\big) . \tag{7.100}$$

From Equations (7.93b), (7.97b) and (7.98), a recursive relation to compute the workload at arrival times of customers is derived.

$$\begin{aligned} u_{n+1}(k) &= \pi_0 \left[\sigma^L[u_n(k)] * b_n(k) * a_n(-k) \right] + \pi_0 \left[\sigma_L[u_n(k)] * a_n(-k) \right] \\ &= \pi_0 \left[\left(\sigma^L[u_n(k)] * b_n(k) + \sigma_L[u_n(k)] \right) * a_n(-k) \right] \end{aligned} \tag{7.101}$$

In terms of random variables, we express this as follows.

$$U_{n+1} = \begin{cases} \max(U_{n,0} + B_n - A_n, 0) & \text{with probability } P(U_n < L) \\ \max(U_{n,1} - A_n, 0) & \text{with probability } P(U_n \geq L) \end{cases} \qquad (7.102)$$

Using Equation (7.101), an algorithm for the calculation of the workload prior to customer arrivals can be found for both stationary and non-stationary traffic conditions. The computational diagram is shown in Figure 7.34.

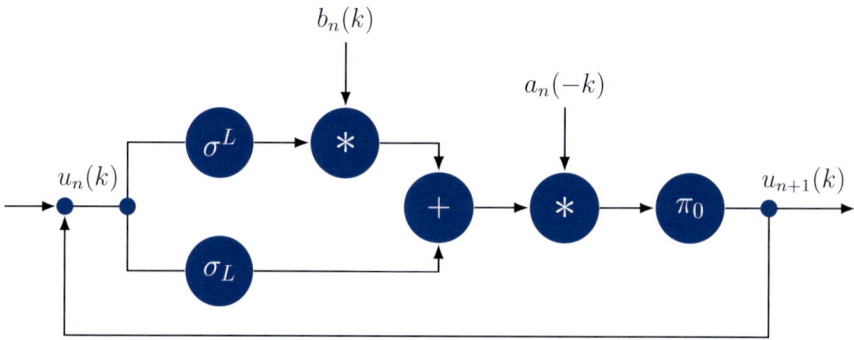

Figure 7.34: Computational diagram for the GI/GI/1 system with feedback control.

The blocking probability of the n-th arriving customer is thus

$$p_{B,n} = \sum_{i=L}^{\infty} u_n(i) . \qquad (7.103)$$

7.6.3 Numerical Results

The impact of the overload control threshold L on the system behavior is discussed. In particular, the mean waiting time and the blocking probability are observed. The discrete time axis is scaled to $\Delta t = 1$. The offered traffic intensity is denoted by $\rho_n = E[B_n]/E[A_n]$ which depends on the n-th customer arrival. Figure 7.35 provides different overload situations. First, consider a sudden increase of the load at $n_1 = 40$ which decreases over time until $n_2 = 75$ (labeled 'peak' in Figure 7.35). This may be caused by some external events like flash-crowd events. Second, consider a constant overload situation between $n_1 = 40$ and $n_2 = 75$ (labeled 'constant' in Figure 7.35). The third overload situation is a triangular load curve. In all three overload situations, the average load $\bar{\rho}$ is chosen to be the same – which is $\bar{\rho} = \sum_{n=n_1}^{n_2} \rho_n = 1.569$ in this numerical example. Before $(n < n_1)$ and after $(n \geq n_2)$ the overload situation, the regular load is $\rho^* = 0.75$.

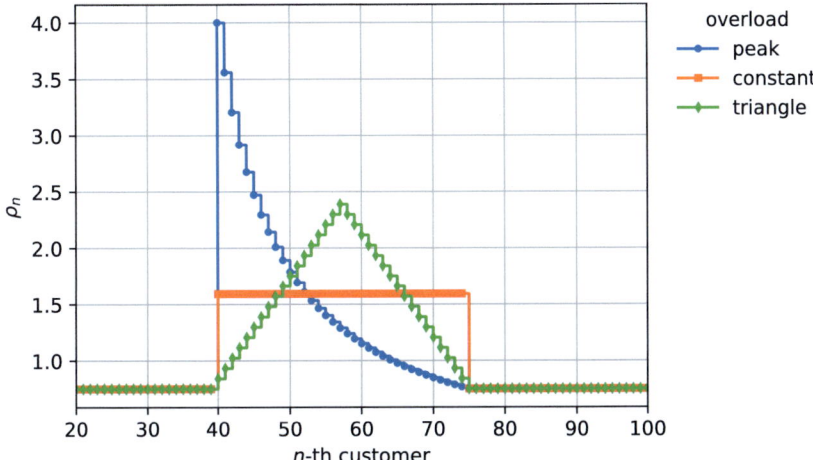

Figure 7.35: Overload scenario. Due to the stochastic nature of the arrival process, the
n-th customer arrival is marked on the x-axis instead of time.

As already pointed out, such an overload situation may be caused by external
events (increased number of arrivals) or internal events (increased service times
within the server). Both types of events lead to an increased load or even overload
situation with $\rho_n > 1$. In our results, we consider an increased number of arrivals
due to external events and adapt A_n over time to obtain a certain load ρ_n, while B_n
follows the same distribution for any n.

Since the overload only happens for a finite time, the system may recover from
the overload. In this context, the overload recovery time is of interest, i.e., the time
until the system reaches the regular system behavior before the overload situation. To
define such an overload recovery time Φ and "regular system behavior", we identify
the number n of customers until the expected waiting time $E[W_n]$ after the overload
situation ($n \geq n_2$) reaches the expected waiting time $E[W^*] = E[W_{n_1-1}]$ just before
the overload happened ($n < n_1$).

$$\Phi = \arg\min_{n \geq n_2} \left(|E[W_n] - E[W^*]| < \varepsilon \right) - n_2 \tag{7.104}$$

To obtain a parametric representation of random process types, we consider the
interarrival and service times having distributions given by their two parameters, e.g.
the mean and the coefficient of variation, whereby the negative binomial distribution
is employed (cf. Section 2.4.1.4).

For a random variable X with mean $E[X]$ and coefficient of variation c_X, we obtain

$$x(k) = \binom{y+k-1}{k} p^y (1-p)^k , \qquad 0 \le p < 1, \; y \in \mathbb{R} , \tag{7.105a}$$

$$p = \frac{1}{E[X] \cdot c_X^2} , \quad y = \frac{E[X]}{E[X] \cdot c_X^2 - 1} , \quad E[X] \cdot c_x^2 > 1 . \tag{7.105b}$$

In our numerical results, we use $B \sim \text{NEGBIN}(y,p)$ for any n. It is $E[B] = 5$ and $c_B = 1$. Hence, the condition $E[B] \cdot c_B^2 > 1$ is fulfilled. The interarrival times follow also the negative binomial distribution with $c_{A_n} = 1$ for any n, but varying mean interarrival time $E[A_n]$. We have $A_n \sim \text{NEGBIN}(y_n, p_n)$ with $\rho_n = E[B]/E[A_n]$ according to Figure 7.35 and Equation (7.105). We assume further that the first customer $(n = 0)$ finds an empty system.

We investigate the system reaction for $L = 5$ and $L = 500$ in terms of customer-individual blocking probability and the mean waiting time to short-term overload patterns. Figure 7.36 shows the expected waiting time $E[W_n]$ for the n-th arriving customer in the system for a very large threshold $L = 500$, which has very low impact on the system behavior, and is thus similar to a GI/GI/1 delay system without threshold control. The maximum blocking probability is at most 1×10^{-14} in both scenarios. The constant overload situation causes a constant increase of the mean waiting time during the overload situation $(n = 40, \ldots, 73)$. The waiting queue gets filled and after the overload situation, it takes some time, until the 'overload' work is completed by the single server. However, the expected waiting time is still far away from the threshold $L = 500$. The other scenario ('peak') has a stronger increase of the mean waiting time than the constant overload scenario in the beginning of the overload situation. However, the step-wise decrease of the overload situation leads to $\rho_n < 1$ for $n = 65$, see Figure 7.35. Hence, for $n \ge 65$, there is a high load situation, but no overload anymore. As a consequence, the mean waiting time is again decreasing.

Figure 7.37 shows the mean waiting time for a threshold value $L = 5$. As a result, the mean waiting time is not reaching such high values as for $L = 500$. We can also observe a different shape of the curves which is caused due to blocking of customers. The constant overload situation leads to an almost constant mean waiting time during overload. Since the queue is not filled with many customers due to the threshold L, the overload is quickly compensated. The mean waiting time reaches quickly the same value as before the overload situation. Taking a closer look at the blocking probabilities in Figure 7.38, we observe similar shapes like for the mean waiting times for $L = 5$. For a proper dimensioning of the threshold value of the overload control strategy, the arrival process characteristics must be carefully taken into account.

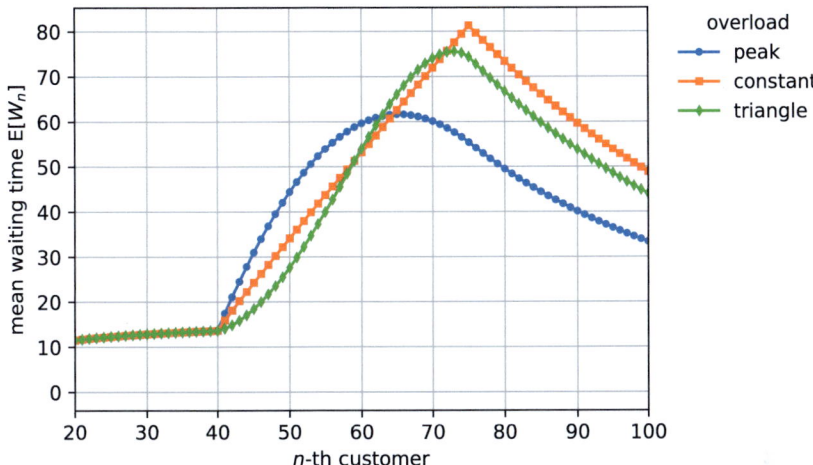

Figure 7.36: Mean waiting time in the overload situations for threshold $L = 500$. The blocking probability is close to zero, and at most 2×10^{-14} in the different overload scenarios; the curves for the blocking probabilities are omitted here.

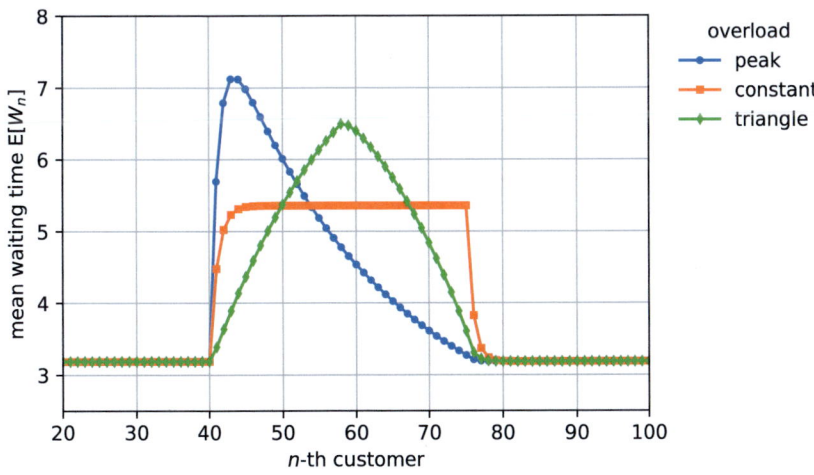

Figure 7.37: Mean waiting time in the overload situations for threshold $L = 5$. The corresponding blocking probabilities are depicted in Figure 7.38.

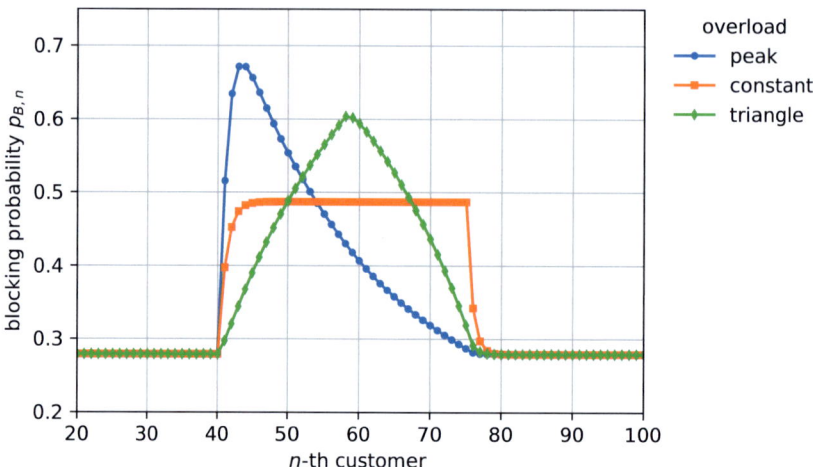

Figure 7.38: Blocking probability $p_{B,n}$ of n-th arriving customer in the overload situations for threshold $L = 5$.

Figure 7.39 visualizes the overload recovery time Φ according to Equation (7.104) depending on the threshold L and the overload pattern. The overload patterns consistently influences Φ, while the threshold L has a major influence on Φ.

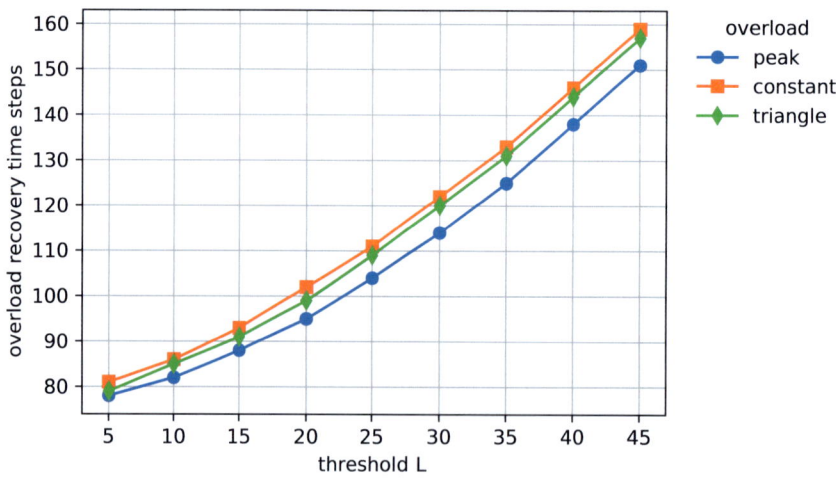

Figure 7.39: Required number of steps to recover from overload situation depending on threshold L.

Bibliography

[1] M. Ackroyd. "Computing the waiting time distribution for the G/G/1 queue by signal processing methods". In: *IEEE Transactions on Communications* 28 (1980), pp. 52–58.

[2] H. Akimaru and K. Kawashima. *Teletraffic – Theory and Applications*. 2nd ed. Telecommunication Networks and Computer Systems. Springer, 1999.

[3] A. S. Alfa. *Applied Discrete-Time Queues*. Springer, 2016.

[4] E. Altman, K. Avrachenkov, and U. Ayesta. "A survey on discriminatory processor sharing". In: *Queueing systems* 53.1-2 (2006), pp. 53–63.

[5] J. Artalejo and G. Falin. "Standard and retrial queueing systems: A comparative analysis". In: *Revista matemática complutense* 15.1 (2002), pp. 101–129.

[6] J. W. Baek, H. W. Lee, S. Ahn, and Y. H. Bae. "Exact time-dependent solutions for the M/D/1 queue". In: *Operations Research Letters* 44.5 (2016), pp. 692–695.

[7] V. E. Benes. *General Stochastic Processes in the Theory of Queues*. Dover Publications, 2017.

[8] D. Bertsimas and G. Mourtzinou. "Transient laws of non-stationary queueing systems and their applications". In: *Queueing Systems* 25.1 (1997), pp. 115–155.

[9] D. Bertsimas and D. Nakazato. "The distributional Little's law and its applications". In: *Operations Research* 43.2 (1995), pp. 298–310.

[10] U. N. Bhat. *An Introduction to Queueing Theory: Modeling and Analysis in Applications*. Birkhäuser, 2015.

[11] U. N. Bhat. "The general queue G/G/1 and approximations". In: *An Introduction to Queueing Theory*. Springer, 2008, pp. 169–183.

[12] G. Bolch. *Leistungsbewertung von Rechensystemen mittels analytischer Warteschlangenmodelle*. Stuttgart: Teubner, 1989.

[13] O. Boxma, A. Löpker, M. Mandjes, and Z. Palmowski. "A multiplicative version of the Lindley recursion". In: *Queueing Systems* (2021), pp. 1–21.

[14] D. Boyle, R. Kolcun, and E. Yeatman. "Energy-efficient communication in wireless networks". In: *ICT – Energy Concepts for Energy Efficiency and Sustainability* (2017).

[15] O. Brun and J.-M. Garcia. "Analytical solution of finite capacity M/D/1 queues". In: *Journal of Applied Probability* (2000), pp. 1092–1098.

[16] H. Bruneel and B. G. Kim. *Discrete-Time Models for Communication Systems including ATM*. Vol. 205. Springer Science & Business Media, 1993.

[17] T. Bu and D. Towsley. "Fixed point approximations for TCP behavior in an AQM network". In: *2001 ACM SIGMETRICS / Int. Conf. on Measurement and Modeling of Computer Systems*. 2001, pp. 216–225.

[18] J. K. Cavers. "On the fast Fourier transform inversion of probability generating functions". In: *Journal of Applied Mathematics* 22 (1978), pp. 275–282.

[19] M. L. Chaudhry and U. C. Gupta. "Modelling and analysis of M/G$^{[a,b]}$/1/N queue – A simple alternative approach". In: *Queueing Systems* 31.1-2 (1999), pp. 95–100.

[20] F. Ciucu and F. Poloczek. "Two extensions of Kingman's GI/G/1 bound". In: *Proc. of the ACM on Measurement and Analysis of Computing Systems* 2.3 (2018), pp. 1–33.

[21] J. W. Cohen. *The Single Server Queue*. North-Holland, 1982. ISBN: 978-0-444-59624-6.

[22] J. Cooley and J. Tukey. "An algorithm for the machine calculation of complex Fourier series". In: *Mathematics of computation* 19 (1965), pp. 297–301.

[23] R. B. Cooper. *Introduction to Queueing Theory*. 2nd ed. New York: North-Holland, 1981. ISBN: 978-0-444-00379-9.

[24] D. R. Cox. *Renewal Theory*. Springer, 1967. ISBN: 978-0-412-20570-5.

[25] D. R. Cox and H. D. Miller. *The Theory of Stochastic Processes*. London: Chapman & Hall, 1965.

[26] J. N. Daigle. *Queueing Theory with Applications to Packet Telecommunication*. Springer, 2005.

[27] D. J. Daley. "Inequalities for moments of tails of random variables, with a queueing application". In: *Zeitschrift für Wahrscheinlichkeitstheorie und verwandte Gebiete* 41.2 (1977), pp. 139–143.

[28] G. Doetsch. *Handbuch der Laplace-Transformation*. Vol. I: Theorie der Laplace-Transformation. Birkhäuser, 1950.

[29]   A. Eckberg. "The single server queue with periodic arrival process and deterministic service times". In: *IEEE Transactions on Communications* 27.3 (1979), pp. 556–562.

[30]   A. Eckberg and L. Green. "Response time analysis for pipelining jobs in a tree network of processors". In: *Applied Probability-Computer Science: The Interface Volume 1*. Springer, 1982, pp. 387–416.

[31]   S.-E. Elayoubi, A. M. Masucci, J. Roberts, and B. Sayrac. "Optimal D2D content delivery for cellular network offloading". In: *Mobile Networks and Applications* 22.6 (2017), pp. 1033–1044.

[32]   A. K. Erlang. "The theory of probabilities and telephone conversations". In: *Nyt. Tidsskr. Mat. Ser. B* 20 (1909), pp. 33–39.

[33]   M. Fasi and N. J. Higham. "An arbitrary precision scaling and squaring algorithm for the matrix exponential". In: *SIAM Journal on Matrix Analysis and Applications* 40.4 (2019), pp. 1233–1256.

[34]   W. Feller. *An Introduction to Probability Theory and its Applications*. 2. New York: Wiley, 1971.

[35]   M. Fiedler, T. Hoßfeld, and P. Tran-Gia. "A generic quantitative relationship between quality of experience and quality of service". In: *IEEE Network* 24.2 (2010), pp. 36–41.

[36]   F. Figueiredo, F. Benevenuto, and J. M. Almeida. "The tube over time: Characterizing popularity growth of YouTube videos". In: *4th ACM Int. Conf. on Web Search and Data Mining*. 2011, pp. 745–754.

[37]   M. Fisz. *Probability Theory and Mathematical Statistics*. 3rd ed. John Wiley & Sons, 1963. ISBN: 978-0-471-26250-3.

[38]   S. B. Fred et al. "Statistical bandwidth sharing: A study of congestion at flow level". In: *ACM SIGCOMM Computer Communication Review* 31.4 (2001), pp. 111–122.

[39]   G. Giambene. *Queuing Theory and Telecommunications*. 3rd ed. Springer, 2021.

[40]   H. Gold and P. Tran-Gia. "Performance analysis of a batch service queue arising out of manufacturing system modelling". In: *Queueing Systems* 14 (1993), pp. 413–426.

[41]   D. Gross, J. F. Shortle, J. M. Thompson, and C. M. Harris. *Fundamentals of Queueing Theory*. 4th ed. Wiley, 2008.

[42] F. Guillemin, V. Q. Rodriguez, and A. Simonian. "A processor-sharing model for the performance of virtualized network functions". In: *31st International Teletraffic Congress (ITC 31)*. 2019, pp. 10–18.

[43] R. Haji and G. F. Newell. "A relation between stationary queue and waiting time distributions". In: *Journal of Applied Probability* 8.3 (1971), pp. 617–620.

[44] G. Haßlinger. "A polynomial factorization approach to the discrete time GI/G/1/(N) queue size distribution". In: *Performance Evaluation* 23.3 (1995), pp. 217–240.

[45] G. Haßlinger and O. Hohlfeld. "The Gilbert-Elliott model for packet loss in real time services on the Internet". In: *14th GI/ITG Conf. on Measurement, Modelling and Evalutation of Computer and Communication Systems*. VDE. 2008, pp. 1–15.

[46] J. Haxhibeqiri, E. De Poorter, I. Moerman, and J. Hoebeke. "A survey of LoRaWAN for IoT: From technology to application". In: *Sensors* 18.11 (2018), p. 3995.

[47] P. E. Heegaard and K. S. Trivedi. "Network survivability modeling". In: *Computer Networks* 53.8 (2009), pp. 1215–1234.

[48] P. Henrici. "Fast Fourier methods in computational complex analysis". In: *SIAM Review* 21 (1979), pp. 481–527.

[49] T. Hoßfeld. "Performance Evaluation of Future Internet Applications and Emerging User Behavior". Doctoral thesis. Universität Würzburg, 2009.

[50] T. Hoßfeld, F. Metzger, and P. E. Heegaard. "Traffic modeling for aggregated periodic IoT data". In: *2018 21st Conf. on Innovation in Clouds, Internet and Networks and Workshops (ICIN)*. IEEE. 2018, pp. 1–8.

[51] T. Hoßfeld, C. Moldovan, and C. Schwartz. "To each according to his needs: Dimensioning video buffer for specific user profiles and behavior". In: *2015 IFIP/IEEE Int. Symposium on Integrated Network Management (IM)*. 2015, pp. 1249–1254.

[52] T. Hoßfeld, R. Schatz, E. Biersack, and L. Plissonneau. "Internet video delivery in YouTube: From traffic measurements to quality of experience". In: *Data Traffic Monitoring and Analysis*. Springer, 2013, pp. 264–301.

[53] T. Hoßfeld, R. Schatz, and U. R. Krieger. "QoE of YouTube video streaming for current Internet transport protocols". In: *Int. Conf. on Measurement, Modelling, and Evaluation of Computing Systems and Dependability and Fault Tolerance*. Springer. 2014, pp. 136–150.

[54] T.-Y. Huang et al. "A buffer-based approach to rate adaptation: Evidence from a large video streaming service". In: *2014 Conf. of the ACM Special Interest Group on Data Communication (SIGCOMM)*. 2014, pp. 187–198.

[55] F. Hübner. "Analysis of a finite-capacity asynchronous multiplexer with deterministic traffic sources". In: *7th ITC Specialist Seminar*. Morristown, NJ, USA, 1990.

[56] V. B. Iversen. "Teletraffic Engineering Handbook". In: *ITU-D SG* 2 (2005), p. 16.

[57] V. B. Iversen and L. Staalhagen. "Waiting time distribution in M/D/1 queueing systems". In: *Electronics Letters* 35.25 (1999), pp. 2184–2185.

[58] N. K. Kim and M. L. Chaudhry. "The use of the distributional Little's law in the computational analysis of discrete-time GI/G/1 and GI/D/c queues". In: *Performance Evaluation* 65.1 (2008), pp. 3–9.

[59] J. F. Kingman. "Inequalities in the theory of queues". In: *Journal of the Royal Statistical Society: Series B (Methodological)* 32.1 (1970), pp. 102–110.

[60] L. Kleinrock. "Internet congestion control using the power metric: Keep the pipe just full, but no fuller". In: *Elsevier Ad hoc networks* 80 (2018), pp. 142–157.

[61] L. Kleinrock. *Queueing Systems*. Vol. 1: Theory. Wiley, 1975. ISBN: 978-0-471-49110-1.

[62] L. Kleinrock. *Queueing Systems*. Vol. 2: Computer Applications. Wiley, 1976. ISBN: 978-0-471-49111-8.

[63] L. Kleinrock. "Time-shared systems: A theoretical treatment". In: *Journal of the ACM* 14.2 (Apr. 1967), pp. 242–261. ISSN: 0004-5411.

[64] H. Kobayashi. *Stochastic Modelling: Queueing Models; Discrete-Time Queueing Systems*. Ed. by G. Louchard and G. Latouche. Academic Press, 1983.

[65] H. Kobayashi and B. L. Mark. *System Modeling and Analysis: Foundations of System Performance Evaluation*. Pearson Education India, 2009. ISBN: 978-0-13-129355-7.

[66] H. Kobayashi, B. L. Mark, and W. Turin. *Probability, Random Processes, and Statistical Analysis*. Cambridge University Press, 2012.

[67] A. Konheim. "An elementary solution of the queueing system GI/G/1". In: *SIAM Journal on Computing* 4 (1975), pp. 540–545.

[68] W. Krämer and M. Langenbach-Belz. "Approximate formulae for the delay in the queueing system GI/G/l". In: *8th International Teletraffic Congress (ITC 8)*. 1976, pp. 235–1.

[69]   P. Kühn. *Tables on Delay Systems*. Stuttgart: Institut für Nachrichtenvermitt-lung und Datenverarbeitung der Universität, 1976.

[70]   J.-Y. Le Boudec. *Performance Evaluation of Computer and Communication Systems*. EPFL Press, 2011.

[71]   D. V. Lindley. "The theory of queues with a single server". In: *Mathematical Proc. of the Cambridge Philosophical Society* 48.2 (1952), pp. 277–289.

[72]   L. V. Lipilina. "The spectral decomposition method for solving the Lindley integral equation and related numerical methods". In: *T-Comm* 14.1 (2020).

[73]   J. D. Little. "Little's Law as viewed on its 50th anniversary". In: *Operations Research* 59.3 (2011), pp. 536–549.

[74]   F. Loh et al. "Is the uplink enough? Estimating video stalls from encrypted network traffic". In: *2020 IEEE/IFIP Network Operations and Management Symposium (NOMS)*. 2020, pp. 1–9.

[75]   K. T. Marshall and R. V. Evans. "Some inequalities in queuing". In: *Operations Research* 16.3 (1968), pp. 651–668.

[76]   B. Melamed and W. Whitt. "On arrivals that see time averages". In: *Operations Research* 38.1 (1990), pp. 156–172.

[77]   M. Menth and S. Muehleck. "Packet waiting time for multiplexed periodic on/off streams in the presence of overbooking". In: *Int. Journal of Communication Networks and Distributed Systems* 4.2 (2010), pp. 207–229.

[78]   C. Metter et al. "Analytical model for SDN signaling traffic and flow table occupancy and its application for various types of traffic". In: *IEEE Transactions on Network and Service Management* 14.3 (2017), pp. 603–615.

[79]   F. Metzger et al. "Modeling of aggregated IoT traffic and its application to an IoT cloud". In: *Proceedings of the IEEE* 107.4 (2019), pp. 679–694.

[80]   L. Niu and Y. Guo. "Enabling reliable data center demand response via aggregation". In: *7th Int. Conf. on Future Energy Systems*. 2016, pp. 1–11.

[81]   L. Oliveira et al. "MAC layer protocols for Internet of Things: A survey". In: *Future Internet* 11.1 (2019), p. 16.

[82]   A. Oppenheim and R. Schafer. *Discrete-Time Signal Processing*. 3rd ed. Pearson India, 2013. ISBN: 978-1-292-03815-5.

[83]   T. J. Ott. "The sojourn-time distribution in the M/G/1 queue with processor sharing". In: *Journal of applied probability* (1984), pp. 360–378.

[84]   N. Papadis et al. "Stochastic models and wide-area network measurements for blockchain design and analysis". In: *2018 IEEE Int. Conf. on Computer Communications (INFOCOM)*. 2018, pp. 2546–2554.

[85] A. Papoulis. *Probability, Random Variables and Stochastic Processes*. New York: McGraw-Hill, 1965.

[86] T. Phung-Duc. *Retrial Queueing Models: A Survey on Theory and Applications*. arXiv: 1906.09560. 2019.

[87] M. Ramalhoto, J. Amaral, and M. T. Cochito. "A survey of J. Little's formula". In: *International Statistical Review/Revue Internationale de Statistique* (1983), pp. 255–278.

[88] G. Ramamurthy and B. Sengupta. "Delay analysis of a packet voice multiplexer". In: *SBT/IEEE Int. Symposium on Telecommunications*. 1990, pp. 155–160.

[89] J. Roberts, U. Mocci, J. Virtamo, and A. T. Andersen. "Broadband network teletraffic: Final report of action COST 242". In: *Broadband Network Teletraffic*. Springer Verlag, 1996.

[90] J. W. Roberts and J. T. Virtamo. "The superposition of periodic cell arrival streams in an ATM multiplexer". In: *IEEE Transactions on Communications* 39.2 (1991), pp. 298–303.

[91] S. M. Ross. *Introduction to Probability Models*. 12th ed. Academic Press London, 2019.

[92] K. Santhi and R. Saravanan. "Performance analysis of cloud computing bulk service using queueing models". In: *Int. Journal of Applied Engineering Research* 12.17 (2017), pp. 6487–6492.

[93] J. Sastre, J. Ibanez, and E. Defez. "Boosting the computation of the matrix exponential". In: *Applied Mathematics and Computation* 340 (2019), pp. 206–220.

[94] A. Saxena, D. Claeys, B. Zhang, and J. Walraevens. "Cloud data storage: A queueing model with thresholds". In: *Annals of Operations Research* 293.1 (2020), pp. 295–315.

[95] L. P. Seelen, H. C. Tijms, and M. H. Van Hoorn. *Tables for Multi-Server Queues*. North-Holland, 1985. ISBN: 978-0-444-87722-2.

[96] M. Seufert et al. "A survey on quality of experience of HTTP adaptive streaming". In: *IEEE Communications Surveys & Tutorials* 17.1 (2014), pp. 469–492.

[97] J. F. Shortle, J. M. Thompson, D. Gross, and C. M. Harris. *Fundamentals of Queueing Theory*. Vol. 399. John Wiley & Sons, 2018.

[98] M. Spiegel. *Laplace-Transformationen - Theorie und Anwendung*. McGraw-Hill (Schaum Publ. Co.), 1977. ISBN: 978-3-89028-930-4.

[99]   U. Sumita and M. Kijima. "Numerical Exploration of a bivariate Lindley process via the bivariate Laguerre transform". In: *Annals of Operations Research* 8.1 (1987), pp. 321–349.

[100] R. Syski. *Introduction to Congestion Theory in Telephone Systems*. North-Holland, 1986. ISBN: 978-0-444-87672-0.

[101] H. Tagaki. *Queueing Analysis: A Foundation of Performance Evaluation – Discrete-Time Systems*. Vol. 3. North-Holland, 1993. ISBN: 978-0-444-81611-5.

[102] L. Takács. "A single server queue with Poisson input". In: *Operations Research* 10 (1962), pp. 388–397.

[103] H. Takagi. *Queueing Analysis: A Foundation of Performance Evaluation*. Vol. 1. North-Holland, 1991. ISBN: 978-0-444-88910-2.

[104] Y. C. Tay. *Analytical Performance Modeling for Computer Systems*. 3rd ed. 1. Morgan & Claypool Publishers, 2018, pp. 1–171.

[105] H. C. Tijms. *Stochastic Models – An Algorithmic Approach*. Chichester: Wiley, 1995. ISBN: 978-0-471-95123-0.

[106] P. Tran-Gia. "Analysis of a Load-driven Overload Control Mechanism in Discrete-Time Domain". In: *12th International Teletraffic Congress (ITC 12)*. 1988.

[107] P. Tran-Gia. "Discrete-Time Analysis for the Interdeparture Distribution of GI/G/1 Queues". In: *Proc. Seminar on Teletraffic Analysis and Computer Performance Evaluation*. June 1986.

[108] P. Tran-Gia. *Analytische Leistungsbewertung verteilter Systeme: Eine Einführung*. Springer-Verlag, 1996.

[109] P. Tran-Gia. "Discrete-time analysis technique and application to usage parameter control modelling in ATM systems". In: *8th Australian Teletraffic Research Seminar*. 1993.

[110] P. Tran-Gia. *Einführung in die Leistungsbewertung und Verkehrstheorie*. Oldenbourg Wissenschaftsverlag, 2009.

[111] P. Tran-Gia and M. Mandjes. "Modeling of customer retrial phenomenon in cellular mobile networks". In: *IEEE Journal on selected areas in communications* 15.8 (1997), pp. 1406–1414.

[112] P. Van Mieghem. *Performance Analysis of Complex Networks and Systems*. Cambridge University Press, 2014.

[113] F. Verdonck, H. Bruneel, and S. Wittevrongel. "Analysis of a 2-state discrete-time queue with stochastic state-period lengths and state-dependent server availability and arrivals". In: *Performance Evaluation* 135 (2019), p. 102026.

[114] J. Virtamo. "Numerical evaluation of the distribution of unfinished work in an M/D/1 system". In: *Electronics Letters* 31.7 (1995), pp. 531–532.

[115] A. D. Wall and D. J. Worthington. "Time-dependent analysis of virtual waiting time behaviour in discrete time queues". In: *European Journal of Operational Research* 178.2 (2007), pp. 482–499.

[116] J. Walraevens, D. Fiems, and H. Bruneel. "Performance analysis of priority queueing systems in discrete time". In: *Network performance engineering*. Springer, 2011, pp. 203–232.

[117] J. Walraevens, D. Fiems, and H. Bruneel. "Time-dependent performance analysis of a discrete-time priority queue". In: *Performance Evaluation* 65.9 (2008), pp. 641–652.

[118] F. Wamser, P. Tran-Gia, S. Geißler, and T. Hoßfeld. "Modeling of traffic flows in internet of things using renewal approximation". In: *Advances in Optimization and Decision Science for Society, Services and Enterprises*. Springer, 2019, pp. 483–492.

[119] W. Whitt. "A review of $L = \lambda W$ and extensions". In: *Queueing Systems* 9.3 (1991), pp. 235–268.

[120] A. Wierman. "Fairness and scheduling in single server queues". In: *Surveys in Operations Research and Management Science* 16.1 (2011), pp. 39–48.

[121] R. Wolff. "Poisson arrivals see time averages". In: *Operations Research* 30 (1982), pp. 223–231.

[122] T. Yang and M. Chaudhry. "On steady-state queue size distributions of the discrete-time GI/G/1 queue". In: *Advances in applied probability* 28.4 (1996), pp. 1177–1200.

[123] S. Yashkov and A. Yashkova. "Processor sharing: A survey of the mathematical theory". In: *Automation and Remote Control* 68.9 (2007), pp. 1662–1731.

[124] Y. Zeng and C. H. Xia. "Optimal bulking threshold of batch service queues". In: *Journal of Applied Probability* 54.2 (2017), p. 409.

[125] M. Zukerman. *Introduction to Queueing Theory and Stochastic Teletraffic Models*. arXiv:1307.2968 [v23]. 2020.

Notation and Symbols

Continuous Random Variables and Related Functions

A continuous non-negative random variable (RV)

$a(t)$ probability density function (PDF)
$$a(t) = \frac{d}{dt} A(t) dt$$

$A(t)$ cumulative distribution function (CDF)
$$A(t) = P(A \leq t) = \int_0^t a(\tau) d\tau$$

$E[A]$ expected value
$$E[A] = \int_0^\infty \tau \cdot a(\tau) d\tau$$

$\Phi_A(s)$ Laplace transform of $a(t)$, Laplace-Stieltjes transform of $A(t)$
$$\Phi_A(s) = \int_0^\infty e^{-st}\, dA(t) = \int_0^\infty e^{-st} a(t)\, dt = E[e^{-sA}]$$

Discrete Random Variables and Related Functions

X discrete non-negative random variable (RV)

$x(k)$ distribution or probabability mass function (PMF)
$$x(k) = P(X = k)$$

$X(k)$ cumulative distribution function (CDF)
$$X(k) = P(X \leq k) = \sum_{i=0}^k x(i)$$

$E[X]$ expected value
$$E[X] = \sum_{i=0}^\infty i \cdot x(i)$$

$X_{GF}(z)$ probability generating function
$$X_{GF}(z) = \sum_{i=0}^\infty x(i) z^i = E[z^X]$$

$X_{ZT}(z)$ Z-transform of the distribution $x(k)$
$$X_{ZT}(z) = \sum_{i=0}^\infty x(i) z^{-i} = E[z^{-X}]$$

$\mathcal{X}_{ZT}(z)$ Z-transform of the CDF $X(k)$
$$X_{ZT}(z) = \sum_{i=0}^\infty X(i) z^{-i}$$

$X_{DFT}(k)$ discrete Fourier transform
$$X_{DFT}(k) = \sum_{k=0}^{N-1} x(k) e^{-(i2\pi n/N)k} \text{ for } n = 0, \ldots, N-1$$

$X_{CEP}(k)$ Cepstrum of the distribution $x(k)$

Expected Value and Moments

X discrete non-negative random variable X

analogous definitions for continuous random variable A

$E[X]$ expected value

$$E[X] = \sum_{i=0}^{\infty} i \cdot x(i)$$

$E[f(X)]$ expected value of a function of a RV

$$E[f(X)] = \sum_{i=0}^{\infty} f(i) \cdot x(i)$$

m_k k-th ordinary moment

$$m_k = E[X^k] = \sum_{i=0}^{\infty} i^k \cdot x(i)$$

μ_k k-th central moment

$$\mu_k = E[(X - m_1)^k] = \sum_{i=0}^{\infty} (i - m_1)^k \cdot x(i)$$

$VAR[X]$ variance of a RV

$$VAR[X] = E[X^2] - E[X]^2$$

$STD[X]$ standard deviation of a RV

$$STD[X] = \sqrt{VAR[X]}$$

c_X coefficient of variation of a RV

$$c_X = STD[X]/E[X]$$

Operators

π_m pi-operator applied to a non-negative discrete random variable X

$$\pi_m\Big(x(k)\Big) = \begin{cases} 0 & k < m \\ \sum\limits_{i=-\infty}^{m} x(i) & k = m \\ x(k) & k > m \end{cases}$$

π_0 pi0-operator provides distribution for $\max(X, 0)$

$$\pi_0\Big(x(k)\Big) = \begin{cases} \sum\limits_{i=-\infty}^{0} x(i) & k = 0 \\ x(k) & k > 0 \end{cases}$$

$*$ convolution of discrete probability distributions X_1, X_2

$$x_1(i) * x_2(i) = \sum_{j=0}^{i} x_1(i - j) \cdot x_2(j) \qquad \text{(sum } X_1 + X_2)$$

$$x_1(i) * x_2(-i) = \sum_{j=0}^{+\infty} x_1(i + j) \cdot x_2(j) \qquad \text{(difference } X_1 - X_2)$$

convolution of continuous random variables A_1, A_2

$$a_1(t) * a_2(t) = \int_{u=0}^{t} a_1(u) a_2(t - u) \, du \qquad \text{(sum } A_1 + A_2)$$

Vectors and Matrices

X discrete non-negative random variable X

$\mathbf{X}$ probability vector $\mathbf{X} = \big(x(0), x(1), \ldots\big)$

$\mathcal{Q}$ rate matrix (transition probability densities) is the infinitesimal generator matrix of a continuous-time Markov process $\mathcal{Q} = \{q_{ij}\}$

$\mathcal{P}$ transition matrix (transition probabilities) $\mathcal{P} = \{p_{ij}\}$

List of Probability Distributions

Continuous Distributions

$A \sim \mathrm{D}(t_0)$
> deterministic distribution takes constant value $t_0 \in \mathbb{R}$
> $A(t) = 0$ for $t < t_0$ and $A(t) = 1$ for $t \geq t_0$

$A \sim \mathrm{EXP}(\lambda)$
> (negative) exponential distribution with rate $\lambda = 1/\mathrm{E}[\,A\,] > 0$
> $A(t) = 1 - e^{-\lambda t}, \quad t \geq 0$

$A \sim \mathrm{E}_k(\lambda)$
> Erlang-k distribution is the sum of k negative exponentially distributed phases, $A_i \sim \mathrm{EXP}(\lambda)$, each with parameter λ: $A = A_1 + A_2 + \ldots + A_k$
> $A(t) = 1 - \sum_{i=0}^{k-1} \frac{(\lambda t)^i}{i!} e^{-\lambda t}, \quad t \geq 0$

$A \sim \mathrm{MIX}(\mathbf{A}, \mathbf{p})$
> mixture distribution A from k independent random variables, as vector $\mathbf{A} = (A_1, \ldots, A_k)$, which are selected with probabilities $\mathbf{p} = (p_1, \ldots, p_k)$
> $A(t) = \sum_{i=1}^{k} p_i \cdot A_i(t)$

$A \sim \mathrm{H}_k(\mathbf{\Lambda}, \mathbf{p})$
> hyperexponential distribution function is a mixture distribution of k exponential phases with parameters $\mathbf{\Lambda} = (\lambda_1, \ldots, \lambda_k)$ and probabilities $\mathbf{p} = (p_1, \ldots, p_k)$; it is $A \sim \mathrm{MIX}((A_1, \ldots, A_k), (p_1, \ldots, p_k))$ with $A_i \sim \mathrm{EXP}(\lambda_i)$
> $A(t) = 1 - \sum_{i=1}^{k} p_i e^{-\lambda_i t}, \quad t \geq 0$

$A \sim U(a, b)$
> (continuous) uniform distribution with $b > a$ and $a, b \in \mathbb{R}$
> $A(t) = \frac{t-a}{b-a}, \quad a \leq t \leq b$

Discrete Distributions

$X \sim \text{BER}(p)$

> Bernoulli distribution with success probability $0 < p < 1$
> (or failure probability $q = 1 - p$)
> $x(0) = 1 - p$ *(failure)* and $x(1) = p$ *(success)*

$X \sim \text{BINOM}(N, p)$

> Binomial distribution as sum of N Bernoulli experiments with success
> probability p, $X = X_1 + X_2 + \ldots X_N$ with $N \in \mathbb{N}$ and $X_i \sim \text{BER}(p)$
> $x(i) = \binom{N}{i} p^i (1 - p)^{N-i}, \quad i = 0, 1, \ldots, N$

$X \sim \text{GEOM}(p)$

> geometric distribution is the number of failures in Bernoulli experiments
> with success probability p before the first success
> $x(i) = (1 - p)^i p, \quad i = 0, 1, \ldots$

$X \sim \text{GEOM}_m(p)$

> shifted geometric distribution with $m \in \mathbb{N}$ for a geometric distribution
> $Y \sim \text{GEOM}(p)$, i.e. $X = Y + m$
> $x(i) = (1 - p)^{i-m} p, \quad i = m, m + 1, \ldots$

$X \sim \text{NEGBIN}(y, p)$

> Negative Binomial Distribution is the y-fold convolution of the geometric
> distribution with itself with $y \in \mathbb{R}$
> $x(i) = \binom{y+i-1}{i} p^y (1 - p)^i, \quad i = 0, 1, \ldots$

$X \sim \text{POIS}(y)$

> Poisson distribution with mean $y \in \mathbb{R}$
> $x(i) = \frac{y^i}{i!} e^{-y}, \quad i = 0, 1, \ldots$

$X \sim \text{DU}(a, b)$

> discrete uniform distribution with $b > a$ and $a, b, \in \mathbb{N}$
> $x(i) = \frac{1}{b-a+1}, \quad i = a, a + 1, \ldots, b - 1, b$

Variables in Queueing Models

A	interarrival time (r.v.)
λ	arrival rate, $\lambda = 1/\mathrm{E}[A]$
R	recurrence time (r.v.)
B	service time (r.v.)
μ	service rate, $\mu = 1/\mathrm{E}[B]$
n	number of servers
S	number of waiting places
a	offered load, $a = \lambda/\mu$
ρ	normalized offered load, $\rho = a/n$
X	number of customers (r.v.)
X_B	number of customers in service stage (r.v.)
X_W	number of customers in waiting room (r.v.)
X_A	system state of an arriving customer (r.v.)
X_D	system state after service termination (r.v.)
X^*	arbitrary-time system state (r.v.)
U	unfinished work (r.v.)
W	waiting time of all customers (r.v.)
W_1	waiting time of waiting customers (r.v.)
Ω	mean queue length
p_W	waiting probability
p_B	blocking probability

Index